TRADING AND REBALANCING, PERFORMANCE EVALUATION, AND GLOBAL INVESTMENT PERFORMANCE STANDARDS

CFA® Program Curriculum
2015 • LEVEL III • VOLUME 6

CFA Institute | WILEY

ISBN 978-1-939515-49-0 (paper)
ISBN 978-1-939515-70-4 (ebk)

10 9 8 7 6 5 4 3 2

Please visit our website at
www.WileyGlobalFinance.com.

CONTENTS

Portfolio Management

◙ indicates an optional segment

Contents

◙ indicates an optional segment

How to Use the CFA Program Curriculum

Congratulations on reaching Level III of the Chartered Financial Analyst (CFA®) Program. This exciting and rewarding program of study reflects your desire to become a serious investment professional. You are embarking on a program noted for its high ethical standards and the breadth of knowledge, skills, and abilities it develops. Your commitment to the CFA Program should be educationally and professionally rewarding.

The credential you seek is respected around the world as a mark of accomplishment and dedication. Each level of the program represents a distinct achievement in professional development. Successful completion of the program is rewarded with membership in a prestigious global community of investment professionals. CFA charterholders are dedicated to life-long learning and maintaining currency with the ever-changing dynamics of a challenging profession. The CFA Program represents the first step toward a career-long commitment to professional education.

The CFA examination measures your mastery of the core skills required to succeed as an investment professional. These core skills are the basis for the Candidate Body of Knowledge (CBOK™). The CBOK consists of four components:

- A broad topic outline that lists the major top-level topic areas (www. cfainstitute.org/cbok);
- Topic area weights that indicate the relative exam weightings of the top-level topic areas (www.cfainstitute.org/level_III);
- Learning outcome statements (LOS) that advise candidates about the specific knowledge, skills, and abilities they should acquire from readings covering a topic area (LOS are provided in candidate study sessions and at the beginning of each reading); and
- The CFA Program curriculum, readings, and end-of-reading questions, which candidates receive upon exam registration.

Therefore, the key to your success on the CFA examinations is studying and understanding the CBOK. The following sections provide background on the CBOK, the organization of the curriculum, and tips for developing an effective study program.

CURRICULUM DEVELOPMENT PROCESS

The CFA Program is grounded in the practice of the investment profession. Using the Global Body of Investment Knowledge (GBIK) collaborative website, CFA Institute performs a continuous practice analysis with investment professionals around the world to determine the knowledge, skills, and abilities (competencies) that are relevant to the profession. Regional expert panels and targeted surveys are conducted annually to verify and reinforce the continuous feedback from the GBIK collaborative website. The practice analysis process ultimately defines the CBOK. The CBOK contains the competencies that are generally accepted and applied by investment professionals. These competencies are used in practice in a generalist context and are expected to be demonstrated by a recently qualified CFA charterholder.

A committee consisting of practicing charterholders, in conjunction with CFA Institute staff, designs the CFA Program curriculum in order to deliver the CBOK to candidates. The examinations, also written by practicing charterholders, are designed to allow you to demonstrate your mastery of the CBOK as set forth in the CFA Program curriculum. As you structure your personal study program, you should emphasize mastery of the CBOK and the practical application of that knowledge. For more information on the practice analysis, CBOK, and development of the CFA Program curriculum, please visit www.cfainstitute.org.

ORGANIZATION OF THE CURRICULUM

The Level III CFA Program curriculum is organized into 10 topic areas. Each topic area begins with a brief statement of the material and the depth of knowledge expected.

Each topic area is then divided into one or more study sessions. These study sessions—18 sessions in the Level III curriculum—should form the basic structure of your reading and preparation.

Each study session includes a statement of its structure and objective and is further divided into specific reading assignments. An outline illustrating the organization of these 18 study sessions can be found at the front of each volume.

The reading assignments are the basis for all examination questions and are selected or developed specifically to teach the knowledge, skills, and abilities reflected in the CBOK. These readings are drawn from content commissioned by CFA Institute, textbook chapters, professional journal articles, research analyst reports, and cases. All readings include problems and solutions to help you understand and master the topic areas.

Reading-specific Learning Outcome Statements (LOS) are listed at the beginning of each reading. These LOS indicate what you should be able to accomplish after studying the reading. The LOS, the reading, and the end-of-reading questions are dependent on each other, with the reading and questions providing context for understanding the scope of the LOS.

You should use the LOS to guide and focus your study because each examination question is based on an assigned reading and one or more LOS. The readings provide context for the LOS and enable you to apply a principle or concept in a variety of scenarios. The candidate is responsible for the entirety of the required material in a study session, which includes the assigned readings as well as the end-of-reading questions and problems.

We encourage you to review the information about the LOS on our website (www.cfainstitute.org/programs/cfaprogram/courseofstudy/Pages/study_sessions.aspx), including the descriptions of LOS "command words" (www.cfainstitute.org/programs/Documents/cfa_and_cipm_los_command_words.pdf).

FEATURES OF THE CURRICULUM

OPTIONAL
SEGMENT

Required vs. Optional Segments   You should read all of an assigned reading. In some cases, though, we have reprinted an entire chapter or article and marked certain parts of the reading as "optional." The CFA examination is based only on the required segments, and the optional segments are included only when it is determined that they might help you to better understand the required segments (by seeing the required material in its full context). When an optional segment begins, you will see an icon and a dashed vertical bar in the outside margin that will continue until the optional segment ends, accompanied by another icon. *Unless the material is specifically marked as optional, you should assume it is required.* You should rely on the required segments and the reading-specific LOS in preparing for the examination.

Problems/Solutions *All questions and problems in the readings as well as their solutions (which are provided directly following the problems) are part of the curriculum and are required material for the exam.* When appropriate, we have included problems within and after the readings to demonstrate practical application and reinforce your understanding of the concepts presented. The questions and problems are designed to help you learn these concepts and may serve as a basis for exam questions. Many of these questions are adapted from past CFA examinations.

Glossary and Index For your convenience, we have printed a comprehensive glossary in each volume. Throughout the curriculum, a **bolded** word in a reading denotes a term defined in the glossary. The curriculum eBook is searchable, but we also publish an index that can be found on the CFA Institute website with the Level III study sessions.

Source Material The authorship, publisher, and copyright owners are given for each reading for your reference. We recommend that you use the CFA Institute curriculum rather than the original source materials because the curriculum may include only selected pages from outside readings, updated sections within the readings, and problems and solutions tailored to the CFA Program.

LOS Self-Check We have inserted checkboxes next to each LOS that you can use to track your progress in mastering the concepts in each reading.

DESIGNING YOUR PERSONAL STUDY PROGRAM

Create a Schedule An orderly, systematic approach to exam preparation is critical. You should dedicate a consistent block of time every week to reading and studying. Complete all reading assignments and the associated problems and solutions in each study session. Review the LOS both before and after you study each reading to ensure that you have mastered the applicable content and can demonstrate the knowledge, skill, or ability described by the LOS and the assigned reading. Use the LOS self-check to track your progress and highlight areas of weakness for later review.

As you prepare for your exam, we will e-mail you important exam updates, testing policies, and study tips. Be sure to read these carefully. Curriculum errata are periodically updated and posted on the study session page at www.cfainstitute.org. You can also sign up for an RSS feed to alert you to the latest errata update.

Successful candidates report an average of more than 300 hours preparing for each exam. Your preparation time will vary based on your prior education and experience. For each level of the curriculum, there are 18 study sessions. So, a good plan is to devote 15–20 hours per week for 18 weeks to studying the material. Use the final four to six weeks before the exam to review what you have learned and practice with topic and mock exams. This recommendation, however, may underestimate the hours needed for appropriate examination preparation depending on your individual circumstances, relevant experience, and academic background. You will undoubtedly adjust your study time to conform to your own strengths and weaknesses and to your educational and professional background.

You will probably spend more time on some study sessions than on others, but on average you should plan on devoting 15–20 hours per study session. You should allow ample time for both in-depth study of all topic areas and additional concentration on those topic areas for which you feel the least prepared.

An interactive study planner is available in the candidate resources area of our website to help you plan your study time. The interactive study planner recommends completion dates for each topic of the curriculum. Dates are determined based on study time available, exam topic weights, and curriculum weights. As you progress through the curriculum, the interactive study planner dynamically adjusts your study plan when you are running off schedule to help you stay on track for completion prior to the examination.

CFA Institute Topic Exams   The CFA Institute topic exams are intended to assess your mastery of individual topic areas as you progress through your studies. After each test, you will receive immediate feedback noting the correct responses and indicating the relevant assigned reading so you can identify areas of weakness for further study. The topic exams reflect the question formats and level of difficulty of the actual CFA examinations. For more information on the topic tests, please visit www.cfainstitute.org.

CFA Institute Mock Exams   Mock examinations mimic the actual CFA examinations not only in question format and level of difficulty, but also in length and topic weight. The three-hour mock exams simulate the morning and afternoon sessions of the actual CFA examination, and are intended to be taken after you complete your study of the full curriculum so you can test your understanding of the curriculum and your readiness for the exam. You will receive feedback at the end of the mock exam, noting the correct responses and indicating the relevant assigned readings so you can assess areas of weakness for further study during your review period. We recommend that you take mock exams during the final stages of your preparation for the actual CFA examination. For more information on the mock examinations, please visit www.cfainstitute.org.

Preparatory Providers   After you enroll in the CFA Program, you may receive numerous solicitations for preparatory courses and review materials. When considering a prep course, make sure the provider is in compliance with the CFA Institute Prep Provider Guidelines Program (www.cfainstitute.org/partners/examprep/Pages/cfa_prep_provider_guidelines.aspx). Just remember, there are no shortcuts to success on the CFA examinations; reading and studying the CFA curriculum is the key to success on the examination. The CFA examinations reference only the CFA Institute assigned curriculum—no preparatory course or review course materials are consulted or referenced.

SUMMARY

Every question on the CFA examination is based on the content contained in the required readings and on one or more LOS. Frequently, an examination question is based on a specific example highlighted within a reading or on a specific end-of-reading question and/or problem and its solution. To make effective use of the CFA Program curriculum, please remember these key points:

1   All pages printed in the curriculum are required reading for the examination except for occasional sections marked as optional. You may read optional pages as background, but you will not be tested on them.

2   All questions, problems, and their solutions—printed at the end of readings—are part of the curriculum and are required study material for the examination.

3   You should make appropriate use of the topic and mock examinations and other resources available at www.cfainstitute.org.

4 Use the interactive study planner to create a schedule and commit sufficient study time to cover the 18 study sessions, review the materials, and take topic and mock examinations.

5 Some of the concepts in the study sessions may be superseded by updated rulings and/or pronouncements issued after a reading was published. Candidates are expected to be familiar with the overall analytical framework contained in the assigned readings. Candidates are not responsible for changes that occur after the material was written.

FEEDBACK

At CFA Institute, we are committed to delivering a comprehensive and rigorous curriculum for the development of competent, ethically grounded investment professionals. We rely on candidate and member feedback as we work to incorporate content, design, and packaging improvements. You can be assured that we will continue to listen to your suggestions. Please send any comments or feedback to info@cfainstitute.org. Ongoing improvements in the curriculum will help you prepare for success on the upcoming examinations and for a lifetime of learning as a serious investment professional.

Portfolio Management

This volume includes Study Sessions 16–18.

TOPIC LEVEL LEARNING OUTCOME

The candidate should be able to prepare an appropriate investment policy statement and asset allocation; formulate strategies for managing, monitoring, and rebalancing investment portfolios; evaluate portfolio performance; and analyze a presentation of investment returns for consistency with Global Investment Performance Standards (GIPS®).

16

Trading, Monitoring, and Rebalancing

Because the investment process is not complete until securities are bought or sold, the quality of trade execution is an important determinant of investment results. The methods by which managers and traders interact with markets, choose appropriate trading strategies and tactics, and measure success in execution are key topics in the first reading.

The second reading discusses the ongoing monitoring and rebalancing of the investment portfolio, integral parts of the portfolio management process. Portfolio managers must understand the reasons for monitoring portfolios and be able to formulate appropriate portfolio rebalancing policies.

READING ASSIGNMENTS

READING

30

Execution of Portfolio Decisions

by Ananth Madhavan, Jack L. Treynor, and Wayne H. Wagner

LEARNING OUTCOMES

Mastery	The candidate should be able to:
☐	a. compare market orders with limit orders, including the price and execution uncertainty of each;
☐	b. calculate and interpret the effective spread of a market order and contrast it to the quoted bid–ask spread as a measure of trading cost;
☐	c. compare alternative market structures and their relative advantages;
☐	d. compare the roles of brokers and dealers;
☐	e. explain the criteria of market quality and evaluate the quality of a market when given a description of its characteristics;
☐	f. explain the components of execution costs, including explicit and implicit costs, and evaluate a trade in terms of these costs;
☐	g. calculate and discuss implementation shortfall as a measure of transaction costs;
☐	h. contrast volume weighted average price (VWAP) and implementation shortfall as measures of transaction costs;
☐	i. explain the use of econometric methods in pretrade analysis to estimate implicit transaction costs;
☐	j. discuss the major types of traders, based on their motivation to trade, time versus price preferences, and preferred order types;
☐	k. describe the suitable uses of major trading tactics, evaluate their relative costs, advantages, and weaknesses, and recommend a trading tactic when given a description of the investor's motivation to trade, the size of the trade, and key market characteristics;
☐	l. explain the motivation for algorithmic trading and discuss the basic classes of algorithmic trading strategies;

(continued)

Managing Investment Portfolios: A Dynamic Process, Third Edition, John L. Maginn, CFA, Donald L. Tuttle, CFA, Jerald E. Pinto, CFA, and Dennis W. McLeavey, CFA, editors. Copyright © 2007 by CFA Institute.

LEARNING OUTCOMES

Mastery	The candidate should be able to:
☐	**m.** discuss the factors that typically determine the selection of a specific algorithmic trading strategy, including order size, average daily trading volume, bid–ask spread, and the urgency of the order;
☐	**n.** explain the meaning and criteria of best execution;
☐	**o.** evaluate a firm's investment and trading procedures, including processes, disclosures, and record keeping, with respect to best execution;
☐	**p.** discuss the role of ethics in trading.

1

INTRODUCTION

The investment process has been described as a three-legged stool supported equally by securities research, portfolio management, and securities trading. Of the three, trading is often the least understood and least appreciated function. As we will show, a deeper appreciation for the trading function can be a powerful help in achieving investment success.

In this reading, we will build the knowledge and explain the concepts needed to understand how managers and traders interact with markets, choose trading strategies and tactics, and measure their success in trading. Our perspective is chiefly that of a portfolio manager (or investment advisor) whose objective is to execute portfolio decisions in the best interests of the client. The portfolio manager's agents in doing so are the firm's traders. These **buy-side traders** are the professional traders employed by investment managers or institutional investors who place the trades that execute the decisions of portfolio managers. The job of such traders is to execute the desired trades quickly, without error, and at favorable prices. Execution is the final, critical step in the interlinked investment process: *The portfolio decision is not complete until securities are bought or sold.*

A portfolio manager is not a professional trader. However, a portfolio manager does need to:

■ communicate effectively with professional traders;

■ evaluate the quality of the execution services being provided for the firm's clients; and

■ take responsibility for achieving best execution on behalf of clients in his or her role as a fiduciary.

To accomplish those goals, the portfolio manager needs a grounding in:

■ the market institutions within which traders work, including the different types of trading venues to which traders may direct orders;

■ the measurement of trading costs; and

■ the tactics and strategies available to the firm's traders and the counterparties with whom they deal, including important innovations in trading technology.

The reading is organized as follows. Section 2 presents essential information for the portfolio manager on the types of orders, the variety of market venues where orders are executed, the roles of dealers and brokers, and the evaluation of market quality.

Section 3 addresses the costs of trading. The next two sections discuss topics relevant to trading strategy: the types of traders and their preferred order types (Section 4) and trade execution decisions and tactics (Section 5). Section 6 discusses serving the client's interests in trading and is followed by concluding remarks (Section 7) and a summary of major points.

THE CONTEXT OF TRADING: MARKET MICROSTRUCTURE

2

The portfolio manager needs to be familiar with **market microstructure**: the market structures and processes that affect how the manager's interest in buying or selling an asset is translated into executed trades (represented by trade prices and volumes).

Knowledge of market microstructure helps a portfolio manager understand how orders will be handled and executed. The formulation of trading strategies depends on accurate microstructure information. Such information can also help the practitioner understand the frictions that can cause asset prices to diverge from full-information expectations of value, possibly suggesting opportunities and pitfalls in trading.

The portfolio manager also needs to understand the characteristics of the major order types as he or she communicates with the trading desk on such matters as the emphasis to put on speed of execution versus price of execution. The next section presents some essential information on order types.

2.1 Order Types

Market orders and limit orders are the two major types of orders that traders use and that portfolio managers need to understand.

1 A **market order** is an instruction to execute an order promptly in the public markets at the best price available.

   For example, an order to buy 10,000 shares of BP p.l.c. directed to the London Stock Exchange (LSE) would execute at the best price available when the order reached that market. Suppose that when the order reaches the LSE, the lowest price at which a seller is ready to sell BP shares is 642p (pence) in quantity up to 8,000 shares (for a buyer, the lower the price, the better). The second-lowest price is 643p in quantity up to 6,000 shares. Thus, 8,000 shares of the market order would be filled (executed) at 642p and the balance of 10,000 − 8,000 = 2,000 shares would fill at 643p.

   A market order emphasizes immediacy of execution. However, a market order usually bears some degree of **price uncertainty** (uncertainty about the price at which the order will execute). In today's markets, most market orders are effectively automated from the point of origin straight through to reporting and clearing.

2 A **limit order** is an instruction to trade at the best price available but only if the price is at least as good as the limit price specified in the order. For buy orders, the trade price must not exceed the limit price, while for sell orders, the trade price must be at least as high as the limit price. An instruction always accompanies a limit order specifying when it will expire.

   Suppose that instead of the market order above, the trader places an order to buy 10,000 shares of BP p.l.c. at 641p limit (which means at a price of 641p or lower), good for one day (the order expires at the end of trading that day). Suppose that this buy order's price is higher than that of any other limit buy order for BP shares at the time. If that is the case, then 641p becomes the best available bid, or **market bid**, for BP shares. If a market sell order for 6,000 shares of BP arrives the instant after the trader's buy limit order for 10,000 shares, it will execute against that limit order. The trader will get a fill (execution) for 6,000 shares at 641p, leaving 4,000 shares of the order unfilled. At that point, favorable news on BP might reach the market. If so, the price of BP could move up sharply and not trade at or below 641p for the remainder of the day. If that is the case, at the end of the day, the trader will have 4,000 shares of his or her order unfilled and the order, which was good for one day, will expire.

By specifying the least favorable price at which an order can execute, *a limit order emphasizes price*. However, limit orders can execute only when the market price reaches the limit price specified by the limit order. The timing of the execution, or even whether the execution happens at all, is determined by the ebb and flow of the market. Limit orders thus have **execution uncertainty**.

Each trading venue specifies the types of orders permitted and other trading protocols. The professional trader needs to know the range of order types permitted. The list of all possible kinds of orders is long, but most order types represent variations on the elemental market and limit orders.[1] Some of these order types may serve to enlist the experience, presence, and knowledge of the trader's agent (broker) in executing a trade. Others may serve to conceal the quantity of a security that the trader wants to buy or sell, or serve some other purpose. A few additional important order types are as follows:

- **Market-not-held order**. This type of order is relevant for trades placed on certain **exchanges** (regulated trading venues) where an order may be handled by an agent of the trader in executing trades (a **broker**). This variation of the market order is designed to give the agent greater discretion than a simple market order would allow. "Not held" means that the broker is not required to trade at any specific price or in any specific time interval, as would be required with a simple market order. Discretion is placed in the hands of a representative of the broker (such as a **floor broker**—an agent of the broker who, for certain exchanges, physically represents the trade on the exchange). The broker may choose not to participate in the flow of orders on the exchange if the broker believes he or she will be able to get a better price in subsequent trading.

- **Participate (do not initiate) order**. This is a variant of the market-not-held order. The broker is to be deliberately low-key and wait for and respond to initiatives of more active traders. Buy-side traders who use this type of order hope to capture a better price in exchange for letting the other side determine the timing of the trade.

- **Best efforts order**. This type of order gives the trader's agent even more discretion to work the order only when the agent judges market conditions to be favorable. Some degree of immediacy is implied, but not immediacy at any price.

- Undisclosed limit order, also known as a reserve, hidden, or iceberg order. This is a limit order that includes an instruction not to show more than some maximum quantity of the unfilled order. For example, a trader might want to buy 200,000 shares of an issue traded on Euronext Amsterdam. The order size would represent a substantial fraction of average daily volume in the issue, and the trader is concerned that share price might move up if the full extent of his

---

1 See Harris (2003) for an in-depth treatment of order types.

or her interest were known. The trader places an undisclosed limit order to buy the 200,000 shares, specifying that no more than 20,000 shares of the unfilled order be shown to the public at a time.

- **Market on open order**. This is a market order to be executed at the opening of the market. Similarly, a **market on close order** is a market order to be executed at the market close. These are examples of orders with an instruction for execution at a specific time. The rationale for using these two types of orders is that the opening and close in many markets provide good liquidity.

The above types of orders describe how an order to buy or sell will be presented to the market. The following describe special types of trades:

- **Principal trade**. A principal trade is a trade with a broker in which the broker commits capital to facilitate the prompt execution of the trader's order to buy or sell. Principal trades are used most frequently when the order is larger and/or more urgent than can be accommodated within the normal ebb and flow of exchange trading. A price concession provides an incentive for the broker acting as a principal in the trade.

- **Portfolio trade** (or program trade or basket trade). A portfolio trade involves an order that requires the execution of purchases (or sales) in a specified basket (list) of securities at as close to the same time as possible. For example, an S&P 500 index fund manager with new cash to invest could execute a portfolio trade to buy the S&P 500 (the shares in the S&P 500 in their index weights). Portfolio trades are often relatively low cost because the diversification implied by multiple security issues reduces the risk to the other side of the trade.

With some essential information on order types in hand, we can discuss market structures for trading.

2.2 Types of Markets

Markets are organized to provide **liquidity** (the ability to trade without delay at relatively low cost and in relatively large quantities), **transparency** (availability of timely and accurate market and trade information), and **assurity of completion** (trades settle without problems under all market conditions—**trade settlement** involves the buyer's payment for the asset purchased and the transfer of formal ownership of that asset).

In what follows, we describe the chief ways trading is organized:

- Quote-driven (or dealer) markets, in which members of the public trade with dealers rather than directly with one another.

- Order-driven markets, in which members of the public trade with one another without the intermediation of dealers.

- Brokered markets, in which the trader relies on a broker to find the other side of a desired trade.

These distinctions are valuable in understanding the dynamics of trading and price formation, although, as we discuss later, the lines between the categories are often blurry. Furthermore, markets evolve, and the portfolio manager needs to keep abreast of important new developments.

Fixed-income and equity markets have evolved very rapidly over the 1990s and 2000s. There are many more choices as to where to trade such bonds and equities than was the case historically—a phenomenon that has been called **market fragmentation**. Another trend is the increasing amount of trading that is partly or fully automated, in the sense that the execution of a trader's order after entry requires minimal or no human intervention or trader-to-trader communication. Reflecting the concern to minimize settlement errors and costs in security markets, the settlement of the trade after execution may also be automated within a given trading system or venue (**straight-through processing**, or STP).

Forward and futures markets are also in transition. For example, at the Chicago Board of Trade (a US commodities exchange), an automated trading system (e-cbot) operates alongside a type of market dating back centuries (an **open outcry auction market**). In an open outcry auction market, representatives of buyers and sellers meet at a specified location on the floor of an exchange, with voices raised ("open outcry") so they can be heard, to conduct auctions to fill customers' orders.

Alternative investment markets have also been affected by changes. For example, hedge funds (loosely regulated pooled investment vehicles) have been aggressive in exploiting advances in trading technology.

All the above developments are better understood when the structures by which trading is organized are grasped. The first type of market that we will discuss is called a quote-driven or dealer market.

2.2.1 Quote-Driven (Dealer) Markets

Quote-driven markets rely on dealers to establish firm prices at which securities can be bought and sold. These markets are therefore also called dealer markets, as trades are executed with a dealer. A **dealer** (sometimes referred to as a market maker) is a business entity that is ready to buy an asset for inventory or sell an asset from inventory to provide the other side of an order to buy or sell the asset.

In the traditional view, market makers or dealers passively provide immediacy or bridge liquidity, the price of which is the **bid–ask spread** (the ask price minus the bid price). A dealer's (or any trader's) **bid price** (or **bid**) is the price at which he or she will buy a specified quantity of a security. A dealer's (or any trader's) **ask price** (or ask, or offer price, or offer) is the price at which he or she will sell a specified quantity of a security. On the principle of buying low and selling high, a dealer's ask price is greater than his bid price. The quantity associated with the bid price is often referred to as the **bid size**; the quantity associated with the ask price is known as the **ask size**. From the perspective of a trader executing an order to *buy* a security from a dealer, a *lower ask* from the dealer is favorable to the trader. If the trader is executing an order to *sell* a security to a dealer, a *higher bid* from the dealer is favorable to the trader.

Suppose that a portfolio manager gives the firm's trading desk an order to buy 1,000 shares of Economical Chemical Systems, Inc. (ECSI), which is traded in a dealer market, and that three dealers (coded A, B, and C) make a market in those shares. At the time the trader views the market in ECSI on his computer screen, 10:22 a.m., the three dealers have put in the following quotes:

- Dealer A: *bid*: 98.85 for 600 shares; *ask*: 100.51 for 1,000 shares
- Dealer B: *bid*: 98.84 for 500 shares; *ask*: 100.55 for 500 shares
- Dealer C: *bid*: 98.82 for 700 shares; *ask*: 100.49 for 800 shares

Thus, the bid–ask spreads of Dealers A, B, and C are, respectively,

- 100.51 − 98.85 = 1.66
- 100.55 − 98.84 = 1.71
- 100.49 − 98.82 = 1.67

The trader might see the quote information organized on his screen as shown in Exhibit 1. In Exhibit 1, the bids and asks are ordered from best to worst and time-stamped. These are actually limit orders because the prices at which the dealers are ready to trade are specified. Because Exhibit 1 lists limit orders, it is called a **limit order** book. The **inside bid**, or **market bid**, which is the highest and best bid, is 98.85 from Dealer A. However, Dealer C is quoting the **inside ask**, or **market ask**, which is the lowest ask, at 100.49. The **inside quote**, or **market quote**, is therefore 98.85 bid, 100.49 ask. The **inside bid–ask spread**, or **market bid–ask spread** (or **inside spread** or **market spread** for short), is 100.49 − 98.85 = 1.64, which in this case is lower than any individual dealer's spread. (Prevailing is also used for *inside* or *market* in all these expressions.) The trader also notes that the **midquote** (halfway between the market bid and ask prices) is (100.49 + 98.85)/2 = 99.67.

Exhibit 1	The Limit Order Book for Economical Chemical Systems, Inc.						
Bid				**Ask**			
Dealer	**Time Entered**	**Price**	**Size**	**Dealer**	**Time Entered**	**Price**	**Size**
A	10:21 a.m.	98.85	600	C	10:21 a.m.	100.49	800
B	10:21 a.m.	98.84	500	A	10:21 a.m.	100.51	1,000
C	10:19 a.m.	98.82	700	B	10:19 a.m.	100.55	500

Note: The bids are ordered from highest to lowest, while the asks are ordered from lowest to highest. These orderings are from best bid or ask to worst bid or ask.

If the trader executes a market buy order for 1,000 shares, the trader would purchase 800 shares from Dealer C at 100.49 per share and 200 shares from Dealer A at 100.51 per share. However, in some markets, it is also possible for the trader to direct the buy order to a specific dealer—for example, Dealer A. The trader may do so for a variety of reasons. For example, the trader may believe that Dealer A is reliable in standing behind quotes but that Dealer C is not. As one example, currency markets are dealer markets, and institutions active in those markets may screen counterparties on credit criteria.

In some dealer markets, a public trader might not have real-time access to all quotes in the security as in our example; that is, the limit order book is not "open," meaning visible in real time to the public. In such **closed-book markets**, the trader would rely on a broker to locate the best ask price, paying the broker a commission. Another notable point concerns limit orders. Historically, in dealer markets, rules would restrict a limit order from a public trader from competing with dealers' bids and asks for other public trades. In a "pure" dealer market, a dealer is a counterparty to every trade. However, in some quote-driven markets, such as the US NASDAQ market for equities, public traders' limit orders are displayed and compete with dealers' bids and asks.[2]

If the portfolio manager communicated that he or she had a focus on price rather than immediacy, the trader might consider placing a limit order within the market spread—for example, an order to buy 1,000 shares at 100 limit. The trader's limit order in a market such as NASDAQ would establish a new market bid at 100, and the revised market quote would be 100 bid, 100.49 ask. If nothing else had changed, an incoming market order to sell ECSI shares would "hit" the trader's bid of 100. The trader might also hope that one of the dealers would revise the ask downward and fill part or all of the trader's order. On the other hand, it is also possible that the trader's limit order would expire unfilled.

Dealers have played important roles in bond and equity markets because *dealers can help markets operate continuously*. Bond markets, in particular, are overwhelmingly dealer markets. The explanation lies in a lack of natural liquidity for many bonds. (**Natural liquidity** is an extensive pool of investors who are aware of and have

---

2 The display of public limit orders on NASDAQ followed a US reform in 1997 that was triggered by a controversy about dealer collusion in setting quotes.

a potential interest in buying and/or selling a security.) Many bonds are extremely infrequently traded. If an investor wanted to buy such a bond, the investor might have a very long wait before the other side of the trade (an interest to sell) appeared from the public. Dealers help markets in such securities operate more nearly continuously by being ready to take the opposite side of a trade.

An examination of the US corporate bond markets highlights the lack of natural liquidity in these markets. In the second quarter of 2011, the average daily volume of corporate bond trades was $15.8 billion, which was only 0.21% of the dollar amount of bonds outstanding at that time.[3] A 2007 study of bond liquidity found that, for the bonds that traded during the time period 2003-2005, the median number of trades was less than one a day. Only 1 percent of active bonds traded more than 20 times per day.[4] Even in the relatively frequently traded issues, an opportunity is thus created for an entity—the dealer—to "make" the market (i.e., create liquidity when no natural liquidity exists). A market is made when the dealer stands ready to provide bridge liquidity by buying securities offered by a seller and holding them until a buyer arrives, in return for earning a spread.

Similar considerations often operate in equities. For example, the London Stock Exchange has a quote-driven, competing dealer market called SEAQ for infrequently traded shares. Dealers also play important roles in markets requiring negotiation of the terms of the instrument, such as forward markets and swap markets, where otherwise finding a counterparty to the instrument would often not be feasible.

The size of the *quoted* bid–ask spread (reflecting the market quote), particularly as a proportion of the quote midpoint, is one measure of trading costs. However, the quoted bid–ask spread may be different from the spread at which a trader actually transacts. The trader's focus is therefore often on the *effective* spread.

The **effective spread** is two times the deviation of the actual execution price from the midpoint of the market quote at the time an order is entered. (If parts of the order execute at different prices, the weighted-average execution price is used in computing the deviation from the midpoint.) The quoted spread is the simplest measure of round-trip transaction costs for an average-size order. The effective spread is a better representation of the true cost of a round-trip transaction because it captures both **price improvement** (i.e., execution within the quoted spread at a price such that the trader is benefited) and the tendency for larger orders to move prices (**market impact**).[5] Exhibit 2 gives the market bid–ask in a hypothetical common equity issue that we can use to illustrate the difference between these two kinds of spreads.

Exhibit 2 A Market Bid–Ask at 10:03:14 (Order Entry)			
Bid Price	**Bid Size**	**Ask Price**	**Ask Size**
$19.97	400	$20.03	1,000

With the information in Exhibit 2 before him, a trader with instructions to buy 500 shares with minimal delay enters a market order for 500 shares. As the order is received in the system at 10:03:18, a dealer in the issue enters a quote of $19.96 bid (bid size: 100 shares) and $20.01 ask (ask size: 500 shares) to improve on ("step

---

3 www.sifma.org/research/statistics.aspx, Accessed 27 September 2011.
4 See Edwards, Harris, and Piwowar (2007), Table 2.
5 Price improvement happens when a trader improves on (or "steps in front of") the best current bid or ask price to take the other side of an incoming market order.

in front of") the prior best ask price of $20.03 and take the incoming market order. This can happen because the dealer quickly decides that the profit from the trade is satisfactory. Exhibit 3 shows the market bid–ask at 10:03:18, when the order executes.

Exhibit 3   A Market Bid–Ask at 10:03:18 (Order Execution)

Bid Price	Bid Size	Ask Price	Ask Size
$19.97	400	$20.01	500

Thus, 500 shares of the trader's market order execute at $20.01, which represents a price improvement of $0.02 relative to the market ask of $20.03 that the trader saw when the order was entered. (The lower purchase price represents a price improvement for the buyer.)

From Exhibit 2 we see that the quoted bid–ask spread is $20.03 − $19.97 = $0.06. The midquote is ($20.03 + $19.97)/2 = $20.00. The effective spread is 2 × ($20.01 − $20.00) = 2 × $0.01 = $0.02, which is $0.06 − $0.02 = $0.04 less than the quoted spread. *The price improvement has resulted in an effective spread that is lower than the quoted spread.*

The **average effective spread** is the mean effective spread (sometimes dollar weighted) over all transactions in the stock in the period under study. The average effective spread attempts to measure the liquidity of a security's market.

EXAMPLE 1

The Effective Spread of an Illiquid Stock

Charles McClung, portfolio manager of a Canadian small-cap equity mutual fund, is reviewing with his firm's chief trader the execution of a ticket to sell 1,000 shares of Alpha Company. The ticket was split into three trades executed in a single day as follows:

A   A market order to sell 200 shares was executed at a price of C$10.15. The quote that was in effect at that time was as follows:

Ask Price	Ask Size	Bid Price	Bid Size
C$10.24	200	C$10.12	300

B   A market order to sell 300 shares was executed at a price of C$10.11. The quote that was in effect at that time was as follows:

Ask Price	Ask Size	Bid Price	Bid Size
C$10.22	200	C$10.11	300

C   A market order to sell 500 shares was executed at an average price of C$10.01. The quote that was in effect at that time was as follows:

Ask Price	Ask Size	Bid Price	Bid Size
C$10.19	200	C$10.05	300

This order exceeded the quoted bid size and "walked down" the limit order book (i.e., after the market bid was used, the order made use of limit order(s) to buy at lower prices than the market bid).

1 For each of the above market orders, compute the quoted spread. Also, compute the average quoted spread for the stock for the day.

2 For each of the above, compute the effective spread. Also, compute the average effective spread and the share-volume-weighted effective spread for the stock for the day.

3 Discuss the relative magnitudes of quoted and effective spreads for each of the three orders.

Solution to 1:

The quoted spread is the difference between the ask and bid prices. So, for the first order, the quoted spread is C\$10.24 − C\$10.12 = C\$0.12. Similarly, the quoted spreads for the second and third orders are C\$0.11 and C\$0.14, respectively. The average quoted spread is (C\$0.12 + C\$0.11 + C\$0.14)/3 = C\$0.1233.

Solution to 2:

Effective spread for a sell order = 2 × (Midpoint of the market at the time an order is entered − Actual execution price).

For the first order, the midpoint of the market at the time the order is entered = (C\$10.12 + C\$10.24)/2 = C\$10.18. So, the effective spread = 2 × (C\$10.18 − C\$10.15) = C\$0.06.

The effective spread for the second order = 2 × [(C\$10.11 + C\$10.22)/2 − C\$10.11] = C\$0.11.

The effective spread for the third order = 2 × [(C\$10.05 + C\$10.19)/2 − C\$10.01] = C\$0.22.

The average effective spread = (C\$0.06 + C\$0.11 + C\$0.22)/3 = C\$0.13. The share-volume-weighted effective spread = [(200 × C\$0.06) + (300 × C\$0.11) + (500 × C\$0.22)]/(200 + 300 + 500) = (C\$12.00 + C\$33.00 + C\$110.00)/1,000 = C\$155.00/1,000 = C\$0.155.

Solution to 3:

In the first trade, there was a price improvement because the shares were sold at a price above the bid price. Therefore, the effective spread is less than the quoted spread. In the second trade, there was no price improvement because the shares were sold at the bid price. Also, there was no impact on the execution price because the entire order was fulfilled at the quoted bid. Accordingly, the effective and quoted spreads are equal. In the third trade, the effective spread is greater than the quoted spread because the order size was greater than the bid size and the order had to walk down the limit order book, resulting in a lower average price for the sale and therefore a higher effective spread.

Empirical research confirms that effective bid–ask spreads are lower in higher-volume securities because dealers can achieve faster turnaround in inventory, which reduces their risk. Spreads are wider for riskier and less liquid securities. Later research provided a deeper understanding of trading costs by explaining variation in bid–ask spreads as part of intraday price dynamics. This research showed that market makers are not simply passive providers of immediacy but must also take an active role in price setting to rapidly turn over inventory without accumulating significant positions on one side of the market.

Price may depart from expectations of value if the dealer is long or short relative to desired (target) inventory, giving rise to transitory price movements during the day—and possibly over longer periods. This intuition drives the models of inventory control developed by, among others, Madhavan and Smidt (1993).

2.2.2 *Order-Driven Markets*

Order-driven markets are markets in which transaction prices are established by public limit orders to buy or sell a security at specified prices. Such markets feature trades between public investors, *usually without intermediation by designated dealers* (market makers). The limit order book shown in Exhibit 1 for the hypothetical Economical Chemical Systems, Inc., would also be a possible limit order book for the company if it were traded in an order-driven market, but typically with public traders replacing dealers (dealers may trade in order-driven markets but do so alongside other traders). There might be more competition for orders, because a trader does not have to transact with a dealer (as in a "pure" dealer market). But it is also possible that a trader might be delayed in executing a trade or be unable to execute it because a dealer with an inventory of the security is not present. Orders from the public "drive," or determine, liquidity, explaining the term *order-driven markets*. In order-driven markets, a trader cannot choose with whom he or she trades because a prespecified set of rules (based on factors such as price and time of order entry) mechanically governs the execution of orders submitted to the market.

Examples of order-driven markets include the Toronto Stock Exchange for equities, the International Securities Exchange for options, and Hotspot FX for foreign exchange. For equity markets, a worldwide trend has favored order-driven markets at the expense of quote-driven markets. Various types of order-driven markets are distinguished:

Electronic Crossing Networks   Electronic crossing networks are markets in which buy and sell orders are batched (accumulated) and crossed at a specific point in time, usually in an anonymous fashion. Electronic crossing networks execute trades at prices taken from other markets. An example of a crossing network is the POSIT trading system, which matches buyers and sellers at the average of prevailing bid and ask prices at fixed points in the day. Crossing networks serve mainly institutional investors.[6]

In using crossing networks, both buyer and seller avoid the costs of dealer services (the bid–ask spread), the effects a large order can have on execution prices, and information leakage. Commissions are paid to the crossing network but are typically low. However, crossing participants cannot be guaranteed that their trades will find an opposing match: The volume in a crossing system is determined by the smallest quantity submitted.

To illustrate how trades on a crossing network are executed, we will suppose that an investment manager, coded A in Exhibit 4, wishes to buy 10,000 shares of a stock. At the same time, two different mutual fund traders, coded B and C, wish to sell 3,000 and 4,000 shares, respectively. The crossing of orders occurs at 12:00 p.m. on each business day. The market bid and ask prices of the stock are €30.10 and €30.16, respectively.

---

6 In discussions of US equity markets in particular, a term that is occasionally used for direct trading of securities between institutional investors is the **fourth market**; the fourth market would include trading on electronic crossing networks.

Exhibit 4	Electronic Crossing Network: Crossing of Orders at 12:00 p.m. (Numerical Entries Are Numbers of Shares)		
	Trader Identity	Buy Orders	Sell Orders
A		10,000	
B			3,000
C			4,000

In this example, total volume is 7,000 shares and the execution price is at the **midquote** (halfway between the prevailing bid and ask prices) of €30.13 = (€30.10 + €30.16)/2. Both sellers have their orders executed in full, but buyer A receives a **partial fill** of 7,000 shares. The buyer has the option of sending the remaining 3,000 shares back to the crossing system for another attempt at execution at the next scheduled crossing or trying to trade this remainder in the open market. None of the participants observes the identities or original submission sizes of the others in the match pool.

Crossing networks provide no price discovery. **Price discovery** means that transaction prices adjust to equilibrate supply and demand. Because the crossing network did not provide price discovery, price could not adjust upward to uncover additional selling interest and fully satisfy trader A's demand to buy.

Auction Markets Many order-driven markets are auction markets—that is, markets in which the orders of multiple buyers compete for execution. Auction markets can be further categorized into **periodic auction markets** or **batch auction markets** (where multilateral trading occurs at a single price at a prespecified point in time) and **continuous auction markets** (where orders can be executed at any time during the trading day). Examples of batch auction markets are the open and close of some stock exchanges and the reopening of the Tokyo Stock Exchange after the midday lunch break; at these times, orders are aggregated for execution at a single price. In contrast to electronic crossing markets, auction markets provide price discovery, lessening the problem of partial fills that we illustrated above for crossing networks.

Automated Auctions (Electronic Limit-Order Markets) These are computer-based auctions that operate continuously within the day using a specified set of rules to execute orders. **Electronic communications networks (ECNs)**, such as the NYSE Arca Exchange in the United States and the Paris Bourse in France, are examples of automated auctions for equities. Like crossing networks, ECNs provide anonymity and are computer-based. In contrast to crossing networks, ECNs operate continuously and, as auction markets, provide price discovery. (Following usual practice, the acronym "ECN" is reserved to refer to electronic communications networks.)

Automated auctions have been among the fastest-growing segments in equity trading. ECNs in particular have blurred the traditional difference between order-driven markets and quote-driven dealer markets. In an ECN, it can be difficult to distinguish between participants who are regulated, professional dealers and other participants who, in effect, are also attempting to earn spread profits by providing liquidity. Hedge funds or day traders, for example, might actively supply liquidity to the market to capture the dealer-like spread profits. From the perspective of an investor, the result is added liquidity and tighter spreads.[7]

---

[7] For further reading on this subject, see Wagner (2004).

2.2.3 Brokered Markets

A broker is an agent of the buy-side trader who collects a commission for skillful representation of the trade. The broker may represent the trade to dealers in the security or to the market order flow. However, the term **brokered markets** refers specifically to markets in which transactions are largely effected through a search-brokerage mechanism away from public markets.[8] Typically, these markets are important in countries where the underlying public markets (e.g., stock exchanges) are relatively small or where it is difficult to find liquidity in size. Consequently, brokered markets are mostly used for block transactions.

Brokers can help locate natural counterparties to a difficult order—for example, a block order. A **block order** is an order to sell or buy in a quantity that is large relative to the liquidity ordinarily available from dealers in the security or in other markets. The trader might use the services of a broker to carefully try to uncover the other side of the trade in return for a commission; the broker might occasionally position a portion of the block. (To **position a trade** is to take the other side of it, acting as a principal with capital at risk.) Brokers can also provide a reputational screen to protect uninformed or liquidity-motivated traders. For example, the broker might "shop the block" only to those potential counterparties that the broker believes are unlikely to **front-run** the trade (trade ahead of the initiator, exploiting privileged information about the initiator's trading intentions). These attributes of brokerage markets facilitate trading and hence add value for all parties to the transaction.

EXAMPLE 2

Market Classifications Are Simplifications

Although it is convenient to equate the dealer function with the activities of professional market makers, many parties can and do perform parts of the dealer function. As discussed, brokerage firms' "upstairs" trading desks may commit capital to support clients' trading desires. Thus, these firms are often called broker/dealers, recognizing that they function as both brokers and dealers. Equally important, investors can compete with dealers. Buy-side traders can reduce their trading costs by providing accommodative, dealer-like services to other market participants—for example, by submitting limit orders that other participants may "hit" to fulfill liquidity needs.

2.2.4 Hybrid Markets

Hybrid markets are combinations of the previously described market types. A good example is the New York Stock Exchange (NYSE), which offers elements of batch auction markets (e.g., the opening) and continuous auction markets (intraday trading), as well as quote-driven markets (the important role of NYSE dealers, who are known as specialists).

---

8 In the United States, brokered equity markets were traditionally referred to as upstairs markets. The reference is to trades executed not on the floor of an exchange ("downstairs") but via communications "upstairs" in brokerage firms' offices.

2.3 The Roles of Brokers and Dealers

Having discussed the types of markets, we now discuss the roles of brokers and dealers, because it is essential that portfolio managers and traders understand their different roles.[9]

A broker is an agent of the investor. As such, in return for a commission, the broker provides various execution services, including the following:

- **Representing the order**. The broker's primary task is to represent the order to the market. The market will accommodate, usually for a price, someone who feels he or she must trade immediately.

- **Finding the opposite side of a trade**. If interest in taking the opposite side of a trade is not currently evident in the market, it usually falls to the broker to try to locate the seller for the desired buy, or the buyer for the desired sale. Often this service requires that the broker act as a dealer and actively buy or sell shares for the broker's own account. The broker/dealer does not bear risk without compensation. Depending on the dealer's inventory position, this service may come at a high cost.

- **Supplying market information**. Market information includes the identity of buyers and sellers, the strength of buying and selling interest, and other information that is relevant to assessing the costs and risks of trading. This market intelligence, which can be provided by the broker, is very valuable to buy-side traders as they consider their trading tactics.

- **Providing discretion and secrecy**. Buy-side traders place great value on preserving the anonymity of their trading intentions. Notice, however, that such secrecy does not extend to the selected broker, whose stock in trade is the knowledge of supply and demand. That an investor is willing to trade is a very valuable piece of information the broker gains as result of his or her relationship with the trader.

- **Providing other supporting investment services**. A broker may provide a range of other services, including providing the client with financing for the use of leverage, record keeping, cash management, and safekeeping of securities. A particularly rich set of supporting services, often including introduction to potential clients, is provided in relationships that have come to be known as **prime brokerage**.

- **Supporting the market mechanism**. Brokerage commissions indirectly assure the continuance of the needed market facilities.

In contrast to the agency relationship of the broker with the trader, the relationship between the trader and a dealer is essentially adversarial. Like any other merchant, the dealer wants to sell merchandise at a higher price (the ask) than the purchase price (the bid). Holding trade volume constant, a dealer gains by wider bid–ask spreads while the trader gains by narrower bid–ask spreads. The dealer is wary of trading with a better-informed counterparty. Consider a portfolio manager who has concluded through new and original analysis that a bond issue currently in the portfolio has more credit risk than the rest of the market perceives. The dealer who makes a market in the company's bonds has set a bid price unaware of the fact that the bond's credit rating may be too high. The dealer's bid is too high relative to the true credit risk of the bond. The portfolio manager's trader liquidates the portfolio position in the bond issue at the dealer's bid price. The dealer's inventory in the bond issue increases, and subsequently the bond's price trends down as the rest of the market becomes aware

---

9 Many sell-side firms are both brokers and dealers. A given firm may deal in a security at the same time that it collects an agency commission for representing an order in it.

of the bond's actual credit risk. The dealer has just experienced **adverse selection risk** (the risk of trading with a more informed trader). Dealers want to know who is active in the market, how informed traders are, and how urgent their interest in transacting with the dealer is, in order to manage profits and adverse selection risk. The tension occurs because the informed or urgent trader does not want the dealer to know those facts.

Buy-side traders are often strongly influenced by sell-side traders such as dealers (the **sell side** consists of institutions that sell services to firms such as investment managers and institutional investors). The buy-side trader may have more interaction with dealers than with other units of the trader's own firm (which might simply communicate computer files of orders). In contrast, the sell-side trader, who possesses information vital to the buy-side trader's success, is a constant verbal window on the world. Over the years, the buy-side trader may build a reservoir of trust, friendship, comfort, and goodwill with his or her sell-side counterparts. It is often necessary to rely on the sell side's reputation for integrity and its long-term desire to maintain relationships. The trader should manage the relationships with dealers, remembering that the buy-side trader's first allegiance must always be to the firm's clients, for whom the trader acts in a fiduciary capacity.

We now have an overview of how markets function and have discussed in some detail the differences between the roles of brokers and dealers. But how *well* does a market function? Does a particular trading venue deserve order flow? The next section provides some ways to think about these questions.

2.4 Evaluating Market Quality

Markets are organized to provide liquidity, transparency, and assurity of completion, so they may be judged by the degree to which they have these qualities in practice. In detail, a liquid market is one that has the following characteristics:[10]

- **The market has relatively low bid–ask spreads**. Such a market is often called tight. Quoted spreads and effective spreads are low. The costs of trading small amounts of an asset are themselves small. As a result, investors can trade positions without excessive loss of value. If bid–ask spreads are high, investors cannot profitably trade on information except when the information is of great value.

- **The market is deep**. Depth means that big trades tend not to cause large price movements. As a result, the costs of trading large amounts of an asset are relatively small. Deep markets have high **quoted depth**, which is the number of shares available for purchase or sale at the quoted bid and ask prices.

- **The market is resilient**. A market is resilient (in the sense used here) if any discrepancies between market price and intrinsic value tend to be small and corrected quickly.

The great advantage of market liquidity is that traders and investors can trade rapidly without a major impact on price. This, in turn, makes it easy for those with relevant information to bring their insights and opinions into the price of securities. Corporations can then attract capital because investors can see that prices efficiently reflect the opportunities for profit and that they can buy and sell securities at will at relatively low cost. Liquidity adds value to the companies whose securities trade on the exchange. Investors will pay a premium for securities that possess the valuable trait of liquidity. Higher security prices enhance corporate value and lower the cost of capital.

---

10 This list follows a well-known analysis and definition of liquidity by Kyle (1985).

Many factors contribute to making a market liquid:

- **Many buyers and sellers**. The presence of many buyers and sellers increases the chance of promptly locating the opposite side of a trade at a competitive price. Success breeds success in that the liquidity resulting from many buyers and sellers attracts additional participants to the market. Investors are more willing to hold shares that they can dispose of whenever they choose to do so.

- **Diversity of opinion, information, and investment needs among market participants**. If the investors in a given market are highly alike, they are likely to want to take similar investment actions and make similar trades. Diversity in the factors described above increases the chance that a buyer of a security, who might have a positive opinion about it, can find a seller, who might have a negative opinion about it or a need for cash. In general, a large pool of investors enhances diversity of opinion.

- **Convenience**. A readily accessible physical location or an easily mastered and well-thought-out electronic platform attracts investors.

- **Market integrity**. Investors who receive fair and honest treatment in the trading process will trade again. The ethical tone set by professional market operatives plays a major role in establishing this trust, as does effective regulation. For example, audits of the financial condition and regulatory compliance of brokers and dealers operating in a market increase public confidence in the market's integrity, as do procedures for the disinterested investigation of complaints about the execution of trades.

Transparency means that individuals interested in or transacting in the market can quickly, easily, and inexpensively obtain accurate information about quotes and trades (**pretrade transparency**), and that details on completed trades are quickly and accurately reported to the public (**post-trade transparency**). Without transparency, the chance that the integrity of the trading process can be compromised increases. Assurity of completion depends on **assurity of the contract** (the parties to trades are held to fulfilling their obligations). To ensure the certainty of trade completion, participating brokers or clearing entities may guarantee the trade to both buyer and seller and be subject to standards of financial strength to ensure that the guarantee has "bite."

EXAMPLE 3

Assessing Market Quality after a Market Structure Change

US equity markets switched from price increments in sixteenths of a dollar to one-cent price increments in the first half of 2001. This decimalization of the US markets has received a lot of attention. Several studies have examined the changes that have taken place on the NYSE and NASDAQ (the major dealer market for US equities) as a consequence of decimalization, and some of their findings regarding the changes are as follows.[11]

A   Quoted spreads have declined from the predecimalization period to the postdecimalization period.

B   Effective spreads have declined.

C   Quoted depths have declined.

---

11 See Bacidore, Battalio, Jennings, and Farkas (2001), Bessembinder (2003), Chakravarty, Wood, and Van Ness (2004), and Oppenheimer and Sabherwal (2003).

For each of the above changes, state whether it suggests an improvement or deterioration in market quality after decimalization, and justify your assertion.

Solution to A:

This change suggests an improvement in market quality. Lower quoted spreads are consistent with lower trading costs, which suggest greater liquidity and an improvement in market quality.

Solution to B:

This change also suggests an improvement in market quality. Lower effective spreads are consistent with lower trading costs, which suggest greater liquidity and an improvement in market quality. Effective spreads are a more accurate measure of trading costs than quoted spreads. One would need to examine changes in commission costs (if any) subsequent to decimalization to get a more complete picture of the changes in trading costs that resulted from decimalization.

Solution to C:

Reduced quoted depths imply that large investors placing large orders are forced to split their orders more often after decimalization. Though small investors who place small orders are not likely to be affected by reduced depths, the trading costs for institutional investors could increase due to reduced depths. By itself, a decline in quoted depths after decimalization implies reduced liquidity supply and deterioration in market quality.

EXAMPLE 4

The Market Quality of Electronic Crossing Networks

Electronic crossing networks offer participants anonymity and low cost through the avoidance of dealer costs and the effect of large orders on execution price. For example, a large sell order in an auction market may be interpreted as conveying negative information and cause bid prices to be revised downward, lowering execution prices. These qualities of crossing networks are particularly valuable for the large trades institutional investors often need to make. As a result of these market quality positives, electronic crossing networks have won significant market share.

Understanding and judging the available alternatives in trading is the new challenge to the buy-side trader. One of the key elements in assessing these alternatives is their costs. Effectively measuring the trading experience over time provides another valuable piece of information to the portfolio manager: On average, how much information advantage do I need to recover the hurdle-rate costs of implementing my decisions? The costs of trading are the subject of the next section.

THE COSTS OF TRADING

3

The view of investment managers on the importance of measuring and managing trading costs has evolved over time. Into the 1970s, trading was viewed as inexpensive and unimportant when contrasted to the hoped-for benefits of securities research.

In those early days, portfolio managers were highly dependent on sell-side firms for investment intelligence and ideas. The traditional way to reward the broker for investment ideas was to channel the resultant trading activity to the broker.

In the early 1970s, several important trends converged to change buy-side trading forever. As pension fund assets grew, the prevailing use of fixed commission schedules for trades on exchanges created an unjustifiable bonanza for the exchange community. Buy-side investors exerted pressure to bring commission charges more in line with the cost of providing trading services. The result was a move to fully negotiated commissions, beginning in 1975 in the United States and continuing worldwide.[12] As a result, different levels of execution services could be bought for different commission charges, presenting the buy-side trader with new choices.

In addition, the first practical applications of the efficient market hypothesis (EMH) came to life in the form of index funds. Index fund managers strongly disagreed with the then-traditional view of trading as being "just a cost of doing business." Since index fund managers have no expectation of recovering trading costs through security selection, reducing these costs is a paramount goal for them. Traders are often the most "active" part of the passive management team.

As the 1980s progressed, trading processes were subjected to analytical thinking. The theory of trading costs measurement received attention. Investors continued to be concerned that trading costs were too high and exacted too great a penalty on investment performance. This concern encouraged a view that trading tactics need to be carefully designed and tailored to the investment decision with due attention paid to managing trading costs.

Today, the prevalent view is that all costs of trading are negative performance. The lower the transaction costs, the more portfolio management ideas that can be executed to add value to the portfolio. The management of transaction costs is today a leading concern of investors and many other market participants. Fund sponsors track transaction costs as part of their responsibility to conserve assets. Investment managers do so both to document their performance in managing costs and to gain information for improving the trading function. Brokers, exchanges, and regulators are also concerned with measuring and evaluating trading costs. Transaction cost measurement not only provides feedback on the success of the trading function; today, its concepts are used in setting trading strategy. An overview of the topic is one building block for our later discussion of trading strategy.

3.1 Transaction Cost Components

Trading costs can be thought of as having two major components: explicit costs and implicit costs. Explicit costs are the direct costs of trading, such as broker commission costs, taxes, stamp duties, and fees paid to exchanges. They are costs for which a trader could be given a receipt. Implicit costs, by contrast, represent indirect trading costs. No receipt could be given for implicit costs; they are real nonetheless. Implicit costs include the following:[13]

- The **bid–ask spread**.
- **Market impact** (or price impact) is the effect of the trade on transaction prices. For example, suppose a trader splits a purchase of 400 bonds into two equal market orders when the quote for a bond is 100.297 to 100.477. The first order executes at the ask price of 100.477, after which the market quotation becomes

---

12 Some adoption dates for negotiated commissions were 1983 in Canada, 1986 in the United Kingdom, and 1999 in Japan.
13 Not every trade will incur each of these costs.

100.300 to 100.516. The second order is placed and executes at 100.516. The trader moved the price obtained in the second order up by $100.516 - 100.477 = 0.039$, or \$0.39 per thousand dollars of face value.

■ **Missed trade opportunity costs** (or unrealized profit/loss) arise from the failure to execute a trade in a timely manner. For example, suppose a futures trader places a limit order to buy 10 contracts at a price of 99.00 (or better), good for one day, when the market quote is 99.01 to 99.04. The order does not execute, and the contract closes at 99.80. The difference $(99.80 - 99.04 = \$0.76)$ reflects the missed trade opportunity cost per contract.[14] By trading more aggressively, the trader might have avoided these costs. Missed trade opportunity costs are difficult to measure. In the example, the time frame (one day) was arbitrary, and the estimate could be quite sensitive to the time frame chosen for measurement.

■ **Delay costs** (also called slippage) arise from the inability to complete the desired trade immediately due to its size and the liquidity of markets. Delay costs are often measured on the portion of the order carried over from one day to the next. One reason delay can be costly is that while a trade is being stretched out over time, information is leaking into the market.

Most traders measure implicit costs (i.e., costs excluding commissions) with reference to some price benchmark or reference point. We have already mentioned one price benchmark: the time-of-trade midquote (quotation midpoint), which is used to calculate the effective spread. When such precise information is lacking, the price benchmark is sometimes taken to be the **volume-weighted average price** (VWAP). The VWAP of a security is the average price at which the security traded during the day, where each trade price is weighted by the fraction of the day's volume associated with the trade. The VWAP is an appealing price benchmark because it allows the fund sponsor to identify when it transacted at a higher or lower price than the security's average trade price during the day. For example, if a buy order for 500 shares was executed at €157.25 and the VWAP for the stock for the day was €156.00, the estimated implicit cost of the order would be $500 \times (€157.25 - €156.00) = €625$.[15] If explicit costs were €25, the total estimated cost would be €650. Alternative price benchmarks include the opening and closing prices for a security, which use less information about prices and are less satisfactory. Although VWAP involves a data-intensive calculation, a number of vendors supply it.[16]

VWAP is less informative for trades that represent a large fraction of volume. In the extreme, if a single trading desk were responsible for all the buys in a security during a day, that desk's average price would equal VWAP and thus appear to be good, however high the prices paid. Another limitation of VWAP (and of the effective spread) is that a broker with sufficient discretion can try to "game" this measure. (To *game* a cost measure is to take advantage of a weakness in the measure, so that the value of the measure may be misleading.) Furthermore, VWAP is partly determined at any point in the day; by using weights based on volume to that point in the day, a trader can estimate the final value of VWAP. The accuracy of such an estimate would tend to increase as the close of trading approaches. By comparing the current price to that estimate, the trader can judge the chances of doing better than VWAP.

---

14 The comparison to closing price is for illustrative purposes and only one alternative. For example, the Plexus Group, acquired in 2006 by ITG, would calculate the missed trade opportunity costs with respect to the price of the instrument 30 days after the decision to trade was made.

15 Were this a sell order, in the calculation, we would subtract the trade price from the benchmark price; in this example, we would calculate $500 \times (€156.00 - €157.25) = -€625$. Executing a sell order at a price above the VWAP is good.

16 For example, Bloomberg terminals report VWAPs.

EXAMPLE 5

Taking Advantage of Weaknesses in Cost Measures

Reginald Smith is consulting to Apex Wealth Management on the use of transaction cost measures. Smith correctly explains to Apex's CIO:

> A broker who has flexibility on how aggressively to fill an order can try to game the effective spread measure by waiting for the trade to come to him—that is, by offering liquidity. The broker with a buy order can wait until an order to sell hits his bid; with a sell order, he can wait until an order to buy hits his ask. By executing buys at the bid and sells at the ask, the broker will always show negative estimated transaction costs if performance is measured by the effective spread. However, the delay costs of this approach to the client may be high. A broker with discretion on timing can also try to improve performance relative to a VWAP benchmark, because VWAP is partly determined at any point into the day. For example, if a buy order is received near the end of the day and the stock's ask price exceeds the VWAP up to that point, the broker might try to move the order into the next day, when he will be benchmarked against a fresh VWAP.

The CIO asserts: "I see your point. Nevertheless, using the opening price as a benchmark might be much more vulnerable to gaming than using VWAP." Critique the CIO's statement.

Solution:

The CIO's statement is correct. In contrast to the VWAP, which is partly determined as the trading day progresses, the opening price is known with certainty at any point into the trading day, making it easier to game.

To address the possibility of gaming VWAP, VWAP could be measured over multiple days (spanning the time frame over which the order is executed), because traders would often be expected to try to execute trades within a day. However, the cost of measuring VWAP over a longer time frame is less precision in estimating trading costs.

Probably the most exact approach to cost measurement—and one not vulnerable to gaming—is the implementation shortfall approach. This approach is also attractive because it views trading from an investment management perspective: What does it cost to actuate investment decisions? This view was first articulated by Andre Perold of the Harvard Business School,[17] following ideas first put forward by Jack Treynor.[18] The approach involves a comparison of the actual portfolio with a paper portfolio, using a price benchmark that represents the price when the decision to trade is made (when the trade list is cut).

Implementation shortfall is defined as the difference between the money return on a notional or paper portfolio in which positions are established at the prevailing price when the decision to trade is made (known as the **decision price**, the arrival price, or the strike price) and the actual portfolio's return. The implementation shortfall method correctly captures all elements of transaction costs. The method takes into account not only explicit trading costs, but also the implicit costs, which are often significant for large orders.

---

17 Perold (1988).
18 See Treynor (1987).

Implementation shortfall can be analyzed into four components:

1 *Explicit costs*, including commissions, taxes, and fees.

2 *Realized profit/loss*, reflecting the price movement from the decision price (usually taken to be the previous day's close)[19] to the execution price for the part of the trade executed on the day it is placed.

3 *Delay costs* (*slippage*), reflecting the change in price (close-to-close price movement) over the day an order is placed when the order is not executed that day; the calculation is based on the amount of the order actually filled subsequently.

4 *Missed trade opportunity cost* (unrealized profit/loss), reflecting the price difference between the trade cancellation price and the original benchmark price based on the amount of the order that was not filled.

Market movement is a component of the last three of these costs. However, market movement is a random element for which the trader should not bear responsibility. It is now common to adjust implementation shortfall for market movements. An illustration of the calculation of implementation shortfall might be helpful. Consider the following facts:

- On Monday, the shares of Impulse Robotics close at £10.00 per share.

- On Tuesday, before trading begins, a portfolio manager decides to buy Impulse Robotics. An order goes to the trading desk to buy 1,000 shares of Impulse Robotics at £9.98 per share or better, good for one day. The benchmark price is Monday's close at £10.00 per share. No part of the limit order is filled on Tuesday, and the order expires. The closing price on Tuesday rises to £10.05.

- On Wednesday, the trading desk again tries to buy Impulse Robotics by entering a new limit order to buy 1,000 shares at £10.07 per share or better, good for one day. That day, 700 shares are bought at £10.07 per share. Commissions and fees for this trade are £14. Shares for Impulse Robotics close at £10.08 per share on Wednesday.

- No further attempt to buy Impulse Robotics is made, and the remaining 300 shares of the 1,000 shares the portfolio manager initially specified are never bought.

The paper portfolio traded 1,000 shares on Tuesday at £10.00 per share. The return on this portfolio when the order is canceled after the close on Wednesday is the value of the 1,000 shares, now worth £10,080, less the cost of £10,000, for a net gain of £80. The real portfolio contains 700 shares (now worth $700 \times £10.08 = £7,056$), and the cost of this portfolio is $700 \times £10.07 = £7,049$, plus £14 in commissions and fees, for a total cost of £7,063. Thus, the total net gain on this portfolio is –£7. The implementation shortfall is the return on the paper portfolio minus the return on the actual portfolio, or £80 – (–£7) = £87. More commonly, the shortfall is expressed as a fraction of the total cost of the paper portfolio trade, or £87/£10,000 = 87 basis points.

We can break this implementation shortfall down further:

- Commissions and fees are calculated naturally as £14/£10,000 = 0.14%.

- Realized profit/loss reflects the difference between the execution price and the relevant decision price (here, the closing price of the previous day). The calculation is based on the amount of the order actually filled:

$$\frac{700}{1,000}\left(\frac{10.07 - 10.05}{10.00}\right) = 0.14\%$$

---

19 The midquote at the time the decision is made is another possible benchmark price.

- Delay costs reflect the price difference due to delay in filling the order. The calculation is based on the amount of the order actually filled:

$$\frac{700}{1,000}\left(\frac{10.05 - 10.00}{10.00}\right) = 0.35\%$$

- Missed trade opportunity cost reflects the difference between the cancellation price and the original benchmark price. The calculation is based on the amount of the order that was not filled:

$$\frac{300}{1,000}\left(\frac{10.08 - 10.00}{10.00}\right) = 0.24\%$$

- Implementation cost as a percent is 0.14% + 0.14% + 0.35% + 0.24% = 0.87%, or 87 bps.

The shortfall computation is simply reversed for sells (for sells, the return on the paper portfolio is subtracted from the return on the actual portfolio).

In this example, shortfall was positive, but this will not always be the case, especially if the effect of the return on the market is removed. To illustrate the adjustment for market return using the market model, suppose that the market had risen 100 basis points (1 percent) over the period of trading and the beta of Impulse Robotics is 1.0. The market model is $\hat{R}_i = \alpha_i + \beta_i R_M$, where $\hat{R}_i$ is the predicted return on asset i, R_M is the return on the market portfolio, α_i is the average return on asset i unrelated to the market return, and β_i is the sensitivity of the return on asset i to the return on the market portfolio. In practice, with daily returns, α_i will be often very close to 0, and $\hat{R}_i \approx \beta_i R_M$. With a beta of 1.0, the predicted return on the shares would be 1.0 × 1% = 1%, and the **market-adjusted implementation shortfall** would be 0.87% − 1.0% = −0.13%. Here, the shortfall is actually negative. By contrast, pretrade cost estimates are always positive.

Exhibit 5 provides an illustration of trading costs for various global equity markets during the third quarter of 2008 and the first quarter of 2011.[20] The trading costs here reflect commissions, the realized profit/loss, and the delay cost components of implementation shortfall.[21]

---

20 Note that these transaction cost totals, particularly in the earlier period, are large enough to explain the 0.50 percent to 0.75 percent one-way transaction costs inferred from the difference between active and passive management.

21 Estimates of missed trade opportunity costs are not often published and in practice, their measurement is subjective. Some firms use a future stock price that differs from the trade cancellation price. The timing of the future stock price measurement can have a large effect on missed trade opportunity cost estimates. Additionally, different firms use different terms for trading cost components. For example, ITG's "IS Costs" include delay costs and realized profit/loss, but not explicit costs or missed trade opportunity costs. ITG's "broker costs" represent market impact costs, which are measured as the realized profit/loss is defined here.

Exhibit 5 Global Equity Trading Costs in Basis Points

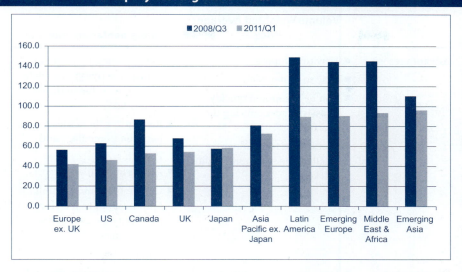

Source for data: ITG's Global Cost Review, 2011/Q1.

Equity trading costs are lower in the developed world, with Europe (excluding the United Kingdom) recently having the lowest costs, followed by the United States and Canada. The highest costs of trading are in the emerging regions. Note, however, that trading costs have declined substantially in most emerging markets. The largest decline in trading costs occurred in Latin America, where costs fell by 60 basis points from 1.50% to 0.90%. The large decline in emerging equity trading costs is perhaps not surprising, given the flight to quality during the 2008 financial crisis.

A smaller decline in trading costs occurred in developed markets, with the exception of Japan, where costs slightly increased. Canada experienced the largest decline in developed equity trading costs as costs fell 34 basis points from 0.87% to 0.53%. In general, the costs of implementing investment ideas has declined significantly across global equity markets.

As a complement to implementation shortfall, some investment management firms measure shortfall with respect not to the above paper portfolio, but with respect to a portfolio in which all trades are transacted in expected markets and the component costs are at expected levels. This approach accounts for the anticipated cost of the trades.[22]

The application of the implementation shortfall approach is hampered when an asset trades infrequently because the decision price is then hard to determine. If the market closing price of a security is "stale"—in the sense of reflecting a trade that happened much earlier—it is not valid. The application of a benchmark price based on trading cost measures, including implementation shortfall, VWAP, and effective spread, is also compromised when a market lacks transparency (accurate price and/or quote information).

Having illustrated trade cost measurement using VWAP and implementation shortfall, we now compare these two major approaches to trade cost measurement in Exhibit 6. VWAP has theoretical disadvantages compared to implementation shortfall but is readily obtained and interpreted and is a useful measure of quality of execution for smaller trades in nontrending markets in particular. The portfolio manager should be familiar with both measures.

---

22 See Cheng (2003).

Exhibit 6	Comparison of VWAP and Implementation Shortfall	
	Volume Weighted Average Price	**Implementation Shortfall**
Advantages	■ Easy to compute. ■ Easy to understand. ■ Can be computed quickly to assist traders during the execution. ■ Works best for comparing smaller trades in nontrending markets.	■ Links trading to portfolio manager activity; can relate cost to the value of investment ideas. ■ Recognizes the tradeoff between immediacy and price. ■ Allows attribution of costs. ■ Can be built into portfolio optimizers to reduce turnover and increase realized performance. ■ Cannot be gamed.
Disadvantages	■ Does not account for costs of trades delayed or canceled. ■ Becomes misleading when trade is a substantial proportion of trading volume. ■ Not sensitive to trade size or market conditions. ■ Can be gamed by delaying trades.	■ Requires extensive data collection and interpretation. ■ Imposes an unfamiliar evaluation framework on traders.

EXAMPLE 6

Commissions: The Most Visible Part of Transaction Costs (1)

Implementation shortfall totals can be divided into categories that define the nature of trading costs. Each component cost is as real as the other costs. Nevertheless, brokerage commissions are the most visible portion of trading costs. The dealer spreads and responses to market pressures are more difficult to gauge. The commissions, however, are printed on every ticket. For better or worse, efforts to reduce transaction costs focus first on commissions.

A good deal of attention has focused on the use of commissions to buy services other than execution services—that is, a practice known as **soft dollars** (or soft dollar arrangements, or soft commissions). Many investment managers have traditionally allocated a client's brokerage business to buy research services that aid portfolio management. In those cases, commissions pay for research received and execution, with clerical personnel assigned to the trade desk managing the commission budget. However, the practice of soft dollars makes accounting for transaction costs less exact and can be abused. CFA Institute in 1998 issued *Soft Dollar Standards* to provide disclosure standards and other guidance related to soft dollar arrangements.[23] Furthermore, individuals who are CFA Institute members or candidates have an overriding responsibility to adhere to the Code of Ethics and Standards of Professional Conduct. Standard III: Duties to Clients, (A) Loyalty, Prudence, and Care, specifies that CFA Institute members using soft dollars should develop policies and procedures with respect to the use of client brokerage, including soft dollars, and that those policies and procedures should reflect that members and candidates must seek best execution for their clients, among other duties.[24]

EXAMPLE 7

Commissions: The Most Visible Part of Transaction Costs (2)

Transaction costs can be thought of as an iceberg, with the commission being the tip most visible above the water's surface. Large parts of transaction costs are unobservable. They do not appear in accounting statements, and they appear only indirectly in manager evaluations. Extensive data collection and analysis are required to gauge the size and relative importance of transaction cost components. Exhibit 7 illustrates the concept with data from ITG's Global Cost Review, 2011/Q1. For comparison purposes, data are provided for both large-capitalization and micro-capitalization US stocks during the first quarter of 2011.

The exhibit shows that trading costs for large-capitalization and micro-capitalization stocks are very different. Total costs for large-capitalization stocks were 39 (7 + 15 + 17) basis points, versus 158 (26 + 23 + 109) basis points for micro-capitalization stocks. The least visible component—delay costs—were the largest component of trading costs, especially for micro-capitalization stocks. For micro-capitalization stocks, delay costs were 109 basis points, or 69 percent (109/158) of total costs. For large-capitalization stocks, delay costs were almost half of total costs, at 44 percent. For both large-capitalization and micro-capitalization stocks, the most visible component of equity transaction costs—commissions—average only about 17 percent of total costs.

---

23 See www.cfainstitute.org for any updates. As of late 2011, no substantive revisions had been made to the 1998 release.
24 See the *Standards of Practice Handbook*, 10th ed. (Charlottesville, VA: CFA Institute, 2010). See www. cfainstitute.org for any updates.

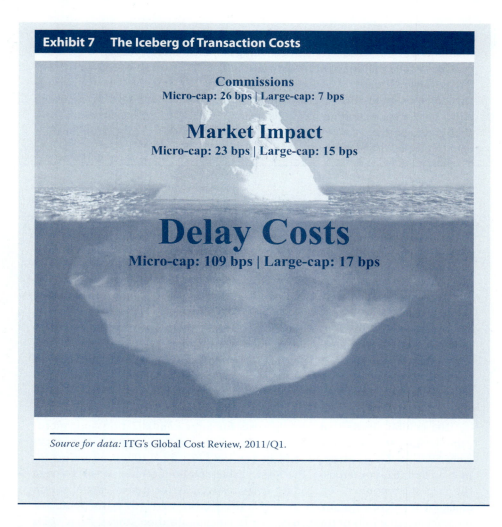

Exhibit 7   The Iceberg of Transaction Costs

Commissions
Micro-cap: 26 bps | Large-cap: 7 bps

Market Impact
Micro-cap: 23 bps | Large-cap: 15 bps

Delay Costs
Micro-cap: 109 bps | Large-cap: 17 bps

Source for data: ITG's Global Cost Review, 2011/Q1.

3.2 Pretrade Analysis: Econometric Models for Costs

Given post-trade shortfall estimates, we can build reliable pretrade estimates using econometric models. The theory of market microstructure suggests that trading costs are systematically related to certain factors, including the following:[25]

- stock liquidity characteristics (e.g., market capitalization, price level, trading frequency, volume, index membership, bid–ask spread);

- risk (e.g., the volatility of the stock's returns);

- trade size relative to available liquidity (e.g., order size divided by average daily volume);

- momentum (e.g., it is more costly to buy in an up market than in a down market);

- trading style (e.g., more aggressive styles using market orders should be associated with higher costs than more passive styles using limit orders).

---

[25] See Madhavan (2000, 2002). More recently, Brownlees, Cipollini, and Gallo (2011) develop a model to predict trading volume and minimize trading costs.

Given these factors, we can estimate the relation between costs and these variables using regression analysis. Since theory suggests a nonlinear relationship, we can use nonlinear methods to estimate the relationship. The key point to note is that the estimated cost function can be used in two ways:

- to form a pretrade estimate of the cost of trading that can then be juxtaposed against the actual realized cost once trading is completed to assess execution quality, and
- to help the portfolio manager gauge the right trade size to order in the first place.

For example, a portfolio manager may want to invest in a stock with an expected excess return target of 5 percent relative to the manager's benchmark over the intended holding period. Initially, a trade of 200,000 shares is proposed with a price currently at $10 per share. However, based on pretrade cost estimates, the cost of a 200,000-share position is 2.5 percent, so that expected round-trip transaction costs are 2 × 2.5% = 5%, which would fully erode the excess return. The optimal trade size will be much smaller than the 200,000 shares initially proposed.

Quantitative managers will balance three factors—return, risk, and cost—in selecting the optimal trade size. But even nonquantitative managers need to make the right choices in terms of balancing expected return against expected entry and exit costs.

EXAMPLE 8

An Econometric Model for Transaction Costs

Several Canadian companies' stocks are listed not only on the Toronto Stock Exchange (TSE), but also on the New York Stock Exchange (NYSE). There are no legal restrictions on cross-border ownership and trading of these stocks. Some of the clients of an American brokerage firm have occasionally asked the brokerage firm for execution of trades in some of the Canadian stocks cross-listed in the United States. These trades can be executed on either the NYSE or TSE, and the American brokerage firm has entered into an alliance with a TSE member firm to facilitate execution of trades on the TSE if desired. John Reynolds is an economist at the brokerage firm. Reynolds has identified 55 of the cross-listed Canadian companies as those in which the firm's clients typically execute trades. Reynolds observes that the implicit transaction costs for some trades in these stocks are lower on the NYSE than on the TSE, or vice versa. Reynolds has built an econometric model that can be used for pretrade assessment of the difference in the implicit costs of transacting on the two exchanges, so that traders can direct trades to the lower-cost venue. Using historic data on trade and firm characteristics and transaction costs, Reynolds developed the following model:

$$\text{Pred. } \Delta\text{Cost} = 0.25 + 1.31 \ln(\text{Mkt Cap}) - 14.91(\text{US Share})$$
$$+ 1.64 \ln(\text{Order Size}) - 1.40(\text{High Tech})$$

where

Pred. ΔCost = Predicted difference between the implicit transaction costs on the NYSE and TSE in basis points

Mkt Cap = Market capitalization of the company in millions of US dollars

US Share = Proportion (stated as a decimal) of total trading in the stock in the United States and Canada that occurs in the United States

Order Size = Number of shares ordered

High Tech is an industry dummy with a value of 1 if the company is a high-tech company and 0 otherwise.

Reynolds has also concluded that the *explicit* transaction costs for the stocks he has analyzed are lower on the NYSE than on the TSE by about 12 bps.

1 Consider an order to sell 50,000 shares of a non-high-tech company that was included in the companies analyzed by Reynolds. The company has a market capitalization of US$100 million, and the US share of overall trading volume in the company is 0.30. Based on the model estimated above and the assessment of the explicit transaction costs, recommend where the order should be placed.

2 Consider an order to sell 1,000 shares of a high-tech company that was included in the companies analyzed by Reynolds. The company has a market capitalization of US$100 million, and the US share of overall trading volume in the company is 0.50. Based on the model estimated above and the assessment of the explicit transaction costs, recommend where the order should be placed.

Solution to 1:

Pred. ΔCost = 0.25 + 1.31 ln(Mkt Cap) − 14.91 (US Share) + 1.64 ln(Order Size) − 1.40 (High Tech) = 0.25 + 1.31 ln(100) − 14.91 (0.30) + 1.64 ln(50,000) − 1.40 (0) = 19.6 bps. The econometric model suggests that the implicit cost of executing this trade is greater on the NYSE than on the TSE by almost 20 bps. Thus, since the explicit transaction costs are lower on the NYSE by about 12 bps, the total cost of executing the trade on the TSE is expected to be less than the cost on the NYSE by almost 8 bps. The recommendation would be to direct the order to the TSE.

Solution to 2:

Pred. ΔCost = 0.25 + 1.31 ln(Mkt Cap) − 14.91 (US Share) + 1.64 ln(Order Size) − 1.40 (High Tech) = 0.25 + 1.31 ln(100) − 14.91 (0.50) + 1.64 ln(1,000) − 1.40 (1) = 8.8 bps. The econometric model suggests that the implicit cost of executing this trade is greater on the NYSE than on the TSE by about 9 bps. However, since the explicit transaction costs are lower on the NYSE by about 12 bps, the total cost of executing the trade on the NYSE is expected to be less than the cost on the TSE by about 3 bps. The recommendation would be to direct the order to the NYSE.

4   TYPES OF TRADERS AND THEIR PREFERRED ORDER TYPES

Beginning with this section and continuing with Section 5, we discuss traders, trading objectives, strategies, and tactics. We first need to understand how investment style affects trading objectives. Implementation strategy and cost are direct consequences of investment management style. Some investment strategies are inherently inexpensive to implement—for example, contrarian, passive, and other "slow idea" strategies. Other strategies, particularly those based on stock price momentum or widely disseminated "news," are inherently more expensive to implement.

The success of the investment strategy depends on whether the information content of the decision process is sufficient relative to the costs of executing the strategy, including trading costs. Thus, the keystone of the buy-side trader's choice of trading strategy is the **urgency of the trade** (the importance of certainty of execution). Is the decision based on slow changes in fundamental value, valuable new information, or the need to increase cash balances? Will the value of completing the trade disappear or dissipate if it is not completed quickly?

From the portfolio manager's perspective, the key to effective trading is to realize that the portfolio decision is not complete until securities are bought or sold. Because execution is so important, market information is critical. When a trade is first seriously contemplated, the trader needs to ask: How sensitive is the security to buying or selling pressure? How much volume can be accumulated without having the price move out of the desirable range? Are there any special considerations (e.g., news, rumors, competing buyers, or anxious sellers) that make this a particularly good or particularly poor time to deal in this stock? In other words, how resilient is the market? Is the price being driven to a level at which a dealer wants to reduce or increase inventory (i.e., the dealer's layoff or buy-in position, respectively)? Armed with this tactical information, the portfolio manager fine-tunes his interest in the security.

The trader can use the answers to these questions to increase his or her awareness of market conditions and security trading behavior. The crucial function of the trading desk is to achieve the best price–time trade-off for the impending transaction given current market circumstances. This trade-off may change rapidly because of market conditions, dealer inventories, news, and changes in the portfolio manager's desires.

The above considerations regarding investment style and the urgency of the trade in particular lead to the following classification of traders according to their motivation in trading.

4.1 The Types of Traders

Traders can be classified by their motivation to trade, as follows.

Information-motivated traders trade on information that has limited value if not quickly acted upon. Accordingly, they often stress liquidity and speed of execution over securing a better price. They are likely to use market orders and rely on market makers to accommodate their desire to trade quickly. They must execute their orders before the information on which they are buying or selling becomes valueless.

Information traders often trade in large blocks. Their information frequently concerns the prospects of one stock, and they seek to maximize the value of the information. Successful information-motivated traders are wary of acquiring a public reputation for astute trading, because if they did, who would wish to trade against them? Accordingly, information traders often use deceptive actions to hide their intentions.

Value-motivated traders act on value judgments based on careful, sometimes painstaking research. They trade only when the price moves into their value range. As explained earlier, they trade infrequently and are motivated only by price and value. They tend to accumulate and distribute large positions quietly over lengthy trading horizons. Value-motivated traders are ready to be patient to secure a better price.

Liquidity-motivated traders do not transact to reap profit from an information advantage of the securities involved. Rather, liquidity-motivated transactions are more a means than an end; such transactions may, for example, release cash proceeds to facilitate the purchase of another security, adjust market exposure, or fund cash needs. Lacking the information sensitivity of the information and value traders, liquidity-motivated traders tend to be natural trading counterparties to more knowledgeable traders. Thus, they need to be aware of the value their liquidity brings to knowledgeable traders.

Passive traders, acting on behalf of passive or index fund portfolio managers, similarly seek liquidity in their rebalancing transactions, but they are much more concerned with the cost of trading. They tend to use time-insensitive techniques in the hope of exchanging a lack of urgency for lower-cost execution. Passive traders have the flexibility to use lower-cost trading techniques. Because of the types of orders and markets they use, these traders resemble dealers in the sense that they allow the opposing party to determine the timing of the trade in exchange for determining the acceptable trade price.

Other types of traders do not fit exactly into the above categories. Dealers, whose profits depend on earning bid–ask spreads, have short trading time horizons like information-motivated traders. Given that a transaction is profitable, however, they have no specific emphasis on time versus price. Arbitrageurs are sensitive to both price of execution and speed of execution as they attempt to exploit small price discrepancies between closely related assets trading in different markets. **Day traders** rapidly buy and sell stocks in the hope that the stocks will continue to rise or fall in value for the seconds or minutes they are ready to hold a position. Like dealers, they often seek to profitably accommodate the trading demands of others.

Exhibit 8 summarizes the attitudes toward trading displayed by the various traders in the market. In the exhibit, the final column gives the trader's emphasis on price or time (i.e., avoiding delay in execution).

Exhibit 8	Summary of Trading Motivations, Time Horizons, and Time versus Price Preferences		
Trader	**Motivation**	**Trading Time Horizon**	**Time versus Price Preference**
Information-motivated	New information	Minutes to hours	Time
Value-motivated	Perceived valuation errors	Days to weeks	Price
Liquidity-motivated	Invest cash or divest securities	Minutes to hours	Time
Passive	Rebalancing, investing/divesting cash	Days to weeks	Price
Dealers and day traders	Accommodation	Minutes to hours	Passive, indifferent

This classification of traders is relevant to both equity markets and fixed-income markets.

Alternative investments tend to be characterized by infrequent trading and illiquidity; day traders are not relevant as a trader type in such markets, in general. However, the thematic differences among the major types of traders (information-motivated, value-motivated, liquidity-motivated, and passive) still have recognizable counterparts in many alternative investment markets, although the relevant time horizons are longer. For example, in real estate, information concerning planned future construction, perceived valuation errors, and the need for liquidity can motivate transactions, and some investors may seek long-term, broad, diversified exposure, corresponding roughly to the passive trader type.

4.2 Traders' Selection of Order Types

All of the orders discussed in earlier sections above, as well as others discussed in advanced treatments, are used tactically by buy-side traders as warranted by market conditions and the motivations of the portfolio manager.

4.2.1 Information-Motivated Traders

Information traders believe that they need to trade immediately and often trade large quantities in specific names. Demands for high liquidity on short notice may overwhelm the ready supply of stock in the market, triggering adverse price movements as the effect of these demands reverberates through the market. Information traders may use fast action principal trades. By transacting with a dealer, the buy-side trader quickly secures execution at a guaranteed price. The major cost of these trades arises because the dealer demands a price concession to cover the inventory risks undertaken. Furthermore, information-motivated traders fear that the price may move quickly to embed the information, devaluing their information edge. They are aware that their trading often moves the market, but they believe their information justifies the increased trading cost. Accordingly, information-motivated traders may wish to disguise their anxious trading need. Where possible, they use less obvious orders, such as market orders, to disguise their trading intentions. This behavior has led information traders to be called "wolves in sheep's clothing."

4.2.2 Value-Motivated Traders

The value-motivated trader develops an independent assessment of value and waits for market prices to move into the range of that assessment. Thus, the market comes with excess inventory to the trader and presents him with attractive opportunities.

The typical value-motivated trader uses limit orders or their computerized institutional market equivalent. An attractive price is more important than timely activity. Thus, price is controlled but timing is not. Even though value-motivated traders may act quickly, they are still accommodative and pay none of the penalties of more anxious traders. As Treynor (1987) pointed out, value traders can sometimes operate as "the dealer's dealer," buying stock when dealers most want to sell stock.

4.2.3 Liquidity-Motivated Traders

The commitment or release of cash is the primary objective of liquidity-motivated traders. The types of orders used include market, market-not-held, best efforts, participate, principal trades, portfolio trades, and orders on ECNs and crossing networks. Low commissions and small impact are desirable, and liquidity traders can often tolerate somewhat more uncertainty about timely trade completion than can information-motivated traders.

Many liquidity-motivated traders believe that displaying their true liquidity-seeking nature works in their favor. When trading with a liquidity-motivated trader, dealers and other market participants can relax some of the protective measures that they use to prevent losses to informed traders.

4.2.4 Passive Traders

Low-cost trading is a strong motivation of passive traders, even though they are liquidity-motivated in their portfolio-rebalancing operations. As a result, these traders tend to favor limit orders, portfolio trades, and crossing networks. The advantages, in addition to certainty of price, are low commissions, low impact, and the possible reduction or elimination of bid–ask spread costs. The major weakness is the uncertainty of whether trades will be completed within a reasonable time frame. These orders and markets are best suited to trading that is neither large nor heavily concentrated.

5   TRADE EXECUTION DECISIONS AND TACTICS

The diversity of markets, order types, and characteristics of the particular securities that must be traded means that the task of selecting a trading strategy and promptly executing it is quite complex. In the following, we first discuss decisions related to the handling of a trade. Then, we address objectives in trading and trading tactics, including automated trading.

5.1 Decisions Related to the Handling of a Trade

Trading costs are controllable, necessitating thoughtful approaches to trading strategies. Poor trading involving inattentive or inappropriate trading tactics leads to higher transaction costs. Conversely, good trading lowers transaction costs and improves investment performance.

A head trader thinking about how to organize his or her team needs to develop a daily strategy which balances the trading needs of the portfolio manager(s) and the condition of the market. The head trader, of course, controls neither but has to devise a strategy for trading the daily blotter. Considerations that come into play include the following:

- Small, liquidity-oriented trades can be packaged up and executed via direct market access and algorithmic trading. **Direct market access** (DMA) refers to platforms sponsored by brokers that permit buy-side traders to directly access equities, fixed income, futures, and foreign exchange markets, clearing via the broker. Trades executed via DMA now represent a substantial fraction of buy-side equity order volume in a number of developed markets. Algorithmic trading, a type of automated electronic trading, will be discussed later. Larger trades can receive custom handling. Why waste the talent of senior traders and the most competent brokers on trades in which it is not possible to make an economically significant difference?

- Large, information-laden trades demand immediate skilled attention. Senior traders are needed to manage the tradeoff between impact and delay costs by releasing the minimum amount of information into the market that is required to get the trade done.

- In addition to best execution, the trader must be cognizant of client trading restrictions, cash balances, and brokerage allocations, if any.

Once the strategy is determined and traders are handed their assignments, the problem of best execution practice becomes tactical. Of course, trading tactics change in response to the market conditions encountered. Each trader, while working orders, should be asking the following questions:

1   What is the right trading tactic for this particular trade at this point in time?

2   Is the trade suitable for DMA or algorithmic trading, or is manual handling of the trade appropriate?

3   If a broker is used, by my experience and measurement, which broker is best suited to handle this order?

4   What is the expected versus experienced cost for this type of trading tactic?

5   Where is the lowest-cost liquidity likely to be found?

6   If the low-cost alternatives fail, where should I go to increase the aggressiveness of the trading?

7   Is the market responding as I would expect, or are there messages that should be conveyed to portfolio management?

8 How can I find out as much as possible about the market situation while revealing as little as possible of my own unfulfilled intentions?

9 What can be done to minimize any negative tax consequences of the trade (such as earmarking specifically the lot of securities being sold so as to control their cost basis)?

The process starts with an order-by-order understanding of the urgency and size constraints. These constraints determine the appropriate processes that the desk can use. Order tactics, in turn, determine the market venues that represent the best alternative. At that point, specific order handling depends on the desk's commitments, activity by brokers currently trafficking in the name, and the desk's comfort with the specific broker or electronic venue.

In summary, the key function of trade desk organization is to prioritize trading. Good desks quickly identify the dangerous trades and assign the priority. They know how their managers think, in general and in relation to the specific individual trade. They attune the mix of brokers to their trading needs, often concentrating trading to increase their clout. Finally, they are constantly innovating and experimenting, trying new trade routes and refining desk processes.

5.2 Objectives in Trading and Trading Tactics

How does a trader decide which type of order to use? Earlier in this reading, the strategic decision of the trade was identified as one of buying or selling time (deciding how much urgency to attach to trade completion). Perhaps the most common trader errors are selling time too cheaply when executing value-motivated transactions and buying time too expensively when executing information-motivated transactions. A third error, and the most serious error for a liquidity trader, is to act in a manner that evokes protective or exploitative responses from dealers and other market participants who sense an information motivation or other time-sensitive motivation.

One tactical decision faced by buy-side traders is the type of order to be used. Few portfolio managers base their investment decisions solely on value, information, or liquidity. Most managers mix strategic goals in response to client agreements, manager perceptions, and market cycles. For example, clients may require full investment in equities at all times, regardless of whether superior investment alternatives are available. Accordingly, trading tactics may at times appear inconsistent with the stated long-term strategic investment objectives. Thus, all buy-side traders need to understand, and occasionally use, the full range of trading techniques. The subsections that follow discuss a categorization of similarities and differences among various trading techniques.

5.2.1 *Liquidity-at-Any-Cost Trading Focus*

Information traders who believe they need to trade in institutional block size with immediacy use these trading techniques. The problem, of course, is that everyone is wary of trading with an informed trader. On the other hand, dealers are mightily interested in finding out whether these anxious traders have any valuable information. Thus, these traders can usually attract brokers willing to represent their order, but often at a high commission rate or price concession.

These trades demand high liquidity on short notice. They may overwhelm the available liquidity in the market and cause prices to move when their presence is detected. Traders who use these techniques usually recognize that these methods are expensive but pay the price in order to achieve timely execution.

On occasion, urgency will place a normally nonaggressive trader into this category. A mutual fund with unusual end-of-day sales, for example, may need to liquidate security positions whatever the cost.

5.2.2 *Costs-Are-Not-Important Trading Focus*

Market orders and the variations on this type (such as market on close) are examples of orders resulting from a costs-are-not-important focus. Some investors seldom consider using anything other than market orders when trading securities. Market orders work acceptably well for most mixes of investment strategies, in which it is difficult to assign pure information, value, or liquidity motivation. They also serve to mask trading intention, since all market orders look alike.

Traders who use market orders trust the competitive market to generate a fair price. For many orders, fair market price is a reasonable assumption. Exchanges encourage market orders and set up elaborate procedures to assure that these orders receive fair "best execution" prices. Active control of the order is not required.

Market orders work best for smaller trades and more liquid stocks. They are sometimes called "no-brainers" because they require little trading skill on the part of the buy-side trader or the broker. Because they require little effort or risk taking by market makers, they are inexpensive for a broker to execute and have been used to produce "soft dollar" commissions in exchange for broker-supplied services.

Traders who use these orders pay ordinary spreads and commissions to have their orders executed rapidly. Trade costs are accepted without question; indeed, they are seldom even considered.

The weakness of market orders is that all trader discretion is surrendered. The trader has no control over the trade, and the broker exercises only the most rudimentary cautions. The marketplace processes are viewed as sufficient to assure fair treatment. To retain discretion, such a trader may also consider using an aggressive limit order—for example, a limit buy order that improves on the best bid or a limit sell order that improves on the best ask price.

5.2.3 *Need-Trustworthy-Agent Trading Focus*

Buy-side traders often need to execute larger orders than the exchange can accommodate at any given moment, particularly when dealing with thinly traded issues. They recognize that their orders may create adverse impact if they are not handled carefully. Accordingly, these traders engage the services of a carefully selected floor broker to skillfully "work" such orders by placing a best efforts, market-not-held, or participate order. The advantage of these trades is that they match trading desires to interest in taking the other side of the trade as such interest is uncovered or arrives in the market. Orders are usually completed through a series of partial trades. Obviously, immediate execution is not of primary importance, so such orders are less useful for information-motivated traders.

These orders are the epitome of the agency relationship. The trader passes control of the order to the broker, who then controls when and at what price the orders execute. The trader frequently does not know how much of an order was cleared until after the market closes.

The agent, however, may serve multiple masters, including other clients and even the agent's own brokerage firm. The valuable information that a buyer or seller exists is revealed to the broker. It is difficult for the trader to know whether that information is used exclusively in the trader's best interests.

5.2.4 *Advertise-to-Draw-Liquidity Trading Focus*

Advertising is an explicit liquidity-enhancing technique used with initial public offerings (IPOs), secondary offerings, and **sunshine trades**, which publicly display the trading interest in advance of the actual order. If publicity attracts enough traders taking the opposite side, the trade may execute with little or no market impact.

Implied in agency orders is an authorization to do some low-level advertising on the exchange floor. Advertising lets the market know that a willing buyer or seller is around. That presence may draw out the other side of the trade. However, such an order may also bear the risk of trading in front of the order. For example, if a large block purchase order is announced, traders may take long positions in the security in the hope of realizing a profit by selling the stock at a higher price.

5.2.5 *Low-Cost-Whatever-the-Liquidity Trading Focus*

Limit orders are the chief example of this type of order, particularly limit orders that specify prices that are "behind the market": either a limit buy order at a price below the best bid, or a limit sell order at a price above the best ask price. The objective is to improve on the market bid or the market ask, respectively. Minimizing trading costs is the primary interest of buy-side traders who use this type of order. There may not be a counterparty to the trader's order who is willing to trade on the terms suggested. This order type is best suited to passive and value-motivated trading situations.

The advantages of such orders are low commissions, low impact, and possibly the elimination of the market maker spread. One major weakness, of course, is execution uncertainty (the uncertainty of whether any trades will be made at all). Traders could end up "chasing the market" if the market moves away from the limit price. Furthermore, if the limit price becomes "stale" because significant new information on the security reaches the public, the trader could find that a trade has been executed before he or she has been able to revise the limit price. For example, a limit buy order specifying a price that is well below the most recent transaction price runs the risk of being executed only if major negative news relating to the security reaches the public. If that happens, the security could trade down to even lower levels.

5.2.6 *Trading Technique Summary*

Exhibit 9 summarizes the uses, costs, advantages, and weaknesses of these trading techniques.

Exhibit 9   Objectives in Trading

Focus	Uses	Costs	Advantages	Weaknesses
Liquidity at any cost (I must trade)	Immediate execution in institutional block size	High cost due to tipping supply/demand balance	Guarantees execution	High potential for market impact and information leakage
Need trustworthy agent (Possible hazardous trading situation)	Large-scale trades; low-level advertising	Higher commission; possible leakage of information	Hopes to trade time for improvement in price	Loses direct control of trade
Costs are not important	Certainty of execution	Pays the spread; may create impact	Competitive, market-determined price	Cedes direct control of trade; may ignore tactics with potential for lower cost
Advertise to draw liquidity	Large trades with lower information advantage	High operational and organizational costs	Market-determined price for large trades	More difficult to administer; possible leakage to front-runners
Low cost whatever the liquidity	Non-informational trading; indifferent to timing	Higher search and monitoring costs	Low commission; opportunity to trade at favorable price	Uncertainty of trading; may fail to execute and create a need to complete at a later, less desirable price

5.3 Automated Trading

Trading strategy will vary according to the specifics of the trade and the markets in which the trade might be executed. For example, traders attempting to trade very large orders relative to typical trading volume may involve brokers to avail themselves of the brokers' network of contacts and market knowledge in locating counterparties. By contrast, traders in quote-driven markets will typically try to negotiate trades with dealers, attempting to find the best possible quotes for their trades. As noted earlier, the rapid evolution of market structure worldwide toward order-driven systems, and electronic automated auctions in particular, has important implications for the trading process. Indeed, one of the more important implications of the growth of automated venues is the rapid expansion in algorithmic trading.

Algorithmic trading refers to automated electronic trading subject to quantitative rules and user-specified benchmarks and constraints. Related, but distinct, trading strategies include using portfolio trades, in which the trader simultaneously executes a set of trades in a basket of stocks, and **smart routing**, whereby algorithms are used to intelligently route an order to the most liquid venue. The term **automated trading** is the most generic, referring to any form of trading that is not manual, including trading based on algorithms.

Estimates of automated trading usage vary widely, and some estimates put it as high as 25 percent of average share volume. Informed commentators all agree that this share is increasing, with some projecting algorithmic volume growing at a 30–35 percent rate per annum over the next few years.[26] This revolution raises natural questions: How do algorithmic systems work? What goes inside the "black box" of algorithmic trading? Will algorithmic systems displace human traders, or can savvy human traders infer the logic of the algorithm and profit by gaming the computer? Do algorithms always work as advertised, or do traders put too much trust in them? Are algorithms really effective in controlling transaction costs and hence adding alpha? What is the future of algorithmic trading? The following discussion sheds light on these issues and focuses on an in-depth analysis of the anatomy of algorithmic trading.

5.3.1 The Algorithmic Revolution

The rapid growth of algorithmic trading by institutional traders reflects complex regulatory and technological factors. In the United States, decimalization (the use of a minimum price increment of 0.01, for US currency $0.01) has led to a dramatic reduction in spreads in US equities but has also reduced quoted depths. Average trade size in many US markets, including the New York Stock Exchange and NASDAQ, which constitute a substantial fraction of world equity market value, has fallen dramatically.[27] For institutions with large orders, these changes greatly complicate the task of trading. Institutional orders are typically large relative to normal trading volume. *The underlying logic behind algorithmic trading is to exploit market patterns of trading volume so as to execute orders with controlled risk and costs.* This approach typically involves breaking large orders up into smaller orders that blend into the normal flow

---

26 It was estimated in December 2010 that algorithmic trading accounted for 30% of institutional trading in the United States. *Source*: Investment Technology Group, *Algorithmic Trading Usage Patterns and their Costs*, May 2011. www.itg.com/news_events/papers/Algorithmic_Trading.pdf, accessed 27 September 2011.
27 According to the *NYSE Fact Book* (various editions), the average number of shares per trade peaked at 2,568 in June 1988 and then began to decline. The number of shares per trade remained in the low 1,000s for most of the late 1990s, falling below 1,000 shares in March of 2001, the year of decimalization, and steadily declining since. In August 2011, the average was 251 shares per trade. Decimalization, adopted by the United States and Canada during the early 2000s, has long been the international standard in equity marketplaces.

of trades in a sensible way to moderate price impact. For active equity trading desks, algorithmic or automated trading is the only recourse for efficiently handling increased volumes given increasingly smaller average trade size.

EXAMPLE 9

The Changing Roles of Traders

Algorithmic trading involves programming a computer to "slice and dice" a large order in a liquid security into small pieces, then meters the pieces into an automated exchange using FIX communications technology (FIX is a messaging protocol in equity markets that facilitates electronic trading).

Trading in 400-share nibbles may sound inefficient, but it is not. Due to the speed of the analytics and the connectivity, trading engines can execute many trades per minute, all without human intervention or human error. Algorithmic trading has changed the role of the trader. Today's traders have become strategists and tacticians, whereas in the past, the primary task of a trader was managing broker relationships.

Of course, the role of the broker also changes when the buy-side institution takes active control of the order. Brokers have in many cases been eliminated from trades they would have formerly been given responsibility for executing. Rather than serving as agents or dealers, brokers increasingly compete on the basis of the quality of their analytic engine.

EXAMPLE 10

Order Fragmentation: The Meat-Grinder Effect[28]

The following trade in the Oracle Corporation (NASDAQ: ORCL) illustrates both order fragmentation and electronic trading.

Before the market opening, a momentum manager sent a 1,745,640-share buy order to his trading desk, and the process unfolded as follows. The desk fed the order to Bloomberg B-Trade, one of several ECNs available to the trade desk. Trading in the issue began at 9:53 a.m. The order was small, in the sense that it was slightly less than 3 percent of Oracle's trading volume that day, and was completed in just 51 minutes in 1,014 separate executions. At times, there were up to 153 executions per minute—more than any human could handle. Average trade size was about 1,700 shares, roughly a 1,000:1 fragmentation ratio (i.e., the ratio of the size of the order to average trade size). The largest execution was roughly 64,000 shares and occurred in a cluster of rapid trading when almost 190,000 shares were executed in less than one minute. The smallest execution was for 13 shares. Seventeen percent of the executions were for 100 shares or less, and 44 percent were for less than 1,000 shares. Implementation shortfall was $0.15 per share, including $0.14 from market impact and delay and $0.01 per share commissions.

---

28 This example is based on Wagner (2003).

> The aggressive trading strategy paid off: ORCL rose at the close to yield a trading profit for the day of 4.1 percent, or $785,538. In order for the 1,700,000-odd-share order to be executed, it had to be forced through a constriction 1,700 shares wide on average. This is the meat-grinder effect: In order for a large equity order to get done, it must often be broken up into many smaller orders.

Ever-faster trade message speed and increased volumes in automated trading systems or electronic limit order books, such as the International Securities Exchange for options and Hotspot FX for foreign exchange, have spurred the development of algorithmic systems. The 2006 merger between the NYSE and the Archipelago Exchange has also promoted greater use of algorithmic systems.

Automated trading requires constant monitoring to avoid taking unintentional risk. For example, if the process executes the easiest trades first, the portfolio manager might wind up later in the day with an unbalanced portfolio or unintended exposure to certain sectors or industries. Algorithmic execution systems that skillfully participate in order flow over time are well adapted to control such portfolio risks.

5.3.2 *Classification of Algorithmic Execution Systems*

Algorithmic trading has gained considerable popularity among more sophisticated institutional traders looking for a technological solution to a complex, fast-moving, and fragmented market environment. These strategies are typically offered through algorithmic execution systems from institutional brokers, although some institutions and hedge funds have developed their own internal algorithms.

Algorithmic trading has its roots in the simple portfolio trades of the 1980s, in which large baskets of stocks were bought and sold (often as part of an index arbitrage strategy) with the push of a button. In the 1990s, automated systems such as ITG's QuantEX™ allowed for so-called rules-based trading. One example of rules-based trading is "pairs trading," in which the trading engine will automatically enter into (or exit from) a long and short position in a predesignated pair of stocks if certain conditions are met. The user can, for instance, specify a rule that calls for buying XYZ and simultaneously selling ABC if the price ratio of the two stocks crosses a certain threshold. The success of rules-based trading gave rise in the late 1990s to algorithmic trading, in which decisions regarding trading horizon, style, and even venue are automatically generated by a computer using specified algorithms based on specified inputs and then executed electronically. Before we delve into the details of how algorithms actually work, it is useful to develop a classification of algorithmic strategies.

Exhibit 10	**Algorithmic Trading Classification**		
Logical Participation Strategies		Opportunistic Strategies	Specialized Strategies
Simple Logical Participation Strategies	Implementation Shortfall Strategies		

The most common class of algorithms in use is **logical participation strategies**, protocols for breaking up an order for execution over time.

Simple Logical Participation Strategies   Institutional traders use the following simple logical participation strategies to participate in overall market volumes without being unduly visible.

- One of the most popular logical participation strategies involves breaking up an order over time according to a prespecified volume profile. The objective of this **volume-weighted average price (VWAP) strategy** is to match or improve upon the VWAP for the day.

    In a VWAP strategy, the trader attempts to match the expected volume pattern in the stock, typically over the whole day. Forecasts of the volume pattern are generally based on historical data (e.g., 21-day stock-specific or industry averages); increasingly, these forecasts are based on forward-looking volume predictors. Since the actual volume for the day is unknown before the end of the day, however, dynamic predictors are quite volatile.

- The **time-weighted average price (TWAP) strategy** is a particularly simple variant that assumes a flat volume profile and trades in proportion to time.

    The TWAP strategy breaks up the order over the day in proportion to time, which is useful in thinly traded assets whose volume patterns might be erratic. The objective here is normally to match or beat a time-weighted or equal-weighted average price. The participation strategy trades at a constant fraction of volume (usually 5–20 percent), attempting to blend in with market volumes. This strategy can be reactive if based on past trades or proactive if based on a dynamic forecast of incoming volume.

- Another common participation strategy is a **percentage-of-volume strategy**, in which trading takes place in proportion to overall market volume (typically at a rate of 5–20 percent) until the order is completed.

Implementation Shortfall Strategies   Recently, a newer logical participation strategy, the so-called **implementation shortfall strategy** (or arrival price strategy), has gained popularity. Unlike simple logical participation strategies, implementation shortfall strategies solve for the optimal trading strategy that minimizes trading costs as measured by the implementation shortfall method.

As discussed earlier, implementation shortfall is defined as the difference between the return on a notional or paper portfolio, in which positions are executed at a price representing the prevailing price when the decision to trade is made, and the actual portfolio's return.

Implementation shortfall strategies seek to minimize implementation shortfall or overall execution costs, usually represented by a weighted average of market impact and opportunity costs. Opportunity costs are related to the risk of adverse price movements, which increases with trading horizon. Consequently, implementation shortfall strategies are typically "front-loaded" in the sense of attempting to exploit market liquidity early in the trading day. Implementation shortfall strategies are especially valuable for portfolio trades, in which controlling the risk of not executing the trade list is critical. They are also useful in transition management (handing over a portfolio to a new portfolio manager), where multiperiod trading is common and there is a need for formal risk controls.

Interest in implementation shortfall strategies is also driven by an increased awareness of the limitations of traditional simple logical participation strategies using VWAP as an objective or benchmark. In addition, the objective of implementation shortfall strategies is consistent with the mean–variance framework used by many quantitative managers, a point we expand upon below. The majority of the value of algorithmically traded orders is executed using simple logical participation and implementation shortfall strategies. Exhibit 11 shows the hypothetical trade schedule for an implementation shortfall algorithmic order. Notice that the order is traded aggressively to minimize a weighted average of market impact costs and trade risk. The black line shows the cumulative fraction of the order that is complete, with the order fully complete by noon EST.

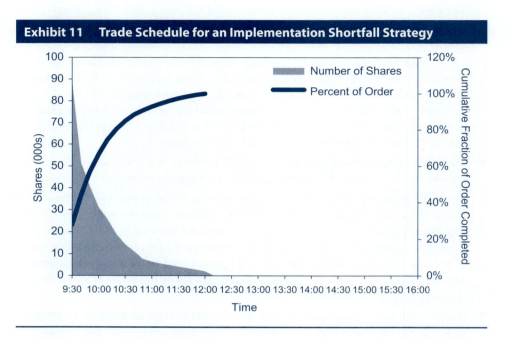

Exhibit 11   Trade Schedule for an Implementation Shortfall Strategy

The remaining major types of algorithmic trading are opportunistic participation strategies and specialized strategies.

Opportunistic Participation Strategies   Opportunistic participation strategies also involve trading over time. The opportunistic trading strategy involves passive trading combined with the opportunistic seizing of liquidity. The most common examples are pegging and discretion strategies, in which the trader who wishes to buy posts a bid, hoping others will sell to him or her, yielding negative implicit trading costs. If the bid–offer spread is sufficiently small, however, the trader might buy at the ask. This strategy typically involves using reserve or hidden orders and crossing (internally or externally) to provide additional sources of liquidity at low cost. Because trading is opportunistic, the liquidity strategy is not a true participation strategy.

Specialized Strategies   Other strategies include passive order strategies, which do not necessarily guarantee execution; "hunter" strategies, which opportunistically seek liquidity when it is offered; and more specialized strategies that target particular benchmarks. Market-on-close algorithms that target the closing price are an example of this last category. Smart routing, in which algorithms are used to intelligently route an order to the most liquid venue, can be viewed as a specialized form of algorithmic trading.

The next section gives further insight into the reasoning behind the main type of algorithmic trading, logical participation strategies.

5.3.3 *The Reasoning behind Logical Participation Algorithmic Strategies*

To take simple logical participation strategies first, underlying such strategies is the implicit assumption that participating in proportion to the actual trading volume can minimize trading costs. A large body of empirical evidence suggests that the price impact of equity trades is an increasing function of order size. Breaking up the order into smaller sub-blocks may therefore yield a lower average market or price impact.

This approach is intuitive, as the cost of an immediate demand for a large amount of liquidity is likely to be quite high, whereas if the same order were spread out in time, more liquidity providers could supply the needed opposite party, lessening the adverse price effects. Under certain assumptions (e.g., if prices are linearly related to the order size), breaking up the order in proportion to expected market liquidity yields lower market impact cost.

An implementation shortfall strategy involves minimizing a weighted average of market impact costs and missed trade opportunity costs. Missed trade opportunity cost refers to the risk of not executing a trade because of adverse price movements. A common proxy for such costs is the volatility of trade value or trade cost, which increases with trading horizon. Intuitively, the sooner an order is made available to the market, the greater the opportunity it usually has to find the opposing side of the trade. Consequently, implementation shortfall strategies are typically front-loaded, in the sense that they can involve trading significant fractions of market volume in the early periods of trading, in contrast to simple logical participation strategies.[29]

The logic for implementation shortfall strategies differs from that of the more traditional participation strategy. Recall that breaking up an order yields the lowest market impact cost. However, there is a cost to extending trade duration by breaking the order very finely, namely, risk. The implementation shortfall strategy—after the user specifies a weight on market impact cost and opportunity cost or risk—solves for the optimal trading strategy.[30] The intuition is straightforward. If the trader is very risk averse, then the strategy will trade aggressively in early periods to complete the order quickly to avoid undue risk. The more formal problem solved by the implementation shortfall algorithm can be expressed mathematically as

$$\text{Min}\{S_1,S_2,\ldots,S_T\}\,\text{Expected cost}(S_1,S_2,\ldots,S_T) + \lambda\,\text{Var}\big[\text{Cost}(S_1,S_2,\ldots,S_T)\big]$$

where T is the horizon (some algorithms actually solve for this), S_t represents the shares to be traded in trading interval (or bucket) t, λ is the weight placed on risk (aversion parameter), and Var[Cost] represents the variance of the cost of trading. The expression given is an **objective function** (a quantitative expression of the objective or goal of a process). In words, the objective function states that an implementation shortfall algorithm selects the set of trades that minimizes a quantity equal to the expected total cost of the trades and a penalty term that increases with the variance of the possible cost outcomes for the set of trades. The penalty term reflects the trader's desire for certainty as to costs.

Observe the close correspondence between this problem and the classic mean–variance portfolio optimization problem. Indeed, for a quantitative manager using a mean–variance optimization approach, it is logical to use an implementation short-fall algorithm. Implementation shortfall costs directly reduce the portfolio's return and hence are part of the expected return component in the portfolio optimization problem. Transaction costs are an integral element of portfolio performance because the variance of cost is ultimately manifested in the variance of portfolio returns, and expected costs directly reduce alpha. Although many managers do not recognize this dependence, it is quantitatively important. For example, a small-capitalization fund rebalancing daily might easily incur costs of trading of, say, 80 bps, with a standard deviation of 150–200 bps. On an annualized basis, these figures are large relative to the expected returns and risks of the portfolio. The implementation shortfall algorithm is thus consistent with the ultimate portfolio optimization problem.

29 The exception might occur when there is significant volume expected at the end of the day that the strategy takes into consideration.
30 See, for example, Almgren and Chriss (2000/2001).

Choosing among algorithms and setting the right parameters are difficult tasks. A simple illustration can help us understand the types of considerations that enter into selecting tactics. Exhibit 12 shows summary output from a trader's order management system (OMS) or trade blotter indicating trade size (in shares), various market attributes, and an urgency level from the portfolio manager. (A **trade blotter** is a device for entering and tracking orders to trade and trade executions.)

Exhibit 12	Order Management System					
Symbol	**Side**	**Size (Shares)**	**Avg. Daily Volume**	**Price**	**Spread (%)**	**Urgency**
ABC	B	100,000	2,000,000	55.23	0.05	Low
DEF	S	30,000	60,000	10.11	0.55	Low
GHIJ	B	25,000	250,000	23.45	0.04	High

What tactics are appropriate for each order? Although the first order in ABC is the largest in shares and value, it is actually the smallest as a percentage of average daily volume, and given the low spreads and low urgency level, it is ideally suited for algorithmic execution, probably with a VWAP algorithm using the entire day's liquidity. Similarly, the order in GHIJ is just 10 percent of average daily volume, but given the high urgency, an implementation shortfall algorithm might be preferred with a high urgency setting to aggressively execute the purchase. By contrast, the order in DEF is large relative to average daily volume and would likely be traded using a broker or crossing system to mitigate the large spreads.

EXAMPLE 11

A Trading Strategy

Charles Lee is discussing execution strategy with Rachel Katz, the head of equity trading at his investment management firm. Lee has decided to increase the position in Curzon Enterprises for growth-oriented equity accounts. Katz shows Lee Exhibit 13, which depicts the execution of a buy order in Curzon Enterprises that established the initial position in it. In Exhibit 13, the black line shows the cumulative fraction of the order that is complete as the trading day progresses, with the order fully complete by the close at 4:00 p.m. EST. The shaded area represents trading volume over half-hour intervals.

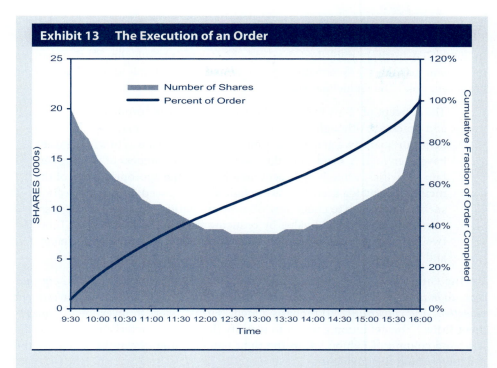

Exhibit 13   The Execution of an Order

Using the information in Exhibit 13, address the following:

1   Interpret the pattern of intraday trading in Curzon Enterprises.

2   Identify and evaluate the execution strategy depicted in Exhibit 13.

Solution to 1:

Trading in Curzon Enterprises follows a U shape, with highest volume at the opening and close and lowest volume at midday.

Solution to 2:

The exhibit depicts a VWAP algorithmic order. The execution strategy split the order up into pieces to be executed throughout the day. The curve indicating the cumulative fraction executed has a steeper slope earlier and later in the day than in midsession, indicating that the volume of orders the algorithm sent to the market was highest near the opening and the close, following the lead of the U-shaped trading volume, which indicates greatest volume at those times.

SERVING THE CLIENT'S INTERESTS

6

For the portfolio manager and buy-side trader, the effectiveness with which portfolio decisions are executed has an impact on the investment performance delivered to the client. The following sections discuss important issues related to protecting the client's interests.

6.1 CFA Institute Trade Management Guidelines

In 2004, CFA Institute published the Trade Management Guidelines[31] that provide investment managers "a systematic, repeatable, and demonstrable approach to seeking best execution." The Guidelines state:

> The concept of "Best Execution" is similar to that of "prudence" in intent and practice. Although prudence and Best Execution may be difficult to define or quantify, a general determination can be made as to whether they have been met. ... Prudence addresses the appropriateness of holding certain securities, while Best Execution addresses the appropriateness of the methods by which securities are acquired or disposed. Security selection seeks to add value to client portfolios by evaluating future prospects; Best Execution seeks to add value by reducing frictional trading costs. These two activities go hand in hand in achieving better investment performance and in meeting standards of prudent fiduciary behavior.

The Guidelines define best execution as *"the trading process Firms apply that seeks to maximize the value of a client's portfolio within the client's stated investment objectives and constraints."* (Emphasis added; "Firms" refers to investment management firms.) The definition goes on to identify the four characteristics shown in the left-hand column of Exhibit 14. In the right-hand column, the authors amplify the thinking behind the guidelines.

Exhibit 14 Best Execution	
Characteristic	**Explanation**
Best execution is intrinsically tied to portfolio-decision value and cannot be evaluated independently.	The purpose of trading is to capture the value of investment decisions. Thus, the definition has strong symmetry to the definition of prudent expert that guides fiduciary decisions.
Best execution is a prospective, statistical, and qualitative concept that cannot be known with certainty *ex ante*.	Trading is a negotiation, with each side of the trade having equal standing. Both buyer and seller—or their appointed agents—jointly determine what "best execution" is for every trade.
Best execution has aspects that may be measured and analyzed over time on an *ex post* basis, even though such measurement on a trade-by-trade basis may not be meaningful in isolation.	Trading occurs in a volatile environment subject to high statistical variability. One would not evaluate a card player on an individual hand; one would need to observe a sequence of hands to determine skill; similarly for traders. Despite the variability, overall trades contain some information useful in evaluating the process. By compiling trade data, one can deduce useful information about the quality of the process.
Best execution is interwoven into complicated, repetitive, and continuing practices and relationships.	Trading is a process, not an outcome. The standards are behavioral.

---

31 See www.cfainstitute.org for any updates.

The Trade Management Guidelines are divided into three areas: processes, disclosures, and record keeping:

1 *Processes.* Firms should establish formal policies and procedures that have the ultimate goal of maximizing the asset value of client portfolios through best execution. A firm's policies and procedures should provide guidance to measure and manage effectively the quality of trade decisions.

2 *Disclosures.* Firms should disclose to clients and prospects 1) their general information regarding trading techniques, venues, and agents and 2) any actual or potential trading-related conflicts of interest. Such disclosure provides clients with the necessary information to help them assess a firm's ability to deliver best execution.

3 *Record keeping.* Firms should maintain proper documentation that supports 1) compliance with the firm's policies and procedures and 2) the disclosures provided to clients. In addition to aiding in the determination of best execution, the records may support a firm's broker selection practices when examined by applicable regulatory organizations.

At the time these guidelines were written, the state of the art in transaction cost measurement was such that it was not possible to specify specific methodologies for transaction cost measurement. Rather, the guidelines are a compilation of recommended practices and not standards.

In the end, best execution is primarily an exercise in serving the needs of the investment management clients. Adherence to standards of documentation and disclosure, as important as these are to ensuring best practices, is simply a means to achieving this overriding objective.[32]

6.2 The Importance of an Ethical Focus

"My word is my honor." The code of both buy-side and sell-side traders is that verbal agreements will be honored. The code is self-enforcing: Any trader who does not adhere to it quickly finds that no one is willing to deal with him.

Nonetheless, valuable information is the stock-in-trade of market participants, and the temptations are great. One of the side effects of the explosion of trading techniques and trading alternatives is that it is difficult to trace the uses to which information is being put. It is often necessary to rely on the strength of a trader's reputation and his or her avid desire to maintain and build long-term relationships.

Trading can be looked at as a "zero-sum game" in which one trader's losses are another trader's gains. The near disappearance of the brokerage commission has caused more trading costs to be implicit rather than explicit. Markets are thus becoming more adversarial and less agency-oriented, making it more difficult to align investor or buy-side interests with broker/dealer or sell-side interests.

In every case, the ethical focus for the portfolio manager and the buy-side trader must be the interests of the client. As previously mentioned, the buy-side trader acts in a fiduciary capacity, with access to the client's assets. Loyalties to the trader's own firm and relationships with sell-side traders must be consistent with the trader's fiduciary responsibilities.

---

[32] For further background on the subject, see Wagner and Edwards (1993), Wagner (2003), and Schwartz and Wood (2003).

7 CONCLUDING REMARKS

The ability of the sell-side system of brokers and exchanges to adapt and create solutions to investment requirements is impressive. In general, and increasingly, traders get the trading services they demand. Different order types and different venues serve investors with different motives and trading needs. In return, the broker/dealers and exchanges earn a competitive price for providing the services.

Technological advances continue to play a major role in reducing transaction costs. Faster dissemination of information, improved public access, more sophisticated analysis, and eventually the replacement of exchange floor trading by electronic trading can be expected. These efficiencies will reduce the cost of running the exchange system, but they will not necessarily reduce the cost of dealer services provided. Nor will the pressure to reduce costs and improve portfolio performance diminish.

Because of the intensity of competition and the readiness to adapt and innovate, costs continue to fall. Buy-side traders who demand the facilities and conveniences provided by the exchange community must expect to pay the costs. To reduce trading costs, an ever-evolving understanding of the trading process and its implied costs is essential. Sponsors and investment advisors may face make-or-buy decisions concerning future trading and trading-subsidized services. High-speed connectivity and algorithmic trading are clear examples of how costs can be effectively reduced by removing extraneous middlemen from the trading process.

Investors and traders are accustomed to a market that handles the duties, costs, and risks of trading. In addition, the sell side delivers an array of valuable but sometimes dimly related services without additional charge. Such services do not come free, however. In the future, pension plan sponsors and other clients will demand that portfolio managers and traders make more informed choices that reconcile trade costs with benefits received. Sponsors and other clients pay the costs of trading and are entitled to—and are increasingly demanding—a clear accounting of benefits derived.

SUMMARY

The portfolio decision is not complete until securities are bought or sold. How well that last step is accomplished is a key factor affecting investment results. This reading has made the following points.

■ Market microstructure refers to the particular trading protocols that govern how a trader's latent demands are translated into executed trades. Knowledge of market microstructure helps investors understand how their trades will be executed and how market frictions may give rise to discrepancies between price and full-information expectations of value.

■ Order-driven markets are those in which prices are established by public limit orders and include auction markets and electronic crossing networks (where trading occurs at prespecified points in time), as well as automated auctions (where trading takes place continuously). Quote-driven markets rely on market makers or dealers to establish prices at which securities can be bought and sold. Brokered markets are markets in which transactions are largely effected by brokers through a search mechanism. Hybrid markets are those, such as the NYSE, that incorporate features of more than one type of market.

■ Execution services secured through a broker include the following: representing the order, finding the buyer, market information for the investor, discretion and secrecy, escrow, and support of the market mechanism. A trader's broker stands in an agency relationship to the trader, in contrast to dealers. Dealers provide bridge liquidity to buyers and sellers in that they take the other side of the trade when no other liquidity is present.

- The effective spread is two times the deviation of the price received or paid from the midpoint of the market at the time an order is entered to the actual execution price. The bid–ask spread is the difference between the bid and the ask prices. The effective spread is a better representation of the true cost of trading than the bid–ask spread because it captures both price improvement and price impact.

- Market quality is judged by the following criteria, which are positives for a market's liquidity: many buyers and sellers; diversity of opinion, information, and investment needs; a readily accessible location; continuous operation during convenient market hours; a reasonable cost of transacting; market integrity, in effect the honesty of market participants; assurity of the contract's integrity.

- Transaction costs include explicit costs and implicit costs. Explicit costs are the direct costs of trading and include broker commission costs, taxes, stamp duties, and fees. Implicit costs include indirect costs such as the impact of the trade on the price received.

- Implementation shortfall is an estimate of transaction costs that amounts to subtracting the all-in transaction costs from the market price at the time the decision was made to buy or sell the security.

- Econometric models for costs are useful for obtaining pretrade estimates of the costs of a trade. These models may use variables such as stock liquidity, risk, trade size relative to available liquidity, momentum, and trading style.

- The major types of traders are information-motivated traders (who trade on information with limited time value), value-motivated traders (who trade on valuation judgments), liquidity-motivated traders (who trade based on liquidity needs), and passive traders (who trade for indexed portfolios). Information-motivated and liquidity-motivated traders have very short trading time horizons and are more sensitive to time than price in execution. By contrast, value-motivated and passive traders have longer trading time horizons and are more sensitive to price than time in execution.

- The two major order types are market orders (for prompt execution in public markets at the best price available) and limit orders (specifying a price at which the order becomes executable). Market orders are among the order types preferred by information-motivated and liquidity-motivated traders because of their time preference. Limit orders are among the order types preferred by value-motivated and passive traders because they are sensitive to price.

- Major focuses influencing the choice of trading strategy include the following: liquidity needed at any cost, need trustworthy agent for possibly hazardous trading situation, costs are not important, advertise to draw liquidity, and low cost whatever the liquidity.

- Algorithmic trading refers to automated electronic trading subject to quantitative rules and user-specified benchmarks and constraints. Three broad categories of algorithmic trading strategies are logical participation strategies (which involve protocols for breaking up an order for execution over time), opportunistic strategies (which involve passive trading combined with the opportunistic seizing of liquidity), and specialized strategies (which cover a range of strategies that serve special purposes).

PRACTICE PROBLEMS

1   An analyst is estimating various measures of spread for Amazon, Inc. (NASDAQ: AMZN). The following is the bid and ask quote for a trade in September 2011.

Bid Price ($)	Ask Price ($)
226.10	226.22

A buyer-initiated trade in was executed at a price of $226.17. For this trade, answer the following:

A   What is the quoted spread?

B   What is the effective spread?

C   When would the effective and quoted spreads be equal?

2   Zhou (2011) examines ownership structure and liquidity using trade data from the NYSE Trade and Quote (TAQ) database. The quoted spreads and effective spreads for trades in the shares of firms with the highest and lowest proportions of institutional ownership are shown below.

Spread (Cents)	Highest	Lowest
Quoted spread	14.47	21.61
Effective spread	9.13	14.61

Source: Zhou, Dan. 2011. "Ownership Structure, Liquidity, and Trade Informativeness." *Journal of Finance and Accountancy.* Vol. 6: 1–17.

On the basis of the above results, address the following:

A   Determine whether the dealers ("specialists") for these NYSE trades provided price improvements.

B   Contrast the price improvement provided for high institutional ownership trades versus that provided for low institutional ownership trades.

3   POSIT is an electronic crossing network providing liquidity in global equities. After stock orders are crossed, there are some stocks for which there are unmatched buy quantities and some stocks with unmatched sell quantities. Discuss whether POSIT should disclose these unmatched quantities after a cross is run.

4   For each of the following, discuss which of the two orders in shares of Sunny Corporation will have a greater market impact. Assume that all other factors are the same.

A   **i.** An order to buy 5,000 shares placed by a trader on the NYSE.

    ii. An order to buy 50,000 shares placed by the same trader on the NYSE.

B   **i.** An order to buy 25,000 shares placed by a trader on the NYSE.

    ii. An order to buy 25,000 shares placed on the NYSE by another trader who is believed to represent informed investors in the stock.

C   **i.** An order to sell 20,000 shares placed by a trader on the NYSE.

ii. An order to sell 20,000 shares placed by the same trader on POSIT, an electronic crossing network.

5   An investment manager placed a limit order to buy 500,000 shares of Alpha Corporation at $21.35 limit at the opening of trading on 8 February. The closing market price of Alpha Corporation on 7 February was also $21.35. The limit order filled 40,000 shares, and the remaining 460,000 shares were never filled. Some good news came out about Alpha Corporation on 8 February, and its price increased to $23.60 by the end of that day. However, by the close of trading on 14 February, the price had declined to $21.74. The investment manager is analyzing the missed trade opportunity cost using the closing price on 7 February as the benchmark price.

   A   What is the estimate of the missed trade opportunity cost if it is measured at a one-day interval after the decision to trade?

   B   What is the estimate of the missed trade opportunity cost if it is measured at a one-week interval after the decision to trade?

   C   What are some of the problems in estimating the missed trade opportunity cost?

6   A portfolio manager would like to buy 5,000 shares of a very recent IPO stock. However, he was not able to get any shares at the IPO price of £30. The portfolio manager would still like to have 5,000 shares, but not at a price above £45 per share. Should he place a market order or a limit order? What would be the advantage and disadvantage of each type of order, given his purposes?

7   An asset management firm wants to purchase 500,000 shares of a company. It decides to shop the order to various broker/dealer firms to see which firm can offer the best service and lowest cost. Discuss the potential negatives of shopping the order.

8   Google Inc. is listed on NASDAQ (symbol: GOOG). A trader sold 100 shares of GOOG on 27 September 2011 at 12:42 at a price of $542.23 per share. Assume that the trades for GOOG below encompass all trades for that day.

Time	Trade Price ($)	Shares Traded
9:30	$538.20	300
9:48	$538.72	200
12:28	$543.61	600
12:42	$542.23	100
12:58	$543.44	300
13:58	$545.84	500
15:59	$539.34	300

Source: Yahoo Finance.

The trader is analyzing the implicit costs of the trade, focusing on the bid–ask spread and market impact using specified price benchmarks.

   A   What would be the estimated implicit transaction costs using each of the following as the price benchmark?

   i. Opening price.

   ii. Closing price.

   iii. Volume-weighted average price (VWAP).

B   Evaluate the effect on estimated implicit transaction costs of the choice of benchmark price.

9   A client of a broker evaluates the broker's performance by measuring transaction costs with a specified price benchmark. The broker has discretion over the timing of his trades for the client. Discuss what the broker could do to make his performance look good to the client (even though the broker's execution decisions may not be in the best interests of the client) if the price benchmark used by the client for evaluation is the:

   A   opening price.

   B   closing price.

   C   volume-weighted average price (VWAP).

10   A trader decided to sell 30,000 shares of a company. At the time of this decision, the quoted price was €53.20 to €53.30. Because of the large size of the order, the trader decided to execute the sale in three equal orders of 10,000 shares spread over the course of the day. When she placed the first order, the quoted price was €53.20 to €53.30, and she sold the shares at €53.22. The trade had a market impact, and the quoted price had fallen to €53.05 to €53.15 when she placed the next order. Those shares were sold at €53.06. The quoted price had fallen to €52.87 to €52.98 when she placed the last order. Those shares were sold at €52.87. Suppose this was the market closing price of the shares that day. Answer the following questions. Ignore commissions.

   A   Estimate the total transaction cost of the sale of 30,000 shares if the closing price is used as the price benchmark.

   B   What is the implementation shortfall estimate of the total cost of executing the sale?

   C   Discuss and compare the answers to A and B above. Which of the two approaches is appropriate for the situation in this problem?

11   Suppose 1,000 shares of Acme Co. stock are ordered to be bought on Monday with a benchmark price of $10.00. On Monday, 600 shares are purchased at $10.02 per share. Commissions and fees are $20. On Monday, the closing price is $9.99 per share. On Tuesday, 100 more shares are purchased at $10.08 per share. Commissions and fees are $12. Shares for Acme close on Tuesday at $10.01 per share. The remaining shares are not purchased, and the order is canceled on Wednesday just as the market closes at $10.05 per share.

   A   Calculate the implementation shortfall for this trade.

   B   Calculate the components of the implementation shortfall for this trade.

12   Jane Smith manages an equity fund. She has decided to undertake a major portfolio restructuring by increasing the exposure of the fund to the telecommunications sector. The implementation of her decision would involve investing more than $2 million in the stocks of about 20 telecommunications companies. Contrast the use of a portfolio trade to the use of purchase orders for these stocks placed individually (stock by stock) in terms of the probable market impact of the two approaches.

13   Famed Investments has a C$25 million portfolio. It follows an active approach to investment management and, on average, turns the portfolio over twice a year. That is, it expects to trade 200 percent of the value of the portfolio over the next year. Every time Famed Investments buys or sells securities, it incurs execution costs of 75 basis points, on average. It expects an annual return before execution costs of 8 percent. What is the expected return net of execution costs?

14 Several British stocks trade on both the London Stock Exchange and the New York Stock Exchange. Due to the time difference between London and New York, these stocks trade for six hours every day in London only, followed by the opening of the NYSE and a two-hour period when both markets are open before London closes. Menkveld (2008) found that the volatility of prices in London is much higher during the two-hour period when both markets are open than during the preceding six-hour period when only London is open. What could be an information-motivated reason for this finding? Assume that US traders do not trade in London.

15 An employee retirement fund manager believes he has special information about a particular company. Based on this information, he believes the company is currently undervalued and decides to purchase 50,000 shares of the company. The manager decides that he will not place a large single order for 50,000 shares but will instead place several medium-sized orders of 2,500–5,000 shares spread over a period of time. Why do you think the manager chooses to follow this strategy?

16 Consider some stocks that trade in two markets, with a trader being able to trade in these stocks in either market. Suppose that the two markets are identical in all respects except that bid–ask spreads are lower and depths (the number of shares being offered at the bid and ask prices) are greater in one of the two markets. State in which market liquidity-motivated and information-motivated traders would prefer to transact. Justify your answer.

17 A trader has been given two trades to execute with the following characteristics. What tactics do you recommend?

Trade	Size (Shares)	Average Daily Volume (ADV)	Price	Spread (%)	Urgency
A	200,000	6,000,000	10.00	0.03	High
B	150,000	200,000	10.00	0.60	High

18 A trader must rebalance a pension plan's actively managed $500 million US small-cap equity portfolio to an S&P 500 indexed portfolio in order to effect a change in the plan's strategic asset allocation. He is told that his primary goal is to minimize explicit costs in this rebalance. What should his trading strategy be?

Questions 19–25 relate to Mel Rojas[1]

Mel Rojas is a risk manager for Deep Asset Management (DAM). DAM prides itself on its investment process, which is characterized by low turnover, a long investment horizon, and deep research into company fundamentals. Rojas has recently been tasked with evaluating DAM's trading desk processes and procedures to evaluate the efficacy of the desk in carrying out trades.

Rojas reviews DAM's purchase of Arachnid Mining (ARCM), which trades on an order-driven market. DAM's trader considered using a market order to buy 5,000 shares, a limit order to buy 5,000 shares at $46.50 or better, or an iceberg order to only show 500 shares at a time. The portfolio manager instructed the trader that he was interested in establishing the position quickly, and that his estimate of fair value

1 This item set was developed by Jeremy Heer, CFA (Brookfield, IL, USA).

for ARCM was $100/share. When the order was placed, the best offer for ARCM was $47.25 for 4,400 shares. Average daily trading volume in ARCM over the previous 10 days has been 98,200 shares.

Rojas then reviews a recent trade in which DAM bought Enviroscrape (NVRO) stock, adding to an existing position. NVRO's price was $17.05 when the decision to add to the position was made. NVRO trades on a quote-driven dealer market, and has an average daily volume of 10,000,000 shares. When the order was placed with the desk on Tuesday at 11:50am, the order book appeared as follows:

Exhibit 1 NVRO Order Book, Tuesday

	Bid				Ask		
Dealer	**Time**	**Price**	**Size**	**Dealer**	**Time**	**Price**	**Size**
C	11:49am	17.02	300	C	11:49am	17.05	3200
A	11:37am	17.00	1000	B	11:45am	17.09	2500
B	11:35am	16.95	5400	D	11:43am	17.15	4500
D	11:33am	16.90	9000	A	11:37am	17.20	500

The desk placed a limit order to buy 10,000 shares at $17.05 or better. After buying 3,200 shares at $17.05, the market traded up and closes at $17.20. No further shares were bought that day. DAM paid $64 in commissions, and the VWAP for the day's trading was 17.00.

The next day, Wednesday, the desk buys another 3,000 shares at $17.25. The market closes at $17.50 and no further action is taken. The desk pays $0.02 per share in commissions for these trades.

A week later, DAM decides to take a much larger position in NVRO. They intend to buy 50,000 shares. First, they decide to enter a 50,000 share buy order on an Electronic Crossing Network (ECN). This network trades once a day at 4:00pm New York time. On the day in question, despite entering in a 50,000 share buy order, DAM is only able to buy 2,000 shares.

The next day, rather than going back to the ECN, the trading desk decides to work with a broker to improve their execution of their NVRO purchase. The broker reviews three different algorithmic trading strategies with DAM: Volume Weighted Average Price (VWAP), Time Weighted Average Price (TWAP), and Percentage-of-Volume (POV).

19 Based on the ARCM market, the trader's choice of order type to buy ARCM was *most likely*:

   A a limit order.

   B a market order.

   C an iceberg order.

20 Based on Exhibit 1, if the DAM trader places a market order to buy 5,700 shares of NVRO at 11:50am, and the order is filled at an average price of $17.07, he will have paid an effective spread *closest* to:

   A $0.02.

   B $0.03.

   C $0.07.

21 Which of the following is the *most likely* reason DAM turned to a broker after failing to execute their 50,000 share order of NVRO with the ECN?

A DAM values price discovery in the marketplace.

B DAM wants to minimize market impact on NVRO.

C NVRO is a very liquid stock and DAM's order would have little market impact.

22 For Tuesday's trading, assuming that DAM uses VWAP as the price benchmark, DAM's implicit transaction cost on the NVRO trade was *closest* to:

A $96.

B $160.

C $256.

23 At the end of Wednesday, DAM's implementation shortfall on the NVRO trade is *closest* to:

A $1,084.

B $2,434.

C $4,376.

24 DAM is *most likely* to be characterized as:

A a value-motivated trader.

B a liquidity-motivated trader.

C an information-motivated trader.

25 Which of the following statements *most likely* explains why the broker recommended a VWAP strategy in order to get the 50,000-share NVRO order executed?

A The stock is thinly traded with erratic volume.

B DAM prefers to execute as close to the closing price as possible.

C The order is a low percentage of the average daily volume of the stock.

SOLUTIONS

1   **A**   The quoted spread is the difference between the ask and bid prices in the quote prevailing at the time the trade is entered. The bid is $226.10 and the ask is $226.22. So, the quoted spread = Ask − Bid = $226.22 − $226.10 = $0.12.

    B   The time-of-trade quotation midpoint = ($226.10 + $226.22)/2 = $226.16. Effective spread = 2 × (Trade price − Time-of-trade quotation midpoint) = 2 × ($226.17 − $226.16) = 2 × $0.01 = $0.02.

    C   The effective and quoted spreads would be equal if a purchase took place at the ask price or a sale took place at the bid price.

2   **A**   The difference between quoted spreads and effective spreads reflects the price improvement provided by dealers. If the effective spreads are lower than the quoted spreads, dealers are providing price improvements. Since the effective spreads are lower than the quoted spreads for both the highest and lowest proportion of institutional ownership firms, dealers provided price improvements for both types of trades.

    B   The difference between the quoted and effective spreads is greater for the lowest institutional ownership firms (7.00 cents) than for the highest institutional ownership firms (5.34 cents). Therefore, on an absolute dollar basis, dealers provided greater price improvement for the lowest institutional ownership firms.

3   POSIT should not disclose unmatched quantities. Crossing networks maintain complete confidentiality not only in regard to the size of the orders and the names of the investors placing the orders, but also in regard to the unmatched quantities. If POSIT were to disclose the unmatched quantities, it would provide useful information to other parties that would affect the supply and demand of these stocks in which clients want to transact. As a result of the information leakage, transaction costs for its clients would likely rise.

4   **A**   The second order will have a greater market impact because it is bigger in size.

    B   The second order will have a greater market impact because the trader placing it has a reputation of representing informed investors in the stock. Thus, other traders may believe that the stock's intrinsic value differs from the current market price and adjust their quotations accordingly. In contrast to most other situations in which a reputation of being smart is beneficial, in stock trading, it is not to one's advantage.

    C   By definition, orders executed on crossing networks, such as POSIT, avoid market impact costs because the orders are crossed at the existing market price determined elsewhere, regardless of size. Therefore, the first order will have greater market impact. Note, however, that a part of a large order may go unfilled on the crossing network.

5   **A**   Missed trade opportunity cost is the unfilled size times the difference between the subsequent price and the benchmark price for buys (or times the difference between the benchmark price and the subsequent price for sells). So, using the closing price on 8 February as the subsequent price, the estimated missed trade opportunity cost is 460,000 × ($23.60 − $21.35) = $1,035,000.

B Using the closing price on 14 February as the subsequent price, the estimated missed trade opportunity cost is 460,000 × ($21.74 − $21.35) = $179,400.

C One of the problems in estimating missed trade opportunity cost is that the estimate depends upon when the cost is measured. As the solutions to Parts A and B of this problem indicate, the estimate could vary substantially when a different interval is used to measure the missed trade opportunity cost. Another problem in estimating the missed trade opportunity cost is that it does not consider the impact of order size on prices. For example, the estimates above assume that if the investment manager had bought the 500,000 shares on 8 February, he would have been able to sell these 500,000 shares at $23.60 each on 8 February (or at $21.74 each on 14 February). However, an order to sell 500,000 shares on 8 February (or on 14 February) would have likely led to a decline in price, and the entire order of 500,000 shares would not have been sold at $23.60 (or at $21.74). Thus, the missed trade opportunity costs above are likely to be overestimates.

6 Since the portfolio manager does not want to pay more than £45 per share, he should place a limit order to buy 5,000 shares at no more than £45 per share. An advantage of placing the limit order is that he avoids the risk of paying too high a price and then suffering substantial losses if the stock price subsequently declines. However, a disadvantage is that his order may not be filled because the market price may never touch his limit order price of £45, incurring a missed trade opportunity cost. For example, consider a situation in which the stock's ask price is £47 when the order to buy at £45 limit is placed and the stock trades up to £80. If the portfolio manager had placed a market order, he would have been able to purchase the stock at £47 and make a profit by selling the stock at the current price of £80. An advantage of a market order is certainty of execution. The disadvantage of a market order is uncertainty concerning the price at which the order will be executed. Because the portfolio manager's chief focus is on execution price, the limit order would be preferred.

7 One negative of shopping the order is that it could delay the execution of the order, and the stock price could increase in the meantime. Another important negative of shopping the order is that it leaks information to others about the buying intention of the asset management firm. This information leakage could result in an adverse price movement in the shares that the asset management firm wants to buy because the broker/dealers could revise their quotes or trade based on the information gained.

8 A Estimated implicit costs = Trade size × (Trade price − Benchmark price) for a buy, or Trade size × (Benchmark price − Trade price) for a sale. In this problem, Trade size = 100 and Trade price = $542.23.

   i. Opening price = $538.20

   Estimated implicit costs = 100 × ($538.20 − $542.23) = −$403

   ii. Closing price = $539.34

   Estimated implicit costs = 100 × ($539.34 − $542.23) = −$289

   iii. We need to first calculate the VWAP.

   VWAP = Dollar volume/Trade volume

   Dollar volume = (300 × $538.20) + (200 × $538.72) + (600 × $543.61) + (100 × $542.23) + (300 × $543.44) + (500 × $545.84) + (300 × $539.34) = $1,247,347.00

   Trade volume = 300 + 200 + 600 + 100 + 300 + 500 + 300 = 2,300 shares

So, VWAP = $1,247,347.00/2,300 = $542.3248 per share. Estimated implicit costs = 100 × ($542.3248 − $542.23) = $9.48

B Using VWAP as a benchmark, implicit costs are $9.48, whereas implicit costs are −$403 (−$289) if the opening price (closing price) is used as a benchmark. Estimated implicit costs may be quite sensitive to the choice of benchmark.

9 A If the order is received late in the day, the broker would act based on how the prices have changed during the day. If the order is a sell order and prices have increased since the opening, the broker would immediately fill the order so that the sale price is greater than the benchmark price. If prices have fallen during the day, the broker would wait until the next day to avoid recording a low-priced sale on a day when the market opened higher. The broker would do the opposite if the order is a buy order. If prices have increased since the opening, the broker would wait until the next day to avoid recording a high-priced buy on a day when the market opened lower. If the prices have fallen during the day, the broker would immediately fill the order so that the purchase price is lower than the benchmark price.

B The broker would execute the order just before closing so that the transaction price is the same as the closing price.

C The broker would split the order and spread its execution throughout the day so that the transaction price is close to the market VWAP.

10 A For a sale, Estimated cost = Trade size × (Benchmark price − Trade price). Using €52.87 as the benchmark price, the transaction cost estimate of the first trade is 10,000 × (€52.87 − €53.22) = −€3,500. The transaction cost estimate of the second trade is 10,000 × (€52.87 − €53.06) = −€1,900. The transaction cost estimate of the third trade is 10,000 × (€52.87 − €52.87) = €0. The total transaction cost estimate = −€3,500 + (−€1,900) + €0 = −€5,400.

B The quotation midpoint that prevailed at the time of the decision to trade was €53.25. This is the benchmark price, and the implementation shortfall estimate of the cost of executing the first order is 10,000 × (€53.25 − €53.22) = €300. The implementation shortfall estimate of the cost of executing the second order is 10,000 × (€53.25 − €53.06) = €1,900. The implementation shortfall estimate of the cost of executing the third order is 10,000 × (€53.25 − €52.87) = €3,800. So, the implementation shortfall estimate of the total cost of executing the three orders is €300 + €1,900 + €3,800 = €6,000.

C The estimated transaction cost using the closing price as the benchmark is negative. This result makes it seem as if the trader had a trading profit. This conclusion is not reasonable because the trader did pay the bid–ask spread and her trades had a market impact, making prices less favorable in her subsequent trades. For example, in the first trade, the trader sold the shares close to the bid price and the trade resulted in a decline in prices. Overall, the use of closing price as the benchmark is not appropriate in this problem because the benchmark itself is significantly affected by the large size of the order.

In contrast, the implementation shortfall estimate uses a benchmark which is determined before the order has an impact on prices. The implementation shortfall approach, which results in a reasonable estimate of €6,000 as the total cost of executing the sale, is the appropriate approach in this problem.

11 A The paper portfolio traded 1,000 shares on Monday for $10.00 per share. The value of the portfolio at the close on Wednesday is $10,050. The net value is $50.

The real portfolio contains only 700 shares and was traded over the course of two days. On Wednesday's close, it is worth 700 × $10.05 = $7,035.

The cost of the portfolio is $7,052:

Monday: 600 × $10.02 = $6,012 + $20 commissions = $6,032

Tuesday: 100 × $10.08 = $1,008 + $12 commissions = $1,020

The net value of the real portfolio is $7,035 − 7,052 = −$17. Thus, the implementation shortfall is $50 − (−$17) = $67, or 67 bps.

B   Implementation shortfall broken into components is as follows:

- Delay

    Monday: 600/1,000 × [($10.00 − $10.00)/$10.00] = 0.00%

    Tuesday: 100/1,000 × [($9.99 − $10.00)/$10.00] = −0.01%

- Realized profit and loss

    Monday: 600/1,000 × [($10.02 − $10.00)/$10.00] = 0.12%

    Tuesday: 100/1,000 × [($10.08 − $9.99)/$10.00] = 0.09%

- Missed trade opportunity cost

    300/1,000 × [($10.05 − $10.00)/$10.00] = 0.15%

Commissions are 0.20% + 0.12% = 0.32%.

Total implementation shortfall is 0.67%, or 67 bps.

12 Portfolio trades involve the purchase or sale of a basket of stocks, with the buy or sell orders placed as a coordinated transaction. Jane Smith could ask a broker for a quote for the entire basket of telecommunications stocks that she wants to purchase. Because there are multiple stocks in the basket being purchased, it is clear to the counterparty that the purchase is not motivated by information about a particular stock and the market impact of the trade is likely to be less. As a consequence, the cost of trading the basket of stocks is expected to be lower than the total trading cost of buying each stock individually.

13 The average execution cost for a purchase of securities is 75 basis points, or 0.75 percent, and the average execution cost for a sale of securities is also 0.75 percent. So, the average execution for a round-trip trade is 2 × 0.75%, or 1.5%. Since the portfolio is expected to be turned over twice, expected execution costs are 1.5% × 2 = 3%. Therefore, the expected return net of execution costs is 8% − 3% = 5%.

14 Just as some traders in London possess information about stocks that traders in New York may not, some New York–based traders possess information that London-based traders may not. When New York–based traders begin to trade with the opening of US markets, their trades reveal new information. The new information is incorporated into prices not only in New York but also in London during the hours of overlap between the markets. This incorporation of additional information from New York in London results in higher volatility of prices in London after the opening of the US markets.

15 One reason the manager may have chosen not to trade more aggressively is that he does not think there are other informed traders who have the same information he has about the company's stock. That is, he does not expect other traders to trade in the stock based on information, thus quickly eliminating his informational advantage. By trading in smaller sizes over a period of time, the manager attempts to reduce the chance that other traders will infer that the fund manager is trading based on special information. By spreading his trades over time, the manager is trying to reduce the price impact of trading by not revealing his full trading intentions.

16 Liquidity-motivated traders transact only to meet liquidity needs and desire low transaction costs. So, they would prefer the market with the lower bid–ask spreads. The information-motivated traders trade strategically to maximize the profits from their information. Some of their profits are made in trades in which liquidity-motivated traders are the counterparty. Since the liquidity-motivated traders trade in the market with the lower spreads, information-motivated traders will trade with them in that market. Also, information-motivated traders prefer to place larger orders to profit from any superior information they have. Such traders with large orders are particularly concerned about the market impact cost in the form of a price change for large trades. Since the quoted prices are firm for only a fixed depth, larger orders may move the bid (ask) price downward (upward). In a market with greater depth, the market impact cost is less. Thus, the market with greater depths would be preferred by information-motivated traders. Overall, between the two alternate trading venues, the one with lower spreads and greater depths would be preferred by both types of traders.

17 *Trade A*: In spite of the high urgency level, this trade represents 3 percent ADV. This trade is suitable for an implementation shortfall algorithm.

Trade B: This trade represents 75 percent ADV and has high spreads. It is not suitable for an algorithmic trade and should be traded using a broker.

18 Although the goal is to minimize explicit transaction costs, the trader needs also to consider the opportunity cost of not being invested in the S&P 500 portfolio. The trader should use an implementation shortfall strategy to control the risk of this rebalance. In short, he should minimize explicit costs by waiting for trades to cross in an electronic crossing network, such as the POSIT trading system, but he should also submit names not likely to cross to a broker in order to minimize opportunity costs. Such a strategy would balance the costs of a delay in implementing a strategic asset allocation against the concern to minimize explicit transaction costs.

19 B is correct. The portfolio manager wanted the order executed quickly and the order would have little impact on the market. Under such circumstances a market order makes sense as it eliminates execution uncertainty at the expense of price uncertainty.

20 C is correct. The effective spread is two times the deviation of the actual execution price from the midpoint of the market quote at the time of the order.

$$2\left(17.07 - \frac{17.05 + 17.02}{2}\right)$$

21 B is correct. Their attempt to use an ECN indicates they value low cost and low market impact above all, and by letting a broker shop an order or use an algorithmic method, they can minimize these costs.

22 B is correct. The implicit cost estimate is the difference between the actual execution price and the VWAP. This is given as

Cost = shares × (executed price − VWAP)
    = 3,200 × ($17.05 − $17.00)
    = $160

23 B is correct. At the end of the second day, DAM wanted to own 10,000 shares of NVRO at $17.05. Their gross paper profit/loss is thus

10,000 × ($17.50 − $17.05) = $4,500

Their actual position was long 3,200 shares at $17.05 and 3,000 shares at $17.25, and they paid $0.02*6,200 shares = $124 in commissions. Thus their actual profit/loss was

$$3,200 \times (\$17.50 - \$17.05) + 3,000 \times (\$17.50 - \$17.25) - \$124 = \$2,066$$

The implementation shortfall is just the difference between these, $4,500 − $2,066 = $2,434.

24 A is correct. Value-motivated traders are patient, infrequent traders driven by differences between price and value.

25 C is correct. A VWAP algorithmic trade is best suited for an order that is a low percentage of the average daily volume of the stock. The 50,000-share order is a small percentage of the average daily volume of 10,000,000 shares.

Monitoring and Rebalancing

by Robert D. Arnott, Terence E. Burns, CFA, Lisa Plaxco, CFA, and Philip Moore

LEARNING OUTCOMES

Mastery	The candidate should be able to:
☐	**a.** discuss a fiduciary's responsibilities in monitoring an investment portfolio;
☐	**b.** discuss the monitoring of investor circumstances, market/economic conditions, and portfolio holdings and explain the effects that changes in each of these areas can have on the investor's portfolio;
☐	**c.** recommend and justify revisions to an investor's investment policy statement and strategic asset allocation, given a change in investor circumstances;
☐	**d.** discuss the benefits and costs of rebalancing a portfolio to the investor's strategic asset allocation;
☐	**e.** contrast calendar rebalancing to percentage-of-portfolio rebalancing;
☐	**f.** discuss the key determinants of the optimal corridor width of an asset class in a percentage-of-portfolio rebalancing program;
☐	**g.** compare the benefits of rebalancing an asset class to its target portfolio weight versus rebalancing the asset class to stay within its allowed range;
☐	**h.** explain the performance consequences in up, down, and nontrending markets of 1) rebalancing to a constant mix of equities and bills, 2) buying and holding equities, and 3) constant proportion portfolio insurance (CPPI);
☐	**i.** distinguish among linear, concave, and convex rebalancing strategies;
☐	**j.** judge the appropriateness of constant mix, buy-and-hold, and CPPI rebalancing strategies when given an investor's risk tolerance and asset return expectations.

Managing Investment Portfolios: A Dynamic Process, Third Edition, John L. Maginn, CFA, Donald L. Tuttle, CFA, Jerald E. Pinto, CFA, and Dennis W. McLeavey, CFA, editors. Copyright © 2007 by CFA Institute.

1 INTRODUCTION

After a portfolio manager has worked closely with a client to document investment objectives and constraints in an investment policy statement (IPS), agreed on the strategic asset allocation that best positions the client to achieve stated objectives, and executed the strategic asset allocation through appropriate investment strategies for each asset class segment, the manager must constantly monitor and rebalance the portfolio. The need arises for several reasons.

First, clients' needs and circumstances change, and portfolio managers must respond to these changes to ensure that the portfolio reflects those changes. Life-cycle changes are expected for individual investors, so the portfolio manager must plan for these changes and respond to them when they occur. Institutional investors face changing circumstances just as commonly. A pension fund may receive a mandate from its trustees to assume less volatility. A university endowment may need to react to higher-than-anticipated inflation in faculty salaries.

Second, capital market conditions change. Portfolio managers must monitor such changes, adjust their capital market expectations appropriately, and reflect changed expectations in how the portfolio is invested. For example, if a client's return requirement is 8 percent but the strategic asset allocation promises to return on average 6.5 percent in the current climate, what changes should a portfolio manager recommend in light of the anticipated 150 bps shortfall?

Third, fluctuations in the market values of assets create differences between a portfolio's current asset allocation and its strategic asset allocation. These differences may be trivial on a daily basis; over longer periods of time, however, they can result in a significant divergence between the intended and actual allocations. When and how a portfolio manager rebalances the portfolio to the strategic asset allocation is one of the primary focuses of this reading.

For a portfolio manager, designing and building a portfolio is only the beginning of the dynamic and interactive process that lasts for as long as she is the client's trusted advisor. As markets evolve, maintaining the alignment between a client's portfolio and his investment objectives requires constant vigilance. Therefore, monitoring and rebalancing the portfolio is one of the most important elements of the dynamic process of portfolio management.

We divide this reading into two major sections, the first covering monitoring and the second covering rebalancing.

2 MONITORING

To monitor something means to systematically keep watch over it to collect information that is relevant to one's purpose. In investments, the purpose is to achieve investment goals. And a reality of investing is that what you don't know *can* hurt you. An overlooked fact may mean not reaching a goal. A portfolio manager should track everything affecting the client's portfolio. We can categorize most items that need to be monitored in one of three ways:

- investor circumstances, including wealth and constraints;
- market and economic changes; and
- the portfolio itself.

Monitoring investor-related factors sometimes results in changes to a client's investment policy statement, strategic asset allocation, or individual portfolio holdings. Monitoring market and economic changes sometimes results in changes to the strategic asset allocation (when they relate to long-term capital market expectations), tactical asset allocation adjustments (when they relate to shorter-term capital market expectations), changes in style and sector exposures, or adjustments in individual holdings. Monitoring the portfolio can lead to additions or deletions to holdings or to rebalancing the strategic asset allocation.

Fiduciaries need to pay particular attention to adequate monitoring in fulfilling their ethical and legal responsibilities to clients. Investment managers for individual and/or institutional separate accounts; managers of pooled funds (including mutual funds and unit trusts); and trustees of private trusts, pension plans, and charitable organizations are all fiduciaries because of their positions of trust with respect to the management of assets owned by or benefiting others. Fiduciaries have a range of ethical, reporting, auditing, disclosure, and other responsibilities to clients. But germane to this discussion, when taking investment actions, fiduciaries must consider the appropriateness and suitability of the portfolio relative to 1) the client's needs and circumstances, 2) the investment's basic characteristics, or 3) the basic characteristics of the total portfolio. These factors change over time. Only by systematic monitoring can a fiduciary secure an informed view of the appropriateness and suitability of a portfolio for a client.

The following sections provide a fuller explanation of monitoring.

2.1 Monitoring Changes in Investor Circumstances and Constraints

Each client has needs and circumstances that will most likely change over time. A successful portfolio manager makes every effort to remain sensitive to client needs and to anticipate events that might alter those needs. Periodic client meetings are an ideal time to ask whether needs, circumstances, or objectives have changed. If they have, the manager may need to revise the IPS and bring the portfolio into line with the revisions. In many cases, minor changes are needed that do not require revising the IPS. In the field of private wealth management, reviews are usually semiannual or quarterly. In institutional investing, the asset allocation review is a natural time for reviewing the range of changes in circumstance. Such reviews are often held annually. In all contacts with any type of client, however, the advisor should be alert to new client circumstances.

When a review is undertaken, what areas should be covered? Changes in investor circumstances and wealth, liquidity requirements, time horizons, legal and regulatory factors, and unique circumstances all need to be monitored.

2.1.1 *Changes in Investor Circumstances and Wealth*

Changes in circumstances and wealth often affect a client's investment plans. For private wealth clients, events such as changes in employment, marital status, and the birth of children may affect income, expenditures, risk exposures, and risk preferences. Each such change may affect the client's income, expected retirement income, and perhaps risk preferences. The responsibilities of marriage or children have repercussions for nearly all aspects of a client's financial situation. Such events often mark occasions to review the client's investment policy statement and overall financial plan. For institutional clients, operating performance, constituent pressures (such as demands for increased support from the beneficiaries of endowments), and changes in governance practices are among the factors that may affect income, expenditures, risk exposures, and risk preferences. A portfolio manager should communicate regularly with the client to become aware of such changes.

Wealth or net worth is one client factor that is central to investment plans. Wealth, when evaluated in the context of an investor's other circumstances, is both a measure of achieved financial success and an influence on future investment planning. Changes in wealth result from saving or spending, investment performance, and events such as gifts, donations, and inheritances. The investor's return requirements may change as a result, as financial goals recede or move closer to achievement, and risk tolerance may change too. Utility theory suggests that increases in wealth allow investors to increase their level of risk tolerance, accepting more systematic risk with its attendant expected reward. In reality, however, portfolio managers should consider only substantial and permanent changes in wealth in establishing the client's risk tolerance, even though client risk perceptions can vary quite substantially with recently experienced market performance. The portfolio manager's appraisal of a client's risk tolerance should be largely unaffected by transient changes in wealth. The investment manager thus has a difficult role to moderate some investors' desire to dramatically change asset allocations in response to market volatility. In contrast, more-conservative investors may be unprepared to increase their risk tolerance even when a substantial increase in wealth suggests an increased capacity for bearing risk. Such a client's goal may become merely preserving gains that they never expected to have despite the opportunity costs. The portfolio manager should try to understand this mindset and, working within the client's comfort level, seek to restrain its excesses.

2.1.2 *Changing Liquidity Requirements*

When a client needs money to spend, the portfolio manager should strive to provide it. A liquidity requirement is a need for cash in excess of new contributions or savings as a consequence of some event, either anticipated or unanticipated.

Individual clients experience changes in liquidity requirements as a result of a variety of events, including unemployment, illness, court judgments, retirement, divorce, the death of a spouse, or the building or purchase of a home. Changes in liquidity requirements occur for a variety of reasons for institutional clients, such as the payment of claims by insurers or of retirement benefits by defined-benefit pension plans, or the funding of a capital project by a foundation or endowment.

The possibility of major withdrawals may constrain a portfolio manager's commitments to illiquid investments because of the costs in exiting those investments quickly. Managers who do not face major withdrawals are better positioned to earn the return premium such investments supply. Managers who do face major withdrawals near term may need to hold some part of their portfolio in liquid and low-price-risk assets such as money market instruments.

2.1.3 *Changing Time Horizons*

Individuals age and pension funds mature. Reducing investment risk is generally advisable as an individual moves through the life cycle and his time horizon shortens; bonds become increasingly suitable investments as this process occurs. Today's life-cycle mutual funds reflect that principle in their asset allocations. In contrast to individuals, some entities such as endowment funds have the hope of perpetual life; the passage of time in and of itself does not change their time horizon, risk budgets, or appropriate asset allocation.

Many private wealth clients have multistage time horizons. For example, a working person typically faces an accumulation stage up to retirement in which she builds wealth through saving and investment, followed by a retirement stage in which she spends wealth and ultimately bequeaths it to heirs. Accumulating funds for a child's higher education can create one or more stages before retirement. Changes in investment policy are usually needed as one time horizon (for example, reaching retirement or selling a closely-held family business) is reached and another begins.

Although some changes in time horizon are forecastable, time horizons can also shift abruptly. For instance, when the last income beneficiary of a trust dies and the **residue** (remaining funds) passes to the **remaindermen** (beneficiaries with a claim on the trust's residue), investment policy, as well as the portfolio, should be adjusted promptly. Annuitizing the benefits for older participants in a pension plan can result in an abrupt change in the plan's remaining liability stream. That should lead to an overhaul of the asset structure and rebalancing to a portfolio structure that more closely fits the new needs. The untimely death of an income-earning spouse requires immediate attention. Portfolio managers need to think about how they will respond to these changes and events and must monitor the client's circumstances for changes in time horizon. Example 1 addresses a change in investment horizon for an individual investor.

EXAMPLE 1

Monitoring a Change in Investment Horizon

William and Mary deVegh, both 32 years old, met and married when they were university students. They each embarked on promising and highly demanding executive careers after leaving college. They are hoping to retire at age 55 to travel and otherwise enjoy the fruits of their hard work. Now well established at their companies, they also want to start a family and are expecting the birth of their first child in two months. They hope the child will follow their tracks and obtain a four-year private university education. The deVeghs anticipate supporting their child through college. Assume that the deVeghs will each live to age 85.

1 Compare and contrast the deVeghs' investment time horizons prior to and immediately subsequent to the birth of their first child.

2 Interpret the challenges the birth will present to their retirement objectives and discuss approaches to meeting those challenges, including investing more aggressively.

Solution to 1:

Prior to the birth of their child, the deVeghs have a two-stage time horizon. The first horizon extends from age 32 up to age 55. This first time horizon could be described as an accumulation period in which the deVeghs save and invest for early retirement. The second time horizon is their retirement and is expected to extend from age 55 to age 85. After the birth of their child, they will have a three-stage time horizon. The first stage extends from age 32 through age 50, when they expect their child to enter university at age 18. During this period, the deVeghs must accumulate funds both for retirement and their child's university education. The second stage extends from age 51 up to age 55. In this period the deVeghs must anticipate disbursing substantial funds for tuition, room and board, and other expenses associated with a private university education. The third stage is retirement, expected to extend from age 55 to age 85 as before.

Solution to 2:

The birth of the child creates a four-year period of heavy expenses immediately prior to the deVeghs' intended retirement date. Those expenses could put their intended retirement date at risk. The most direct way to mitigate this risk is to increase the amount of money saved and to invest savings for the child's education in a tax-efficient way (tax-advantaged education saving vehicles are available in certain tax jurisdictions). Can the deVeghs mitigate their risk by increasing their risk tolerance? The need for a larger future sum of money does not in itself increase an investor's ability to take risk, although it may affect the investor's willingness to do so. There is no indication that the child's birth will be accompanied by a salary raise or other event increasing the ability to take risk. If the deVeghs' stated risk tolerance prior to the child's birth accurately reflects their ability to bear risk, investing more aggressively after the child's birth will not help them meet the challenges the event poses to their retirement objective.

2.1.4 *Tax Circumstances*

Taxes are certain; the form they will take and their amount in the future are uncertain. Taxable investors should make all decisions on an after-tax basis. Managers for taxable investors must construct portfolios that deal with each client's current tax situation and take future possible tax circumstances into account. For taxable investors, holding period length and portfolio turnover rates are important because of their effect on after-tax returns. In evaluating investment strategies to meet a taxable investor's changed objective, a portfolio manager will take into account each strategy's **tax efficiency** (the proportion of the expected pretax total return that will be retained after taxes). Monitoring a client's tax situation may suggest the following actions, for example:

■ Deferring the realization of income from a higher-tax year to an anticipated lower-tax year.

■ Accelerating expenses to a high-tax year.

■ Realizing short-term losses at year-end to offset realized short-term gains in the same year.

■ Deploying assets with high unrealized gains so as to use a step-up in tax basis from original cost to market value (a break allowed investors for certain trans-actions in some tax jurisdictions). For example, if the client intends to make a charitable donation, making the contribution in appreciated securities may be tax advantageous in some tax jurisdictions.

■ Reducing or increasing commitments to tax-exempt securities, where available.

2.1.5 *Changes in Laws and Regulations*

Laws and regulations create the environment in which the investor can lawfully operate, and the portfolio manager must monitor them to ensure compliance and understand how they affect the scope of the advisor's responsibility and discretion in managing client portfolios. For example, in the United States in recent years, corporate trustees have reevaluated how they manage investment portfolios for trust clients in light of the adoption of the Uniform Prudent Investor Rule (versus the traditional prudent man rule) and the Uniform Principal and Income Act.

Besides that necessity, portfolio managers should seek to grasp the implication of such legal and regulatory changes for current portfolio holdings and investment opportunities. Portfolio managers for both taxable and tax-exempt investors should monitor changes in tax regulations because such changes typically affect not only taxes but the equilibrium relationships among assets.

2.1.6 *Unique Circumstances*

A unique circumstance is an internal factor (other than a liquidity requirement, time horizon, or tax concern) that may constrain portfolio choice. The client may present the portfolio manager with a variety of challenges in this respect. For example, some clients direct portfolio managers to retain concentrated stock positions because of an emotional attachment to the particular holding, because the client must maintain the stock position to demonstrate his or her commitment as an officer of the company, or because the concentrated position effectively has an extremely large unrealized capital gain. Is it feasible and appropriate to hedge or monetize the position through one of several special strategies? If not, given the volatility and concentrated risk of this single holding, how should the portfolio manager allocate the balance of the client's portfolio? As a portfolio manager, what investment actions will you recommend or implement when the emotional attachment is gone, when the client is no longer an officer of the company, or when the client's heirs receive the position?

Institutional clients may have a range of special concerns. For example, a client may adopt principles of socially responsible investing (often referred to by its acronym, SRI). Endowments and public employee pension plans often have been particularly active in SRI. As an example, a fund may decide to reduce or eliminate holdings in "sin" stocks, such as gaming, alcohol, and tobacco. SRI constraints have tended to tilt a portfolio away from large companies, which introduces non-market-related risks and causes a small-capitalization stock bias. In the mid-1980s, when small-cap stocks were demonstrating a return advantage over large-cap stocks, SRI seemed a costless (even profitable) strategy. However, the client should be aware of the potential costs in adopting an SRI policy.

Institutional clients are focusing significant attention on evaluating and fostering improvements in corporate governance, believing that those efforts will in the long run enhance return and/or reduce portfolio risk. Indeed, European fund managers themselves have demanded better integration of extrafinancial issues such as corporate governance, human capital management, value creation or destruction during mergers and acquisitions, and global environment challenges in sell-side analysis.[1] Portfolio managers must respect such client concerns in evaluating the appropriateness of investments.

In Example 2, an investment advisor determines an appropriate investment recommendation for an inheritance and later, a new investment advisor makes changes to the client's IPS in light of dramatically changed needs. This example shows the detailed analysis and judgment that enters into revising an IPS.

EXAMPLE 2

Monitoring Changes in an Investor's Circumstances and Wealth[2]

John Stern, 55 years old and single, is a dentist. Stern has accumulated a $2.0 million investment portfolio with a large concentration in small-capitalization US equities. Over the last five years, the portfolio has averaged 20 percent annual total return on investment. Stern does not expect to retire before age 70. His current income is more than sufficient to meet his expenses. Upon retirement, he plans to sell his dentistry practice and use the proceeds to purchase an annuity to cover his retirement cash flow needs. He has no additional long-term goals or needs.

In consultation with Stern, his investment advisor, Caroline Roppa, has drawn up an investment policy statement with the following elements. (Roppa's notes justifying each item are included.)

---

1 In 2004, four major European fund managers representing €330 billion under management announced an Enhanced Analytics Initiative in which 5 percent of brokerage commissions would be awarded on the basis of the integration of these concerns in brokerage house analysis.
2 Adapted from the 2001 Level III CFA examination.

Elements of Stern's Investment Policy Statement

Risk tolerance: Stern has above-average risk tolerance. *Roppa's notes*:

- Stern's present investment portfolio and his desire for large returns indicate a high *willingness* to take risk.
- His financial situation (large current asset base, ample income to cover expenses, lack of need for liquidity or cash flow, and long time horizon) indicates a high *ability* to assume risk.

Return objective: The return objective is an average total return of 10 percent or more with a focus on long-term capital appreciation. *Roppa's notes*: Stern's circumstances warrant an above-average return objective that emphasizes capital appreciation for the following reasons:

- Stern has a sizable asset base and ample income to cover his current spending; therefore, the focus should be on growing the portfolio.
- Stern's low liquidity needs and long time horizon support an emphasis on a long-term capital appreciation approach.
- Stern does not rely on the portfolio to meet living expenses.

The numerical objective of 10 percent represents an estimate of a target Stern can aim for rather than a minimum return required to meet a specific financial goal.

Liquidity: Stern's liquidity needs are low. *Roppa's notes*:

- Stern has no regular cash flow needs from the portfolio because the income from his dentistry practice meets all current spending needs.
- No large, one-time cash needs are stated. However, it could be considered appropriate to keep a small cash reserve for emergencies.

Time horizon: Stern's time horizon is long term and consists of two stages:

- The first stage consists of the time until his retirement, which he expects to be 15 years.
- The second consists of his lifetime following retirement, which could range from 10 to 20 years.

Roppa has also summarized Stern's current portfolio in Exhibit 1.

Exhibit 1	Summary of Stern's Current Portfolio			
	Value	Percent of Total	Expected Annual Return	Expected Annual Standard Deviation
Short-term bonds	$200,000	10%	4.6%	1.6%
Domestic large-cap equities	600,000	30	12.4	19.5
Domestic small-cap equities	1,200,000	60	16.0	29.9
Total portfolio	$2,000,000	100%	13.8%	23.1%

Stern expects to soon receive an inheritance of $2.0 million. Stern and Roppa sit down to discuss its investment in one of four index funds. Given Stern's already above-average risk tolerance and level of portfolio risk, Roppa and Stern have concluded that the risk tolerance description in the current IPS remains valid; they do not want to contemplate a further increase in portfolio risk. On the other hand, they do not wish to reduce expected return. Roppa is evaluating the four index funds shown in Exhibit 2 for their ability to produce a portfolio that will meet the following two criteria relative to the current portfolio:

- maintain or enhance expected return, and
- maintain or reduce volatility.

Each fund is invested in an asset class that is not substantially represented in the current portfolio as shown in Exhibit 1. Exhibit 2 presents statistics on those index funds.

Exhibit 2	Index Fund Characteristics		
Index Fund	Expected Annual Return	Expected Annual Standard Deviation	Correlation of Returns with Current Portfolio's Returns
Fund A	15%	25%	+0.80
Fund B	11	22	+0.60
Fund C	16	25	+0.90
Fund D	14	22	+0.65

1 Recommend the most appropriate index fund to add to Stern's portfolio. Justify your recommendation by describing how your chosen fund *best* meets both of the stated criteria. No calculations are required.

Twenty years later, Stern is meeting with his new financial advisor, Jennifer Holmstrom. Holmstrom is evaluating whether Stern's investment policy remains appropriate for his new circumstances.

- Stern is now 75 years old and retired. His spending requirements are expected to increase with the rate of general inflation, which is expected to average 3.0 percent annually.
- Stern estimates his current living expenses at $150,000 annually. An annuity, purchased with the proceeds from the sale of his dentistry practice, provides $20,000 of this amount. The annuity is adjusted for inflation annually using a national price index.
- Because of poor investment performance and a high level of spending, Stern's asset base has declined to $1,200,000 exclusive of the value of the annuity.
- Stern sold all of his small-cap investments last year and invested the proceeds in domestic bonds.

- Because his past international equity investments have performed poorly, Stern has become markedly uncomfortable with holding international equities.

- Stern plans to donate $50,000 to a charity in three months.

2   Discuss how *each* of the following components of Stern's investment policy statement should now reflect the changes in his circumstances.

   i. Risk tolerance.

   ii. Return requirement.

   iii. Liquidity needs.

   iv. Time horizon.

   Note: Your discussion should focus on, but not be limited to, the *direction* and *magnitude of change* in each component rather than on a specific numeric change.

Stern's investment portfolio at age 75 is summarized in Exhibit 3.

Exhibit 3	Stern's Investment Portfolio at Age 75		
	Current Allocation	Expected Return	Expected Standard Deviation
Cash equivalents	2%	5%	3%
Fixed income	75	7	8
Domestic equities	10	10	16
International equities	3	12	22
Domestic real estate	10	10	17

3   Given Stern's changed circumstances, state whether the current allocation to *each* asset class should be lower, the same, or higher. Justify your response with *one* reason for *each* asset class. No calculations are required.

   i. Cash equivalents.

   ii. Fixed income.

   iii. Domestic equities.

   iv. International equities.

   v. Domestic real estate.

   Note: Your response should be based only on Stern's changed circumstances and the information in Exhibit 3.

4   Explain one way in which Stern might seek to reduce the tension between his current return requirement and his current risk tolerance.

Solution to 1:

Fund D represents the single *best* addition to complement Stern's current portfolio, given the selection criteria. Fund D's expected return (14.0 percent) has the potential to increase the portfolio's return somewhat. Second, Fund D's relatively low correlation coefficient with his current portfolio (+0.65) indicates that it will provide larger diversification benefits than any of the other alternatives except Fund B. The result of adding Fund D should be a portfolio with about the same expected return and somewhat lower volatility compared to the original portfolio.

The other three funds have shortcomings in either expected return enhancement or volatility reduction through diversification:

- Fund A offers the potential for increasing the portfolio's return but is too highly correlated with other holdings to provide substantial volatility reduction through diversification.

- Fund B provides substantial volatility reduction through diversification but is expected to generate a return well below the current portfolio's return.

- Fund C has the greatest potential to increase the portfolio's return but is too highly correlated with other holdings to provide substantial volatility reduction through diversification.

Solution to 2:

i. *Risk tolerance.* Stern's risk tolerance has declined as a result of investment losses and the material erosion of his asset base. His *willingness* to accept risk as reflected in his portfolio holdings and aversion to international equities has declined. Also, Stern's return requirement has risen sharply at the same time that assets available to generate that return are lower. Thus, Stern's *ability* to accept risk has also declined. Investments should emphasize less volatile securities.

ii. *Return requirement.* Stern now has a return requirement that represents an increase in both dollar and percentage terms from his return objective of 20 years earlier. In contrast to his prior situation, Stern now must use investments to meet normal living expenses.

Stern's annual expenses not covered by annuity payments total $130,000 (10.8 percent of his now reduced assets). His expenses are increasing at a rate at least as high as the 3 percent general inflation rate. To stay ahead of inflation without eroding the principal value of his portfolio, Stern needs to earn 13.8 percent. This percentage will increase to 14.3 percent after the $50,000 charitable donation occurs, because this distribution will further diminish Stern's asset base.

iii. *Liquidity needs.* Stern will require $50,000 (4.2 percent of assets) in three months for a charitable donation. In addition, Stern's need to fund a large part of his living expenses from his portfolio has created a substantial ongoing liquidity need. Investments should emphasize liquid securities in part to meet any unplanned near-term expenses without incurring substantial transaction costs.

iv. *Time horizon.* Stern is now 20 years older than when his initial investment policy was written. Assuming his life expectancy is normal, Stern's time horizon remains long term (i.e., in excess of 10 years) but shorter than when the initial policy was drafted.

Solution to 3:

i. Cash equivalents should have a substantially higher weight than 2 percent. Stern requires $50,000 (4.2 percent of assets) in three months for the charitable donation. Compared with his position 20 years ago, his willingness and ability to accept volatility have decreased, his liquidity needs have increased, and his time horizon is now shorter. Stern needs a larger portion of his portfolio in low-risk, highly liquid assets.

ii. Fixed income should have a lower weight than 75 percent. Bonds are expected to provide a greater return than cash equivalents, which would help to meet Stern's return requirement. To meet additional liquidity needs and provide higher returns for expenses and inflation, however, a lower allocation is warranted.

iii. Domestic equities should have a higher weight than 10 percent. Stern requires fairly high returns and protection from inflation. Domestic equity investments would help meet those needs, but his lower ability and willingness to assume risk suggest only a moderate allocation to this somewhat volatile asset class, although higher than the current allocation.

iv. International equities should be eliminated. Although international equities may provide higher returns and diversification benefits, Stern is uncomfortable with holding international equities because of his experience with them. In the interests of respecting client wishes, Holmstrom should thus eliminate this asset class from the portfolio.

v. Domestic real estate should have a lower weight than 10 percent because of Stern's substantial liquidity requirements and reduced risk tolerance. Domestic equities have the same expected return as real estate with lower expected standard deviation and generally greater liquidity; therefore, domestic equities would be favored over domestic real estate among the higher expected return asset classes. Nevertheless, a smaller (i.e., less than 10 percent) real estate allocation could be maintained to obtain diversification benefits, to possibly generate income, and as a potential hedge against inflation.

Solution to 4:

Based on his current expenses of $150,000 annually, Stern has a very high return requirement in relation to his current risk tolerance. The most direct way to reduce this tension would be to decrease annual expenses, although that might involve a change in living arrangements or lifestyle. For example, if annual expenses were cut by one-third to $100,000, only $80,000 would need to be supplied by investments after annuity payments. That would represent $80,000/$1,200,000 = 6.7% of assets, resulting in a return requirement of 9.7% prior to the charitable contribution. All else equal, the higher the return requirement relative to actual returns earned, the greater the need to spend principal and the greater **longevity risk** (the risk that one will outlive one's funds). Reducing expenses would mitigate that risk.

High-net-worth individuals often face the issue of concentrated stock holdings, which may be complicated by the issue of high unrealized capital gains. In Example 3, a change in client circumstances leads an investment advisor to search for the appropriate means to address the problem.

EXAMPLE 3

An Investor with a Concentrated Stock Position

Jonathan Wiese, CFA, serves as investment counsel for the Lane family. Franklin Lane, 62 years old, has a 2,000,000 share position in Walton Energy, Inc. (WEI), an actively traded mid-cap energy company, accumulated through five years' service on its board of directors and earlier service as chief operating officer. At current market prices, the position is worth $24,000,000, representing 40 percent of Lane's total portfolio of $60,000,000. Another 20 percent of his portfolio is invested in other common equities, with the balance of 40 percent invested in Treasury inflation-protected and government agency securities. The cost basis of the WEI position is $2,400,000, and the sale of the position would trigger a tax liability exceeding $3.2 million. In the past Lane has insisted on maintaining his position in WEI shares to show his commitment to the company, but with Lane's recent retirement from WEI's board Wiese has suggested that a portfolio review is appropriate. WEI shares are part of a mid-cap stock index, and Lane's position is substantial compared to average daily trading volume of WEI. Techniques to deal with concentrated stock positions fall under the rubric of hedging and monetization strategies. Wiese has organized several of these strategies in Exhibit 4, one or more of which may be appropriate to deal with Lane's concentrated position.

Exhibit 4 Hedging and Monetization Strategies

Strategy and Description	Advantages	Drawbacks
Zero-premium collar. Simultaneous purchase of puts and sale of call options on the stock. The puts are struck below and the calls are struck above the underlying's market price. The call premiums fund the cost of the puts.	■ Locks in a band of values for the stock position. ■ Defers capital gains until stock is actually sold.	■ Hedge lasts only the duration of the option's life. ■ Involves commissions. ■ Provides downside protection but gives away most of upside.
Variable prepaid forward. In effect, combines a collar with a loan against the value of the shares. When the loan comes due (often in two to four years), shares are sold to pay off the loan and part of any appreciation is shared with the lender.	■ Converts 70 to 90 percent of the value of the position to cash. ■ Defers capital gains until stock is actually sold.	■ Involves commissions and interest expenses. ■ Surrenders part of any appreciation in the stock.
Exchange fund. Fund into which several investors place their different share holdings in exchange for shares in the diversified fund itself. At the end of a period of time (often seven years), the fund distributes assets to shareholders pro rata.	■ Diversifies holdings without triggering tax consequences.	■ Expense ratio often 2 percent and other fees usually apply. ■ Diversification may be incomplete.

(continued)

Exhibit 4	(Continued)	

Strategy and Description	Advantages	Drawbacks
Private exchange. Shares that are a component of an index are exchanged for shares of an index mutual fund in a privately arranged transaction with the fund.	■ Exchange is tax free. ■ Low continuing expenses. ■ Greatly increases diversification.	■ Shares usually must be part of an index so not generally applicable. ■ Share position must be very substantial. ■ Concession to market value of shares exchanged may need to be offered. ■ May not be possible to arrange because fund interest may be lacking.

Note: Zero-premium collars and variable prepaid forwards may involve a tax liability; the taxation of these strategies varies across tax jurisdictions.

Lane faces no liquidity requirements, at least in the short term. At the review, Wiese and Lane agree that a 60/40 stock/bond mix remains appropriate for Lane.

1   Identify and evaluate Lane's primary investment need and the primary constraint on addressing that need.

2   Determine and justify the two strategies that most directly address the need identified in Part 1.

Solution to 1:

Lane's primary need is for diversification of his concentrated stock position. Having ended his last ties to WEI, Lane should be in a position to satisfy that need. The tax liability that would result from a sale of WEI stock, however, acts as a constraint on addressing that need: Selling the WEI position and investing the proceeds in a diversified stock portfolio would incur a tax liability of about $3.2 million.

Solution to 2:

The exchange fund and private exchange options most directly address Lane's diversification need. The zero-premium collar would hedge the value of WEI position but would not diversify Lane's equity position. Also, the zero-premium collar would essentially convert the WEI holding into a position with volatility not dissimilar to short-term bonds, over the collar's duration, changing the effective asset allocation. The variable prepaid forward would convert a large fraction of the value of the position to cash, which could then be invested in a diversified equity position; so that instrument could be used to address the diversification need. Because of the huge built-in tax liability, however, Lane would need to roll over the forward indefinitely with the attendant expenses. The exchange fund is a costly option because of its fee structure, but it does address Lane's needs more directly and on a longer-term basis. The same can be said of the private exchange option, which appears to be more cost effective than the exchange fund while achieving a similar purpose.

2.2 Monitoring Market and Economic Changes

In addition to changes in individual client circumstances, the economic and financial markets contexts of investments also require monitoring. Those contexts are not static. The economy moves through phases of expansion and contraction, each with some unique characteristics. Financial markets, which are linked to the economy and expectations of its future course, reflect the resulting changing relationships among asset classes and individual securities.[3] A portfolio manager's monitoring of market and economic conditions should be broad and inclusive. Changes in asset risk attributes, market cycles, central bank policy, and the yield curve and inflation are among the factors that need to be monitored.

2.2.1 Changes in Asset Risk Attributes

The historical record reflects that underlying mean return, volatility, and correlations of asset classes sometimes meaningfully change. An asset allocation that once promised to satisfy an investor's investment objectives may no longer do so after such a shift. If that is the case, investors will need either to adjust their asset allocations or to reconsider their investment objectives. Monitoring changes in asset risk attributes is thus essential. Fiduciaries also owe their clients a duty to understand the risk factors in individual investments as such factors evolve.

Changes in asset risk attributes also present investment opportunities. Market prices for all assets reflect consensus perceptions of risk and reward. Changes in those perceptions produce immediate gains or losses. Successful active managers assess differences between actual risk and perceived risk of an investment and embrace that investment when the consensus view is unduly pessimistic.

Investment theoreticians and practitioners have long recognized the risk–reward trade-off. Long-run incremental rewards are generally unattainable without incurring incremental risk. Conversely, an investor must sacrifice some return when seeking to minimize risk. Systematic risk, which diversification cannot eliminate, is the most likely type of risk to promise reward according to asset pricing theory. Although a link exists between systematic risk and return, it is less consistent than pure theory suggests. For active managers, the key to exploiting inconsistencies lies in determining when risk is already priced into an asset and when perceptions of risk deviate enough from quantifiable risk so that a courageous investor can profit from favorable mispricings and avoid the others. In equity markets historically, increasing volatility has signaled opportunity more often than not, providing buying opportunities when fear prompts others to sell.

2.2.2 Market Cycles

Investors monitor market cycles and valuation levels to form a view on the short-term risks and rewards that financial markets offer. Based on these opinions, investors may make tactical adjustments to asset allocations or adjust individual securities holdings.

Tactically, the markets' major swings present unusual opportunities to be either very right or very wrong. When things are going well, securities eventually perform too well; during economic weakness, stock prices often decline excessively. Weakness engenders an environment that may foreshadow extraordinary profits, while ebullient markets provide unusual opportunities to sell, reinvesting elsewhere. Although this point is easily illustrated by looking over our shoulders at the US stock market in 1999 and 2000, it should be remembered that it was only the extremeness of the 1999–2000 market peak that is notable; these cycles recur nearly every decade or so. Market veterans may recall the environment of late 1974 as one of extraordinary

---

3 See the reading on capital market expectations for more information.

opportunity. At one point the earnings yield of the US stock market was 600 bps higher than bond yields, a difference not seen since the early 1950s. Conversely, in 1980 and 1981 and again in 1999 and 2000, bond yields exceeded earnings yields by a wide margin. That cyclical top presented another historic tactical opportunity as well as a shining example of the power and speed of mean reversion of asset-class returns. Reducing exposure to outperforming asset classes and increasing exposure to underperforming asset classes at the asset-class level—selling the stocks that had proven so comfortable and buying the bonds that the investment world seemed then to abhor—would have had a profound positive influence on total portfolio risk and return during those times.

Individual securities routinely show similar excesses. There are always securities whose issuers have either received such laudatory notices or suffered such unremitting adversity that their prices depart from reality. It is difficult to isolate those securities and then to act; only those investors suitably prepared and armed with courage will accept the challenge.

2.2.3 Central Bank Policy

Central banks wield power in the capital markets through the influence of their monetary and interest rate decisions on liquidity and interest rates. Their influence is felt in both bond and stock markets.

In bond markets, the most immediate impact of monetary policy is on money market yields rather than long-term bond yields. A central bank's influence on bond market *volatility*, however, is profound.

An example of this influence occurred in 1979, when the board of the US Federal Reserve Bank under Paul Volcker changed its focus from controlling interest rates to controlling monetary growth. Previously the board had adjusted the discount rate in response to movements in the money supply, while simultaneously trying to manage that supply. Interest rates took a back seat in the board's deliberations, and T-bill rates rose from 9 percent to 14 percent in an eight-month period. The effect was dramatic. Volatility in the bond market exploded between late 1979 and mid-1982 (at which time policy was quietly reversed to combat recession). High-yielding bonds provided a compelling alternative to stocks, putting downward pressure on stock prices until the summer of 1982, when rallying bond prices and declining bond yields finally eased the pressure, making stocks again more attractive.

Turning to the stock market, "Do not fight the Fed" has been a longstanding warning from Martin Zweig—a warning that it can be problematic to invest in the market when the Fed is tightening the money supply. Jensen, Johnson, and Mercer (2000) and Conover, Jensen, Johnson, and Mercer (2005) have documented that in the United States, stock returns are on average higher during periods of expansionary monetary policy than in periods of restrictive monetary policy, as indicated by decreases and increases in the discount rate, respectively.[4]

These lessons bear repetition. Fed policy does matter and should not be ignored: Restricted credit and higher interest rates usually hurt stock returns; eased credit and lower interest rates usually enhance stock returns.

2.2.4 The Yield Curve and Inflation

The default-risk-free yield curve reflects investors' required return at various maturities. It incorporates not only individuals' time preferences for current versus future real consumption but also expected inflation and the maturity premium demanded.

---

4 The discount rate is the rate a Federal Reserve member bank pays for borrowing reserves from the Federal Reserve system. Along with open market operations (the purchase and sale of government securities by the Fed) and changes in reserve requirement, discount rate policy is one of the three tools of US monetary policy.

Yield curve changes reflect changes in bond values, and bond value changes affect equity values through the competition that bonds supply to equities. Thus investors closely monitor the yield curve.

The premium on long-term bonds over short-term bonds tends to be countercyclical (i.e., high during recessions and low at the top of expansions) because investors demand greater rewards for bearing risk during bad times. By contrast, short-term yields tend to be procyclical because central banks tend to lower short rates in an attempt to stimulate economic activity during recessions. Yield curves thus tend to become steeply upward-sloping during recessions, to flatten in the course of expansions, and to be downward sloping (inverted) before an impending recession. In the United States, for example, nearly every recession after the mid-1960s was predicted by an inverted yield curve within six quarters of the recession; only one inverted yield curve was not followed by a recession during this period.[5] Thus the evidence suggests that the yield curve contains information about future GDP growth. Theory also suggests that the yield curve reflects expectations about future inflation.

Investors monitor a number of variables to gauge opportunities in bond markets. If relative yields of lower-quality issues exceed historical norms, the prospect of higher returns by investing in bonds of lower quality is enhanced. Even a measure as simple as the slope of the bond market yield curve is an indicator of bond performance relative to (short-term) cash equivalents.

Looking back at the late 1970s and early 1980s and focusing on yield curve slope rather than height, the spread between bond yields and cash yields steepened, starting with a flat to mildly inverted yield curve from late 1978 through mid-1981 and increasing to a 4 percent bond risk premium by July 1982. This increased bond risk premium preceded the bond rally of August–October 1982, during which 30-year Treasuries rallied 29 percent in three months. Although it is the rise in interest rates that catalyzes subsequent stock bear markets, it is the spread between long-term and short-term rates that presages bond rallies. If the yield curve is unusually steep (i.e., if bond yields are high relative to cash equivalent yields), the outlook tends to be good for bonds. This relationship is significant when either cash yield or the inflation rate is used as a proxy for the underlying risk-free rate.[6]

This interpretation of steep yield curves is unconventional. The usual fear is that the forward curve[7] foreshadows rising yields and falling bond prices. Empirical evidence tends to refute any basis for that apprehension.

Inflation has a pervasive influence on investors' ability to achieve their financial and investment objectives. On the one hand, it affects the nominal amount of money required to purchase a given basket of goods and services. On the other hand, inflation influences returns and risk in capital markets. When inflation rises beyond expectations, bond investors face a cut in *real yield.* As nominal yields rise in turn to counteract this loss, bond prices fall. Unexpected changes in the inflation rate are highly significant to stock market returns as well.

---

5 See Ang, Piazzesi, and Wei (2006).

6 T-bills and other cash instruments are not truly risk free, as they have both nonzero durations and nonzero standard deviations. Although they are generally an excellent reflection of the theoretical risk-free rate, the inflation rate can sometimes be preferable as a proxy for the risk-free rate, because it is not directly subject to manipulation by a central bank.

7 A "forward curve" shows the incremental yield earned by going one step further out on the yield curve. Suppose a one-year bond yields 2 percent and an equivalent-credit two-year bond yields 4 percent. The two-year bond must have a one-year forward yield of approximately 6 percent during its second year in order for its two-year average yield to be 4 percent. A steep yield curve implies an expectation of rising future bond yields.

2.3 Monitoring the Portfolio

Monitoring a portfolio is a continuous process that requires the manager to evaluate 1) events and trends affecting the prospects of individual holdings and asset classes and their suitability for attaining client objectives and 2) changes in asset values that create unintended divergences from the client's strategic asset allocation. The former tend to lead to changes in investment policy or to substitutions of individual holdings; the latter lead directly to rebalancing to the existing strategic asset allocation.

In a perfect-markets world, we could hold portfolio managers to a demanding standard: If a portfolio manager were to begin building a portfolio afresh today, would it mirror the existing portfolio? If not, he should consider changing the existing portfolio. Of course, taxes and transaction costs, discussed later, mean managers do not continuously revise portfolios. After even one day no portfolio is exactly optimal; however, the costs of adjustment may well outweigh any expected benefits from eliminating small differences between the current portfolio and the best possible one.

New information on economic and market conditions or on individual companies may lead a portfolio manager to take a variety of investment actions in an effort to add value for the client. The following examples offer some perspectives for the practitioner to consider as he or she translates monitoring into investment action.

EXAMPLE 4

How Active Managers May Use New Analysis and Information

As portfolio managers gather and analyze information that leads to capital market expectation revisions, they may attempt to add value through at least three types of portfolio actions:

- **Tactical asset allocation.** The portfolio manager may, in the short term, adjust the target asset mix within the parameters of the investment policy statement by selling perceived overpriced asset classes and reinvesting the proceeds in perceived underpriced asset classes in an attempt to profit from perceived disequilibria. When an investor's long-term capital market expectations change, however, the manager must revisit the strategic asset allocation.

- **Style and sector exposures.** Portfolio managers may alter investment emphasis within asset classes because of changes in capital market expectations. For example, a portfolio manager may lengthen the duration in the fixed-income allocation based on expectations of a sustained period of declining interest rates or adjust the style of the equity portfolio based on expectations that an economy is entering a period of sustained economic growth. Portfolio managers also may adjust the exposure to certain sectors back to or closer to historical weightings to reduce sector exposure relative to the index. For example, consider the impact on portfolio risk and return of reducing the exposure to the technology sector (within the large-cap US equity allocation) in January 2000, when technology represented more than 31 percent of the S&P 500 Index relative to the historical average of about 17 percent.

- **Individual security exposures.** A portfolio manager may trade an individual issue for one that seems to offer better value or reduce the exposure of a specific security as the returns of a single security begin to contribute a greater proportion of the total return than the manager believes to be appropriate.

EXAMPLE 5

The Characteristics of Successful Active Investors

Ironic gaps exist between the theory of revising portfolios and its practice. Some managers persist in constantly juggling the asset mix and churning portfolios in response to their basic emotions, clouded thinking, classic behavioral finance errors, and the desire to maximize fee revenue—often shrouding their "illusion of action" with marketing glitz. Clients tend to hire managers after recent success and fire them after recent disappointment. This chasing of investment performance, which reflects human nature, infrequently benefits investment results. What then are the elements of investment success?

Successful active investors stray from established roles. Nature conditions us to feel that what has been working will continue to work and that failure heralds failure. In investments, experience belies this notion. Consider investment managers who scramble to find a fix when their style is out of fashion. Often they (and their clients) change their approach during a period of disappointment, just before results rebound. We see the same pattern in customers' decisions to hire and fire managers. These costly errors stem from a quest for comfort that capital markets rarely reward and a lack of discipline to remain committed to long-term strategy as defined in the investment policy statement. Investors crave the solace that companionship affords. In the investment business, when one has too much company, success is improbable.

Successful active investors are not swayed by the crowd. The cultures of successful corporations and winning investors are profoundly different. Corporations, which are cooperative enterprises, prize teamwork and reward triumph while dismissing failure. The exceptional investor pursues an opposite course, staying far from the crowd and seeking opportunities in overlooked areas while avoiding excesses of the crowd. Investing in areas that are not popular while refusing to join in trends sets the successful investor apart.

Successful active investors are disciplined. There is a subtle pattern in the trading of successful investors and a key ingredient of investment success—discipline. Successful investors make disciplined changes even when they are performing well, and they often are willing to endure disappointment patiently.

Opportunistic investors must steel themselves against discomfort. Only knowledge and discipline can give them the confidence needed to transact. Indeed, even then, consideration for clients (or fears of their reactions) may inhibit the profitable move. Many investors fear the consequences of acting contrary to recent market experience. Disciplined investment decision processes add value by providing an *objective* basis for having confidence in an uncomfortable investment action.

As we shall discuss in more detail later, disciplined rebalancing to the strategic asset allocation reinforces the strategy of selling high and buying low or reducing exposure to outperforming asset classes and increasing exposure to underperforming asset classes. That behavior and discipline unfortunately is at odds with human nature. When investments have performed poorly, less successful investors and portfolio managers tend to address the problem by making changes for the sake of change or by abandoning a strategy altogether! If investments are doing well, the tendency is to coast with the winning strategy. These common patterns can often make underperformance problems significantly worse (i.e., selling near the bottom) or result in forgoing some portion of handsome market gains (i.e., not selling near the top).

EXAMPLE 6

The Nonfinancial Costs of Portfolio Revision

When a portfolio manager revises a portfolio, he obviously incurs financial costs as detailed later in Section 3.1.2. Financial costs will indeed be a focus of the section on rebalancing. But the costs of transacting can also take nonfinancial forms. If a client grows uncomfortable with portfolio turnover she considers excessive, the portfolio manager may lose credibility and the client may limit future trading. Even if trading is timely and likely to be profitable, it may impose subjective costs that are all too real. Finance theory recognizes these costs by directing managers to focus on optimizing client satisfaction rather than maximizing return. Even the most profitable strategy or investment process is useless if the client abandons it.

3   REBALANCING THE PORTFOLIO

Monitoring and rebalancing a portfolio is similar to flying an airplane: The pilot monitors and adjusts, if necessary, the plane's altitude, speed, and direction to make sure that the plane ultimately arrives at the predetermined destination. Just as a pilot makes in-flight adjustments, so does the portfolio manager. An important question in this regard is how far off course can the plane get before the pilot must make an adjustment? In the following sections we address that issue, but we first must be clear on the scope of what we will discuss under the rubric of rebalancing.

The term "rebalancing" has been used in the literature of investing to cover a range of distinct actions including 1) adjusting the actual portfolio to the current strategic asset allocation because of price changes in portfolio holdings; 2) revisions to the investor's target asset class weights because of changes in the investor's investment objectives or constraints, or because of changes in his capital market expectations; and 3) tactical asset allocation (TAA). For pedagogical reasons and because subjects such as TAA are covered in other readings, in this section we use "rebalancing" to refer only to the first type of action: rebalancing to the strategic asset allocation in reaction to price changes. Both individual and institutional investors need to set policy with respect to this type of action.

3.1 The Benefits and Costs of Rebalancing

Portfolio rebalancing involves a simple trade-off: the cost of rebalancing versus the cost of not rebalancing.

3.1.1 *Rebalancing Benefits*

Clients and their investment managers work hard to have their normal asset policy mix reflect an educated judgment of their appetite for reward and their aversion to risk. That having been done, however, the mix often drifts with the tides of day-to-day market fluctuations. If we assume that an investor's strategic asset allocation is optimal, then any divergence in the investor's portfolio from this strategic asset allocation is undesired and represents an expected utility loss to the investor. Rebalancing benefits the investor by reducing the present value of expected losses from not tracking the optimum. In theory, the basic cost of not rebalancing is this present value of expected utility losses.[8] Equivalently, the cost of not rebalancing is the present value of expected utility losses from straying from the optimum.

There are also several practical risk management benefits to rebalancing. First, if higher-risk assets earn higher returns on average and we let the asset mix drift, higher-risk assets will tend to represent ever-larger proportions of the portfolio over time. Thus the level of portfolio risk will tend to drift upward.[9] Portfolio risk will tend to be greater than that established for the client in the investment policy statement. Rebalancing controls drift in the overall level of portfolio risk. Second, as asset mix drifts, the *types* of risk exposures drift. Rebalancing maintains the client's desired systematic risk exposures. Finally, not rebalancing may mean holding assets that have become overpriced, offering inferior future rewards. A commitment to rebalance to the strategic asset allocation offers an effective way to dissuade clients from abandoning policy at inauspicious moments. Once signed on to the concept, clients are more likely to stay the course.

Example 7 illustrates the benefits of disciplined rebalancing judged against the do-nothing alternative of letting asset mix drift.

EXAMPLE 7

An Illustration of the Benefits of Disciplined Rebalancing

Although portfolios can be rebalanced using a variety of methods, it is important to recognize that, in comparison to letting an asset mix drift, any disciplined approach to rebalancing tends to add value over a long-term investment horizon by enhancing portfolio returns and/or reducing portfolio risk.

For example, assume an institutional client wishes to maintain the stated policy mix of 60 percent stocks and 40 percent bonds and requires monthly rebalancing to the equilibrium 60/40 mix. That asset mix is not uncommon for North American pension funds and provides a reasonable baseline from which to quantify the likely benefits from disciplined rebalancing. Transaction costs of 10 bps on each side of a trade are assumed to be attainable using futures.

In the four decades (1973–2010) summarized in Exhibits 5 and 6, simple monthly rebalancing produced an average annual return of 9.29 percent versus 9.02 percent for a drifting mix—a 27 bp enhancement. Furthermore,

---

8 See Leland (2000).
9 This type of drift will be more acute for portfolios with asset classes with dissimilar volatility and/or with low correlations.

the incremental return involved significantly less risk. That is, the rebalanced portfolio's standard deviation during that time period was 11.96 percent versus 13.66 percent—170 bps less than that of the drifting mix!

Analyzing the results of the two strategies across time adds additional insight. Examining Exhibit 6 gives rise to some significant return differences. First, the rebalancing strategy significantly underperformed the drifting mix strategy in the late 1990s as the tech bubble began to build. During this period, the equity market experienced large gains attributable mainly to technology stocks. As equity prices kept climbing, the drifting mix portfolio held higher and higher percentages of its assets in equity. As long as the price of equities continued to rise, the drifting mix benefitted from its skewed asset allocation. As the tech bubble burst in 2000, however, the benefit of disciplined rebalancing becomes obvious. With the drastic price declines in stocks, the drifting mix portfolio suffers substantial losses in 2000, 2001, and 2002. Meanwhile, the rebalanced portfolio, which held a significant portion of assets in bonds throughout the tech bubble, is not as exposed to the bursting of the tech bubble and performs relatively well compared with the drifting mix portfolio.

A second trend evident in Exhibit 6 is the outperformance by the rebalanced portfolio during the recent economic crisis. The intuition for this outperformance is similar to the explanation of the tech boom and bust above. With strong positive stock returns in the mid- 2000s, especially in 2003 and 2006, the drifting mix portfolio again becomes heavily invested in equities. With the equity market's precipitous drop in 2008, the drifting mix experiences a significant loss. The rebalanced portfolio, by retaining a healthy mix of stocks and bonds, avoids some of this exposure and performs relatively well.

In the most recent 16-year period (1995–2010), rebalancing appears to be even more beneficial. As seen in Exhibit 7, the additional average annual return for a monthly rebalanced portfolio over a drifting mix portfolio is 68 bps for the period. This incremental return is over twice as large as the 27 bps difference observed over the entire period from 1973–2010 (see Exhibit 5). Exhibit 7 illustrates that the risk (standard deviation of return) during the last 16 years is significantly higher than the risk measured for the entire 38-year period. However, consistent with the full-period findings, rebalancing during this more recent period results in substantially lower risk than the drifting mix approach (the difference in risk is 184 bps). Relative to the full-period, the recent 16-year period shows lower overall average returns and higher risk, yet the benefits of rebalancing remain consistent. This most recent period provides an obvious example of the benefit of rebalancing. By rebalancing, investors are able to retain a diversified mix of assets and avoid over-exposure to extreme price fluctuations in individual asset classes. Over the last 16 years, a rebalanced portfolio would have allowed investors to avoid some of the losses associated with the bursting of the tech bubble and the most recent financial crisis.

Exhibit 5	Full-Period Rebalancing Results January 1973– December 2010		
	Rebalancing Return	Drifting Mix Return	Difference
Average	9.29%	9.02%	0.27%
Maximum	35.25	35.75	
Minimum	−15.71	−13.57	

Exhibit 5	(Continued)		
	Rebalancing Return	Drifting Mix Return	Difference
Standard deviation	11.96	13.66	
Reward/Risk ratio	0.78	0.66	

Exhibit 6	Rebalancing Returns vs. Drifting Mix Returns By Year		
Year	Rebalancing	Drifting Mix	Difference
1973	−10.22%	−10.19%	−0.03%
1974	−15.71	−13.57	−2.14
1975	24.87	21.66	3.21
1976	20.80	20.15	0.65
1977	−5.10	−4.62	−0.48
1978	3.28	2.51	0.77
1979	8.00	7.15	0.85
1980	16.09	15.46	0.63
1981	−1.51	−1.99	0.48
1982	29.40	28.90	0.50
1983	13.14	13.39	−0.25
1984	9.91	9.38	0.53
1985	32.41	32.29	0.12
1986	20.43	19.99	0.44
1987	2.73	1.30	1.43
1988	13.27	13.45	−0.18
1989	26.54	26.93	−0.39
1990	1.36	0.78	0.58
1991	26.26	26.74	−0.48
1992	7.64	7.55	0.09
1993	12.97	12.49	0.48
1994	−1.90	−1.36	−0.54
1995	35.25	35.75	−0.50
1996	13.58	16.23	−2.65
1997	26.38	29.00	−2.62
1998	24.45	26.60	−2.15
1999	9.12	15.72	−6.60
2000	−0.29	−6.98	6.69
2001	−5.17	−8.47	3.30
2002	−7.83	−12.88	5.05
2003	17.47	18.11	−0.64
2004	7.06	7.31	−0.25
2005	2.54	2.57	−0.03

(continued)

Exhibit 6   (Continued)

Year	Rebalancing	Drifting Mix	Difference
2006	9.86	10.58	−0.72
2007	5.79	5.19	0.60
2008	−23.75	−25.37	1.62
2009	17.93	16.85	1.08
2010	9.65	9.18	0.47

Exhibit 7   Portfolio Returns January 1995–December 2010

	Rebalancing	Drifting Mix	Difference
Average	8.88%	8.20%	0.68%
Maximum	35.25	35.75	
Minimum	−23.75	−25.37	
Standard deviation	14.38	16.22	
Reward/Risk ratio	0.62	0.51	

Example 7 reinforces the point that disciplined rebalancing has tended to reduce risk while incrementally adding to returns. "Tended" means just that: It does not work in every year or even in every market cycle, but it should work over long-term investment horizons. Historically, the benefit of rebalancing has justified the minimal activity involved with implementing the approach. Studies such as Arnott and Lovell (1993), Plaxco and Arnott (2002), and Buetow et al. (2002) have supported this conclusion using both historical and simulated data. Rebalancing to a fixed asset mix—because it involves both selling appreciated assets and buying depreciated assets—can be viewed as a contrarian investment discipline that can be expected to earn a positive return for supplying liquidity.

3.1.2 Rebalancing Costs

Despite its benefits, rebalancing exacts financial costs. These costs are of two types—transaction costs and, for taxable investors, tax costs.

Transaction Costs   Transaction costs can never be recovered, and their cumulative erosion of value can significantly deteriorate portfolio performance. Transaction costs offset the benefits of rebalancing. Yet the true trade-off is not easy to gauge because transaction costs are difficult to measure.

Relatively illiquid investments such as private equity and real estate have become increasingly important in the portfolios of investors such as endowments and pension funds. These investments pose special challenges to rebalancing because the costs of rebalancing these investments represent a high hurdle. At the same time, the valuations given such assets often underestimate their true volatility because the valuations may be based on appraisals. If rebalancing requires reducing the value of illiquid holdings, this reduction may sometimes be accomplished through reinvestment of cash flows from them.[10] At the same time, portfolio managers cannot increase the allocations of these assets as quickly as in liquid asset markets.

Focusing on more liquid markets such as public equities, we can estimate transaction costs but only with error. There is in fact no exact answer to the question of what the transaction costs of a trade are. Transaction costs consist of more than just explicit costs such as commissions. They include implicit costs, such as those related to the bid–ask spread and market impact. Market impact is the difference between realized price and the price that *would have prevailed in the absence of the order.* That cost is inherently unobservable. In an analogy to the Heisenberg principle in physics, the process of executing a trade masks what would exist without the trade taking place. Furthermore, the trades one seeks but fails to execute impose yet another tariff—an opportunity cost. This missed trade opportunity cost may be more onerous than the others, and it is equally unobservable. Trading costs take on the character of an iceberg: Commissions rise above the surface, visible to all, while the submerged leviathan encompasses the market impact of trades and the imponderable cost of the trades that never happened.

A useful analogy can be drawn from the bond market. Most bond portfolios are priced from matrix prices, which may better represent "fair value" than actual transaction prices.[11] Bond transaction prices can be too dependent on the idiosyncratic meeting of one buyer and one seller. The same curious conclusion can be drawn for equities. Actual prices are set by the marginal seller and buyer who represent not a consensus but the strongest motivation to transact at a particular point in time.[12]

Because unaffected prices are unobservable, market impact costs can never be more than indirectly estimated. Still, this is not a fatal flaw: Total transaction costs can be estimated to a useful degree of accuracy, relative to the imprecision of other financial measurements (e.g., beta, value or future internal rate of return).

Tax Costs   In rebalancing, a portfolio manager sells appreciated asset classes and buys depreciated asset classes to bring the asset mix in line with target proportions. In most jurisdictions the sale of appreciated assets triggers a tax liability for taxable investors and is a cost of rebalancing for such investors.[13] The US tax code distinguishes between long- and short-term capital gains based on the length of the holding period (as of 2004, holding periods greater than 12 months qualify as long-term). As of 2004 the maximum tax rates applicable to short- and long-term capital gains in the United States, 35 percent and 15 percent respectively, differed significantly. For a US taxable investor, therefore, a rebalancing trade that realizes a short-term rather than long-term capital gain can be very costly. However, an appreciated asset class may contain assets with not only unrealized short- and long-term capital gains but also short- and long-term capital losses. Realizing short-term losses, long-term capital losses, long-term capital gains, and lastly short-term gains, in that order, would usually be the tax-efficient priority in selling. In contrast to the difference between long-and short-term capital gains, the value of the deferral of a long-term capital gain is generally much less in magnitude.[14]

---

10 See Horvitz (2002).

11 **Matrix prices** are prices determined by comparisons to other securities of similar credit risk and maturity.

12 The need to outbid competitive traders suggests that market impact can even be negative. Prices would always be the same or lower without the most motivated buyer's willingness to buy. Prices similarly would always be the same or higher without the most motivated seller's willingness to sell.

13 Some tax jurisdictions such as Jamaica, Hong Kong, and Singapore do not impose taxes on capital gains. See Ernst & Young (2005).

14 See Horvitz (2002). The value of tax deferral of X years is the tax bill if the sale is today (call this Y) minus the present value of Y to be paid in X years, using a default-risk-free tax-exempt rate.

3.2 Rebalancing Disciplines

A rebalancing discipline is a strategy for rebalancing. In practice, portfolio managers have most commonly adopted either calendar rebalancing or percentage-of-portfolio rebalancing.

3.2.1 Calendar Rebalancing

Calendar rebalancing involves rebalancing a portfolio to target weights on a periodic basis, for example, monthly, quarterly, semiannually, or annually. Quarterly rebalancing is one popular choice; the choice of rebalancing frequency is sometimes linked to the schedule of portfolio reviews.[15]

If an investor's policy portfolio has three asset classes with target proportions of 45/15/40, and his investment policy specifies rebalancing at the beginning of each month, at each rebalancing date asset proportions would be brought back to 45/15/40. Calendar rebalancing is the simplest rebalancing discipline. It does not involve continuously monitoring portfolio values within the rebalancing period. If the rebalancing frequency is adequate given the portfolio's volatility, calendar rebalancing can suffice in ensuring that the actual portfolio does not drift far away from target for long periods of time. A drawback of calendar rebalancing: It is unrelated to market behavior. On any given rebalancing date, the portfolio could be very close to or far away from optimal proportions. In the former case, the portfolio would be nearly optimal and the costs in rebalancing might swamp the benefits. In the latter case, an investor might incur unnecessarily high costs in terms of market impact by rebalancing.

3.2.2 Percentage-of-Portfolio Rebalancing

Percentage-of-portfolio rebalancing (also called percent-range or interval rebalancing) offers an alternative to calendar rebalancing. Percentage-of-portfolio rebalancing involves setting rebalancing thresholds or trigger points stated as a percentage of the portfolio's value. For example, if the target proportion for an asset class is 40 percent of portfolio value, trigger points could be at 35 percent and 45 percent of portfolio value. We would say that 35 percent to 45 percent (or 40% ± 5%) is the corridor or tolerance band for the value of that asset class. The portfolio is rebalanced when an asset class's weight first passes through one of its rebalancing thresholds, or equivalently, outside the corridor.

For example, consider a three-asset class portfolio of domestic equities, international equities, and domestic bonds. The target asset proportions are 45/15/40 with respective corridors 45% ± 4.5%, 15% ± 1.5%, and 40% ± 4%. Suppose the portfolio manager observes the actual allocation to be 50/14/36; the upper threshold (49.5%) for domestic equities has been breached. The asset mix would be rebalanced to 45/15/40.

Rebalancing trades can occur on any calendar date for percentage-of-portfolio rebalancing, in contrast to calendar rebalancing. Compared with calendar rebalancing (particularly at lower frequencies such as semiannual or annual), percentage-of-portfolio rebalancing can exercise tighter control on divergences from target proportions because it is directly related to market performance.

Percentage-of-portfolio rebalancing requires monitoring of portfolio values at an agreed-upon frequency in order to identify instances in which a trigger point is breached. To be implemented with greatest precision, monitoring should occur

---

[15] In practice, some portfolio managers will rebalance a portfolio just before a scheduled client meeting so the portfolio manager appears to be fulfilling his or her responsibility, although that practice may reflect more the concerns of the portfolio manager than the concerns of the client. By contrast, other portfolio managers may rebalance a portfolio just after the client meeting so the client or investment committee has the opportunity to approve the manager's actions.

daily. Daily monitoring obviously requires having an efficient custodian, one who can accurately monitor and quickly process and communicate portfolio and asset class valuations.

An obvious and important question is: How are the corridors for asset classes determined?

Investors sometimes set ad hoc corridors. We have already illustrated an example of one well-known yet ad hoc approach, based on a hypothetical portfolio of domestic equities, international equities, and domestic bonds. The corridors were set according to a formula based on a percentage of the target allocation, target ± (target allocation × $P\%$), where $P\%$ was 10% (but could be another percentage such as 5%). Following that formula, a corridor of 45% ± (45% × 10%) = 45% ± 4.5% applied to domestic stocks, 15% ± 1.5% applied to international equities, and 40% ± 4% applied to domestic bonds. However, *ad hoc* approaches such as this one are open to several criticisms. The approach illustrated does not account for differences in transaction costs in rebalancing these three asset classes, for example.

The literature suggests that at least five factors should play a role in setting the corridor for an asset class:

- transaction costs;
- risk tolerance concerning tracking risk versus the strategic asset allocation;
- correlation with other asset classes;
- volatility;
- volatilities of other asset classes.

The more expensive it is to trade an asset class (or the lower its liquidity), the wider its corridor should be, because the marginal benefit in rebalancing must at least equal its marginal cost. The higher the risk tolerance (i.e., the lower the investor's sensitivity to straying from target proportions), the wider corridors can be.

Correlations also should be expected to play a role. In a two asset-class case, a higher correlation should lead to wider tolerance bands. Suppose one asset class has moved above its target allocation (so the other asset class is below its target weight). A further increase in value has an expected smaller effect on asset weights if the assets classes' returns are more highly positively correlated because the denominator in computing the asset class's weight is the sum of the values of the two asset classes. That denominator's value is likely to be higher for a given up-move of the asset class of concern if the two asset classes' returns are positively correlated. In a multi-asset-class case, all pairwise asset class correlations would need to be considered, making the interpretation of correlations complex. To expand the application of the two-asset case's intuition, one simplification involves considering the balance of a portfolio to be a single hypothetical asset and computing an asset class's correlation with it.[16]

A higher volatility should lead to a narrower corridor, all else equal. It hurts more to be a given percent off target for a more highly volatile asset class because it has a greater chance of a further large move away from target. In a two-asset case the more volatile the second asset, the more risk there is in being a given percent off target for the first asset class, all else equal. All asset classes' volatilities would affect the optimal corridor in the multi-asset-class case. Again, a simplification is to treat the balance of the portfolio as one asset. Exhibit 8 summarizes the discussion. (It applies to the two-asset-class case, or to the multi-asset-class case with the simplification of treating all other asset classes—the balance of the portfolio—as one asset class.)

---

16 As in Masters (2003).

Exhibit 8	Factors Affecting Optimal Corridor Width	
Factor	**Effect on Optimal Width of Corridor (All Else Equal)**	**Intuition**
Factors Positively Related to Optimal Corridor Width		
Transaction costs	The higher the transaction costs, the wider the optimal corridor.	High transaction costs set a high hurdle for rebalancing benefits to overcome.
Risk tolerance	The higher the risk tolerance, the wider the optimal corridor.	Higher risk tolerance means less sensitivity to divergences from target.
Correlation with rest of portfolio	The higher the correlation, the wider the optimal corridor.	When asset classes move in synch, further divergence from targets is less likely.
Factors Inversely Related to Optimal Corridor Width		
Asset class volatility	The higher the volatility of a given asset class, the narrower the optimal corridor.	A given move away from target is potentially more costly for a high-volatility asset class, as a further divergence becomes more likely.
Volatility of rest of portfolio	The higher this volatility, the narrower the optimal corridor.	Makes large divergences from strategic asset allocation more likely.

EXAMPLE 8

Tolerance Bands for an Asset Allocation

An investment committee is reviewing the following strategic asset allocation:

Domestic equities	50% ± 5%
International equities	15% ± 1.5%
Domestic bonds	35% ± 3.5%

The committee views the above corridors as appropriate if each asset class has identical risk and transaction-cost characteristics. It now wants to account for differences among the asset classes in setting the corridors.

Evaluate the implications of the following sets of facts on the stated tolerance band (set off by italics), given an all-else-equal assumption in each case:

1   Domestic bond volatility is much lower than that of domestic or international equities, which are equal. *Tolerance band for domestic bonds.*

2   Transaction costs in international equities are 10 percent higher than those for domestic equities. *Tolerance band for international equities.*

3   Transaction costs in international equities are 10 percent higher than those for domestic equities, and international equities have a much lower correlation with domestic bonds than do domestic equities. *Tolerance band for international equities.*

4 The correlation of domestic bonds with domestic equities is higher than their correlation with international equities. *Tolerance band for domestic equities.*

5 The volatility of domestic bonds has increased. *Tolerance band for international equities.*

Solution to 1:

The tolerance band for domestic bonds should be wider than 35% ± 3.5%.

Solution to 2:

The tolerance band for international equities should be wider than 15% ± 1.5%.

Solution to 3:

Transaction costs point to widening the tolerance band for international equities, but correlations to narrowing it. The overall effect is indeterminate.

Solution to 4:

The tolerance band for domestic equities should be wider than 50% ± 5%.

Solution to 5:

The tolerance band for international equities should be narrower than 15% ± 1.5%.

3.2.3 *Other Rebalancing Strategies*

The investment literature includes rebalancing disciplines other than those discussed above. Calendar rebalancing can be combined with percentage-of-portfolio rebalancing (as described in Buetow et al.). In this approach (which may be called **calendar-and-percentage-of-portfolio rebalancing**), the manager monitors the portfolio at regular frequencies, such as quarterly. The manager then decides to rebalance based on a percentage-of-portfolio principle (has a trigger point been exceeded?). This approach mitigates the problem of incurring rebalancing costs when near the optimum that can occur in the calendar rebalancing.

McCalla (1997) describes an **equal probability rebalancing** discipline. In this discipline, the manager specifies a corridor for each asset class as a common multiple of the standard deviation of the asset class's returns. Rebalancing to the target proportions occurs when any asset class weight moves outside its corridor. In this discipline each asset class is equally likely to trigger rebalancing if the normal distribution describes asset class returns. However, equal probability rebalancing does not account for differences in transaction costs or asset correlations.

Goodsall and Plaxco (1996) and Plaxco and Arnott (2002) discuss as **tactical rebalancing** a variation of calendar rebalancing that specifies less frequent rebalancing when markets appear to be trending and more frequent rebalancing when they are characterized by reversals. This approach seeks to add value by tying rebalancing frequency to expected market conditions that most favor rebalancing to a constant mix.

3.2.4 *Rebalancing to Target Weights versus Rebalancing to the Allowed Range*

In the descriptions of rebalancing strategies, we have presented the standard paradigm in which a rebalancing involves adjusting asset class holdings to their target proportions. The alternative, applicable to rebalancing approaches that involve corridors, is to rebalance the asset allocation so that all asset class weights are within the allowed range but not necessarily at target weights. The rebalancing may follow a rule, such as adjusting weights halfway back to target (e.g., if an asset class's corridor is 50% ± 5% and the asset class's weight is 57 percent, reducing the weight to 52.5%), or to some judgmentally determined set of proportions. Compared with rebalancing to target weight, rebalancing to the allowed range results in less close alignment with target proportions but lower transaction costs; it also provides some room for tactical adjustments. For example, suppose that a US investor's target allocation to non-US equities is 15 percent and that its weight moves above its corridor on the upside. During an expected transitory period of a depreciating US dollar, the portfolio manager may want to rebalance the exposure only part way to the target proportion to take advantage of the apparent exchange rate tactical opportunity. The discipline of rebalancing to the allowed range also allows portfolio managers to better manage the weights of relatively illiquid assets.

A number of studies have contrasted rebalancing to target weights to rebalancing to the allowed range based on particular asset classes, time periods, and measures of the benefits of rebalancing. They have reached a variety of conclusions which do not permit one to state that one discipline is unqualifiedly superior to the other.

3.2.5 *Setting Optimal Thresholds*

The optimal portfolio rebalancing strategy should maximize the present value of the *net* benefit of rebalancing to the investor. Equivalently, the optimal strategy minimizes the present value of the sum of two costs: expected utility losses (from divergences from the optimum) and transaction costs (from rebalancing trades). Despite the apparent simplicity of the above formulations, finding the optimal strategy in a completely general context remains a complex challenge:

- If the costs of rebalancing are hard to measure, the benefits of rebalancing are even harder to quantify.

- The return characteristics of different asset classes differ from each other, and at the same time interrelationships (correlations) exist among the asset classes that a rebalancing strategy may need to reflect.

- The optimal rebalancing decisions at different points in time are linked; one decision affects another.

- Accurately reflecting transaction costs may be difficult; for example, transaction costs can be nonlinear in the size of a rebalancing trade.

- The optimal strategy is likely to change through time as prices evolve and new information becomes available.

- Rebalancing has tax implications for taxable investors.

Researchers are beginning to make headway in addressing optimal rebalancing in a general context.[17] At some future date, investors may be able to update optimal rebalancing thresholds in real time based on a lifetime utility of wealth formulation, including a transaction costs penalty component. Implementing such a system lies in the future rather than present of industry practice. If reasonable simplifying assumptions are permitted, some models are currently available to suggest specific values for optimal corridors, although no industry standard has been established yet.

3.3 The Perold–Sharpe Analysis of Rebalancing Strategies

Prior sections discussed rebalancing to a strategic asset allocation for a portfolio of many risky asset classes. That discipline of rebalancing, which can also be called a constant-mix strategy, is a bread-and-butter topic for investment practitioners. The following sections share the insights of Perold and Sharpe's (1988) analysis contrasting constant mix with other strategies. To make its points, the Perold–Sharpe

---

17 See Leland (2000) and Donohue and Yip (2003).

analysis assumes a simple two-asset class setting in which just one asset class is risky. Nevertheless, the analysis throws light on the underlying features of the strategies and what market dynamics and investor attitudes to risk favor or disfavor each of them.

3.3.1 *Buy-and-Hold Strategies*

A buy-and-hold strategy is a passive strategy of buying an initial asset mix (e.g., 60/40 stocks/Treasury bills) and doing absolutely nothing subsequently. Whatever the market does, no adjustments are made to portfolio weights. It is a "do-nothing" strategy resulting in a drifting asset mix.

The investment in Treasury bills (bills, for short) is risk-free and for the sake of simplicity is assumed to earn a zero return; it is essentially cash. In a buy-and-hold strategy, the value of risk-free assets represents a floor for portfolio value. For instance, take €100 and invest it initially according to 60/40 stocks/cash asset allocation. If the value of the stock allocation were to fall to zero, we would still have the €40 invested in cash. Therefore, the following expression pertains:

Portfolio value = Investment in stocks + Floor value

For a 60/40 stock/cash allocation the equation is

Portfolio value = Investment in stocks + Floor value of €40

Portfolio value is a linear function of the investment in stocks (the risky asset). If the buy-and-hold strategy has a floor, it is also true that there is no limit on upside potential so long as the portfolio is above the floor. The higher the initial allocation to stocks, the greater the increase (decrease) in value when stocks outperform (underperform) bills.

The amount by which portfolio value exceeds the investment in cash is the cushion (i.e., a buffer of value above the floor value). For a buy-and-hold strategy, the value of the investment in stocks moves 1:1 with the value of the cushion, as can be seen from rearranging the previous expression for portfolio value:

Investment in stocks = Cushion = Portfolio value − Floor value   **(1)**

In our one-risky-asset portfolio, the portfolio return (the percent change in portfolio value over a given holding period) equals the fraction of assets in stocks multiplied by the return on stocks (under the assumption of a zero return on bills).

Portfolio return = (Percent in stocks) × (Return on stocks)

For example, if stocks earn a 10 percent return, the value of stocks rises by 6 from 60 to 66; the value of the portfolio goes up by 6 from 100 to 106 (equal to 66 + 40). For the portfolio, that represents a 6 percent return as 6/100 = 6%. And 6% = 0.6 × 10%.

The investor's percent allocation to stocks is directly related to stock performance. For example if stocks earn a −100 percent return, the stock/bills allocation goes from 60/40 to 0/100 (the cushion is zero, the value of the portfolio is 40, which is the amount invested in bills). If stocks earn a +100 percent return, the asset allocation goes from 60/40 to 75/25 (the value of stocks goes from 60 to 120, increasing portfolio value from 100 to 160; 120/160 = 0.75 or 75%, which becomes the new stock allocation). A higher allocation to stocks reflects a greater risk tolerance. Therefore, a buy-and-hold strategy would work well for an investor whose risk tolerance is positively related to wealth and stock market returns.

To summarize, for a buy-and-hold strategy the following holds:

- Upside is unlimited, but portfolio value can be no lower than the allocation to bills.

- Portfolio value is a linear function of the value of stocks, and portfolio return is a linear function of the return on stocks.

- The value of stocks reflects the cushion (above floor value) 1:1.

- The implication of using this strategy is that the investor's risk tolerance is positively related to wealth and stock market returns. Risk tolerance is zero if the value of stocks declines to zero.

3.3.2 Constant-Mix Strategies

What we have called rebalancing to the strategic asset allocation in prior sections is a constant-mix strategy in the terminology of Perold–Sharpe. Constant mix is a "do-something" (or "dynamic") strategy in that it reacts to market movements with trades. An investor decides, for example, that his portfolio will be 60 percent equities and 40 percent bills and rebalances to that proportion regardless of his level of wealth. In particular, the target investment in stocks in the constant-mix strategy is

Target investment in stocks = m × Portfolio value   (2)

where m is a constant between 0 and 1 that represents the target proportion in stocks. If the equity market moves up, the actual stock proportion increases, but then it is adjusted down to m. If the equity market moves down, the actual stock proportion decreases, but then it is adjusted up to m.

Although a constant-mix strategy is "do-something," its effect is to maintain stable portfolio systematic risk characteristics over time, in contrast to a buy-and-hold strategy and the other "do-something" strategies that we will discuss shortly.

So far as returns alone are concerned, the adjustment policy of a constant-mix strategy will prove inferior to a buy-and-hold strategy if returns either move straight up, or move straight down. Strong bull and bear markets favor a buy-and-hold strategy. In the bull market case, the investor is cutting back on the shares of stock through rebalancing prior to further moves upwards. The buy-and-hold investor, by contrast, would profit by holding the number of shares constant (actually representing an increasing fraction of the portfolio invested in stocks). In the bear market case, the investor buys more shares prior to further moves down. The buy-and-hold investor does better by not changing his share holdings.

On the other hand, the constant-mix strategy tends to offer superior returns compared with buy-and-hold strategies if the equities returns are characterized more by reversals than by trends. For example, suppose the corridor for equities is 60% ± 5%. The stock market drops and the equity allocation falls below 55 percent; the equity allocation is rebalanced to 60 percent by selling bills and purchasing shares. The stock market then appreciates to its initial level (i.e., a return reversal occurs). The shares purchased in rebalancing under a constant-mix strategy show a gain. On the other hand, if the stock market first goes up, triggering a sale of shares and purchase of bills, and then drops back to its initial level, the constant-mix strategy also realizes a gain. Either returns reversal pattern is neutral for the buy-and-hold strategy. The constant-mix strategy is contrarian and supplies liquidity. Buying shares as stock values fall and selling shares as stock values rise are actions that supply liquidity because the investor is taking the less popular side of trades.

A constant-mix strategy is consistent with a risk tolerance that varies proportionately with wealth.[18] An investor with such risk tolerance desires to hold stocks at all levels of wealth.

---

18 That is, with a constant-mix strategy, the amount of money invested in risky assets increases with increasing wealth, implying increasing risk tolerance. Because the amount of money held in risky assets increases to maintain a constant ratio of risky assets to wealth, risk tolerance increases proportionately with wealth (constant *relative* risk tolerance or constant *relative* risk aversion).

3.3.3 *A Constant-Proportion Strategy: CPPI*

A constant-proportion strategy is a dynamic strategy in which the target equity allocation is a function of the value of the portfolio less a floor value for the portfolio. The following equation is used to determine equity allocation:

$$\text{Target investment in stocks} = m \times (\text{Portfolio value} - \text{Floor value}) \tag{3}$$

where m is a fixed constant. Constant-proportion strategies are so called because stock holdings are held to a constant proportion of the cushion. A characteristic of constant-proportion strategies is that they are consistent with a zero tolerance for risk (and hence no holdings in stocks) when the cushion is zero. Comparing Equation 1 with Equation 3, we see that a buy-and-hold strategy is a special case of a constant-proportion strategy in which $m = 1$. (For a buy-and-hold strategy, there is no distinction between the actual and target investment in stocks. The desired investment is whatever the actual level is.) When m exceeds 1, the constant-proportion strategy is called constant-proportion portfolio insurance (CPPI).[19]

CPPI is consistent with a higher tolerance for risk than a buy-and-hold strategy (when the cushion is positive), because the investor is holding a larger multiple of the cushion in stocks. Whereas a buy-and-hold strategy is do-nothing, CPPI is dynamic, requiring a manager to sell shares as stock values decline and buy shares as stock values rise. The floor in a buy-and-hold strategy is established with a fixed investment in bills; by contrast, in a CPPI strategy it is established dynamically. When stock values are trending up, the investment in stocks increases more than 1:1 with the increase in the value of stocks. The holding of bills may be minimal. When stocks are trending down, the allocation to stocks decreases more than 1:1 with the decrease in the value of stocks. The holding in bills rapidly increases until it reaches the floor value.

To manage transaction costs, a CPPI strategy requires some rules to determine when rebalancing to the stated multiple of the cushion should take place. One approach transacts when the portfolio value changes by a given percentage. At this point, the portfolio incurs transaction costs to rebalance. Because taxes can be a material consideration for taxable investors, they create a need for a rebalancing rule.

We expect a CPPI strategy to earn high returns in strong bull markets because the share purchases as the cushion increases are profitable. In a severe bear market, the sale of shares also is profitable in avoiding losses on them. By contrast, CPPI performs poorly in markets characterized more by reversals than by trends. CPPI requires a manager to sell shares after weakness and buy shares after strength; those transactions are unprofitable if drops are followed by rebounds and increases are retraced. The CPPI strategy is just the opposite of the constant-mix strategy in using liquidity and being momentum oriented.

3.3.4 *Linear, Concave, and Convex Investment Strategies*

A buy-and-hold strategy has been called a linear investment strategy because portfolio returns are a linear function of stock returns. The share purchases and sales involved in constant-mix and CPPI strategies introduce nonlinearities in the relationship. For constant-mix strategies, the relationship between portfolio returns and stock returns is concave; that is, portfolio return increases at a decreasing rate with positive stock returns and decreases at an increasing rate with negative stock returns.[20] In contrast, a CPPI strategy is convex. Portfolio return increases at an increasing rate with positive stock returns, and it decreases at a decreasing rate with negative stock returns.[21] Concave and convex strategies graph as mirror images of each other on

---

19 A value of m between 0 and 1 (and a floor value of zero) represents a constant-mix strategy.
20 The graph of portfolio return against stock return would have an inverted saucer shape.
21 The graph of portfolio return against stock return has a saucer shape.

either side of a buy-and-hold strategy. Convex strategies represent the purchase of portfolio insurance, concave strategies the sale of portfolio insurance. That is, convex strategies dynamically establish a floor value while concave strategies provide or sell the liquidity to convex strategies.

3.3.5 Summary of Strategies

Exhibit 9 summarizes the prior discussion of Perold–Sharpe analysis. The multiplier refers to Equation 3 which integrates all the models discussed.

Exhibit 9	Relative Return Performance of Different Strategies in Various Markets		
	Constant Mix	**Buy and Hold**	**CPPI**
Market Condition			
Up	Underperform	Outperform	Outperform
Flat (but oscillating)	Outperform	Neutral	Underperform
Down	Underperform	Outperform	Outperform
Investment Implications			
Payoff curve	Concave	Linear	Convex
Portfolio insurance	Selling insurance	None	Buying insurance
Multiplier	$0 < m < 1$	$m = 1$	$m > 1$

It is important to recognize that we have focused the discussion of performance in Exhibit 9 and the reading on return performance, not risk (except to mention the downside risk protection in the CPPI and stock/bills buy-and-hold strategies).

Finally, the appropriateness of buy-and-hold, constant-mix, and constant-proportion portfolio insurance strategies for an investor depends on the investor's risk tolerance, the types of risk with which she is concerned (e.g., floor values or downside risk), and asset-class return expectations, as Example 9 illustrates.

EXAMPLE 9

Strategies for Different Investors

For each of the following cases, suggest the appropriate strategy:

1   Jonathan Hansen, 25 years old, has a risk tolerance that increases by 20 percent for each 20 percent increase in wealth. He wants to remain invested in equities at all times.

2   Elaine Cash has a $1 million portfolio split between stocks and money market instruments in a ratio of 70/30. Her risk tolerance increases more than proportionately with changes in wealth, and she wants to speculate on a flat market or moderate bull market.

3   Jeanne Roger has a €2 million portfolio. She does not want portfolio value to drop below €1 million but also does not want to incur the drag on returns of holding a large part of her portfolio in cash equivalents.

Solution to 1:

Given his proportional risk tolerance (constant relative risk tolerance) and desire to remain invested in equities at all times, a constant-mix strategy is appropriate for Hansen.

Solution to 2:

Her risk tolerance is greater than that of a constant-mix investor, yet Cash's forecasts include the possibility of a flat market in which CPPI would do poorly. A buy-and-hold strategy is appropriate for Cash.

Solution to 3:

The concern for downside risk suggests either a buy-and-hold strategy with €1 million in cash equivalents as a floor or dynamically providing the floor with a CPPI strategy. The buy-and-hold strategy would incur the greater cash drag, so the CPPI strategy is appropriate.

3.4 Execution Choices in Rebalancing

In our discussion of rebalancing we have skirted the important issue of transaction execution. The particulars of execution depend on the specific asset classes held, the availability of relevant derivative markets in addition to cash markets, and the tax consequences of different execution means for taxable investors. The major choices are to rebalance by selling and buying portfolio assets (cash market trades) or by overlaying derivative positions onto the portfolio (derivative trades).

3.4.1 *Cash Market Trades*

Cash market trades represent the most direct means of portfolio rebalancing. Such trades represent adjustment at the "retail" level of risk because they typically involve buying and selling individual security positions.[22] If the investor employs active managers, then such adjustments need to be executed with care to minimize the impact on active managers' strategies. Cash market trades generally are more costly, and slower to execute, than equivalent derivative trades. For taxable investors, however, tax considerations may favor cash market trades over derivative market trades. First, there may be no exact derivative market equivalent to a cash market trade on an after-tax basis. Second, in some tax jurisdictions such as the United States, derivative market trades may have unfavorable tax consequences relative to cash market trades.[23] In addition, even if differences in taxation are irrelevant (as in the case of tax-exempt investors), not all asset class exposures can be closely replicated using derivatives, and individual derivative markets may have liquidity limitations. To some extent, the level of granularity with which asset classes have been defined affects the availability of adequate derivative equivalents.

3.4.2 *Derivative Trades*

Portfolio managers can also often use derivative trades involving instruments such as futures contracts and total return swaps for rebalancing. Trades are carried out so that the total exposure to asset classes (portfolio and derivative positions) closely mimics the effect of rebalancing by buying and selling underlying assets.

---

22 An exception would be rebalancing a passive exposure through an available exchange-traded fund (ETF) or basket trade.

23 See Horvitz (2002) for some details.

Rebalancing through derivatives markets, for the portion of the portfolio that can be closely replicated through derivative markets, has a number of major advantages:

- lower transaction costs;

- more rapid implementation—in derivative trades one is buying and selling systematic risk exposures rather than individual security positions; and

- leaving active managers' strategies undisturbed—in contrast to cash market trades, which involve trading individual positions, derivative trades have minimal impact on active managers' strategies.[24]

Besides the possibility that an asset class exposure may not be closely replicable with available derivatives, individual derivatives markets may have liquidity limits. Many investors, including tax-exempt investors, find it appropriate to use both cash and derivative trades in rebalancing their portfolios.

4 · CONCLUDING REMARKS

Managers must accord markets the respect they deserve. Implementation of portfolio strategies and tactics must be as rigorous as the investment decision process. A manager should understand his or her clients. Nothing is more important than a client's inherent tolerance for risk. Each client is unique; so should be the manager's understanding of the client's needs. When those needs change sufficiently, transaction costs assume a secondary role.

A portfolio manager must constantly monitor changes in investor circumstances, market and economic changes, and the portfolio itself, making sure that the IPS, asset allocation, and individual holdings continue to appropriately address the client's situation and investment objectives. The manager must serve as the client's champion in the investment realm, understand changes in the client's needs, and incorporate those changes into the dynamic management of the portfolio.

Legitimate chances to improve on diversified portfolios are rare. It pays to be wary of the multitude of vendors whose commercial interest argues otherwise.

A predetermined policy portfolio designed to be the continuing ideal and standard for an investor's combination of objectives, risk tolerance, and available asset classes, while hardly sacred, is the beacon one should generally steer toward.

SUMMARY

Even the most carefully constructed portfolios do not manage themselves. In this reading we have discussed two ingredients to ensuring an investment program's continuing relevancy: monitoring and rebalancing.

- Portfolio managers need to monitor everything that is relevant to positioning a portfolio to satisfy the client's objectives and constraints. Three areas that the portfolio manager must monitor are changes in investor circumstances and wealth, market and economic changes, and the portfolio itself.

---

24 There may also be tactical advantages to using futures. For example, futures may trade cheaply in relation to the underlying cash market when the cash market is falling. See Kleidon and Whaley (1992).

- Fiduciaries have an ethical and legal responsibility for adequate monitoring. Only by systematic monitoring can the fiduciary secure an informed view of the appropriateness and suitability of a portfolio for a particular client.

- Rebalancing to an investor's strategic asset allocation has benefits and costs. If the target asset class proportions of an investor's strategic asset allocation represent his optimum, any divergence from the target proportions represents an expected utility loss to the investor. The benefit in rebalancing equals the reduction in the present value of expected utility losses from not tracking the optimum. Rebalancing is a risk-control discipline that helps ensure an appropriate level of portfolio risk.

- The costs of rebalancing include transaction costs and, for taxable investors, tax costs (tax liabilities that are triggered by rebalancing trades).

- Calendar rebalancing involves rebalancing the portfolio to target weights on a periodic basis such as monthly, quarterly, semiannually, or annually. Calendar rebalancing is the simplest rebalancing discipline; it has the drawback of being unrelated to market performance. Yet it can suffice in ensuring that the actual portfolio does not drift far away from target for long periods of time if the rebalancing frequency is adequate given the portfolio's volatility.

- Percentage-of-portfolio rebalancing involves setting rebalancing thresholds (trigger points) that define a corridor or tolerance band for the value of that asset class such as 50% ± 5%. Compared with calendar rebalancing (particularly at lower frequencies such as semiannually or annually), percentage-of-portfolio rebalancing can exercise tighter control on divergences from target proportions because it is directly related to market performance.

- In rebalancing, two disciplines are rebalancing to target weights and rebalancing to the allowed range. The former exercises tighter discipline on risk exposures, the latter allows for more control of costs and for tactical adjustment.

- Factors positively related to optimal corridor width for an asset class include transaction costs, risk tolerance, and correlation with the rest of the portfolio. The greater these factors, the wider the optimal corridor, in general.

- Factors negatively related to optimal corridor width for an asset class include the asset class's volatility and the volatility of the rest of the portfolio. The greater these factors, the narrower the optimal corridor, in general.

- Three contrasting strategies are buy and hold, constant mix (rebalancing to the strategic asset allocation), and constant proportion (which includes constant-proportion portfolio insurance).

- A buy-and-hold strategy is a passive strategy of buying an initial asset mix (e.g., 60/40 stocks/bills) and doing absolutely nothing subsequently. It is synonymous with a drifting asset mix. A constant-mix strategy involves rebalancing so that the investment in stocks is a constant fraction of portfolio value. A constant-proportion portfolio insurance strategy involves making trades so the investment in stocks represents a constant multiple of the cushion of portfolio value above a floor value.

- In strong bull markets, CPPI outperforms a buy-and-hold strategy, while a buy-and-hold strategy outperforms a constant-mix strategy, in general. In strong bear markets, the same priority of performance holds. In a market characterized more by reversals than by trends, a constant-mix strategy tends to do best, followed by buy-and-hold and then CPPI strategies.

PRACTICE PROBLEMS

1 Evaluate the most likely effects of the following events on the investor's investment objectives, constraints, and financial plan.

  A A childless working married couple in their late 20s adopts an infant for whom they hope to provide a college education.

  B An individual decides to buy a house in one year. He estimates that he will need $102,000 at that time for the down payment and closing costs on the house. The portfolio from which those costs will be paid has a current value of $100,000 and no additions to it are anticipated.

  C A foundation with a €150,000,000 portfolio invested 60 percent in equities, 25 percent in long-term bonds, and 15 percent in absolute return strategies has approved a grant totaling €15,000,000 for the construction of a radio telescope observatory. The foundation anticipates a new contribution from a director in the amount of €1,000,000 towards the funding of the grant.

2 Duane Rogers, as chief investment officer for the Summit PLC defined benefit pension scheme, has developed an economic forecast for presentation to the plan's board of trustees. Rogers projects that UK inflation will be substantially higher over the next three years than the board's current forecast.

Rogers recommends that the board immediately take the following actions based on his forecast:

  A Revise the pension scheme's investment policy statement to account for a change in the UK inflation forecast.

  B Reallocate pension assets from domestic (UK) to international equities because he also expects inflation in the United Kingdom to be higher than in other countries.

  C Initiate a program to protect the pension scheme's financial strength from the effects of UK inflation by indexing benefits paid by the scheme.

State whether *each* recommended action is correct or incorrect. Justify *each* of your responses with *one* reason.

The following two interpretative monitoring questions (3–4) are presented as two-part narratives: initial client circumstances, which comprise the gist of a client's IPS and the detailed information going into its formulation, followed by the changed client circumstances.

3 **Initial Client Circumstances** Claire Wisman, a vice president for Spencer Design, is a 42-year-old widow who lives in the United States. She has two children: a daughter, age 21, and a son, age 7. She has a $2,200,000 portfolio; half of the portfolio is invested in Spencer Design, a publicly traded common stock, which has a cost basis of $350,000. Despite a substantial drop in the value of her portfolio over the last two years, her long-term annual total returns have averaged 7 percent before tax. The recent drop in value has caused her great anxiety, and she believes that she can no longer tolerate an annual decline greater than 10 percent.

Wisman intends to retire in 20 years and her goals for the next 20 years, in order of priority, are as follows. The present values given are gross of taxes.

- Funding the cost of her daughter's upcoming final year of college, which has a present value of $26,000, and her son's future college costs, which have a present value of $130,000.

- Increasing the portfolio to a level that will fund her retirement living expenses, which she estimates to be $257,000 for the first year of her retirement.

- Building her "dream house" in five years, the cost of which (including land) has a present value of $535,000.

- Giving, if possible, each of her children $1,000,000 when they reach age 40.

After subtracting the present value (before tax) of her children's education costs and her homebuilding costs, the present value of her portfolio is $1,509,000. With returns from income and gains taxable at 30 percent and with continued annual growth of 7 percent before tax (7% × (1 − 0.30) = 4.9% after taxes), the portfolio's value will be approximately $3,928,000 net of taxes at the end of 20 years.

Wisman's annual salary is $145,000, her annual living expenses are currently $100,000, and both are expected to increase at an inflation rate of 3 percent annually. Taxes on income and short-term capital gains (holding period one year or less) are substantially higher than taxes on long-term capital gains (holding period greater than one year). For planning purposes, however, Wisman wants to assume that her average tax rate on all income and gains is 30 percent. The inflation and tax rates are expected to remain constant. Currently, Wisman rents a townhouse, has no debt, and adamantly intends to remain debt-free. Spencer Design has no pension plan but provides company-paid medical insurance for executives for life and for their children to age 25. After taxes, Wisman's salary just covers her living expenses and thus does not allow her to make further meaningful capital contributions to her portfolio.

Wisman's current investment policy statement has the following elements:

Return requirement. A total return objective of 7 percent before tax is sufficient to meet Claire Wisman's educational, housing, and retirement goals. If the portfolio earns total return of 7 percent annually, the value at retirement ($3.93 million) should be adequate to meet ongoing spending needs then ($257,000/$3,928,000 = 6.5 percent spending rate) and fund all Wisman's extraordinary needs (college and homebuilding costs) in the meantime. The million-dollar gifts to her children are unrealistic goals that she should be encouraged to modify or drop.

Risk tolerance. Wisman has explicitly stated her limited (below average) willingness to take risk. Wisman appears to have an average ability to take risk. Her portfolio has some flexibility, because her expected return objective of 7 percent will meet her goals of funding her children's education, building her "dream house," and funding her retirement. Overall her risk tolerance is below average.

Time horizon. Her time horizon is multistage. The time horizon could be described as three-stage (the next 5 pre-retirement years defined by work/housing costs; the subsequent 15 pre-retirement years defined by work/college costs; and beyond 20 years postretirement).

Liquidity. Wisman has only a minor liquidity need ($26,000 in present value terms) to cover education expenses for her daughter next year. After that she has no liquidity need for the next five years. Only then ($535,000 in present value terms, for home construction) and in Years 11 through 14 ($130,000 in present value terms, for her son's education) will significant liquidity concerns exist.

Taxes. Taxes are a critical concern because Wisman needs to fund outlays with after-tax dollars.

Unique circumstances. A significant unique circumstance is the large concentration (50 percent of her assets) in Spencer Design stock. Another factor is her desire to build a new home in five years yet incur no debt. Also, she would "like" to give each child $1 million, but this goal is unrealistic and should not drive portfolio decisions.

Wisman indicates that Spencer Design has a leading and growing market share. The company has shown steady fundamental growth trends, and Wisman intends to hold her Spencer Design stock, which is expected to return at least 9 percent annually before tax with a standard deviation of returns of 20 percent.

Changed Client Circumstances Claire Wisman, now 47 years old, has recently married a coworker at Spencer Design. Wisman and her husband are buying their dream house at a total cost of $700,000, and they have decided to make an immediate down payment of $430,000 and finance the remainder over 15 years. Wisman also indicates that her son has contracted a rare disease, requiring major surgery; the disease will prevent him from attending college. Although Wisman and her husband have medical insurance that will pay her son's ongoing medical expenses, her son's surgery will cost an additional $214,000 immediately. The cost of medical expenditures is expected to grow at a rate exceeding the general inflation rate for the foreseeable future. Wisman has decided to quit work to care for her son, whose remaining life expectancy is 40 years. She also insists on the need to provide care for her son when she and her husband are no longer capable of doing so. Wisman's parents died one year ago, and her daughter is now financially independent. Wisman's husband intends to retire in 25 years.

Given these circumstances, the investment portfolio held by Wisman and her husband will need to provide an amount equal to $1,713,000 (present value) to meet their living expenses until his retirement. They also want their portfolio to grow enough to cover their living expenses at retirement, which they estimate to be $400,000 annually. They believe they will need a before-tax portfolio growth rate of approximately 8 to 10 percent annually to achieve this goal. Based on a retirement spending goal of $400,000, their corresponding effective postretirement spending rate will be approximately 6 to 7 percent annually.

Wisman summarizes her new financial information in Exhibit 1 below. She indicates that her portfolio and her husband's portfolio should be considered as one. She further states that her husband has taken well above-average risk in the past but he is now willing to leave the investment management decisions to her.

Exhibit 1	New Financial Information			
	Claire Wisman	**Husband**	**Combined**	**Current Allocation Percentage of Combined Portfolio**
Salary	$0	$150,000	$150,000	—
Assets				
Money market	$61,000	$27,000	$88,000	2.4%
Diversified bond fund	$1,129,000	$0	$1,129,000	30.5%

Exhibit 1   (Continued)

	Claire Wisman	Husband	Combined	Current Allocation Percentage of Combined Portfolio
Equities				
Large-capitalization equities	$385,000	$0	$385,000	10.4%
Emerging market equities	$0	$407,000	$407,000	11.0%
Spencer Design common stock	$1,325,000	$122,000	$1,447,000	39.1%
Undeveloped commercial land	$0	$244,000	$244,000	6.6%
Total portfolio	**$2,900,000**	**$800,000**	**$3,700,000**	**100.0%**

A   Indicate how *each* component of Wisman's investment policy statement should change as a result of Wisman's new circumstances. Justify *each* of your responses with *two* reasons based on Wisman's new circumstances.

B   Recommend whether the current allocation percentage (given in the exhibit) for *each* of the following assets should be decreased or increased as a result of Wisman's new circumstances. Justify *each* of your responses with *one* reason based on Wisman's new circumstances.

   i. Spencer Design common stock.

   ii. Money market.

   iii. Diversified bond fund.

   iv. Large-capitalization equities.

   v. Emerging market equities.

   vi. Undeveloped commercial land.

4   Initial Client Circumstances Both parents of 12-year-old Andrew Campbell recently died in an accident. The parents had been supporting Andrew and his grandmother, Lisa Javier, age 77. The parents' accumulated assets prior to their death were $640,000 in a diversified common stock (both domestic and international) portfolio and $360,000 in the common stock of Newman Enterprises, a publicly traded company founded by Javier's husband. The parents' assets will now be held in a single US-based trust—the Javier–Campbell Trust (the Trust)—to benefit both Javier and Campbell. In addition to these assets, the Trust received life insurance proceeds of $2,000,000.

Newman Enterprises will continue to provide medical coverage for Javier until her death. Campbell has government-provided healthcare until he reaches age 22. Campbell will attend university for four years beginning at age 18. In addition to normal living expenses, initial annual university costs are projected to be $38,000, rising 8 percent annually.

According to the provisions of the Trust document:

- The Trust should provide for Javier's and Campbell's annual living expenses, currently estimated to total $78,000 per year (after tax). The Trust portfolio should earn a return sufficient to cover the living expenses of Javier and Campbell, taking taxes into consideration and allowing for inflation (expected to be 2 percent annually). Income and capital gains are taxed at 30 percent, and this tax treatment is not expected to change.

- The Trust should limit shortfall risk (defined as expected total return minus two standard deviations) to no lower than a −10 percent return in any one year.

- Campbell is entitled to receive distributions from the Trust until he reaches age 32. At that point, the Trust will continue making distributions for Javier's living expenses.

- Upon Javier's death, the Trust's assets will go to Campbell, provided he is at least 32 years old. If Campbell is not yet aged 32 when Javier dies, the Trust will then distribute income and principal to Campbell until he reaches age 32, at which point the Trust will terminate and the assets will be distributed to Campbell.

- The Newman Enterprises common stock cannot be sold without Javier's approval for as long as she is alive. Javier has stated her strong desire to retain the Newman stock indefinitely, to fulfill a promise she made to her husband.

- The Trust must hold in cash equivalents an amount equal to nine months of living expenses (on a pretax basis) for Javier and Campbell.

- In the unlikely event that Campbell dies before Javier, distributions will continue for Javier's benefit until she dies, at which point any remaining Trust assets will be distributed to several charities.

As a result of poor financial advice, Javier lost all of her inheritance from her husband's estate. Because her assets are nearly depleted, she wants to minimize any future losses in the Trust portfolio; in fact, she has expressed serious concerns about the Trust's ability to meet Campbell's and her needs during her lifetime.

The risk tolerance and return requirement elements of the Javier–Campbell Trust's IPS are as follows:

Risk Tolerance

Ability. The Trust has average ability to assume risk, largely because of its substantial asset base in relation to its spending needs. Because the portfolio is Javier's only source of support, the Trust's ability to assume risk is lower than it might otherwise be.

Willingness. The Trust has below-average willingness to assume risk. The Trust document requires that the account be invested so that shortfall risk (defined as expected total return minus two standard deviations) is limited to a −10 percent return in any one year. This limitation implies that the Trust will be unwilling to tolerate any substantial volatility in portfolio returns.

Overall risk tolerance. The Trust has below-average risk tolerance and will continue to have it for many years, especially while Javier is alive.

Return Requirement

The return requirement reflects two major factors: the need to cover living expenses and the need to protect the portfolio from the adverse effects of inflation. Specifically, the Trust must generate a total before-tax return of at least 6.57 percent on an annual basis to meet these return requirements.

The living expenses, estimated at $78,000 per year, represent a $78,000/$3,000,000 = 2.6 percent spending rate. However, because the Trust is taxed at 30 percent, it will need to earn a pretax return of (2.6% + 2%)/(1 − 0.30) = 6.57 percent to meet Javier and Campbell's living expenses.

Changed Client Circumstances Ten years have now passed, and the Javier–Campbell Trust portfolio returns over the previous 10 years have failed to meet expectations. Lower returns, coupled with Lisa Javier's and Andrew Campbell's living expenses and Campbell's college costs, have combined to reduce the value of the Trust portfolio to $2,000,000.

Javier, now 87, recently moved to an assisted-living care facility. With her health failing, doctors have determined she will live no longer than three years and will require full-time care for the remaining time until her death. Javier's medical expenses are covered by insurance, but her care and living expenses now require $84,000 per year (after tax and adjusted for inflation) from the Trust. Inflation is expected to be 3 percent annually over the next several years. Javier has no other support and depends on the Trust to meet her financial needs. She has continued to express her concern that the Trust will not provide enough distributions to cover her expenses during her remaining lifetime. She still wishes to retain the Newman Enterprises common stock, which now constitutes 15 percent of the Trust portfolio and has an expected annual yield of 2 percent over the next several years. Legal constraints have not changed, and the Trust still requires nine months of living expenses (on a pretax basis) to be held in reserve.

Campbell, now 22, is a recent college graduate and has accepted a job with Elkhorn Consulting Partners. In the job offer, Elkhorn agreed to pay the cost of Campbell's M.B.A. degree. Campbell also has the opportunity to buy a partnership stake in the company by making equal annual payments of $600,000 per year for five years. He will begin making those payments in ten years. Campbell's starting salary is sufficient to cover his living expenses.

Although Campbell is concerned about providing for Javier, he believes that with the appropriate asset allocation, the Trust assets should be sufficient to take care of her expenditures until she dies and to provide the growth he needs to meet his partnership obligations. Campbell views growth from the Trust to be essential in meeting his long-term goals. Assuming that Campbell lives longer than Javier, the individual assets in the Trust will be distributed to Campbell upon termination of the Trust; the Trust portfolio will become Campbell's portfolio.

The trustee believes that circumstances have changed enough to warrant revising certain components of the investment policy statements for Campbell and the Trust.

Formulate revised statements about the Javier–Campbell Trust's willingness to take risk that reflect the changed circumstances of both Javier and Campbell. Your response should include appropriate supporting justification.

5   A foundation holds an equally weighted portfolio of domestic equities, international equities, private equity, and inflation-protected bonds.

   A   Critique a percentage-of-portfolio discipline that involves establishing a corridor of target percentage allocation ± 5% for each asset class in the foundation's portfolio.

   B   Evaluate the implications of the following sets of facts on the stated corridor, given an all-else-equal assumption in each case:

       i.   The Foundation's risk tolerance has decreased. *Corridor for international equities.*

ii. Transaction costs in international equities are one-half those for private equity. *Corridor for inflation-protected bonds.*

iii. The correlation of private equity with the rest of the portfolio is lower than the correlation of domestic equities with the rest of the portfolio. *Corridor for private equity.*

iv. The volatility of domestic equities is higher than that of inflation-protected bonds. *Corridor for domestic equities.*

6 A Recommend an appropriate rebalancing discipline for an investor who cannot monitor portfolio values on a daily basis yet holds an above-average risk portfolio and low risk tolerance.

B How would the investment results of the recommended rebalancing discipline be affected if markets were nontrending?

7 Marvis University (MU) is a private, multiprogram US university with a $2 billion endowment fund as of fiscal year-end May 31, 2002. With little government support, MU is heavily dependent on its endowment fund to support ongoing expenditures, especially because the university's enrollment growth and tuition revenue have not met expectations in recent years. The endowment fund must make a $126 million annual contribution, which is indexed to inflation, to MU's general operating budget. The US Consumer Price Index is expected to rise 2.5 percent annually, and the US higher education cost index is anticipated to rise 3 percent annually. The endowment has also budgeted $200 million due on January 31, 2003, representing the final payment for construction of a new main library.

In a recent capital campaign, MU met its fundraising goal only with the help of one very successful alumna, Valerie Bremner, who donated $400 million of Bertocchi Oil and Gas common stock at fiscal year-end May 31, 2002. Bertocchi Oil and Gas is a large-capitalization, publicly traded US company. Bremner donated the stock on the condition that no more than 25 percent of the initial number of shares may be sold in any fiscal year. No substantial additional donations are expected in the future.

Given the large contribution to and distributions from the endowment fund, the fund's Investment Committee has decided to revise its investment policy statement.

In the revised IPS, the endowment portfolio manager established that MU's return requirement is 10 percent. MU's average ability to take risk restrains its risk tolerance.

Five years have passed, and the Marvis University endowment fund's willingness and ability to assume risk have increased. The endowment fund's Investment Committee asks its consultant, James Chan, to discuss and recommend a rebalancing strategy to incorporate the new risk tolerance. Chan anticipates a bull market in growth assets over the next three to five years. He also believes that volatility will be below historical averages during that same time period. The Investment Committee directs Chan to incorporate his views into his recommendation. The Committee also does not want the market value of the portfolio to decline more than 15 percent below its current market value.

A Describe the following *three* primary rebalancing strategies:

i. Buy and hold.

ii. Constant mix.

   iii. Constant-proportion portfolio insurance.

B Determine which *one* of the three rebalancing strategies in Part A Chan should recommend for the Marvis University endowment fund. Justify your response with two reasons based on the circumstances described above.

Questions 8 through 15 relate to Heather Daniels, Duane Lee, and Janice Mirimi[1]

Heather Daniels is a financial advisor who recently met with two prospective clients, Duane Lee and Janice Mirimi. Summary information for each prospective client is presented in Exhibit 1.

| Exhibit 1 | Client Summary Information |

Lee Summary:

Duane Lee is 55 years old and has a portfolio valued at $2 million, with $1.6 million in domestic equities and $400,000 in Treasury bills. When he inherited the portfolio from his grandfather 20 years ago, 65% of the portfolio was invested in domestic equities with a cost basis of $500,000 and 35% was invested in Treasury bills. He has not rebalanced his portfolio since he inherited the portfolio.

Mirimi Summary:

Janice Mirimi is 32 years old and has a portfolio valued at $10.5 million. She recently received a large inheritance, and her willingness and her ability to assume risk has increased. Her previous financial advisor rebalanced her portfolio to the optimal strategic allocation whenever one of the asset classes moved outside its rebalancing thresholds.

Exhibit 2 presents the strategic asset allocations and rebalancing thresholds (defining corridors for rebalancing) that Daniels plans to recommend for each client.

| Exhibit 2 | Client Strategic Asset Allocation | | | |

Asset Class	Duane Lee Allocation	Corridor	Janice Mirimi Allocation	Corridor
Domestic equities	50%	0%	55%	±5.5%
International equities	0%	0%	15%	±1.5%
Domestic bond	0%	0%	30%	±3.0%
Treasury bills	50%	0%	0%	0%

Daniels provides the following information to each prospective client.

- Her firm projects a bull market for domestic and international equities for the next five years.

- The volatility of international and domestic equities has recently decreased and is expected to remain at historically low levels over the next several years.

- Transaction costs for domestic bonds are expected to increase in relation to the other asset classes.

- The correlation of domestic bonds with the other asset classes is expected to decrease.

Daniels notes that both prospective clients want to employ a rebalancing strategy. Select client statements pertaining to rebalancing are presented in Exhibit 3.

Exhibit 3   Client Rebalancing Statements

Lee Statement:

"I know I have an emotional attachment to my grandfather's portfolio; however, I am getting closer to retirement and my portfolio needs to be adjusted. I don't need my financial advisor to check my portfolio on a daily basis. I just want my portfolio to be adjusted to my target allocations on a regular basis, such as right before our quarterly meetings.

Mirimi Statement:

"I am comfortable giving my financial advisor flexibility to take advantage of tactical opportunities when it comes to rebalancing my portfolio, but I do want to minimize transaction costs which might occur. Although my risk tolerance has increased, I would like to be diversified across equities and bonds."

8 Based upon the information presented in Exhibit 1, the cost of rebalancing that is *most likely* to have the greatest effect on the value of Lee's portfolio is:

   A tax costs.

   B transaction costs.

   C market impact costs.

9 Based upon the change in volatility of international equities noted by Daniels, the corridor for international equities for Mirimi's portfolio presented in Exhibit 2 would *most likely* be:

   A indeterminate.

   B wider than ± 1.5%.

   C narrower than ± 1.5%.

10 Based upon both the change in transaction costs and the change in the correlation of domestic bonds noted by Daniels, the corridor for domestic bonds for Mirimi's portfolio presented in Exhibit 2 would *most likely* be:

   A indeterminate.

   B wider than ± 3%.

   C narrower than ±3%.

11 Based only upon the forecast for domestic equities and international equities provided by Daniels, which type of rebalancing strategy would result in the best relative return performance?

   A Constant mix.

   B Buy-and-hold.

   C Constant-proportion portfolio insurance.

12 Based upon Mirimi's preferences noted in Exhibit 3, if one of the asset classes increases beyond its corridor for rebalancing, Daniels would *most likely*:

A rebalance the asset class to the allowable range.

B rebalance the asset class to the optimal target weight.

C pursue a passive strategy that reflects a drifting asset mix.

13 According to Lee's statements in Exhibit 3, what would be the *most likely* drawback associated with Lee's preferred rebalancing discipline?

A It is unrelated to market performance.

B It involves continuous monitoring of portfolio values.

C It does not account for differences in transaction costs and asset correlations.

14 Lee's preferred rebalancing strategy described in Exhibit 3 would result in which type of payoff diagram?

A Linear.

B Convex.

C Concave.

15 What type of rebalancing strategy would Daniels *most likely* recommend for Mirimi's portfolio?

A Constant mix.

B Buy-and-hold.

C Constant-proportion portfolio insurance.

SOLUTIONS

1 **A** Accumulating funds for the child's education is a new investment goal. Prior to the adoption, the couple's time horizon was two-stage (preretirement and postretirement). In their late 40s, they will have a period in which they need to pay for the cost of the child's education; this will involve substantial costs for which they must plan. The couple's multistage time horizon now includes the period up to the child's entering college, the child's college years, the remaining period to retirement, and retirement.

 B Given the investor's circumstances, the decision to buy a house in one year's time makes the addition of a shortfall risk objective appropriate. He needs to earn at least 2 percent if he is to have sufficient funds to buy the house. An appropriate shortfall risk objective is to minimize the probability that the return on the portfolio falls below 2 percent over a one-year horizon. The decision also creates a liquidity requirement. The need for $102,000 in cash at the end of the investment period means that the investor cannot tie up his money in a way such that he does not have ready access to it in a year's time.

 C The approval of the grant has created a liquidity requirement of €15,000,000 − €1,000,000 = €14,000,000.

2 The first action ("Revise the investment policy statement of the pension scheme to take into account a change in the forecast for inflation in the United Kingdom") is incorrect. The Investment Policy Statement depends on the client's particular circumstances, including risk tolerance, time horizon, liquidity and legal constraints, and unique needs. Therefore, a change in economic forecast would not affect the Investment Policy Statement. The Investment Policy Statement also considers a client's return requirement. This return requirement may change over the long term if the inflation outlook has changed over the long term. A change in the inflation outlook over a short period, such as in this question, would not necessitate a change in the return portion or any other aspect of the Investment Policy Statement.

 The second action ("Reallocate pension assets from domestic [UK] to international equities because he also expects inflation in the United Kingdom to be higher than in other countries") is correct. A change in economic forecast might necessitate a change in asset allocation and investment strategy. An expectation of increased inflation in the United Kingdom might lead to expectations that UK equity performance will slow and would likely result in both weaker UK equity returns and stronger returns from overseas markets. This would justify an increased allocation to international equities.

 The third action ("Initiate a program to protect the financial strength of the pension scheme from the effects of UK inflation by indexing benefits paid by the scheme") is incorrect. The implementation of an inflation index adjustment program would protect the plan participants, not the plan itself, from the effects of higher UK inflation. With an inflation index adjustment program, Summit's costs of funding the defined benefit scheme would actually increase (thereby weakening the plan's financial position) as UK inflation increases.

3 **A** The return requirement should be higher to:
 - fund her additional living expenses, and
 - meet her new retirement goals.

The following calculations are not required but provide basis for the statement that the return must be higher than the previous 7 percent to generate a retirement portfolio that will support the desired retirement spending level (at a reasonable retirement spending rate). The portfolio must now produce a return of approximately 9 percent, depending on the retirement spending rate assumption made.

Current Portfolio (Gross)	$3,700,000
Less surgery	$214,000
Less house down payment	$430,000
Less living expenses	$1,713,000
Current Portfolio (Net)	$1,343,000
After-tax return = Before-tax return $(1 - T)$ = 9.0% (0.7) = 6.3%	
Years = 25	
Retirement portfolio	$6,185,967 = \$1,343,000(1.063)^{25}$
Retirement spending	$400,000
Spending rate	$6.47\% = \$400,000/\$6,185,967$

Risk tolerance should be higher. Wisman's risk tolerance should be higher because:

- her husband's intention to work for another 25 years gives her the ability to assume more risk, and

- the increase in assets affords her the ability to assume more risk.

Her time horizon is still multistage, but the stages have changed. In the first stage expected to last 25 years, her husband will be working. The second stage is retirement.

The liquidity requirement should be higher. Wisman has a higher liquidity requirement because of the cost of the surgery for her son and the down payment for the house.

B   **i.** The allocation to Spencer Design Stock (currently 39.1 percent) should be decreased. Having a large percentage of her portfolio in one risky and potentially illiquid equity security exposes the portfolio to unnecessary and significant security-specific risk.

  ii. The allocation to cash (currently 2.4 percent) should be increased. Wisman needs $430,000 for a house down payment, $214,000 for her son's surgery, and the current year's portion of the $1,713,000 present value of ongoing living expenses.

  iii. The allocation to the diversified bond fund (currently 30.5 percent) should be increased. The couple's portfolio must support the $1,713,000 present value of ongoing living expenses and can sustain only moderate portfolio volatility. The regular income stream and diversification benefits offered by bonds are consistent with those needs.

  iv. The allocation to large-capitalization equities (currently 10.4 percent) should be increased. Wisman requires growth and inflation protection to meet her current and future spending needs. A diversified equity portfolio is likely to meet these requirements over time without imparting unacceptable volatility to principal values.

  v. The allocation to emerging market equities (currently 11 percent) should be decreased. Wisman requires high returns but cannot afford to sustain large losses. Having a large percentage of total assets in volatile emerging markets securities is too risky for Wisman.

   vi. The allocation to undeveloped commercial land (currently 6.6 percent) should be decreased. Wisman needs income and liquidity to meet ongoing portfolio disbursement requirements. Undeveloped land requires cash payments (taxes, etc.) and is often illiquid.

4 The Javier–Campbell Trust's willingness to take risk is now below average because of its need to have a high probability of covering Javier's living expenses during the remainder of her lifetime, which encompasses a short time horizon. Javier's below-average willingness to take risk (coupled with her short time horizon) dominates Campbell's above-average willingness (coupled with his long time horizon). Of course, once Javier is no longer living, the Trust can reflect Campbell's higher willingness to take risk.

5 **A** The suggested approach has several disadvantages:

- A fixed ±5% corridor takes no account of differences in transaction costs among the asset classes. For example, private equity has much higher transaction costs than inflation-protected bonds and should have a wider corridor, all else equal.
- The corridors do not take account of differences in volatility. Rebalancing is most likely to be triggered by the highest volatility asset class.
- The corridors do not take account of asset class correlations.

  B **i.** The corridor for international equities should be narrower than it was previously.

    ii. The corridor for inflation-protected bonds should be unaffected. The transaction costs should have an effect on the relative widths of the corridors for private equity and international equities.

    iii. The corridor for private equity should be narrower than that for domestic equities.

    iv. The corridor for domestic equities should be narrower than that for inflation-protected bonds.

6 **A** Calendar rebalancing at a relatively high frequency such as weekly or monthly would be appropriate. In contrast to percentage-of-portfolio rebalancing, calendar rebalancing does not require continuous monitoring of portfolio values. The riskiness of the portfolio suggests frequent rebalancing to control drift.

  B Such markets tend to be characterized by reversal and enhance the investment results from rebalancing to the strategic asset allocation, according to Perold–Sharpe analysis.

7 **A** **i.** *Buy and hold.* The buy-and-hold strategy maintains an exposure to equities that is linearly related to the value of equities in general. The strategy involves buying, then holding, an initial mix (equities/bills). No matter what happens to relative values, no rebalancing is required; hence this is sometimes termed the "do nothing" strategy. The investor sets a floor below which he or she does not wish the portfolio's value to fall. An amount equal to the value of that floor is invested in some nonfluctuating asset (e.g., Treasury bills or money market funds). The payoff diagram for a buy-and-hold strategy is a straight line, so the portfolio's value rises (falls) as equity values rise (fall), with a slope equal to the equity proportion in the initial mix. The value of the portfolio will never fall below the specified floor, and the portfolio has unlimited upside potential. Increasing equity prices favor a buy-and-hold strategy; the greater the equity proportion in the initial mix, the better (worse) the strategy will perform when equities outperform (underperform) bills.

The strategy is particularly appropriate for an investor whose risk tolerance above the specified floor varies with wealth but drops to zero at or below that floor. After the initial portfolio transaction, transaction costs are not an issue. The strategy is tax efficient for taxable investors.

ii. *Constant mix.* The constant-mix strategy maintains an exposure to equities that is a constant percentage of total wealth. Periodic rebalancing to return to the desired mix requires the purchase (sale) of equities as they decline (rise) in value. This strategy, which generates a concave payoff diagram, offers relatively little downside protection and performs relatively poorly in up markets. The strategy performs best in relatively flat (but oscillating or volatile) markets and capitalizes on market reversals. The constant-mix strategy performs particularly well in a time period when equity values oscillate greatly but end close to their beginning levels; greater volatility around the beginning values accentuates the positive performance.

The constant-mix strategy is particularly appropriate for an investor whose risk tolerance varies proportionately with wealth; such an investor will hold equities at all levels of wealth. This strategy requires some rule to determine when rebalancing should take place; typical approaches avoid transaction costs until asset-class weights have changed by a given percentage. At this point, transaction costs are incurred to rebalance. Taxes can be material for taxable investors.

iii. *Constant-proportion portfolio insurance.* The constant-proportion portfolio insurance (CPPI) strategy maintains an exposure to equities that is a constant multiple greater than 1 of a "cushion" specified by the investor. The investor sets a floor below which he does not wish assets to fall. Under normal market conditions the value of the portfolio will not fall below this specified floor. As equity values rise (fall), the CPPI strategy requires the investor to purchase (sell) additional equities. Thus following this strategy keeps equities at a constant multiple of the cushion (assets − floor) and generates a convex payoff diagram. The CPPI strategy tends to give good downside protection and performs best in directional, especially up, markets; the strategy does poorly in flat but oscillating markets and is especially hurt by sharp market reversals.

The strategy is particularly appropriate for an investor who has zero tolerance for risk below the stated floor but whose risk tolerance increases quickly as equity values move above the stated floor. To control transaction costs, this strategy requires some rule to determine when rebalancing takes place. One approach avoids transaction costs until the value of the portfolio has changed by a given percentage. At this point, transaction costs are incurred to rebalance. Taxes can be a material consideration for taxable investors.

B The CPPI strategy is the most appropriate rebalancing strategy for the MU endowment fund, taking into account the major circumstances described: the endowment's increased risk tolerance, the outlook for a bull market in growth assets over the next five years, the expectation of lower than normal volatility, and the endowment's desire to limit downside risk.

The CPPI strategy is consistent with higher risk tolerance, because the strategy calls for purchasing more equities as equities increase in value; higher risk tolerance is reflected in the resulting increased allocation to equities over time.

■ The CPPI strategy will do well in an advancing equities market; because equities are purchased as their values rise, each marginal purchase has a high payoff.

■ The CPPI strategy would do poorly in a higher-volatility environment for equities, because the strategy would sell on weakness but buy on strength, only to experience reversals; conversely, the strategy does much better in the face of lower volatility.

■ The CPPI strategy provides good downside protection, because the strategy sells on weakness and reduces exposure to equities as a given floor is approached.

In summary, given that MU receives little other funding, the endowment fund must produce the maximum return for a specified level of risk. Given that the level of acceptable risk is generally higher, although with a very specific downside floor, the market outlook suggests that the constant-proportion strategy is the endowment fund's best rebalancing strategy.

8 A is correct. Lee's market value of equities is $1.6 million and its cost basis is $500,000. He has not rebalanced his portfolio since he inherited the portfolio 20 years ago. Sale of appreciated assets will trigger a tax liability, which is the cost of rebalancing most likely to have the greatest effect on portfolio value if rebalancing occurs.

9 B is correct. Mirimi wants to follow a percentage-of-portfolio rebalancing program and the volatility of international equities is expected to decrease, thus the optimal rebalancing corridor for international equities can be wider than ± 1.5%.

10 A is correct. The increase in transaction costs point to widening the corridor for domestic bonds, but decreasing correlations point to narrowing it. The overall effect is indeterminate.

11 C is correct. The constant-proportion portfolio insurance (CPPI) strategy is expected to earn high returns in bull markets. The CPPI strategy is a convex strategy with portfolio returns increasing at an increasing rate with positive stock returns. Although the buy and hold strategy does well in bull markets, it is a linear investment strategy. Thus, a CPPI strategy outperforms a buy and hold strategy in bull markets.

12 A is correct. Mirimi states that she wants to minimize transaction costs and provide opportunities for tactical adjustments by her financial advisor, which would be appropriate for a strategy that rebalances to the allowable range rather than the optimal target weight.

13 A is correct. Lee prefers his portfolio to be rebalanced to its target weights each quarter, which is calendar rebalancing. The primary drawback to calendar rebalancing is that it is unrelated to market behavior.

14 C is correct. Exhibit 3 notes that Lee wants to rebalance his portfolio to the optimal strategic allocation each quarter, which is a constant mix rebalancing strategy. When following a constant mix strategy, portfolio returns increase at a decreasing rate with positive stock returns and decrease at an increasing rate with negative stock returns. Therefore, a constant mix strategy generates a concave payoff diagram.

15 C is correct. The constant-proportion portfolio insurance (CPPI) strategy is the most appropriate rebalancing strategy given Mirimi's preferences described in Exhibit 1 and Exhibit 3 and the information provided by Daniels. The CPPI strategy is consistent with higher risk tolerance, does well in strong bull markets, and also in markets characterized by lower than normal volatilities. These factors all indicate that the CPPI strategy would be the most appropriate.

17

Performance Evaluation

Performance evaluation addresses three questions that are essential in evaluating the results of the portfolio management process:

- What was the portfolio's performance?
- Why did the portfolio produce the observed performance?
- Was the portfolio's performance due to luck or skill?

These questions are answered by performance measurement, performance attribution, and performance appraisal, respectively. The information developed in performance evaluation provides key inputs to a) assessing compliance with investment policy and progress toward achieving client goals, b) determining whether an investment manager's performance has been consistent with the manager's stated investment discipline, and c) deciding whether to hire, retain, or dismiss an investment manager.

READING ASSIGNMENTS

Reading 32	Evaluating Portfolio Performance *Managing Investment Portfolios: A Dynamic Process*, Third Edition, John L. Maginn, CFA, Donald L. Tuttle, CFA, Jerald E. Pinto, CFA, and Dennis W. McLeavey, CFA, editors

Evaluating Portfolio Performance

by Jeffery V. Bailey, CFA, Thomas M. Richards, CFA, and David E. Tierney

LEARNING OUTCOMES

Mastery	The candidate should be able to:
☐	**a.** demonstrate the importance of performance evaluation from the perspective of fund sponsors and the perspective of investment managers;
☐	**b.** explain the following components of portfolio evaluation: performance measurement, performance attribution, and performance appraisal;
☐	**c.** calculate, interpret, and contrast time-weighted and money-weighted rates of return and discuss how each is affected by cash contributions and withdrawals;
☐	**d.** identify and explain potential data quality issues as they relate to calculating rates of return;
☐	**e.** demonstrate the decomposition of portfolio returns into components attributable to the market, to style, and to active management;
☐	**f.** discuss the properties of a valid performance benchmark and explain advantages and disadvantages of alternative types of benchmarks;
☐	**g.** explain the steps involved in constructing a custom security-based benchmark;
☐	**h.** discuss the validity of using manager universes as benchmarks;
☐	**i.** evaluate benchmark quality by applying tests of quality to a variety of possible benchmarks;
☐	**j.** discuss issues that arise when assigning benchmarks to hedge funds;
☐	**k.** distinguish between macro and micro performance attribution and discuss the inputs typically required for each;
☐	**l.** demonstrate and contrast the use of macro and micro performance attribution methodologies to identify the sources of investment performance;

(continued)

Managing Investment Portfolios: A Dynamic Process, Third Edition, John L. Maginn, CFA, Donald L. Tuttle, CFA, Jerald E. Pinto, CFA, and Dennis W. McLeavey, CFA, editors. Copyright © 2007 by CFA Institute.

LEARNING OUTCOMES

Mastery	The candidate should be able to:
☐	m. discuss the use of fundamental factor models in micro performance attribution;
☐	n. evaluate the effects of the external interest rate environment and active management on fixed-income portfolio returns;
☐	o. explain the management factors that contribute to a fixed-income portfolio's total return and interpret the results of a fixed-income performance attribution analysis;
☐	p. calculate, interpret, and contrast alternative risk-adjusted performance measures, including (in their *ex post* forms) alpha, information ratio, Treynor measure, Sharpe ratio, and M^2;
☐	q. explain how a portfolio's alpha and beta are incorporated into the information ratio, Treynor measure, and Sharpe ratio;
☐	r. demonstrate the use of performance quality control charts in performance appraisal;
☐	s. discuss the issues involved in manager continuation policy decisions, including the costs of hiring and firing investment managers;
☐	t. contrast Type I and Type II errors in manager continuation decisions.

1 INTRODUCTION

The *ex post* analysis of investment performance stands as a prominent and ubiquitous feature of modern investment management practice. Investing involves making decisions that have readily quantifiable consequences and that, at least on the surface, lend themselves to elaborate dissection and review. We broadly refer to the measurement and assessment of the outcomes of these investment management decisions as **performance evaluation**. At the institutional investor level, and to a lesser (but growing) extent on the individual investor level, a large industry has developed to satisfy the demand for performance evaluation services. Although some observers contend that performance evaluation is misguided, frequently misapplied, or simply unattainable with any reasonable degree of statistical confidence, we believe that analytic techniques representing best practices can lead to valid insights about the sources of past returns, and such insights can be useful inputs for managing an investment program.

The purpose of this reading is to provide an overview of current performance evaluation concepts and techniques. Our focus will be on how institutional investors—both fund sponsors and investment managers—conduct performance evaluation. Individual investors tend to use variations of the performance evaluation techniques employed by institutional investors. We define fund sponsors to be owners of large pools of investable assets, such as corporate and public pension funds, endowments, and foundations. These organizations typically retain multiple investment management firms deployed across a range of asset categories. Fund sponsors have the challenge of evaluating not only the performance of the individual managers, but also the investment results within the asset categories and for their total investment programs.

In Section 2 we distinguish between the perspectives of the fund sponsor and the investment manager. Section 3 divides the broad subject of performance evaluation into three components: **performance measurement**, **performance attribution**, and **performance appraisal**. Under the topic of performance measurement, in Section 4 we discuss several methods of calculating portfolio performance. Section 5 introduces the concept of performance benchmarks. Turning to performance attribution, in Section 6 we consider the process of analyzing the sources of returns relative to a designated benchmark both from the total fund (fund sponsor) level and from the individual portfolio (investment manager) level. Our topic in Section 7 is performance appraisal, which deals with assessing investment skill. Section 8 addresses key issues in the practice of performance evaluation, and we conclude with a summary of the reading's key points.

THE IMPORTANCE OF PERFORMANCE EVALUATION   2

Performance evaluation is important from the perspectives of both the fund sponsor and the investment manager.

2.1 The Fund Sponsor's Perspective

A typical fund sponsor would consider its investment program incomplete without a thorough and regular evaluation of the fund's performance relative to its investment objectives. Applied in a comprehensive manner, performance evaluation is more than a simple exercise in calculating rates of return. Rather, it provides an exhaustive "quality control" check, emphasizing not only the performance of the fund and its constituent parts relative to objectives, but the sources of that relative performance as well.

Performance evaluation is part of the feedback step of the investment management process. As such, it should be an integral part of a fund's investment policy and documented in its investment policy statement. As discussed in Ambachtsheer (1986) and Ellis (1985), investment policy itself is a combination of philosophy and planning. On the one hand, it expresses the fund sponsor's attitudes toward a number of important investment management issues, such as the fund's mission, the fund sponsor's risk tolerance, the fund's investment objectives, and so on. On the other hand, investment policy is a form of longterm strategic planning. It defines the specific goals that the fund sponsor expects the fund to accomplish, and it describes how the fund sponsor foresees the realization of those goals.

Investment policy gives an investment program a sense of direction and discipline. Performance evaluation enhances the effectiveness of a fund's investment policy by acting as a feedback and control mechanism. It identifies an investment program's strengths and weaknesses and attributes the fund's investment results to various key decisions. It assists the fund sponsor in reaffirming a commitment to successful investment strategies, and it helps to focus attention on poorly performing operations. Moreover, it provides evidence to fund trustees, who ultimately bear fiduciary responsibility for the fund's viability, that the investment program is being conducted in an appropriate and effective manner.

Fund sponsors are venturing into nontraditional asset categories and hiring a larger assortment of managers exhibiting unique investment styles, with the addition of hedge fund managers representing the latest and perhaps most complex example of this trend. Some fund sponsors are taking more investment decisions into their own hands, such as tactical asset allocation and style timing. Others are taking a quite different direction, giving their managers broad discretion to make asset allocation and security selection decisions. As a consequence of these developments, alert trustee boards are demanding more information from their investment staffs. The staffs, in turn, are seeking to better understand the extent of their own contributions and those of the funds' investment managers to the funds' investment results. The increased complexity of institutional investment management has brought a correspondingly greater need for sophisticated performance evaluation from the fund sponsor's perspective.

2.2 The Investment Manager's Perspective

Investment managers have various incentives to evaluate the performance of the portfolios that they manage for their clients. Virtually all fund sponsors insist that their managers offer some type of accounting of portfolio investment results. In many cases, performance evaluation conducted by the investment manager simply takes the form of reporting investment returns, perhaps presented alongside the returns of some designated benchmark. Other clients may insist on more sophisticated analyses, which the managers may produce in-house or acquire from a third party.

Some investment managers may seriously wish to investigate the effectiveness of various elements of their investment processes and examine the relative contributions of those elements. Managing investment portfolios involves a complex set of decision-making procedures. For example, an equity manager must make decisions about which stocks to hold, when to transact in those stocks, how much to allocate to various economic sectors, and how to allocate funds between stocks and cash. Numerous analysts and portfolio managers may be involved in determining a portfolio's composition. Just as in the case of the fund sponsor, performance evaluation can serve as a feedback and control loop, helping to monitor the proficiency of various aspects of the portfolio construction process.

3 THE THREE COMPONENTS OF PERFORMANCE EVALUATION

In light of the subject's importance to fund sponsors and investment managers alike, we want to consider the primary questions that performance evaluation seeks to address. In discussing performance evaluation we shall use the term "account" to refer generically to one or more portfolios of securities, managed by one or more investment management organizations. Thus, at one end of the spectrum, an account might indicate a single portfolio invested by a single manager. At the other end, an account could mean a fund sponsor's total fund, which might involve numerous portfolios invested by many different managers across multiple asset categories. In between, it might include all of a fund sponsor's assets in a particular asset category or the aggregate of all of the portfolios managed by an investment manager according to a particular mandate. The basic performance evaluation concepts are the same, regardless of the account's composition.

With the definition of an account in mind, three questions naturally arise in examining the investment performance of an account:

1 What was the account's performance?
2 Why did the account produce the observed performance?
3 Is the account's performance due to luck or skill?

In somewhat simplistic terms, these questions constitute the three primary issues of performance evaluation. The first issue is addressed by performance measurement, which calculates rates of return based on investment-related changes in an account's value over specified time periods. Performance attribution deals with the second issue. It extends the results of performance measurement to investigate both the sources of the account's performance relative to a specific investment benchmark and the importance of those sources. Finally, performance appraisal tackles the third question. It attempts to draw conclusions concerning the quality (that is, the magnitude and consistency) of the account's relative performance.

PERFORMANCE MEASUREMENT

4

To many investors, performance measurement and performance evaluation are synonymous. However, according to our classification, performance measurement is a component of performance evaluation. Performance measurement is the relatively simple procedure of calculating returns for an account. Performance evaluation, on the other hand, encompasses the broader and much more complex task of placing those investment results in the context of the account's investment objectives.

Performance measurement is the first step in the performance evaluation process. Yet it is a critical step, because to be of value, performance evaluation requires accurate and timely rate-of-return information. Therefore, we must fully understand how to compute an account's returns before advancing to more involved performance evaluation issues.

4.1 Performance Measurement without Intraperiod External Cash Flows

The rate of return on an account is the percentage change in the account's market value over some defined period of time (the evaluation period), after accounting for all external cash flows.[1] (External cash flows refer to contributions and withdrawals made to and from an account, as opposed to internal cash flows such as dividends and interest payments.) Therefore, a rate of return measures the relative change in the account's value due solely to investment-related sources, namely capital appreciation or depreciation and income. The mere addition or subtraction of assets to or from the account by the account's owner should not affect the rate of return. Of course, in the simplest case, the account would experience no external cash flows. In that situation, the account's rate of return during evaluation period t equals the market value (MV_1) at the end of the period less the market value at the beginning of the period (MV_0), divided by the beginning market value.[2] That is,

$$r_t = \frac{MV_1 - MV_0}{MV_0} \tag{1}$$

Example 1 illustrates the use of Equation 1.

---

1 The evaluation period in this sense can also be called the measurement period.
2 From the fund sponsor's perspective, the account's market value should reflect the impact of all fees and expenses associated with investing the account's assets. Many managers report the return on accounts that they manage without including the effect of various fees and expenses. This practice is often justified based on the fact that fees vary among clients.

EXAMPLE 1

Rate-of-Return Calculations When There Are No External Cash Flows

Winter Asset Management manages institutional and individual accounts, including the account of the Mientkiewicz family. The Mientkiewicz account was initially valued at $1,000,000. One month later it was worth $1,080,000. Assuming no external cash flows and the reinvestment of all income, applying Equation 1, the return on the Mientkiewicz account for the month is

$$r_t = \frac{\$1,080,000 - \$1,000,000}{\$1,000,000} = 8.0\%$$

Fund sponsors occasionally (and in some cases frequently) add and subtract cash to and from their managers' accounts. These external cash flows complicate rate-of-return calculations. The rate-of-return algorithm must deal not only with the investment earnings on the initial assets in the account, but also with the earnings on any additional assets added to or subtracted from the account during the evaluation period. At the same time, the algorithm must exclude the direct impact of the external cash flows on the account's value.

An account's rate of return may still be computed in a straightforward fashion if the external cash flows occur at the beginning or the end of the measurement period when the account is valued. If a contribution is received at the start of the period, it should be added to (or, in the case of a withdrawal, subtracted from) the account's beginning value when calculating the account's rate of return for that period. The external cash flow will be invested alongside the rest of the account for the full length of the evaluation period and will have the same investment-related impact on the account's ending market value and, hence, should receive a full weighting. Thus, the account's return in the presence of an external cash flow at the beginning of the evaluation period should be calculated as

$$r_t = \frac{MV_1 - (MV_0 + CF)}{MV_0 + CF} \tag{2}$$

If a contribution is received at the end of the evaluation period, it should be subtracted from (or, in the case of a withdrawal, added to) the account's ending value. The external cash flow had no opportunity to affect the investment-related value of the account, and hence, it should be ignored.

$$r_t = \frac{(MV_1 - CF) - MV_0}{MV_0} \tag{3}$$

EXAMPLE 2

Rate-of-Return Calculations When External Cash Flows Occur at the Beginning or End of an Evaluation Period

Returning to the example of the Mientkiewicz account, assume that the account received a $50,000 contribution at the beginning of the month. Further, the account's ending and beginning market values equal the same amounts previously stated, $1,080,000 and $1,000,000, respectively. Applying Equation 2, the rate of return for the month is therefore

$$r_t = \frac{\$1{,}080{,}000 - (\$1{,}000{,}000 + \$50{,}000)}{\$1{,}000{,}000 + \$50{,}000} = 2.86\%$$

If the contribution had occurred at month-end, using Equation 3, the account's return would be

$$r_t = \frac{(\$1{,}080{,}000 - \$50{,}000) - \$1{,}000{,}000}{\$1{,}000{,}000} = 3.00\%$$

Both returns are less than the 8% return reported when no external cash flows took place because we are holding the ending account value fixed at $1,080,000. In the case of the beginning-of-period contribution, the account achieves an ending value of $1,080,000 on a beginning value that is higher than in Example 1, so its return must be less than 8%. In the case of the end-of-period contribution, the return is lower than 8% because the ending value of $1,080,000 is assumed to reflect an end-of-period contribution that is removed in calculating the return. In both instances, a portion of the account's change in value from $1,000,000 to $1,080,000 resulted from the contribution; in Example 1, by contrast, the change in value resulted entirely from positive investment performance by the account.[3]

The ease and accuracy of calculating returns when external cash flows occur, if those flows take place at the beginning or end of an evaluation period, lead to an important practical recommendation: Whenever possible, a fund sponsor should make contributions to, or withdrawals from, an account at the end of an evaluation period (or equivalently, the beginning of the next evaluation period) when the account is valued. In the case of accounts that are valued on a daily basis, the issue is trivial. However, despite the increasing prevalence of daily valued accounts, many accounts are still valued on an audited basis once a month (or possibly less frequently), and the owners of those accounts should be aware of the potential for rate-of-return distortions caused by intraperiod external cash flows.

What does happen when external cash flows occur between the beginning and the end of an evaluation period? The simple comparison of the account's value relative to the account's beginning value must be abandoned in favor of more intricate methods.

4.2 Total Rate of Return

Interestingly, widely accepted solutions to the problem of measuring returns in the presence of intraperiod external cash flows are relatively recent developments. Prior to the 1960s, the issue received little attention, largely because the prevailing performance measures were unaffected by such flows. Performance was typically measured on an income-only basis, thus excluding the impact of capital appreciation. For example, current yield (income-to-price) and yield-to-maturity were commonly quoted return measures.

3 Note that the account's reported return was lower when the contribution took place at the start of the month than at the end. This result occurs because the account had both a positive return and proportionately more assets to invest over the month when the contribution was received at the beginning as opposed to the end. If the account's return had been negative, then, given the same ending value, a contribution at the beginning of the month would have resulted in a less negative reported return than would have resulted from a contribution that occurred at the end of the month.

The emphasis on income-related return measures was due to several factors:

- *Portfolio management emphasis on fixed-income assets.* Particularly in the low-volatility interest rate environment that existed prior to the late 1970s, bond prices tended to be stable. Generally high allocations to fixed-income assets made income the primary source of investment-related wealth production for many investors.

- *Limited computing power.* Accurately accounting for external cash flows when calculating rates of return that include capital appreciation requires the use of computers. Access to the necessary computing resources was not readily available. The income-related return measures were simpler and could be performed by hand.

- *Less competitive investment environment.* Investors, as a whole, were less sophisticated and less demanding of accurate performance measures.

As portfolio allocations to equity securities increased, as computing costs declined, and as investors (particularly larger institutional investors) came to focus more intently on the performance of their portfolios, the demand grew for rate-of-return measures that correctly incorporated all aspects of an account's investment-related increase in wealth. This demand led to the adoption of total rate of return as the generally accepted measure of investment performance.

Total rate of return measures the increase in the investor's wealth due to both investment income (for example, dividends and interest) and capital gains (both realized and unrealized). The total rate of return implies that a dollar of wealth is equally meaningful to the investor whether that wealth is generated by the secure income from a 90-day Treasury bill or by the unrealized appreciation in the price of a share of common stock.

Acceptance of the total rate of return as the primary measure of investment performance was assured by a seminal study performed in 1968 by the Bank Administration Institute (BAI). The BAI study (which we refer to again shortly) was the first comprehensive research conducted on the issue of performance measurement. Among its many important contributions, the study strongly endorsed the use of the total rate of return as the only valid measure of investment performance. For our purposes, henceforth, it will be assumed that rate of return refers to the total rate of return, unless otherwise specified.

4.3 The Time-Weighted Rate of Return

We now return to considering the calculation of rates of return in the context of intraperiod external cash flows. To fully appreciate the issue at hand, we must think clearly about the meaning of "rate of return." In essence, the rate of return on an account is the investment-related growth rate in the account's value over the evaluation period. However, we can envision this growth rate being applied to a single dollar invested in the account at the start of the evaluation period or to an "average" amount of dollars invested in the account over the evaluation period. This subtle but important distinction leads to two different measures: the time-weighted and the money-weighted rates of return.

The **time-weighted rate of return** (TWR) reflects the compound rate of growth over a stated evaluation period of one unit of money initially invested in the account. Its calculation requires that the account be valued every time an external cash flow occurs. If no such flows take place, then the calculation of the TWR is trivial; it is simply the application of Equation 1, in which the change in the account's value is expressed relative to its beginning value. If external cash flows do occur, then the TWR requires computing a set of subperiod returns (with the number of subperiods equaling one plus the number of dates on which external cash flows occur). These subperiod returns must then be linked together in computing the TWR for the entire evaluation period.

EXAMPLE 3

Calculating Subperiod Rates of Return

Returning again to the Mientkiewicz account, let us assume that the account received two cash flows during month t: a contribution of $30,000 on day 5 and a contribution of $20,000 on day 16. Further, assume that we use a daily pricing system that provides us with values of the Mientkiewicz account (inclusive of the contributions) of $1,045,000 and $1,060,000 on days 5 and 16 of the month, respectively. We can then calculate three separate subperiod returns using the rate-of-return computation applicable to situations when external cash flows occur at the end of an evaluation period, as given by Equation 3:

Subperiod 1 = Days 1–5

Subperiod 2 = Days 6–16

Subperiod 3 = Days 17–30

For subperiod 1:

$$r_{t,1} = \left[(\$1,045,000 - \$30,000) - \$1,000,000 \right] / \$1,000,000$$

$$= 0.0150$$

$$= 1.50\%$$

For subperiod 2:

$$r_{t,2} = \left[(\$1,060,000 - \$20,000) - \$1,045,000 \right] / \$1,045,000$$

$$= -0.0048$$

$$= -0.48\%$$

For subperiod 3:

$$r_{t,3} = (\$1,080,000 - \$1,060,000) / \$1,060,000$$

$$= 0.0189$$

$$= 1.89\%$$

The subperiod returns can be combined through a process called **chain-linking**. Chain-linking involves first adding 1 to the (decimal) rate of return for each subperiod to create a set of wealth relatives. A **wealth relative** can be thought of as the ending value of one unit of money (for example, one dollar) invested at each subperiod's rate of return. Next, the wealth relatives are multiplied together to produce a cumulative wealth relative for the full period, and 1 is subtracted from the result to obtain the TWR. Note that this process of chain-linking implicitly assumes that the initially invested dollar and earnings on that dollar are reinvested (or compounded) from one subperiod to the next. The cumulative wealth relative from the chain-linking of the subperiod wealth relatives can be interpreted as the ending value of one dollar invested in the account at the beginning of the evaluation period. Subtracting 1 from this wealth relative produces the TWR for the account:

$$r_{\text{twr}} = (1 + r_{t,1}) \times (1 + r_{t,2}) \times \ldots \times (1 + r_{t,n}) - 1 \tag{4}$$

Note that unless the subperiods constitute a year, the time-weighted rate of return will not be expressed as an annual rate. Example 4 illustrates the calculation of a time-weighted rate of return.

EXAMPLE 4

Calculating the TWR

Continuing with the Mientkiewicz account, its TWR is

$$r_{twr} = (1 + 0.0150) \times (1 + -0.0048) \times (1 + 0.0189) - 1$$
$$= 0.0292$$
$$= 2.92\%$$

The TWR derives its name from the fact that each subperiod return within the full evaluation period receives a weight proportional to the length of the subperiod relative to the length of the full evaluation period. That relationship becomes apparent if each subperiod return is expressed as the cumulative return over smaller time units. In the Mientkiewicz account example, the return in the first subperiod is 0.015 over five days. On a daily compounded basis that return is 0.0030 [= $(1 + 0.015)^{1/5} - 1$]. Performing the same calculation for the other two subperiods yields the following:

$$r_{twr} = (1 + 0.0030)^5 \times (1 + -0.0004)^{11} \times (1 + 0.0013)^{14} - 1$$
$$= 0.0292 = 2.92\% \text{ (allowing for rounding)}$$

From this expression for the TWR, we can see that the subperiods 1, 2, and 3 receive compounding "weights" of 5/30, 11/30, and 14/30, respectively.

4.4 The Money-Weighted Rate of Return

The **money-weighted rate of return** (MWR) measures the compound growth rate in the value of all funds invested in the account over the evaluation period. In the corporate finance literature, the MWR goes by the name **internal rate of return**, or IRR. Of importance for performance measurement, the MWR is the growth rate that will link the ending value of the account to its beginning value plus all intermediate cash flows. With MV_1 and MV_0 the values of the account at the end and beginning of the evaluation period, respectively, in equation form the MWR is the growth rate R that solves

$$MV_1 = MV_0(1 + R)^m + CF_1(1 + R)^{m-L(1)} + \ldots + CF_n(1 + R)^{m-L(n)} \qquad (5)$$

where

> m = number of time units in the evaluation period (for example, the number of days in the month)
>
> CF_i = the ith cash flow
>
> $L(i)$ = number of time units by which the ith cash flow is separated from the beginning of the evaluation period

Note that R is expressed as the return per unit of time composing the evaluation period. For example, in the case of monthly performance measurement, where the constituent time unit is one day, R would be the daily MWR of the account. Extending this thought, $[(1 + R)^m - 1]$ can be seen to be the account's MWR for the entire evaluation period, as $(1 + R)^m = (1 + r_{mwr})$. Therefore, in the case of no external cash flows, with some algebraic manipulation, Equation 5 reduces to Equation 1, the simple expression for rate of return:

$$MV_1 = MV_0(1 + R)^m + 0$$

$$(1 + R)^m = MV_1/MV_0$$

$$(1 + r_{mwr}) = MV_1/MV_0$$

$$r_{mwr} = (MV_1 - MV_0)/MV_0$$

$$= r_t$$

EXAMPLE 5

Calculating the MWR

Consider the Mientkiewicz account again. Its MWR is found by solving the following equation for R:

$$\$1,080,000 = \$1,000,000(1 + R)^{30} + \$30,000(1 + R)^{30-5}$$
$$+ \$20,000(1 + R)^{30-16}$$

There exists no closed-form solution for R. That is, Equation 5 cannot be manipulated to isolate R on the left-hand side. Consequently, R must be solved iteratively through a trial-and-error process. In our example, we begin with an initial guess of $R = 0.001$. The right-hand side of the equation becomes \$1,081,480. Thus our initial guess is too high and must be lowered. Next try a value $R = 0.0007$. In this case the right-hand side now equals \$1,071,941. Therefore our second guess is too low.

We can continue this process. Eventually, we will arrive at the correct value for R, which for the Mientkiewicz account is 0.0009536. Remember that this value is the Mientkiewicz account's daily rate of return during the month. Expressed on a monthly basis, the MWR is 0.0290 [$= (1 + 0.0009536)^{30} - 1$], or 2.90%.

As one might expect, a computer is best suited to perform the repetitious task of calculating the MWR. Spreadsheet software to perform these computations is readily available.

4.5 TWR versus MWR

The MWR represents the average growth rate of all money invested in an account, while the TWR represents the growth of a single unit of money invested in the account. Consequently, the MWR is sensitive to the size and timing of external cash flows to and from the account, while the TWR is unaffected by these flows. Under "normal" conditions, these two return measures will produce similar results. In the example of the Mientkiewicz account, the MWR was 2.90% for the month and the TWR was 2.92%.

However, when external cash flows occur that are large relative to the account's value and the account's performance is fluctuating significantly during the measurement period, then the MWR and the TWR can differ materially.

EXAMPLE 6

When TWR and MWR Differ

Consider the Charlton account, worth $800,000 at the beginning of the month. On day 10 it is valued at $1,800,000 after receiving a $1,000,000 contribution. At the end of the month, the account is worth $3,000,000. As a result, the Charlton account's MWR is 87.5%, while its TWR is only 66.7%.

For subperiod 1:

$$r_{t,1} = \left[(\$1,800,000 - \$1,000,000) - \$800,000 \right] / \$800,000$$

$$= 0.0 \text{ or } 0\%$$

For subperiod 2:

$$r_{t,2} = (\$3,000,000 - \$1,800,000) / \$1,800,000$$

$$= 0.6667 \text{ or } 66.7\%$$

Then

$$r_{\text{twr}} = (1 + 0) \times (1 + 0.667) - 1$$

$$= 0.667 \text{ or } 66.7\%$$

For MWR, we need to solve

$$\$3,000,000 = \$800,000(1 + R)^{30} + \$1,000,000(1 + R)^{30-10}$$

By trial and error, R comes out to be 0.020896. Expressed on a monthly basis, MWR is 0.859709 or 86.0% [$= (1 + 0.020896)^{30} - 1$].

If funds are contributed to an account prior to a period of strong performance (as in the case of the Charlton account in Example 6), then the MWR will be positively affected compared to the TWR, as a relatively large sum is invested at a high growth rate. That is, in the case of the Charlton account, a contribution was made just prior to a subperiod in which a dollar invested in the account earned 66.7%. In the prior subperiod the account earned 0.0%. Thus, on average, the account had more dollars invested earning 66.7% than it had dollars earning 0.0%, resulting in an MWR greater than the TWR. Conversely, if funds are withdrawn from the account prior to the strong performance, then the MWR will be adversely affected relative to the TWR. (The opposite conclusions hold if the external cash flow occurred prior to a period of weak performance.)

As noted, the TWR is unaffected by external cash flow activity. Valuing the account at the time of each external cash flow effectively removes the impact of those flows on the TWR. Consequently, the TWR accurately reflects how an investor would have fared over the evaluation period if he or she had placed funds in the account at the beginning of the period.

In most situations, an investment manager has little or no control over the size and timing of external cash flows into or out of his or her accounts. Therefore, practitioners generally prefer a rate-of-return measure that is not sensitive to cash flows if they want to evaluate how a manager's investment actions have affected an account's value. This consideration led the authors of the Bank Administration Institute study to recommend that the TWR be adopted as the appropriate measure of account performance. That recommendation has received almost universal acceptance since the study's publication. (Note that the Global Investment Performance Standards [GIPS®] generally require a TWR methodology.)

However, one can readily conceive of situations in which the MWR may prove useful in evaluating the returns achieved by an investment manager. The most obvious examples are those situations in which the investment manager maintains control over the timing and amount of cash flows into the account. Managers of various types of private equity investments typically operate under arrangements that permit them to call capital from their investors at the managers' discretion and ultimately to determine when the original capital, and any earnings on that capital, will be returned to investors. In these "opportunistic" situations, it is generally agreed that the MWR is the more appropriate measure of account returns.[4]

4.6 The Linked Internal Rate of Return

Despite its useful characteristics, the TWR does have an important disadvantage: It requires account valuations on every date that an external cash flow takes place. Thus, calculation of the TWR typically necessitates the ability to price a portfolio of securities on a daily basis. Although daily pricing services are becoming more common, marking an account to market daily is administratively more expensive and cumbersome, and potentially more error-prone, than traditional monthly accounting procedures. For these reasons, use of pure TWR is not yet standard practice, with the prominent exception of the mutual fund industry.[5] The MWR, on the other hand, despite its sensitivity to the size and timing of external cash flows, requires only that an account be valued at the beginning and end of the evaluation period and that the amounts and dates of any external cash flows be recorded.

The complementary advantages and disadvantages of the TWR and the MWR led the authors of the BAI study to make an important recommendation: The TWR should be approximated by calculating the MWR over reasonably frequent time intervals and then chain-linking those returns over the entire evaluation period. This process is referred to as the Linked Internal Rate of Return (LIRR) method and originally was developed by Peter Dietz (1966). The BAI study estimated that if the LIRR method were applied to an account experiencing "normal" cash flow activity, then using monthly valuations and daily dating of external cash flows, the calculated rate of return on average would fall within 4 basis points per year of the true TWR.[6] Given the inaccuracies inherent in the pricing of even the most liquid portfolios, this slight difference appears immaterial.

EXAMPLE 7

An Example of LIRR

Suppose, in a given month, the Mientkiewicz account's MWR is calculated each week. These MWRs are 0.021 in week 1, 0.0016 in week 2, −0.014 in week 3, and 0.018 in week 4. The LIRR is obtained by linking these rates:

$$R_{LIRR} = (1 + 0.021) \times (1 + 0.0016) \times (1 + -0.014)$$
$$\times (1 + 0.018) - 1$$
$$= 0.0265 \text{ or } 2.65\%$$

4 For a discussion of the use of the MWR as a performance measure for opportunistic investments, see Tierney and Bailey (1997).
5 Nevertheless, for periods beginning 1 January 2010, firms will be required to value portfolios on the date of all large external cash flows to claim compliance with the GIPS standards. In the interim, the GIPS standards admit the use of acceptable daily weighted methods for estimating the time-weighted rate of return. These methods are presented in the reading on Global Investment Performance Standards.
6 Bank Administration Institute (1968), p. 22.

The BAI study concluded that only under unusual circumstances would the LIRR fail to provide an acceptable representation of the TWR. Specifically, the LIRR would fail if both large external cash flows (generally over 10% of the account's value) and volatile swings in subperiod performance occurred during the evaluation period. With an evaluation period as short as one month, the chances of such a joint event occurring for an account are low. Nevertheless, if it should happen, the BAI study recommended valuing the account on the date of the intramonth cash flow.

4.7 Annualized Return

For comparison purposes, rates of return are typically reported on an annualized basis. As defined here, the annualized return represents the compound average annual return earned by the account over the evaluation period. The calculation is also known as the compound growth rate or geometric mean return. An annualized return is computed by employing the same chain-linking method used to calculate linked internal rates of return, except that the product of the linking is raised to the reciprocal of the number of years covering the evaluation period (or equivalently, taking the appropriate root of the linked product, where the root is the number of years in the measurement period).

EXAMPLE 8

Annualized Return

If in years 1, 2, and 3 of a three-year evaluation period an account earned 2.0%, 9.5%, and −4.7%, respectively, then the annualized return for the evaluation period would be

$$r_a = \left[(1 + 0.02) \times (1 + 0.095) \times (1 - 0.047)\right]^{1/3} - 1$$
$$= 0.021 \text{ or } 2.1\%$$

If twelve quarterly returns had been available for the account instead of three yearly returns, then those quarterly returns would have been similarly linked and the cube root of the product would have been calculated to produce the account's annualized return over the three-year period.

In general, with measurement periods shorter than a full year, it is inadvisable to calculate annualized returns. Essentially, the person calculating returns is extrapolating the account's returns over a sample period to the full year. Particularly for equity accounts, returns can fluctuate significantly during the remaining time in the evaluation period, making the annualized return a potentially unrealistic estimate of the account's actual return over the full year.

4.8 Data Quality Issues

The performance measurement process is only as accurate as the inputs to the process. Often performance report users fail to distinguish between rates of return of high and low reliability. In the case of accounts invested in liquid and transparently priced securities and experiencing little external cash flow activity, the reported rates of return are likely to be highly reliable performance indicators. They will accurately reflect the experience of an investor who entered such an account at the beginning of the evaluation period and liquidated his or her investment at the end of the period. Conversely, for accounts invested in illiquid and infrequently priced assets, the underlying valuations may be suspect, thereby invalidating the reported rates of return. For example, due to the inaccuracy inherent in estimation techniques, quarterly valuations of venture capital funds typically have limited economic content. An investor may not be able to enter or leave the account at a value anywhere near the reported valuations. As a result, monthly or even annual performance measurement of such funds should be viewed with caution.

Various services exist that collect data on recent market transactions for a wide range of fixed-income and equity securities. Particularly for many thinly traded fixed-income securities, a current market price may not always be available. In that case, estimated prices may be derived based on dealer-quoted prices for securities with similar attributes (for example, a security with a similar credit rating, maturity, and economic sector). This approach is referred to as **matrix pricing**. For highly illiquid securities, reasonable estimates of market prices may be difficult or impossible to obtain. Investment managers may carry these securities at cost or the price of the last trade in those securities. It is outside the scope of this discussion to address in detail the subject of account valuation. Suffice it to say that *caveat emptor*—"let the buyer beware"—should be the motto of any user of performance measurement reports who deals with securities other than liquid stocks and bonds.

In addition to obtaining accurate account valuations and external cash flow recognition, reliable performance measurement requires appropriate data collection procedures. For example, account valuations should be reported on a trade-date, fully accrued basis. That is, the stated value of the account should reflect the impact of any unsettled trades and any income owed by or to the account but not yet paid. Such a valuation process correctly represents the best available statement of the account's position at a point in time. Other methods, such as settlement date accounting and the exclusion of accrued income, incorrectly reflect the account's market value.

BENCHMARKS

5

Performance evaluation cannot be conducted in a vacuum. By its nature, performance evaluation is a relative concept. Absolute performance numbers mean little. Even so-called "absolute return" managers should provide some sense of how alternative uses of their clients' money would have performed if exposed to similar risks. Consider how one interprets a 7% return on a well-diversified common stock portfolio during a given month. If you knew that the broad stock market had declined 15% during the month, you might be impressed. Conversely, if the market had advanced 25%, you might be disappointed. If we are to conduct meaningful performance evaluation, then we must develop an appropriate benchmark against which an account's performance can be compared.

5.1 Concept of a Benchmark

The Merriam-Webster Dictionary defines a benchmark as a "standard or point of reference in measuring or judging quality, value, etc." Applying this general definition to investment management, a benchmark is a collection of securities or risk factors and associated weights that represents the persistent and prominent investment characteristics of an asset category or manager's investment process. At the asset category level, we can think of a benchmark as the collection of securities that the fund sponsor would own if the fund sponsor were required to place all of its investments within the asset category in a single, passively managed portfolio. (In other words, the benchmark is the fund sponsor's preferred index fund for the asset category.) At the manager level, we can think of a benchmark as a passive representation of the manager's investment style, incorporating the salient investment features (such as significant exposures to particular sources of systematic risk) that consistently appear in the manager's portfolios. More metaphorically, a manager's benchmark encompasses the manager's "area" of expertise. Just as an angler has a favorite fishing hole, an investment manager also has distinct preferences for certain types of securities and risk exposures. The opportunity set that represents the manager's area of expertise may be broad or narrow, reflecting the resources and investment processes that the manager brings to bear on the portfolio selection problem.

A little algebra succinctly conveys these concepts. Begin with the simple identity of an investment manager's portfolio; that is, any portfolio is equal to itself:[7]

$$P = P$$

Now, consider an appropriately selected benchmark B. If we add and subtract B from the right-hand side of this identity, effectively adding a zero to the relationship, the result is

$$P = B + (P - B)$$

Additionally, if we define the manager's active investment judgments as being the difference between the manager's portfolio P and the benchmark B so that $A = (P - B)$, then the equation just given becomes

$$P = B + A \qquad \text{(6)}$$

Thus, the managed portfolio P can be viewed as a combination of 1) the benchmark B and 2) active management decisions A composed of a set of over-and underweighted positions in securities relative to the benchmark. We can extend this relationship by introducing a market index M. Adding and subtracting M from the right-hand side of Equation 6 gives

$$P = M + (B - M) + A$$

The difference between the manager's benchmark portfolio and the market index $(B - M)$ can be defined as the manager's investment style S. If we let $S = (B - M)$, then the equation just given becomes

$$P = M + S + A \qquad \text{(7)}$$

Equation 7 states that a portfolio has three components: market, style, and active management.

There are several interesting applications of Equation 7. First, note that if the portfolio is a broad market index fund, then $S = (B - M) = 0$ (that is, no style biases) and $A = (P - B) = 0$ (that is, no active management). Consequently, Equation 7 reduces to $P = M$; the portfolio is equivalent to the market index.

Second, if we define the benchmark as the market index [that is, $S = (B - M) = 0$, or no style], then Equation 7 reduces to Equation 6 and substituting M for B gives

$$P = M + A$$

Because many managers and fund sponsors have been willing to define a manager's benchmark as a broad market index (for example, the S&P 500 in the case of US common stock managers), both parties are implicitly stating that they believe that the manager has no distinct investment style. However, most practitioners would agree that the vast majority of managers pursue specific investment styles. Specialization

---

7 The variables used in this section can be interpreted as either rates of return or weights assigned to securities that make up a portfolio.

has become the hallmark of our postindustrial society, and it should not be surprising that, with respect to a subject as complex as portfolio management, many managers have chosen to focus their skills on certain segments of that subject.

EXAMPLE 9

Returns Due to Style and Active Management

Suppose the Mientkiewicz account earns a total return of 3.6% in a given month, during which the portfolio benchmark has a return of 3.8% and the market index has a return of 2.8%. Then the return due to the portfolio manager's style is

$$S = B - M = 3.8\% - 2.8\% = 1\%$$

and the return due to active management is

$$A = P - B = 3.6\% - 3.8\% = -0.2\%$$

5.2 Properties of a Valid Benchmark

Although in practice an acceptable benchmark is simply one that both the manager and the fund sponsor agree fairly represents the manager's investment process, to function effectively in performance evaluation, a benchmark should possess certain basic properties. A valid benchmark is:

- **Unambiguous**. The identities and weights of securities or factor exposures constituting the benchmark are clearly defined.

- **Investable**. It is possible to forgo active management and simply hold the benchmark.

- **Measurable**. The benchmark's return is readily calculable on a reasonably frequent basis.

- **Appropriate**. The benchmark is consistent with the manager's investment style or area of expertise.

- **Reflective of current investment opinions**. The manager has current investment knowledge (be it positive, negative, or neutral) of the securities or factor exposures within the benchmark.

- **Specified in advance**. The benchmark is specified prior to the start of an evaluation period and known to all interested parties.

- **Owned**. The investment manager should be aware of and accept accountability for the constituents and performance of the benchmark. It is encouraged that the benchmark be embedded in and integral to the investment process and procedures of the investment manager.

The failure of a benchmark to possess these properties compromises its utility as an effective investment management tool. A benchmark represents an equivalent risk opportunity cost to the fund sponsor. The properties listed merely formalize intuitive notions of what constitutes a fair and relevant performance comparison. It is interesting to observe that a number of commonly used benchmarks fail to satisfy these properties.

5.3 Types of Benchmarks

At the investment manager level, a benchmark forms the basis of a covenant between the manager and the fund sponsor. It reflects the investment style that the fund sponsor expects the manager to pursue, and it becomes the basis for evaluating the success of the manager's investment management efforts. Many different benchmarks may satisfy the criteria for an acceptable benchmark and, if agreed upon by both parties, could be implemented. In general, there are seven primary types of benchmarks in use.

Absolute   An absolute return can be a return objective. Examples include an actuarial rate-of-return assumption or a minimum return target which the fund strives to exceed. Unfortunately, absolute return objectives are not investable alternatives and do not satisfy the benchmark validity criteria.[8]

Manager Universes   Consultants and fund sponsors frequently use the median manager or fund from a broad universe of managers or funds as a performance evaluation benchmark. As discussed in more detail later, a median manager benchmark fails all the tests of benchmark validity except for being measurable.

Broad Market Indexes   Many managers and fund sponsors use **broad market indexes** as benchmarks. Prominent examples of broad market indexes used by US investors include the S&P 500, Wilshire 5000, and Russell 3000 indexes for US common stocks; the Lehman Aggregate and the Citigroup Broad Investment-Grade (US BIG) Bond Indexes[9] for US investment-grade debt; and the Morgan Stanley Capital International (MSCI) Europe, Australasia, and Far East (EAFE) Index for non-US developed-market common stocks. Market indexes are well recognized, easy to understand, and widely available, and satisfy several properties of valid benchmarks. They are unambiguous, generally investable, and measurable, and they may be specified in advance. In certain situations, market indexes are perfectly acceptable as benchmarks, particularly as benchmarks for asset category performance or for "core" type investment approaches in which the manager selects from a universe of securities similar in composition to the benchmark. However, in other circumstances, the manager's style may deviate considerably from the style reflected in a market index. For example, assigning a micro-capitalization US growth stock manager an S&P 500 benchmark clearly violates the appropriateness criterion.

Style Indexes   Broad market indexes have been increasingly partitioned to create **investment style indexes** that represent specific portions of an asset category: for example, subgroups within the US common stock asset category. Four popular US common stock style indexes are 1) large-capitalization growth, 2) large-capitalization value, 3) small-capitalization growth, and 4) small-capitalization value. (Mid-capitalization growth and value common stock indexes are also available.) The Frank Russell Company,

---

8 As we have used the term, a benchmark is a means to differentiate managers or fund sponsors who add value through investment insights from those who do not. In this sense, a sponsor's liabilities may also be treated as a type of benchmark. That is, institutional investors such as defined-benefit pension plan sponsors and endowment and foundation executives seek to achieve rates of return enabling them, at a minimum, to meet liabilities as they come due without making greater-than-planned additions to fund assets. (Another way to express this financial objective is to say that institutional investors seek at least to maintain a stated level of fund surplus, defined as the present value of assets less the present value of liabilities.) In terms of asset-liability management, or surplus management, the fund's investment objective may be to achieve a rate of return on assets that meets or exceeds the "return" on liabilities—that is, the percentage change in the present value of the liabilities over the evaluation period. Moreover, because a liability, or a stream of liabilities, may be considered a financial asset held short, it is possible, in principle, to construct a custom index representing the fund's liabilities and to use that index as a benchmark at the level of the total fund.
9 Barclays has acquired Lehman Brothers and will maintain the family of Lehman Brothers indices and the associated index calculation, publication, and analytical infrastructure and tools.

Standard & Poor's, and Morgan Stanley Capital International produce the most widely used US common stock style indexes. International common stock style indexes are more recent developments.

Fixed-income style indexes are produced in a similar manner. In many ways, investment-grade bonds are a more convenient asset category for developing style indexes, because the broad market indexes are easily segregated into various types of securities. For example, broad bond market indexes, such as the Lehman Aggregate for US debt, can be broken up into their constituent parts, such as the Lehman Government/Credit Index, the Lehman Mortgage Index, and so on. The Lehman Aggregate can also be decomposed along the lines of maturity (or duration) and quality.

Similar to broad market indexes, investment style indexes are often well known, easy to understand, and widely available. However, their ability to pass tests of benchmark validity can be problematic. Some style indexes contain weightings in certain securities and economic sectors that are much larger than what many managers consider prudent. Further, the definition of investment style implied in the benchmark may be ambiguous or inconsistent with the investment process of the manager being evaluated. Differing definitions of investment style at times can produce rather extreme return differentials. In 1999, the S&P Large Value Index had a return of 12.72%, and the Russell Large Value Index had a return of 7.35%. These large return differences among indexes presumably designed to represent the results of the same investment style are disconcerting. Users of style indexes should closely examine how the indexes are constructed and assess their applicability to specific managers.

Factor-Model-Based   Factor models provide a means of relating one or more systematic sources of return to the returns on an account.[10] As a result, a specified set of factor exposures could potentially be used as a **factor-model-based benchmark**. The simplest form of factor model is a one-factor model, such as the familiar **market model**. In that relationship, the return on a security, or a portfolio of securities, is expressed as a linear function of the return on a broad market index, established over a suitably long period (for example, 60 months):

$$R_p = a_p + \beta_p R_I + \varepsilon_p \tag{8}$$

where R_p represents the periodic return on an account and R_I represents the periodic return on the market index.[11] The market index is used as a proxy for the underlying systematic return factor (or factors). The term ε_p is the residual, or nonsystematic, element of the relationship. The term β_p measures the sensitivity of the returns on the account to the returns on the market index; it is typically estimated by regressing the account's returns on those of the market index. The sensitivity term is called the beta of the account. Finally, the intercept a_p is the "zero factor" term, representing the expected value of R_p if the factor value was zero.

---

10 Factor models are discussed in DeFusco, McLeavey, Pinto, and Runkle (2004) as well as in standard investment textbooks such as Sharpe, Alexander, and Bailey (1999).

11 Although the market model has some resemblances to the capital asset pricing model (CAPM), the market model is not an equilibrium model of asset pricing, as is the CAPM. Under a set of specific assumptions, the CAPM states that investors will act in a manner that generates a unique relationship between the beta of a security or portfolio and the return on the market portfolio. Any security or portfolio with the same beta is expected to produce the same return. The market model, on the other hand, is an empirical relationship between the return on a security or portfolio and a particular market index (as opposed to the market portfolio). See Markowitz (1984) for a discussion of this distinction.

EXAMPLE 10

Returns from a Market Model

Consider an account with a zero-factor value of 2.0% and a beta of 1.5. Applying Equation 8, a return of 8% for the market index generates an expected return on the account of 14% (= 2.0% + 1.5 × 8%).

Some managers hold accounts that persistently display a beta greater than 1.0, while other managers hold accounts with betas persistently less than 1.0. Out of these patterns arises the concept of a benchmark with a "normal beta" consistent with these observed tendencies. For example, suppose that an analysis of past account returns, combined with discussions with the manager, suggests a normal beta of 1.2. This normal beta becomes the basis for the benchmark that specifies the level of return that the account would be expected to generate in the absence of any value added by active management on the part of the manager.

Incorporating multiple sources of systematic risk can enhance the richness of the factor model approach. That is, Equation 8 can be extended to include more than one factor. For example, a company's size, industry, growth characteristics, financial strength, and other factors may have a systematic impact on a portfolio's performance. Generalizing Equation 8 produces

$$R_p = a_p + b_1 F_1 + b_2 F_2 + \dots + b_K F_K + \varepsilon_p$$

where $F_1, F_2, \dots F_K$ represent the values of factors 1 through K, respectively. Numerous commercially available multifactor risk models have been produced. Rosenberg and Marathe (1975) pioneered the development of these models, and their work was extended to create performance evaluation benchmarks. The concept of a "normal beta" in a multifactor context leads to the concept of a normal portfolio. A **normal portfolio** is a portfolio with exposures to sources of systematic risk that are typical for a manager, using the manager's past portfolios as a guide.

Benchmarks based on factor exposures can be useful in performance evaluation. Because they capture the systematic sources of return that affect an account's performance, they help managers and fund sponsors better understand a manager's investment style. However, they are not always intuitive to the fund sponsor and particularly to the investment managers (who rarely think in terms of factor exposures when designing investment strategies), are not always easy to obtain, and are potentially expensive to use. In addition, they are ambiguous. We can build multiple benchmarks with the same factor exposures, but each benchmark can earn different returns. For example, we can construct two different portfolios, each with a beta of 1.2 ("normal beta"), but the portfolios can have materially different returns. Also, because the composition of a factor-based benchmark is not specified with respect to the constituent securities and their weights, we cannot verify all the validity criteria (the benchmark may not be investable, for example).

Returns-Based   Sharpe (1988, 1992) introduced the concept of **returns-based benchmarks**. These benchmarks are constructed using 1) the series of a manager's account returns (ideally, monthly returns going back in time as long as the investment process has been in place) and 2) the series of returns on several investment style indexes over the same period. These return series are then submitted to an allocation algorithm that solves for the combination of investment style indexes that most closely tracks the account's returns.[12]

For example, assume that we have ten years of monthly returns of a US equity mutual fund. Also, assume that we have the monthly returns of four US equity style indexes—1) large-cap growth, 2) large-cap value, 3) small-cap growth, and 4) small-cap value—over the same time period. If we submit these return series to a properly constructed allocation algorithm, we can solve for a particular set of allocation weights for the four style indexes that will track most closely the return series of the manager's actual portfolio. The returns-based benchmark is represented by these allocation weights.

Returns-based benchmarks are generally easy to use and are intuitively appealing. They satisfy most benchmark validity criteria, including those of being unambiguous, measurable, investable, and specified in advance. Returns-based benchmarks are particularly useful in situations where the only information available is account returns. One disadvantage of returns-based benchmarks is that, like the style indexes that underlie the benchmarks, they may hold positions in securities and economic sectors that a manager might find unacceptable. Further, they require many months of observation to establish a statistically reliable pattern of style exposures. In the case of managers who rotate among style exposures, such a pattern may be impossible to discern.

Custom Security-Based   An investment manager will typically follow an investment philosophy that causes the manager to focus its research activities on certain types of securities. The manager will select those securities that represent the most attractive investment opportunities that the research process has identified. As the financial and investment characteristics of securities will change over time, a manager's research universe will similarly evolve.

A **custom security-based benchmark** is simply a manager's research universe weighted in a particular fashion. Most managers do not use a security weighting scheme that is exactly an equal weighting across all securities or one that exactly assigns weights according to market capitalization. Consequently, a custom benchmark reflecting a particular manager's unique weighting approach can be more suitable than a published index for a fair and accurate appraisal of that manager's performance.

The overwhelming advantage of a custom security-based benchmark is that it meets all of the required benchmark properties and satisfies all of the benchmark validity criteria, making it arguably the most appropriate benchmark for performance evaluation purposes. In addition, it is a valuable tool for managers to monitor and control their investment processes and for fund sponsors to effectively allocate or budget risk across teams of investment managers. One major disadvantage is that custom security-based benchmarks are expensive to construct and maintain. In addition, as they are not composed of published indexes, the perception of a lack of transparency can be of concern.

5.4 Building Custom Security-Based Benchmarks

A valid custom security-based benchmark is the product of discussions between the client or the client's consultant and the manager and of a detailed analysis of the manager's past security holdings. The construction of such a benchmark involves the following steps:

- Identify prominent aspects of the manager's investment process.

---

12 The ability to track the account's returns is typically measured by the standard deviation of the monthly return differences of the account and the benchmark, called the tracking error.

- Select securities consistent with that investment process.
- Devise a weighting scheme for the benchmark securities, including a cash position.
- Review the preliminary benchmark and make modifications.
- Rebalance the benchmark portfolio on a predetermined schedule.

For the purpose of custom benchmark construction, an analysis of the manager's past portfolios will identify prominent aspects of the manager's investment process. The selection of benchmark portfolio securities requires both a broad universe of potential candidates and a set of screening criteria consistent with the manager's investment process. Weighting schemes may include aspects of equal weighting and capitalization weighting, depending on the manager's investment process and client restrictions. Following these steps, a preliminary benchmark portfolio is selected. At this point, the benchmark's composition is reviewed and final modifications are made. Ultimately, keeping the benchmark portfolio current with the manager's investment process necessitates rebalancing the portfolio at regularly scheduled intervals.

These steps, though simple in appearance, constitute a complex task. A proper benchmark must make a fine distinction between the manager's "normal" or policy investment decisions and the manager's active investment judgments. Considerable resources are required, including a comprehensive security database, an efficient computer screening capability, a flexible security weighting system, and a means of maintaining the integrity of the benchmark over time.

5.5 Critique of Manager Universes as Benchmarks

Fund sponsors have a natural interest in knowing how their investment results compare to those achieved by similar institutions and how the returns earned by the managers they have selected compare to those earned by managers they might have engaged. To facilitate peer group comparisons, some consulting firms and custodial banks have developed databases or "universes" of account returns ranked in descending order. Fund sponsors often use the median account in a particular peer group as a return benchmark. For instance, the investment policy statement of a public fund might specify that the fund's objective is to perform in the top half of a certain universe of public funds, and the guidelines for a domestic large-cap equity account might state that the manager's results are expected to exceed those of the median account in a certain universe consisting of portfolios with large-cap value mandates or characteristics.

With the exception of being measurable, the median account in a typical commercially available universe does not have the properties of a valid benchmark described above. One of the most significant deficiencies is that, although the universe can be named, the median account cannot be *specified in advance*. Universe compilers can only establish the median account on an *ex post* basis, after the returns earned by all accounts have been calculated and ranked. Prior to the start of an evaluation period, neither the manager nor the fund sponsor has any knowledge of who the median manager will be at period end. In addition, different accounts will fall at the median from one evaluation period to another. For these reasons, the benchmark is not *investable* and cannot serve as a passive alternative to holding the account that is under analysis. Even after the evaluation period concludes, the identity of the median manager typically remains unknown, preventing the benchmark from satisfying the *unambiguous* property. The ambiguity of the median manager benchmark makes it impossible to verify its *appropriateness* by examining whether the investment style it represents adequately corresponds to the account being evaluated. The fund sponsor who chooses to employ universes for peer group comparisons can only rely on the compiler's representations that accounts have been rigorously screened against well-defined criteria for inclusion, the integrity of the input data is scrupulously monitored, and a uniform return calculation methodology has been used for all accounts in all periods.

One other disadvantage merits attention. Because fund sponsors terminate under-performing managers, universes are unavoidably subject to "survivor bias." Consider the hypothetical universe represented in Exhibit 1, where a shaded cell indicates that a particular account existed for a given year and an X indicates that a rate of return can be calculated for the referenced evaluation period.

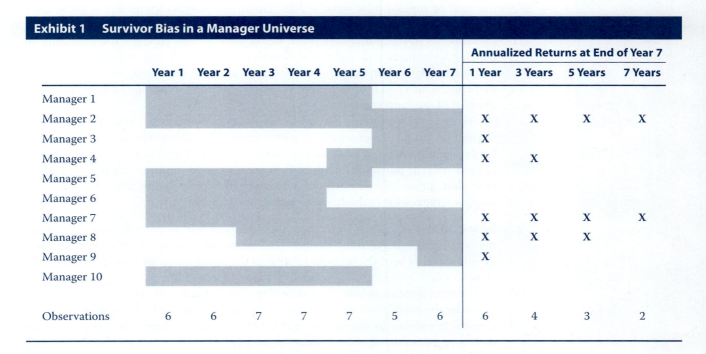

Exhibit 1 Survivor Bias in a Manager Universe

| | Year 1 | Year 2 | Year 3 | Year 4 | Year 5 | Year 6 | Year 7 | Annualized Returns at End of Year 7 | | | |
								1 Year	3 Years	5 Years	7 Years
Manager 1											
Manager 2								X	X	X	X
Manager 3								X			
Manager 4								X	X		
Manager 5											
Manager 6											
Manager 7								X	X	X	X
Manager 8								X	X	X	
Manager 9								X			
Manager 10											
Observations	6	6	7	7	7	5	6	6	4	3	2

In this example, there were six accounts in the universe at the end of Year 1, and there were six at the end of Year 7. They were not all the same accounts, however; in fact, only two have survived for the full period to achieve seven-year returns. The other four in the Year 1 cohort were no longer present because the sponsors reallocated funds or possibly because the managers' performance was unsatisfactory. In any event, it is likely that the two survivors were among the best-performing in the group of accounts that existed in Year 1; sponsors are naturally reluctant to dismiss strong performing managers. Because the survivors' returns were presumably high, the actual median seven-year return for this universe will be higher than the median of a hypothetical return distribution from which no accounts were removed.

Why are these deficiencies of the median manager benchmark of concern? From the perspective of performance evaluation, the question becomes, "To what is the manager expected to add value?" Without a valid reference point, superior performance remains an elusive notion. Placing above the median of a universe of investment managers or funds may be a reasonable investment *objective*, but the performance of a particular manager or fund is not a suitable performance benchmark that can be used to assess investment skill.[13]

---

13 Bailey (1992a) critiques in detail the use of manager universes as benchmarks. Beyond the failure to possess the properties of a valid benchmark and the issue of survivor bias, Bailey also discusses the failure of manager universes to pass tests of benchmark quality. The tests of benchmark quality are summarized in Section 5.6.

5.6 Tests of Benchmark Quality

In many organizations, benchmarks have become an important element of the investment management process. Moreover, benchmark use has expanded beyond performance evaluation. Benchmarks are now an integral part of risk management, at both the investment manager and fund sponsor levels. Most forms of risk budgeting use benchmarks to estimate the risks to which a fund sponsor's investment program is exposed at the asset category and investment manager levels.

Given the important uses of benchmarks, it is in the interests of all parties involved (fund sponsors, consultants, and managers) to identify good benchmarks and to improve or replace poor benchmarks. Good benchmarks increase the proficiency of performance evaluation, highlighting the contributions of skillful managers. Poor benchmarks obscure manager skills. Good benchmarks enhance the capability to manage investment risk. Poor benchmarks promote inefficient manager allocations and ineffective risk management. They also increase the likelihood of unpleasant surprises, which can lead to counterproductive actions and unnecessary expense on the part of the fund sponsor.

Bailey (1992b) presents a heuristic set of benchmark quality criteria designed to distinguish good benchmarks from poor benchmarks. These criteria are based on the fundamental properties of valid benchmarks discussed previously and on a logical extension of the purposes for which benchmarks are used. Although none of the criteria alone provides a definitive indicator of benchmark quality, taken together they provide a means for evaluating alternative benchmarks.

Systematic Biases   Over time, there should be minimal systematic biases or risks in the benchmark relative to the account. One way to measure this criterion is to calculate the historical beta of the account relative to the benchmark; on average, it should be close to 1.0.[14]

Potential systematic bias can also be identified through a set of correlation statistics. Consider the correlation between $A = (P - B)$ and $S = (B - M)$. The contention is that a manager's ability to identify attractive and unattractive investment opportunities should be uncorrelated with whether the manager's style is in or out of favor relative to the overall market. Accordingly, a good benchmark will display a correlation between A and S that is not statistically different from zero.

Similarly, let us define the difference between the account and the market index as $E = (P - M)$. When a manager's style (S) is in favor (out of favor) relative to the market, we expect both the benchmark and the account to outperform (underperform) the market. Therefore, a good benchmark will have a statistically significant positive correlation coefficient between S and E.

Tracking Error   We define tracking error as the volatility of A or $(P - B)$. A good benchmark should reduce the "noise" in the performance evaluation process. Thus, the volatility (standard deviation) of an account's returns relative to a good benchmark should be less than the volatility of the account's returns versus a market index or other alternative benchmarks. Such a result indicates that the benchmark is capturing important aspects of the manager's investment style.

---

14 The historical beta of the account relative to the benchmark is derived from a regression of the account's past returns on the past returns of the benchmark. The resulting slope of the regression line, termed the beta of the regression, indicates the sensitivity of the account's returns to those of the benchmark. Note that a benchmark may fail this test because the manager holds cash in the account, typically for transaction purposes, while the benchmark may reflect a zero cash position. If the account's beta relative to the benchmark would be 1.0 excluding the positive cash position, the overall beta of the account (including the cash position) will be less than 1.0. As a result, the account will have an unfavorable performance bias in an up market and a favorable bias in a down market. The simple solution is to hold cash in the benchmark at a level reflective of the manager's "neutral" cash position.

Risk Characteristics   An account's exposure to systematic sources of risk should be similar to those of the benchmark over time.[15] The objective of a good benchmark is to reflect but not to replicate the manager's investment process. Because an active manager is constantly making bets against the benchmark, a good benchmark will exhibit risk exposures at times greater than those of the managed portfolio and at times smaller. Nevertheless, if the account's risk characteristics are always greater or always smaller than those of the benchmark, a systematic bias exists.

Coverage   Benchmark coverage is defined as the proportion of a portfolio's market value that is contained in the benchmark. For example, at a point in time, all of the securities and their respective weights that are contained in the account and the benchmark can be examined. The market value of the jointly held securities as a percentage of the total market value of the portfolio is termed the coverage ratio. High coverage indicates a strong correspondence between the manager's universe of potential securities and the benchmark. Low coverage indicates that the benchmark has little relationship, on a security level, with the opportunity set generated by the manager's investment process.

Turnover   Benchmark turnover is the proportion of the benchmark's market value allocated to purchases during a periodic rebalancing of the benchmark. Because the benchmark should be an investable alternative to holding the manager's actual portfolio, the benchmark turnover should not be so excessive as to preclude the successful implementation of a passively managed portfolio.

Positive Active Positions   An active position is an account's allocation to a security minus the corresponding weight of the same security in the benchmark. For example, assume an account has a 3% weighting in General Electric (GE). If the benchmark has a 2% weighting in GE, then the active position is 1% (3% − 2%). Thus, the manager will receive positive credit if GE performs well. Actively managed accounts whose investment mandates permit only long positions contain primarily securities that a manager considers to be attractive. When a good custom security-based benchmark has been built, the manager should be expected to hold largely positive active positions for actively managed long-only accounts.[16]

Note that when an account is benchmarked to a published index containing securities for which a long-only manager has no investment opinion and which the manager does not own, negative active positions will arise. A high proportion of negative active positions is indicative of a benchmark that is poorly representative of the manager's investment approach.

5.7 Hedge Funds and Hedge Fund Benchmarks

Hedge funds have become increasingly popular among institutional and high-net-worth investors in recent years. Although the term "hedge fund" covers a wide range of investment strategies, there are some common threads that link these strategies. In general, **hedge funds** attempt to expose investors to a particular investment opportunity while minimizing (or hedging) other investment risks that could impact the outcome. In most cases, hedging involves both long and short investment positions.

---

15 Risk characteristics refer to factors that systematically affect the returns on many securities. We will return to the issue later in the discussion on performance attribution.
16 Violations of this quality criterion often occur when a benchmark is market capitalization weighted. Because many managers do not utilize a market-capitalization weighting scheme in building their portfolios, the possibility of negative active positions can arise when a capitalization-weighted benchmark is assigned.

The term "hedge fund" is believed to have originated as a description of an investment strategy developed by Alfred Winslow Jones.[17] The basic strategy involved shorting stocks that managers considered to be overvalued and using the proceeds to invest in stocks that were deemed to be undervalued. In addition, an incentive fee was established, and Jones committed his own capital to assure investors that his interests were aligned with their interests.

In essence, the Jones strategy is the same as the standard long-only strategy in that, relative to the benchmark, a long-only manager will overweight undervalued securities and underweight overvalued securities. The difference is that the long-only manager is limited to a minimum investment of zero in any security. As a result, the maximum "negative bet" that a long-only manager can place on a security that is rated as overvalued is not to hold it (a weight of zero). For example, because approximately 450 companies in the S&P 500 have weights less than 0.5%, a long-only manager with an S&P 500 benchmark and a negative opinion on any of these stocks would be limited to, at most, a −0.5% active position. By removing the zero weight constraint (that is, allowing shorting), a manager can further exploit overvalued stocks.

There are, however, performance measurement issues as well as numerous administrative and compliance issues that are created when there are short positions in an account. Recall that earlier in the reading (Equation 1), we stated that an account's rate of return is equal to its market value (MV_1) at the end of a period less its market value at the beginning of the period (MV_0), divided by the beginning market value:

$$r_t = \frac{MV_1 - MV_0}{MV_0}$$

In theory, the net assets of a long–short portfolio could be zero; the value of the portfolio's long positions equal the value of the portfolio's short positions. In this case, the beginning market value, MV_0, would be zero and the account's rate of return would be either positive infinity or negative infinity. In the real world of long–short investing, an account will typically have a positive net asset value due to various margin and administrative requirements. However, as the net asset value gets smaller and approaches zero, the account's return will become nonsensically extreme (large positive or large negative).

To address this problem, we need to revise our performance measurement methodology. One approach would be to think in terms of performance impact, which is discussed in more detail later in the reading. That is,

$$r_V = r_p - r_B \qquad\qquad (9)$$

where

r_V = value-added return

r_p = portfolio return

r_B = benchmark return

Here, the term r_V is the value-added return on a long–short portfolio where the active weights sum to zero, which is the same situation as a zero-net asset hedge fund. Although the active weights sum to zero, a return can be determined by summing the performance impacts of the n individual security positions (both long and short).

---

17 See Koh, Lee, and Fai (2002).

$$\sum_{i=1}^{n} w_{vi} = \left(\sum_{i=1}^{n} w_{pi} - \sum_{i=1}^{n} w_{Bi} \right) = 0; \text{ and}$$

$$r_v = \sum_{i=1}^{n} \left[w_{vi} \times r_i \right] = \sum_{i=1}^{n} \left[\left(w_{pi} - w_{Bi} \right) \times r_i \right]$$

$$= \sum_{i=1}^{n} \left(w_{pi} \times r_i \right) - \sum_{i=1}^{n} \left(w_{Bi} \times r_i \right) = r_p - r_B$$

where w_{vi}, w_{pi}, and w_{Bi} are respectively the *active* weight of security i in the portfolio, the weight of security i in the portfolio, and the weight of security i in the benchmark. A return could be calculated for the period during which the individual security positions were maintained. Once an individual security position changed, the return period would end and a new return period would start.[18]

The application of benchmarks to long-only portfolios has reached a mature status. Issues regarding the quality of various benchmark designs and the concerns of overly constraining active management strategies by somehow tying performance too closely to benchmarks remain contentious issues. (For example, see Bernstein 2003.) Nevertheless, it is the rare fund sponsor or investment manager who does not make reference to account performance relative to some benchmark. The advent of hedge funds, however, added a new dynamic to the discussion of the use and design of benchmarks. Some practitioners eschew the use of benchmarks entirely for hedge fund managers, contending that the "absolute return" mandate associated with hedge funds implies that relative performance comparisons are meaningless.

The discussion of hedge fund benchmarks is confounded by the vagueness of the definition of hedge funds. A wide variety of active investment strategies fall under the category of hedge funds. The implications of that diversity for benchmark design are considerable. Underlying all long-only benchmark designs are references to the opportunity set available to the manager. Some hedge fund managers have very clearly definable investment universes composed of highly liquid, daily priced securities. For example, many long-short equity managers also manage long-only portfolios. The universe of securities from which they select on the short side often closely resembles the universe of securities from which they select on the long side. Given information regarding the historical returns and holdings of a long-short equity manager's long and short portfolios, we could use either returns-based or security-based benchmark building approaches to construct separate long and short benchmarks for the manager. These benchmarks could be combined in appropriate proportions to create a valid benchmark. Other hedge fund managers, such as macro hedge fund managers, take rapidly changing long-short leveraged positions in an array of asset categories ranging from equities to commodities, which present significant benchmark building challenges.

The ambiguity of hedge fund manager opportunity sets has led to the widespread use of the Sharpe ratio to evaluate hedge fund manager performance. As discussed later in this reading, the traditional Sharpe ratio is a measure of excess returns (over a risk-free return) relative to the volatility of returns; notably, it can be calculated without reference to the manager's underlying investment universe. Typically, a hedge fund's Sharpe ratio is compared to that of a universe of other hedge funds that have investment mandates assumed to resemble those of the hedge fund under evaluation. Unfortunately, this approach is exposed to the same benchmark validity criticisms

---

18 Another approach to determining a rate of return for a long–short portfolio would be to specify the numerator in Equation 1 as the profit and/or loss resulting from the particular hedge fund strategy. The denominator could be specified as the asset base over which the strategy applies. This could be defined as the amount of assets at risk and could be approximated by the absolute value of all the long positions plus the absolute value of all the short positions.

leveled against standard manager universe comparisons. Further, the standard deviation as a measure of risk (the denominator of the Sharpe ratio) is questionable when an investment strategy incorporates a high degree of optionality (skewness), as is the case for the strategies of many hedge funds.

6   PERFORMANCE ATTRIBUTION

We now move to the second phase of performance evaluation, performance attribution. Fama (1972) proposed the first approach to analyzing the sources of an account's returns. Practitioners use various forms of performance attribution, but the basic concept remains the same: a comparison of an account's performance with that of a designated benchmark and the identification and quantification of sources of differential returns. Further, a unifying mathematical relationship underlies all performance attribution approaches: Impact equals weight times return. We will return to that relationship shortly.

Performance attribution provides an informed look at the past. It identifies the sources of different-from-benchmark returns (**differential returns**) and their impacts on an account's performance. Presuming that one of the objectives of performance attribution is to gain insights helpful for improving the portfolio management process, that process should dictate the method of attribution. The result will be information or a message that will directly relate to the inputs that have gone into the portfolio management process.

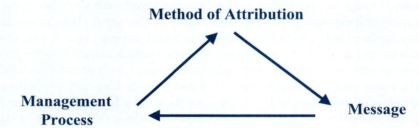

When performance attribution is conducted in this manner, the message will either 1) *reinforce* the effectiveness of the management process or 2) cause a *rethinking* of that process.

Effective performance attribution requires an appropriate analytical framework for decomposing an account's returns relative to those of the benchmark. There is no single correct approach. The appropriate framework will depend on the context of the analysis. In particular, the appropriate framework should reflect the decision-making processes of the organizations involved.

We will consider two basic forms of performance attribution from the standpoints of the fund sponsor and the investment manager. Each form seeks to explain the sources of differential returns. We refer to the performance attribution conducted on the fund sponsor level as **macro attribution**. Performance attribution carried out on the investment manager level we call **micro attribution**. The distinction relates to the specific decision variables involved, as opposed to which organization is actually conducting the performance attribution. While it is unlikely that an investment manager would be in a position to carry out macro attribution, one can easily envision situations in which a fund sponsor may wish to conduct both macro and micro attribution.

6.1 Impact Equals Weight Times Return

A manager can have a positive impact on an account's return relative to a benchmark through two basic avenues: 1) selecting superior (or avoiding inferior) performing assets and 2) owning the superior (inferior) performing assets in greater (lesser) proportions than are held in the benchmark. This simple concept underlies all types of performance attribution. The assets themselves may be divided or combined into all sorts of categories, be they economic sectors, financial factors, or investment strategies. In the end, however, the fundamental rule prevails that impact equals (active) weight times return.

The nature of this concept is illustrated through the following example.

EXAMPLE 11

An Analogy to the Expression for Revenue

Consider a business that sells widgets. Its total revenue is determined by the formula

Revenue = Price × Quantity sold

This year, revenue has risen. The company wants to know why. Based on the above formula, the increase in revenues can be attributed to changes in the unit prices or quantity sold or both (perhaps offsetting to a degree). Exhibit 2 displays the situation in which both price and quantity sold have risen. The old revenue was equal to $P_1 \times Q_1$. The new revenue is equal to $P_2 \times Q_2$. The difference in revenues is a bit more complicated, however. It is due in part to an increase in price [$(P_2 - P_1) \times Q_1$; Area 1], in part to an increase in quantity sold [$(Q_2 - Q_1) \times P_1$; Area 2], and in part to the interaction of both variables [$(P_2 - P_1) \times (Q_2 - Q_1)$; Area 3]. Making the connection to performance attribution, the change in quantity is roughly analogous to a difference in weights between securities held in the account and the benchmark, while the change in price represents the difference in returns between securities held in the account and the benchmark.

Exhibit 2   A Price–Quantity Analogy

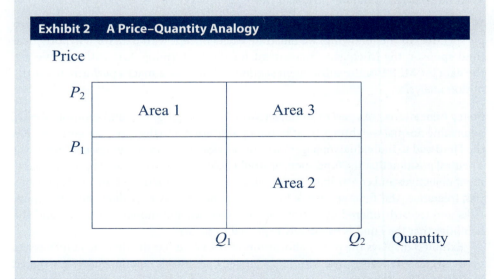

6.2 Macro Attribution Overview

Let us assume for the moment that for a fund sponsor the term "account" refers to a total fund consisting of investments in various asset categories (for example, domestic stocks, international stocks, domestic fixed income, and so on) and that the investments are managed by various investment managers. For ease of exposition, we will call this particular account the "Fund." The fund sponsor controls a number of variables that have an impact on the performance of the Fund. For example, the fund sponsor determines the broad allocation of assets to stocks, bonds, and other types of securities. Further, because the fund sponsor retains multiple investment managers to invest the assets of the Fund, decisions must be made regarding allocations across the various investment styles offered by the managers and allocations to the individual managers themselves.

Macro attribution can be carried out solely in a rate-of-return metric. That is, the results of the analysis can be presented in terms of the effects of decision-making variables on the differential return. Most forms of macro attribution follow that approach. The analysis can be enriched by considering the impacts of the decision-making variables on the differential returns in monetary terms. Consider that it is one thing to report that a fund sponsor's active managers added, say, 0.30% to the Fund's performance last month. It is quite another thing to state that the 30 basis points of positive active management added US$5 million to the value of the Fund. Performance attribution expressed in a value metric (as opposed to a return metric) can make the subject more accessible not only to investment professionals, but particularly to persons not regularly exposed to the subtle issues of performance attribution. We will present examples of both approaches.

6.3 Macro Attribution Inputs

Three sets of inputs constitute the foundation of the macro attribution approach:

1 policy allocations;
2 benchmark portfolio returns; and
3 fund returns, valuations, and external cash flows.

With these inputs in hand we can decompose the Fund's performance from a macro perspective. In the following, we illustrate each concept with data for a hypothetical fund sponsor, the Michigan Endowment for the Performing Arts (MEPA). We use the data for MEPA in the subsequent section to illustrate a macro performance attribution analysis.

Policy Allocations As part of any effective investment program, fund sponsors should determine normal weightings (that is, policy allocations) to the asset categories within the Fund and to individual managers within the asset categories. By "normal" we mean a neutral position that the fund sponsor would hold in order to satisfy long-term investment objectives and constraints. Policy allocations are a function of the fund sponsor's risk tolerance, the fund sponsor's long-term expectations regarding the investment risks and rewards offered by various asset categories and money managers, and the liabilities that the Fund is eventually expected to satisfy.

Exhibit 3 displays the policy allocations of MEPA. It has divided the Fund's assets between two asset categories, with 75% assigned to domestic equities and 25% assigned to domestic fixed income. Within each asset category, MEPA has retained two active managers. It has allocated 65% of the domestic equities to Equity Manager #1 and the remaining 35% to Equity Manager #2. Similarly, the fund sponsor has assigned 55% of the domestic fixed income to Fixed-Income Manager #1 and 45% to Fixed-Income Manager #2.

Exhibit 3	Michigan Endowment for the Performing Arts Investment Policy Allocations	
Asset Category		**Policy Allocations**
Domestic equities		75.0%
Equity Manager #1	65.0	
Equity Manager #2	35.0	
Domestic fixed income		25.0
Fixed-Income Manager #1	55.0	
Fixed-Income Manager #2	45.0	
Total fund		100.0%

Benchmark Portfolio Returns We defined benchmarks earlier. Exhibit 4 presents the benchmarks that MEPA has selected for its two asset categories and the managers within those asset categories. The fund sponsor uses broad market indexes as the benchmarks for asset categories, while it uses more narrowly focused indexes to represent the managers' investment styles.[19]

Exhibit 4	Michigan Endowment for the Performing Arts Benchmark Assignments
Asset Category	**Benchmark**
Domestic equities	S&P 500
Equity Manager #1	Large-Cap Growth Index
Equity Manager #2	Large-Cap Value Index
Domestic fixed income	Lehman Govt./Credit Index
Fixed-Income Manager #1	Lehman Int. Govt./Credit Index
Fixed-Income Manager #2	Lehman Treasury Index

Returns, Valuations, and External Cash Flows Macro attribution in a return-only metric requires fund returns. These returns must be computed at the level of the individual manager to allow an analysis of the fund sponsor's decisions regarding manager selection. If macro attribution is extended to include a value-metric approach, then account valuation and external cash flow data are needed not only to calculate accurate rates of return, but also to correctly compute the value impacts of the fund sponsor's investment policy decision making.

For the month of June 20xx, Exhibit 5 shows the beginning and ending values, external cash flows, and the actual and benchmark returns for MEPA's total fund, asset categories, and investment managers.

---

19 Rather than using broad market indexes as asset category benchmarks, some fund sponsors and consultants construct asset category benchmarks by weighting the managers' benchmarks in accordance with their policy allocations. Under this approach, using the data given in Exhibits 3 and 4, the blended asset category benchmark for domestic equities would consist of a 65% weighting in Large-Cap Growth Index and a 35% weighting in Large-Cap Value Index. However, this approach impairs the sponsor's ability to evaluate the impact of "misfit returns" or "style bias" as described below.

Exhibit 5	Michigan Endowment for the Performing Arts Account Valuations, Cash Flows, and Returns June 20xx				
Asset Category	Beginning Value	Ending Value	Net Cash Flows	Actual Return	Benchmark Return
Domestic equities	$143,295,254	$148,747,228	$(1,050,000)	4.55%	4.04%
Equity Mgr. #1	93,045,008	99,512,122	1,950,000	4.76	4.61
Equity Mgr. #2	50,250,246	49,235,106	(3,000,000)	4.13	4.31
Domestic fixed income	43,124,151	46,069,371	2,000,000	2.16	2.56
Fixed-Income Mgr. #1	24,900,250	25,298,754	0	1.60	1.99
Fixed-Income Mgr. #2	18,223,900	20,770,617	2,000,000	2.91	2.55
Total fund	$186,419,405	$194,816,599	$950,000	3.99%	3.94%

With the inputs for our hypothetical fund sponsor in hand, we turn to an example of a macro performance attribution analysis in the next section.

6.4 Conducting a Macro Attribution Analysis

One can envision a number of different variables of interest when evaluating the fund sponsor's decision-making process. Below, we present six levels or components of investment policy decision making into which the Fund's performance might be analyzed. We do not imply that these are the only correct variables—they are simply logical extensions of a typical fund sponsor's decision-making process.

Specifically, those levels (which we later refer to as "investment strategies" for reasons to become apparent shortly) are:

1   Net Contributions
2   Risk-Free Asset
3   Asset Categories
4   Benchmarks
5   Investment Managers
6   Allocation Effects

Macro attribution analysis starts with the Fund's beginning-of-period and end-of-period values. Simply put, the question under consideration is: How much did each of the decision-making levels contribute, in either a return or a value metric, to the Fund's change in value over an evaluation period? Macro attribution takes an incremental approach to answering this question. Each decision-making level in the hierarchy is treated as an investment strategy, and its investment results are compared to the cumulative results of the previous levels. That is, each decision-making level represents an unambiguous, appropriate, and specified-in-advance investment alternative: in other words, a valid benchmark. The fund sponsor has the option to place all of the Fund's assets in any of the investment strategies. The strategies are ordered in terms of increasing volatility and complexity. Presumably, the fund sponsor will move to a more aggressive strategy only if it expects to earn positive incremental returns. Macro attribution calculates the incremental contribution that the choice to move to the next strategy produces.

In the previous section we gave the inputs necessary to conduct a macro performance attribution analysis for a hypothetical fund sponsor, MEPA, for the month of June 20xx. We apply the macro attribution framework just outlined to MEPA in the following discussion. Exhibit 6 summarizes the results.

Decision-Making Level (Investment Alternative)	Fund Value	Incremental Return Contribution	Incremental Value Contribution
Beginning value	$186,419,405	—	—
Net contributions	187,369,405	0.00%	950,000
Risk-free asset	187,944,879	0.31%	575,474
Asset category	194,217,537	3.36%	6,272,658
Benchmarks	194,720,526	0.27%	502,989
Investment managers	194,746,106	0.01%	25,580
Allocation effects	194,816,599	0.04%	70,494
Total fund	194,816,599	3.99%	8,397,194

Exhibit 6 Michigan Endowment for the Performing Arts Monthly Performance Attribution June 20xx

We now examine each of the six levels in turn.

Net Contributions Exhibit 6 indicates that the starting point of the analysis is the Fund's beginning market value. In our example, at the beginning of June 20xx, the market value of the Fund was $186,419,405. During a given month, the Fund may experience contributions and/or withdrawals. The Net Contributions investment strategy specifies that the net inflows are invested at a zero rate of return and, therefore, the Fund's value changes simply by the total amount of these flows. During June 20xx, net contributions to the Fund were a positive $950,000. Adding this amount to the Fund's beginning value produces a value of $187,369,405 for the Fund under the Net Contributions investment strategy. Although no fund sponsor would deliberately follow this investment strategy, it provides a useful baseline to begin the analysis.

Risk-Free Asset One highly conservative (but certainly reasonable) investment strategy open to a fund sponsor is to invest all of the Fund's assets in a riskfree asset, such as 90-day Treasury bills.[20] Assuming that the Fund's beginning value and its net external cash inflows (accounting for the dates on which those flows occur) are invested at the risk-free rate, the Fund's value will increase by an additional amount over the value achieved under the Net Contributions investment strategy with its zero rate of return. The Risk-Free Asset investment strategy, using a risk-free rate during June 20xx of 0.31%, produces an incremental increase in value of $575,474 (= $187,944,879 – 187,369,405) over the results of the Net Contributions investment strategy, for a total fund value of $187,944,879.[21]

Asset Category Most fund sponsors view the Risk-Free Asset investment strategy as too risk-averse and therefore overly expensive. Instead, they choose to invest in risky assets, based on the widely held belief that, over the long run, the market rewards investors who bear systematic risk. The Asset Category investment strategy assumes that the Fund's beginning value and external cash flows are invested passively in a combination of the designated asset category benchmarks, with the specific allocation to each benchmark based on the fund sponsor's policy allocations to those asset categories.

---

20 Alternatively, a pension fund might identify the risk-free asset as a portfolio of bonds that best hedges its liabilities.
21 The increment of $575,474 cannot be replicated by multiplying $187,369,405 by 0.31% because the $950,000 net contribution (to obtain $187,369,405) was not a single, beginning-of-the-month cash flow.

In essence, this approach is a pure index fund approach. The Fund's value under this investment strategy will exceed or fall below the value achieved under the Risk-Free Asset investment strategy depending on whether the capital markets fulfill the expectation that risk-taking investors are rewarded. From a return-metric perspective, the incremental return contribution is

$$r_{AC} = \sum_{i=1}^{A} w_i \times \left(r_{Ci} - r_f \right)$$

(10)

where r_{AC} is the incremental return contribution of the Asset Category investment strategy, r_{Ci} is the return on the ith asset category, r_f is the risk-free return, w_i is the policy weight assigned to asset category i, and A is the number of asset categories. From a value-metric perspective, the incremental contribution of the Asset Category investment strategy is found by investing each asset category's policy proportion of the Fund's beginning value and all net external cash inflows at the differential rate between the asset category's benchmark rate of return and the risk-free rate, and then summing across all asset categories.

In the Fund's case, investing 75% of the Fund's beginning value and net external cash inflows in the S&P 500 and 25% in the Lehman Brothers Government/Credit Bond Index (for a combined return of 3.67% in the month, or 3.36% above the risk-free rate) increases the Fund's market value by $6,272,658 (= $194,217,537 – $187,944,879) over the value produced by the Risk-Free Asset investment strategy. As a result, the Fund's value totals $194,217,537 under the Asset Category investment strategy.

It would be entirely appropriate for a fund sponsor to stop at the Asset Category investment strategy. In fact, an efficient markets proponent might view this all-passive approach as the most appropriate course of action. Nevertheless, fund sponsors typically choose to allocate their funds within an asset category among a number of active managers, most of whom pursue distinctly different investment styles. Importantly for macro attribution, when fund sponsors hire active managers, they are actually exposing their assets to two additional sources of investment returns (and risks): investment style and active management skill.

An investment manager's performance versus the broad markets is dominated by the manager's investment style. With respect to US common stocks, for example, active managers cannot realistically hope to consistently add more than 2–3 percentage points (if that much) annually to their investment styles, as represented by appropriate benchmarks. Conversely, the difference in performance between investment styles can easily range from 15 to 30 percentage points per year.

Benchmarks   The macro attribution analysis can be designed to separate the impact of the managers' investment styles (as represented by the managers' benchmarks) on the Fund's value from the effect of the managers' active management decisions. In this case, the next level of analysis assumes that the Fund's beginning value and net external cash inflows are passively invested in the aggregate of the managers' respective benchmarks. An aggregate manager benchmark return is calculated as a weighted average of the individual managers' benchmark returns. The weights used to compute the aggregate manager benchmark return are based on the fund sponsor's policy allocations to the managers. From a return-metric perspective,

$$r_{IS} = \sum_{i=1}^{A} \sum_{j=1}^{M} w_i \times w_{ij} \times \left(r_{Bij} - r_{Ci} \right)$$

(11)

where r_{IS} is the incremental return contribution of the Benchmarks strategy, r_{Bij} is the return for the jth manager's benchmark in asset category i, r_{Ci} is the return on the ith asset category, w_i is the policy weight assigned to the ith asset category, w_{ij} is the policy weight assigned to the jth manager in asset category i, and A and M are the number of asset categories and managers, respectively.[22] (Note that summed across all managers and asset categories, $w_i \times w_{ij} \times r_{Bij}$ is the aggregate manager benchmark return.) From a value-metric perspective, the incremental contribution of the Benchmarks strategy is calculated by multiplying each manager's policy proportion of the total fund's beginning value and net external cash inflows by the difference between the manager's benchmark return and the return of the manager's asset category, and then summing across all managers.

In the case of the Fund, the aggregate manager benchmark return was 3.94% in June 20xx. Investing the Fund's beginning value and net external cash inflows at this aggregate manager benchmark return produces an incremental gain of $502,989 (= $194,720,526 − $194,217,537) over the Fund's value achieved under the Asset Category investment strategy. As a result, under the Investment Style investment strategy, the Fund's value grows to $194,720,526.

Paralleling the Asset Category investment strategy, the Benchmarks strategy is essentially a passively managed investment in the benchmarks of the Fund's managers. The difference in performance between the aggregate of the managers' benchmarks and the aggregate of the asset category benchmarks is termed "misfit return" or, less formally, "style bias." In June 20xx, the Fund's misfit return was (3.94% − 3.67%), or a positive 0.27%. Although the expected value of misfit return is zero, it can be highly variable over time. That variability can be particularly large for a fund sponsor who has retained investment manager teams within the fund's various asset categories that display sizeable style biases relative to their respective asset category benchmarks. Some fund sponsors employ special risk-control strategies to keep this misfit risk within acceptable tolerances.

Investment Managers or Value of Active Management   In the next level of analysis, to discern the impact of the managers' active management decisions on the change in the Fund's value, macro attribution analysis calculates the value of the Fund as if its beginning value and net external cash flows were invested in the aggregate of the managers' actual portfolios. Again, the weights assigned to the managers' returns to derive the aggregate manager return will come from the policy allocations set by the fund sponsor. A relationship similar to Equation 11 describes the return-metric contribution of the Investment Managers strategy:

$$r_{IM} = \sum_{i=1}^{A}\sum_{j=1}^{M} w_i \times w_{ij} \times \left(r_{Aij} - r_{Bij}\right) \tag{12}$$

where r_{Aij} represents the actual return on the jth manager's portfolio within asset category i and the other variables are as defined previously.

The difference in the Fund's value under the Investment Managers strategy relative to the Benchmarks strategy will depend on whether the managers, in aggregate, exceeded the return on the aggregate benchmark. In the case of the Fund, the aggregate actual return of the managers (calculated using policy weights) was 3.95%, as opposed to 3.94% return on the aggregate manager investment style benchmark. This modestly positive excess return translates into an incremental increase in the fund's value of $25,580 (= $194,746,106 − $194,720,526) over the value produced under the Benchmarks strategy, for a total value of $194,746,106 under the Investment Managers investment strategy.

It should be emphasized that macro attribution calculates the value added by the Fund's managers based on the assumption that the fund sponsor has invested in each of the managers according to the managers' policy allocations. Of course, the actual allocation to the managers will likely differ from the policy allocations. However, if

---

22 Note: $\sum_{j=1}^{M} w_{ij} = 1$ for all i and $\sum_{i=1}^{A} w_i = 1$.

we wish to correctly isolate the contributions of the various levels of fund sponsor decision making, we must distinguish between those aspects of the Fund's investment results over which the fund sponsor does and does not have control. That is, the fund sponsor sets the allocation of assets to the Fund's managers but has no influence over their investment performance. Conversely, the managers have control over their investment performance, but they do not generally determine the amount of assets placed under their management.

In examining the value added by the Fund's managers, we should assume they were funded at their respective policy allocations and ask the question, "What would the managers have contributed to the Fund's performance if the fund sponsor consistently maintained the stated policy allocations?" On the other hand, in examining the contribution of the fund sponsor, it makes sense to calculate the impact of the differences between the managers' actual and policy allocations on the Fund's performance and thus ask the question, "How did the fund sponsor's decisions to deviate from investment manager policy allocations affect the Fund's performance relative to a strategy of consistently maintaining the stated policy allocations?" The analysis performed at the Investment Managers level attempts to answer the former question. The analysis done at the Allocation Effects level begins to answer the latter question.

Allocation Effects   The final macro attribution component is Allocation Effects. In a sense, the Allocation Effects incremental contribution is a reconciling factor—by definition, it is the difference between the Fund's ending value and the value calculated at the Investment Managers level. If the fund sponsor had invested in all of the managers and asset categories precisely at the established policy allocations, then the Allocation Effects investment strategy's contribution would be zero. However, most fund sponsors deviate at least slightly from their policy allocations, thereby producing an allocation effect. The Fund's actual ending value was $194,816,599, which represents a $70,494 increase (= $194,816,599 − $194,746,106) over the value achieved through the Investment Managers investment strategy. By implication, then, MEPA's actual weightings of the asset categories and managers versus the policy weightings contributed positively to the Fund's value in the month of June 20xx.

6.5 Micro Attribution Overview

As implied by its name, micro attribution focuses on a much narrower subject than does macro attribution. Instead of examining the performance of a total fund, micro attribution concerns itself with the investment results of individual portfolios relative to designated benchmarks. Thus, let us define the term "account" to mean a specific portfolio invested by a specific investment manager which we will refer to as the "Portfolio." The Portfolio can be formed of various types of securities. Our illustrations will initially be based on a portfolio of US common stocks. We shall address fixed-income attribution in Section 6.8, below.

Over a given evaluation period, the Portfolio will produce a return that is different from the return on the benchmark. This difference is typically referred to as the manager's value-added or active return. As shown earlier in Equation 9, a manager's value-added can be expressed as

$$r_v = r_p - r_B$$

Because the return on any portfolio is the weighted sum of the returns on the securities composing the portfolio, Equation 9 can be rewritten as

$$r_v = \sum_{i=1}^{n} w_{pi} r_i - \sum_{i=1}^{n} w_{Bi} r_i \qquad\qquad \text{(13)}$$

where w_{pi} and w_{Bi} are the proportions of the Portfolio and benchmark, respectively, invested in security i, r_i is the return on security i, and n is the number of securities.[23]

Rearranging the last equation demonstrates that the manager's value-added is equal to the difference in weights of the Portfolio and benchmark invested in a security times the return on that security, summed across all n securities in the Portfolio and benchmark:

$$r_v = \sum_{i=1}^{n}\left[\left(w_{pi} - w_{Bi}\right) \times r_i\right]$$

With further manipulation,[24] it can be shown that

$$r_v = \sum_{i=1}^{n}\left[\left(w_{pi} - w_{Bi}\right) \times \left(r_i - r_B\right)\right] \tag{14}$$

where r_B is the return on the Portfolio's benchmark.

Equation 14 offers the simplest form of micro performance attribution: a security-by-security attribution analysis. In this analysis, the manager's value-added can be seen to come from two sources: the weights assigned to securities in the Portfolio relative to their weights in the benchmark and the returns on the securities relative to the overall return on the benchmark.

There are four cases of relative-to-benchmark weights and returns for security i to consider. Exhibit 7 gives those cases and their associated performance impacts versus the benchmark.

Exhibit 7   Relative-to-Benchmark Weights and Returns

	$w_{pi} - w_{Bi}$	$r_i - r_B$	Performance Impact versus Benchmark
1.	Positive	Positive	Positive
2.	Negative	Positive	Negative
3.	Positive	Negative	Negative
4.	Negative	Negative	Positive

A manager can add value by overweighting (underweighting) securities that perform well (poorly) relative to the benchmark. Conversely, the manager can detract value by overweighting (underweighting) securities that perform poorly (well) relative to the benchmark.

Security-by-security micro attribution generally is unwieldy and typically provides little in the way of useful insights. The large number of securities in a well-diversified portfolio makes the impact of any individual security on portfolio returns largely uninteresting. A more productive form of micro attribution involves allocating the value-added return to various sources of systematic returns.

---

[23] For simplicity we assume that the Portfolio's securities are chosen from among the securities in the benchmark. Otherwise n needs to represent the number of securities in the union of the benchmark and the Portfolio.

[24] Note that the sum of the security weights in any portfolio must equal 1.0, or, equivalently, $\sum_{i=1}^{n}\left(w_{pi} - w_{Bi}\right) = 0$. Because zero multiplied by a constant equals zero, $\sum_{i=1}^{n}\left(w_{pi} - w_{Bi}\right) \times r_B = 0$, where r_B is the known return on the benchmark (the constant). Subtracting this expression from the right-hand side of the equation just given yields $r_v = \sum_{i=1}^{n}\left[\left(w_{pi} - w_{Bi}\right) \times \left(r_i - r_B\right)\right]$.

Underlying most micro attributions is a factor model of returns. A factor model assumes that the return on a security (or portfolio of securities) is sensitive to the changes in various factors. These factors represent common elements with which security returns are correlated. Factors can be defined in a number of ways: They might be sector or industry membership variables; they might be financial variables, such as balance sheet or income statement items; or they might be macroeconomic variables, such as changes in interest rates, inflation, or economic growth.

The market model, introduced previously, relates a security's or portfolio's return to movements of a broad market index, with the exposure to that index represented by the beta of the security. Recall that Equation 8 provides one expression of the market model:

$$R_p = a_p + \beta_p R_I + \varepsilon_p$$

Example 12 illustrates the calculation of value-added (active return) relative to a one-factor model.

EXAMPLE 12

Active Return Relative to a One-Factor Model

Assume that the Portfolio has a zero-factor value of 1.0% and a beta of 1.2 at the beginning of the evaluation period. During the period, the return on the market index was 7%. The market model, expressed in Equation 8, states that the Portfolio should return 9.4% (= 1.0% + 1.2 × 7%). Further, assume that the Portfolio was assigned a custom benchmark with its own market model parameters, a zero-factor value of 2.0% and a beta of 0.8, and which thus has an expected return of 7.6% (= 2.0% + 0.8 × 7%). If the Portfolio's actual return was 10.9%, then the differential return of 3.3% could be attributed in part to the Portfolio's differential expected returns. That is, the Portfolio held a zero factor of 1.0 versus the 2.0 of the benchmark, while the Portfolio had a beta of 1.2 versus the benchmark's beta of 0.8. The incremental expected return of the Portfolio versus the benchmark was 1.8% [= (1.0% − 2.0%) + (1.2 − 0.8) × 7%]. The remaining 1.5% of differential return would be attributed to the investment skill of the manager.

6.6 Sector Weighting/Stock Selection Micro Attribution

Many investment managers employ analysts to research securities and portfolio managers to then build portfolios based on that research. With this investment process, managers are interested in an attribution analysis that will disaggregate the performance effects of the analysts' recommendations and the portfolio managers' decisions to over- and underweight economic sectors and industries.

We can define the returns on the Portfolio and its benchmark to be the weighted sums of their respective economic sector returns. Therefore, just as Equation 13 expressed the manager's value-added return as the difference between the weighted average return on the securities in the Portfolio and the benchmark, the manager's value-added return can similarly be expressed as the difference between the weighted average return on the economic sectors in the Portfolio and the benchmark:

$$r_v = \sum_{j=1}^{S} w_{pj} r_{pj} - \sum_{j=1}^{S} w_{Bj} r_{Bj} \qquad (15)$$

where

w_{pj} = Portfolio weight of sector j
w_{Bj} = benchmark weight of sector j
r_{pj} = Portfolio return of sector j
r_{Bj} = benchmark return of sector j
  S = number of sectors

Continuing with the example of one of MEPA's investment managers, Exhibit 8 shows the results of a micro attribution analysis based on partitioning a manager's value-added into a part due to skill in sector selection and a part due to skill in security selection. In this example, the return on the Portfolio for a selected one-month period was 1.12%. During that same month the benchmark return was 0.69%, generating a value-added return of 0.43%.

Exhibit 8   Results of a Micro Attribution Analysis

Economic Sectors	Portfolio Weight (%)	Sector Benchmark Weight (%)	Portfolio Return (%)	Sector Benchmark Return (%)	Performance Attribution			
					Pure Sector Allocation	Allocation/ Selection Interaction	Within-Sector Selection	Total Value-Added
Basic materials	5.97	5.54	−0.79	−0.67	−0.01	0.00	−0.01	−0.01
Capital goods	7.82	7.99	−3.60	−3.95	0.01	0.00	0.03	0.04
Consumer durables	2.90	2.38	0.46	−0.21	0.00	0.00	0.02	0.01
Consumer nondurables	31.78	34.75	1.92	1.97	−0.04	0.00	−0.02	−0.05
Energy	7.15	6.01	0.37	0.14	−0.01	0.00	0.01	0.01
Financial	22.47	20.91	2.92	2.05	0.02	0.01	0.18	0.22
Technology	12.14	16.02	2.00	−0.30	0.04	−0.09	0.37	0.32
Utilities	8.64	6.40	0.46	−0.37	−0.02	0.02	0.05	0.05
Cash and equivalent	1.13	0.00	0.14		−0.01	0.00	0.00	−0.01
Buy/hold + cash	100.00	100.00	1.26	0.69	−0.02	−0.05	0.64	0.57
Trading and other			−0.14					−0.14
Total portfolio			1.12	0.69				0.43

Note that this is a holdings-based or "buy-and-hold" attribution. Each sector's contribution to the total allocation and selection effects depends upon the beginning portfolio and benchmark weights in that sector and the constituent securities' returns due to price appreciation and dividend income. The buy-and-hold approach, which disregards the impact of transactions during the evaluation period, has an important practical advantage: Only the holdings and their returns need be input to the attribution system. There is, however, a disadvantage: The account's buy-and-hold return will not equal its time-weighted total return. For that reason, the attribution analysis shown above includes a reconciling item captioned "Trading and Other." In the example shown in Exhibit 8, "Trading and Other" is the negative 14 basis point (−0.14%) difference between the account's Buy/Hold return of 1.26% and the actual portfolio return of 1.12%. The imputed "trading and other" factor reflects the net impact of cash flows and security purchases and sales during the evaluation period. In actively managed accounts with high turnover, the "trading and other" factor can be significant. Where this is a concern, transaction-based attribution analysis can be employed.[25]

The value-added return can be segmented into the impact of assigning the assets of the portfolio to various economic sectors and the impact of selecting securities within those economic sectors. Equation 15 can be rearranged to form the following relationship:[26]

$$r_v = \underbrace{\sum_{j=1}^{S}\left(w_{pj} - w_{Bj}\right)\left(r_{Bj} - r_B\right)}_{\text{Pure Sector Allocation}} + \underbrace{\sum_{j=1}^{S}\left(w_{pj} - w_{Bj}\right)\left(r_{pj} - r_{Bj}\right)}_{\text{Allocation/Selection Interation}}$$

$$+ \underbrace{\sum_{j=1}^{S} w_{Bj}\left(r_{pj} - r_{Bj}\right)}_{\text{Within-Sector Selection}}$$

(16)

where S is the number of sectors and r_B is the return on the Portfolio's benchmark.

In Equation 16 the **Pure Sector Allocation return** equals the difference between the allocation (weight) of the Portfolio to a given sector and the Portfolio's benchmark weight for that sector, times the difference between the sector benchmark's return and the overall Portfolio's benchmark return, summed across all sectors. The pure sector allocation return assumes that within each sector the manager held the same securities as the benchmark and in the same proportions. Thus, the impact on relative performance is attributed only to the sector-weighting decisions of the manager.

EXAMPLE 13

The Pure Sector Allocation Return for Consumer Nondurables

Exhibit 8 indicates that at the beginning of the month the Portfolio had a 31.78% weight in consumer nondurables, while the benchmark had a 34.75% weight. Because the return of the benchmark consumer nondurables sector was 1.97% and the return of the overall benchmark was 0.69%, the performance impact due to the consumer nondurables sector allocation is −0.04% [= (31.78% − 34.75%) × (1.97% − 0.69%)]. That is, the decision to underweight a sector that performed better than the overall benchmark resulted in a negative contribution to the performance of the Portfolio relative to the overall benchmark. The Pure Sector Allocation return is typically the responsibility of the portfolio managers who determine the Portfolio's relative allocations to economic sectors and industries.

The **Within-Sector Selection return** equals the difference between the return on the Portfolio's holdings in a given sector and the return on the corresponding sector benchmark, times the weight of the benchmark in that sector, summed across all sectors. The Within-Sector Selection return implicitly assumes that the manager weights each sector in the Portfolio in the same proportion as in the overall benchmark,

---

25 See Spaulding (2003). Transaction-based attribution analysis is outside the scope of the present discussion.
26 Equation 16 covers performance attribution in the single-period case. Multiperiod performance attribution, while an extension of the single-period approach, involves considerably more complexity. For a discussion of some of the issues involved in multiperiod performance attribution, see Menchero (2004) and Frongello and Bay (2002).

although *within the sector* the manager may hold securities in different-from-benchmark weights. Thus, the impact on relative performance is now attributed only to the security selection decisions of the manager.

EXAMPLE 14

The Within-Sector Allocation Return for Technology

Exhibit 8 shows that the return of the portfolio's technology sector was 2.00%, while the return of the benchmark's technology sector was −0.30%. Consequently, the performance impact of security selection within the technology sector was +0.37% {= 16.02% × [2.00% − (−0.30%)]}, where 16.02% is the weight of the benchmark's holdings in the technology sector. During the month, the Portfolio held technology stocks that in total performed better than the aggregate performance of the technology stocks contained in the sector benchmark, thereby contributing positively to the Portfolio's performance relative to the overall benchmark. The Within-Sector Selection impact is often the responsibility of the security analysts. Among the securities that they research, they are expected to identify significantly misvalued securities and recommend appropriate action.

The **Allocation/Selection Interaction return** is a more difficult concept, because it involves the joint effect of the portfolio managers' and security analysts' decisions to assign weights to both sectors and individual securities. The Allocation/Selection Interaction equals the difference between the weight of the Portfolio in a given sector and the Portfolio's benchmark for that sector, times the difference between the Portfolio's and the benchmark's returns in that sector, summed across all sectors.

EXAMPLE 15

The Allocation/Selection Interaction Return for Technology

Again referring to Exhibit 8, we can see that the Portfolio's relative underweight in the Technology sector of −3.88% (= 12.14% − 16.02%) and the Portfolio's positive relative performance in the Technology sector of 2.30% [= 2.00% − (−0.30%)] produced an Allocation/Selection Interaction effect of −0.09% during the month.

A decision to increase the allocation to a particular security adds not only to the weight in that security but also to the weight of the sector to which the security belongs, unless there is an offsetting adjustment to securities within that sector. Unless the portfolio manager is careful to make offsetting adjustments, security selection decisions can inadvertently drive sector-weighting decisions. In general, the Allocation/Selection Interaction impact will be relatively small if the benchmark is appropriate—that is, one that is devoid of any material systematic biases. Because the Allocation/Selection Interaction impact is often the source of some confusion and is usually the result of security selection decisions, some practitioners consolidate the Allocation/Selection Interaction impact with the Within-Sector Selection impact.

6.7 Fundamental Factor Model Micro Attribution

As we have noted, some type of factor model underlies virtually all forms of performance attribution. Economic sectors and industries represent only one potential source of common factor returns. Numerous practitioners and academics (for example, see Sharpe 1982 and Fama and French 1992) have investigated other common factor return sources. For example, with respect to common stocks, a company's size, its industry, its growth characteristics, its financial strength, and other factors seem to have an impact on account performance. Often these factors are referred to as fundamental factors. They may be combined with economic sector factors to produce multifactor models that can be used to conduct micro attribution.

As with any form of performance attribution, the exposures of the Portfolio and the benchmark to the factors of the fundamental factor model must be determined at the beginning of the evaluation period. The benchmark could be the risk exposures of a style or custom index, or it could be a set of normal factor exposures that were typical of the manager's portfolio over time. Finally, the performance of each of the factors must be determined.

EXAMPLE 16

Fundamental Factor Model Micro Attribution

Exhibit 9 provides an example of a fundamental factor model micro attribution analysis where a US growth stock manager invests the Portfolio. The performance attribution example covers a one-month period, and during that time the Portfolio generated a 6.02% rate of return, while the normal portfolio and the market index produced returns of 5.85% and 6.09%, respectively. During this particular month, growth stocks performed less well than the market index, largely explaining why the normal portfolio (representing the manager's investment style) underperformed the return on the market index by −0.24%. The performance difference between the Portfolio (6.02%) and the normal portfolio (5.85%) is a measure of the portfolio manager's investment skill (0.17%) or value-added.

The micro attribution analysis shown in Exhibit 9 attributes the manager's investment skill or value-added to four primary sources: 1) market timing, 2) exposures to fundamental factors, 3) exposures to economic sectors, and 4) a specific or unexplained return component. The market-timing component is made up of two performance impacts; one is due to the Portfolio's cash position, and the other relates to the Portfolio's beta. In the example, the combination of these two effects had a negative impact of −0.09%. The second primary performance attribute involves the exposures to the fundamental factors. The Portfolio's fundamental factor exposures are contrasted with "normal" fundamental factor exposures, represented by the manager's benchmark.[27] The Portfolio's actual factor exposures versus its "normal" exposures resulted in a negative return impact of −0.61%. Similarly, the Portfolio's economic sector allocations are contrasted with the Portfolio's "normal" allocations to produce performance attribution impacts. In this case, the active sector weights had a positive impact of 0.15%. Finally, the fundamental factor model was unable to explain a portion

---

27 Exposure to a fundamental factor in this case is measured in terms of standard deviations from the mean, where the mean is determined by the average value of the particular factor for a group of capitalization-weighted stocks.

of the Portfolio's return; in this case, the Portfolio had a specific or unexplained return of +0.72%.[28] This specific return that cannot be explained by the factor model is attributed to the investment manager.

Exhibit 9	Micro Attribution Using a Fundamental Factor Model				
	Portfolio Exposure	Normal Exposure	Active Exposure	Active Impact	Return
Market return					6.09%
Normal portfolio return					5.85
Cash timing	2.36	0.00	2.36	−0.13	
Beta timing	1.02	1.00	0.02	0.04	
Total market timing					−0.09
Growth	1.12	0.85	0.27	−0.15	
Size	−0.26	0.35	−0.61	−0.35	
Leverage	−0.33	−0.60	0.27	0.11	
Yield	−0.03	−0.12	0.09	−0.22	
Total fundamental risk factors					−0.61
Basic industry	14.10	15.00	−0.90	0.04	
Consumer	35.61	30.00	5.61	−0.07	
Energy	8.36	5.00	3.36	0.05	
Financials	22.16	20.00	2.16	−0.02	
Technology	17.42	25.00	−7.58	0.16	
Utilities	2.35	5.00	−2.65	−0.01	
Total economic sectors					0.15
Specific (unexplained)					0.72
Actual portfolio return					6.02%

6.8 Fixed-Income Attribution

The sector weighting/stock selection approach to micro attribution is applicable to fixed-income as well as equity accounts. We mentioned in our remarks on fixed-income style indexes in Section 5.3 that broad fixed-income market indexes may be segregated into their constituent market segments. Accordingly, the sector weighting/stock selection equity attribution analysis can also be adapted for use with fixed-income

---

28 Although this type of performance attribution analysis provides valuable insights to investment practitioners, there is a serious limitation. It involves the ambiguity of the benchmark. If the benchmark is based solely on a set of exposures to investment risk factors, then the benchmark is ambiguous. That is, we can construct multiple portfolios that have the same risk characteristics, but they will not have the same investment return. For example, many portfolios might have the same beta, but they will have different investment returns. The solution to this limitation is to base the attribution analysis on the risk exposures of an appropriate benchmark portfolio, i.e., a portfolio with specified securities and weights. In this case, the benchmark portfolio will have a specific or unexplained return component. The difference between it and the portfolio's specific return is attributed to the investment manager.

accounts by substituting market segments such as government bonds, agency and investment-grade corporate credit bonds, high-yield bonds, and mortgage-backed securities, among others, for the economic sectors such as energy, financial, or utilities.

Nonetheless, bonds are unlike stocks, and an approach that merely isolates allocation and selection effects among bond market sectors will be of limited value in analyzing the sources of fixed-income account returns. Useful attribution analysis captures the return impact of the manager's investment decisions, and fixed-income managers weigh variables that differ in important ways from the factors considered by equity portfolio managers. In the interests of mathematical brevity, we will limit our discussion of fixed-income micro performance attribution to a conceptual overview.[29]

Major determinants of fixed-income results are changes in the general level of interest rates, represented by the government (default-free) yield curve, and changes in sector, credit quality, and individual security differentials, or nominal spreads, to the yield curve. As a general rule, fixed-income security prices move in the opposite direction of interest rates: If interest rates fall, bond prices rise, and vice versa. In consequence, fixed-income portfolios tend to have higher rates of return in periods of falling interest rates and, conversely, lower rates of return in periods of rising interest rates. Consider the example displayed in Exhibit 10, where the US Treasury spot rate yield curve shifted upward across all maturities during the nine-month period ending 30 June 2004, and where the return for the Lehman Brothers US Government Index for the nine-month period was −0.56%. Comparing the yield curves for 30 September 2004 and 30 June 2004, we see that in the third quarter of 2004 the change in the US Treasury yield curve was more complex: Short-term rates rose, while the yields on government securities with terms to maturity longer than two years fell. Reflecting the decline in intermediate and long-term yields, the return on the Lehman Brothers US Government Index for the three-month period was 3.11%.

| Exhibit 10 | Interest Rate Term Structure (US Government Issues—3-Month to 30-Year Maturity) |

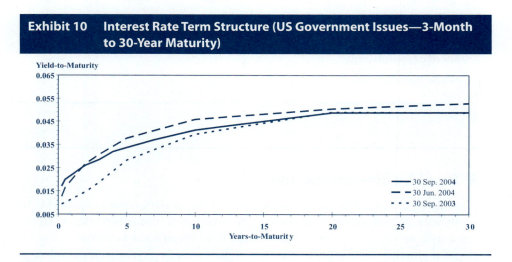

For fixed-income securities that are subject not only to default-free yield-curve movements but also to credit risk, spread changes represent an additional source of interest rate exposure. Companies operating within the same industry face the same business environment, and the prices of the securities they issue have a general tendency to move in the same direction in response to environmental changes. All airlines, for example, are affected by changes in business and leisure travel patterns and the cost of fuel, among other economic factors. In the corporate bond market,

---

29 A more rigorous treatment of this discussion of fixed-income micro attribution can be found in Fong, Pearson, and Vasicek (1983).

such commonalities are reflected in sector spreads, which widen when investors require higher yields in compensation for higher perceived business risk. In addition, rating agencies evaluate the creditworthiness of corporate bond issues, and credit quality spreads vary with changes in the required yields for fixed-income securities of a given rating. Exhibit 11 shows the combined market-based yield effect of the spot rate yield-curve and nominal spread changes for an investor holding AA-rated 10-year industrial bonds. For example, for the nine-month period ending 30 June 2004, increases in the 10-year spot rate and the 10-year AA spread of 0.64 percent and 0.12 percent, respectively, combined to result in a total change of 0.76 percent in the yield of AA-rated 10-year industrial bonds.

Exhibit 11   Yield Curve and Nominal Spread Changes

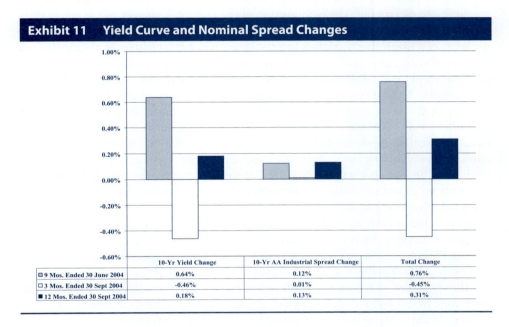

	10-Yr Yield Change	10-Yr AA Industrial Spread Change	Total Change
▣ 9 Mos. Ended 30 June 2004	0.64%	0.12%	0.76%
▢ 3 Mos. Ended 30 Sept 2004	-0.46%	0.01%	-0.45%
■ 12 Mos. Ended 30 Sept 2004	0.18%	0.13%	0.31%

Exhibit 12 shows the total returns of the Lehman US Government and the Lehman AA Industrials Indexes for the same evaluation periods. The AA Industrials Index modestly underperformed the Government Index in the nine-month period ended 30 June 2004, when the yield curve rose and the nominal spread widened, and significantly outperformed in the subsequent quarter, when the yield curve fell and the nominal spread was essentially unchanged. In addition, of course, the spreads of individual 10-year AA-rated industrial bonds may vary from the average reflected by the sector index, and those differences, too, will be reflected in the actual performance of a specific portfolio.

Exhibit 12   Total Returns Data

	Total Returns	
	Lehman US Government Index (%)	**Lehman AA Industrials Index (%)**
9 months ended 30 June 2004	−0.56	−0.58
3 months ended 30 September 2004	3.11	3.71
12 months ended 30 September 2004	2.52	3.11

The impact of interest rate and spread movements on the investment performance of a given portfolio depends upon the nature of the market changes and the interest-sensitive characteristics of the portfolio. We have already seen two types of yield-curve changes: An upward (although nonparallel) shift in the nine-month period ended 30 June 2004, and a twist in the third quarter of 2004 when short-term rates rose and long-term rates fell. Additionally, in both cases, the slope of the yield curve changed. An indicator of the slope is the difference between the 2-year and the 10-year yield-curve rates. The difference was 2.48% on 30 September 2003, 1.90% on 30 June 2004, and 1.52% on 30 September 2004. Thus, over this time frame, the US government spot rate yield curve flattened from one measurement point to the next.

The external interest rate environment is not under the control of the manager; the manager can dictate only the composition of the Portfolio. Subject to the constraints established by the investment mandate and the pertinent policies or guidelines, the manager can adjust the Portfolio's interest-sensitive characteristics in anticipation of forecasted yield-curve and spread changes. Different fixed-income instruments and portfolios will respond diversely to yield-curve movements like those shown above. For example, the resulting adjustment in the valuation of a mortgage-backed portfolio will not be the same as the valuation change of a government bond portfolio. Even portfolios made up of the same types of fixed-income securities (for instance, traditional investment-grade corporate bonds) will have different outcomes, depending upon factors including the maturity, coupon, and option features of their constituent holdings. The manager will modify the Portfolio's interest rate risk profile so as to benefit from expected advantageous movements or to attenuate the return impact of expected adverse changes.

In addition to such interest rate management, other management factors contributing to total portfolio return are the allocation of assets among market segments, economic sectors, and quality grades, and the selection of specific securities within those categories. Trading activity during the evaluation period will also have an impact.

These sources of return are displayed in Exhibit 13.[30] The forward interest rates referred to in this exhibit can be calculated from the points along the spot rate government yield curve at the beginning and the end of the performance evaluation period.

Exhibit 13   Sources of the Total Return of a Fixed-Income Portfolio

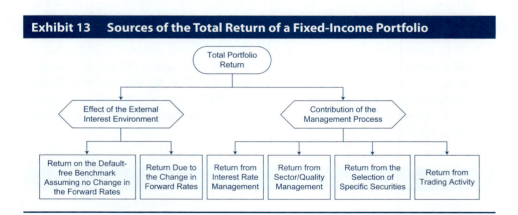

The total return of a fixed-income portfolio can be attributed to the external interest rate effect, on one hand, and the management effect, on the other. The return due to the external interest rate environment is estimated from a term structure analysis of a universe of Treasury securities and can be further separated into the return from the implied forward rates (the expected return) and the difference between the actual

---

30 Fong, Pearson, and Vasicek (1983).

realized return and the market implied return from the forward rates (the unexpected return). The overall external interest rate effect represents the performance of a passive, default-free bond portfolio.

The management effect is calculated by a series of repricings and provides information about how the management process affects the portfolio returns. The management effect can be decomposed into four components:

- **Interest rate management effect**: Indicates how well the manager predicts interest rate changes. To calculate this return, each security in the portfolio is priced as if it were a default-free security. The interest rate management contribution is calculated by subtracting the return of the entire Treasury universe from the aggregate return of these repriced securities. The interest rate management effect can be further broken down into returns due to duration, convexity, and yield-curve shape change, as shown in Exhibit 14.

- **Sector/quality effect**: Measures the manager's ability to select the "right" issuing sector and quality group. The sector/quality return is estimated by repricing each security in the portfolio using the average yield premium in its respective category. A gross return can be then calculated based on this price. The return from the sector/quality effect is calculated by subtracting the external effect and the interest rate management effect from this gross return.

- **Security selection effect**: Measures how the return of a specific security within its sector relates to the average performance of the sector. The security selection effect for each security is the total return of a security minus all the other components. The portfolio security selection effect is the market-value weighted average of all the individual security selection effects.

- **Trading activity**: Captures the effect of sales and purchases of bonds over a given period and is the total portfolio return minus all the other components.

Exhibit 14 Performance Attribution Analysis of Two Fixed-Income Managers for the Windsor Foundation, Year Ending 31 December 20xx

	Evaluation Period Returns (%)		
	Broughton Asset Management	Matthews Advisors	Bond Portfolio Benchmark
I. Interest Rate Effect			
1. Expected	0.44	0.44	0.44
2. Unexpected	0.55	0.55	0.55
Subtotal	0.99	0.99	0.99
II. Interest Rate Management Effect			
3. Duration	0.15	−0.13	0.00
4. Convexity	−0.03	−0.06	0.00
5. Yield-curve shape change	0.04	0.13	0.00
Subtotal (options adjusted)	0.16	−0.06	0.00
III. Other Management Effects			
6. Sector/quality	−0.09	1.15	0.00
7. Bond selectivity	0.12	−0.08	0.00

(continued)

Exhibit 14	(Continued)		
	Evaluation Period Returns (%)		
	Broughton Asset Management	Matthews Advisors	Bond Portfolio Benchmark
8. Transaction costs	0.00	0.00	0.00
Subtotal	0.03	1.07	0.00
IV. Trading activity return	0.10	0.08	0.00
V. Total return (sum of I, II, III, and IV)	1.28	2.08	0.99

Quantifying the absolute return contributions due to the management effect by means of serial portfolio repricings is data- and computation-intensive, and conducting value-added performance attribution relative to a fixed-income benchmark is still more challenging. Fixed-income investment management organizations often use commercially developed performance measurement and attribution systems. The vendor-provided systems available vary substantially in methodology and level of analytical sophistication, and selecting a system is not a trivial exercise, but most models attempt to isolate and measure the impact of environmental and management factors like those discussed here.

The output of a representative fixed-income attribution system can be demonstrated through a brief illustration. Let us consider the case of the investment officer of the Windsor Foundation, whose consultant has analyzed the performance of two of the foundation's external fixed-income managers, Broughton Asset Management and Matthews Advisors. The consultant has prepared an attribution analysis, shown in Exhibit 14, for a particular evaluation period.

The consultant also included in the analysis the following summary of the investment management strategies of the two firms:

▪ Broughton Asset Management states that its investment strategy relies on active interest rate management decisions to outperform the benchmark index. Broughton also seeks to identify individual issues that are mispriced.

▪ Matthews Advisors states that its investment strategy is to enhance portfolio returns by identifying undervalued sectors while maintaining a neutral interest rate exposure relative to the benchmark index. Matthews believes it is not possible to enhance returns through individual bond selection on a consistent basis.

Does the consultant's attribution analysis validate the two firms' self-descriptions of their investment strategies?

In fact, the foundation officer and the consultant can *preliminarily* conclude on the basis of the single year under review that approximately one-half of the incremental return due to Broughton's management process can be attributed to relying on active interest rate management decisions. The total performance contribution for the interest rate management effect—the primary indicator of effective active interest rate management decisions in this analysis—was 16 basis points out of a total of 29 basis points due to the manager's active management process. In addition, the performance contribution for bond selectivity—here, the most direct measure of success in security selection—was 12 basis points. Therefore, nearly all of Broughton's positive performance of 29 basis points (1.28% versus 0.99%) was a result of its stated strategies of interest rate management (16 basis points) and security selection (12 basis points).

Interestingly, a substantial portion of Matthews' performance results are attributable to the firm's success in identifying undervalued sectors. The positive performance contribution for sector and quality was 1.15%, representing a large proportion of Matthews' return relative to the benchmark and indicating success over the evaluation period.

Fixed-income performance attribution is receiving increasing attention from plan sponsors and consultants, but it remains primarily the province of investment managers who have access to the requisite capital market data services as well as the scale of operations to justify the expense and the expertise needed to interpret the results in depth.

PERFORMANCE APPRAISAL   7

The final phase of the performance evaluation process is performance appraisal. The two preceding phases supplied information indicating how the account performed and quantifying the sources of that performance relative to a designated benchmark. Ultimately, however, fund sponsors are concerned with whether the manager of the account has displayed investment skill and whether the manager is likely to sustain that skill. The goal of performance appraisal is to provide quantitative evidence that the fund sponsor can use to make decisions about whether to retain or modify portions of its investment program.

That said, perhaps no issue elicits more frustration on the part of fund sponsors than the subject of appraising manager investment skill. The problem stems from the inherent uncertainty surrounding the outcome of active management decisions. Even the most talented managers can underperform their benchmarks during any given quarter, year, or even multiyear period due to poor luck. Conversely, ineffective managers at times may make correct decisions and outperform their benchmarks simply by good fortune. We will return to this concept later.

What do we mean by the term "investment skill"? We define **investment skill** as the ability to outperform an appropriate benchmark consistently over time. As discussed previously, a manager's returns in excess of his or her benchmark are commonly referred to as the manager's value-added return or active return. Because no manager is omniscient, every manager's value-added returns, regardless of the manager's skill, will be positive in some periods and negative in others. Nevertheless, a skillful manager should produce a larger value-added return more frequently than his or her less talented peers.

We emphasize that a skillful manager may produce a small value-added return very frequently or a larger value-added return less frequently. It is the magnitude of the value-added returns relative to the variability of value-added returns that determines a manager's skill.

When evaluating managers, many fund sponsors focus solely on the level of value-added returns produced while ignoring value-added return volatility. As a consequence, superior managers may be terminated (or not hired) and inferior managers may be retained (or hired) on the basis of statistically questionable performance data.

7.1 Risk-Adjusted Performance Appraisal Measures

Risk-adjusted performance appraisal methods can mitigate the natural fixation on rates of return. There are a number of appraisal measures that explicitly take the volatility of returns into account. A widely accepted principle of investment management theory and practice is that investors are risk averse and therefore require additional expected return to compensate for increased risk. Thus, it is not surprising that measures of performance appraisal compare returns generated by an account manager with the account's corresponding risk. Two types of risk are typically applied to deflate *ex post* returns: the account's market (or systematic) risk, as measured by its beta, and the account's total risk, as measured by its standard deviation.

Three risk-adjusted performance appraisal measures have become widely used: **ex post alpha** (also known as Jensen's alpha), the Treynor measure (also known as reward-to-volatility or excess return to nondiversifiable risk), and the **Sharpe ratio** (also known as reward-to-variability). Another measure, **M²**, has also received some acceptance. A thorough discussion of these measures can be found in standard investment texts such as Sharpe, Alexander, and Bailey (1999), but we present a summary here. We consider these measures in their *ex post* (after the fact) form used to appraise a past record of performance.

***Ex Post* Alpha**   The *ex post* alpha (also known as the *ex post* Jensen's alpha—see Jensen 1968, 1969) uses the *ex post* Security Market Line (SML) to form a benchmark for performance appraisal purposes. Recall that the capital asset pricing model (CAPM) developed by Sharpe (1966), Lintner (1965), and Mossin (1966), from which the *ex post* SML is derived, assumes that on an *ex ante* (before the fact) basis, expected account returns are a linear function of the risk-free return plus a risk premium that is based on the expected excess return on the market portfolio over the risk-free return, scaled by the amount of systematic risk (beta) assumed by the account. That is, over a single period, the *ex ante* CAPM (SML) is

$$E(R_A) = r_f + \beta_A[E(R_M) - r_f] \tag{17}$$

where

$E(R_A)$ = the expected return on the account, given its beta
r_f = the risk-free rate of return (known constant for the evaluation period)
$E(R_M)$ = the expected return on the market portfolio
β_A = the account's beta or sensitivity to returns on the market portfolio, equal to the ratio of covariance to variance as $Cov(R_A, R_M)/Var(R_M)$

With data on the actual returns of 1) the account, 2) a proxy for the market portfolio (a market index), and 3) the risk-free rate, we can produce an *ex post* version of the CAPM relationship. Rearranging Equation 17, a simple linear regression can estimate the parameters of the following relationship:

$$R_{At} - r_{ft} = \alpha_A + \beta_A(R_{Mt} - r_{ft}) + \varepsilon_t \tag{18}$$

where for period t, R_{At} is the return on the account, r_{ft} is the risk-free return, and R_{Mt} is the return on the market proxy (market index).[31] The term α_A is the intercept of the regression, β_A is the beta of the account relative to the market index, and ε is the random error term of the regression equation. The estimate of the intercept term α_A is the *ex post* alpha. We can interpret *ex post* alpha as the differential return of the account compared to the return required to compensate for the systematic risk assumed by the account during the evaluation period. The level of the manager's demonstrated

---

[31] The *ex post* alpha relationship can be expanded to incorporate other sources of risk (for example, the three-factor model developed by Fama and French). See Carhart (1997) for further discussion.

skill is indicated by the sign and value of the *ex post* alpha. Left unsaid is whether the fund sponsor prefers a manager with a large (positive) but highly variable alpha to one that produces a smaller (positive) but less variable alpha.

Treynor Measure   The Treynor measure (see Treynor 1965) is closely related to the *ex post* alpha. Like the *ex post* alpha, the Treynor measure relates an account's excess returns to the systematic risk assumed by the account. As a result, it too uses the *ex post* SML to form a benchmark, but in a somewhat different manner than the *ex post* alpha. The calculation of the Treynor measure is

$$T_A = \frac{\bar{R}_A - \bar{r}_f}{\hat{\beta}_A} \qquad\qquad (19)$$

$\bar{R}_A$ and $\bar{r}_f$ are the average values of each variable over the evaluation period. The Treynor measure has a relatively simple visual interpretation, given that the beta of the risk-free asset is zero. The Treynor measure is simply the slope of a line, graphed in the space of mean *ex post* returns and beta, which connects the average risk-free return to the point representing the average return and beta of the account. When viewed alongside the *ex post* SML, the account's benchmark effectively becomes the slope of the *ex post* SML. Thus, a skillful manager will produce returns that result in a slope greater than the slope of the *ex post* SML.

Both the *ex post* alpha and the Treynor measure will always give the same assessment of the existence of investment skill. This correspondence is evident from the fact that any account with a positive *ex post* alpha must plot above the *ex post* SML. Therefore, the slope of a line connecting the risk-free rate to this account must be greater than the slope of the *ex post* SML, the indication of skill under the Treynor measure.

Sharpe Ratio   Both the *ex post* alpha and Treynor measure compare excess returns on an account relative to the account's systematic risk. In contrast, the Sharpe ratio (see Sharpe 1966) compares excess returns to the total risk of the account, where total risk is measured by the account's standard deviation of returns. The *ex post* Sharpe ratio is traditionally given by

$$S_A = \frac{\bar{R}_A - \bar{r}_f}{\hat{\sigma}_A} \qquad\qquad (20)$$

The benchmark in the case of the Sharpe ratio is based on the *ex post* capital market line (CML). The *ex post* CML is plotted in the space of returns and standard deviation of returns and connects the risk-free return and the point representing the mean return on the market index and its estimated standard deviation during the evaluation period. As with the Treynor measure, a skillful manager will produce returns that place the account above the CML, and hence the slope of the line connecting the risk-free rate and the account will lie above the *ex post* CML. Such a manager is producing more average return relative to the risk-free rate per unit of volatility than is a passive investment in the market index.

M²   Like the Sharpe ratio, M² (see Modigliani and Modigliani 1997) uses standard deviation as the measure of risk and is based on the *ex post* CML. M² is the mean incremental return over a market index of a hypothetical portfolio formed by combining the account with borrowing or lending at the risk-free rate so as to match the standard deviation of the market index. M² measures what the account would have returned if it had taken on the same total risk as the market index. To produce that benchmark, M² scales up or down the excess return of the account over the risk-free rate by a factor equal to the ratio of the market index's standard deviation to the account's standard deviation.

$$M_A^2 = \overline{r}_f + \left(\frac{\overline{R}_A - \overline{r}_f}{\hat{\sigma}_A}\right)\hat{\sigma}_M \qquad (21)$$

Visually, we can consider a line from the average risk-free rate to the point representing the average return and standard deviation of the account. Extending (or retracing) this line to a point corresponding to the standard deviation of the market index allows us to compare the return on the account to that of the market index at the same level of risk. A skillful manager will generate an M^2 value that exceeds the return on the market index.

M^2 will evaluate the skill of a manager exactly as does the Sharpe ratio. Further, as we discussed, the Jensen's alpha and the Treynor measure will produce the same conclusions regarding the existence of manager skill. However, it is possible for the Sharpe ratio and M^2 to identify a manager as not skillful, although the *ex post* alpha and the Treynor measure come to the opposite conclusion. This outcome is most likely to occur in instances where the manager takes on a large amount of nonsystematic risk in the account relative to the account's systematic risk. In that case, one can see by comparing Equations 19 and 20 that while the numerator remains the same, increased nonsystematic risk will lower the Sharpe ratio but leave the Treynor measure unaffected. As the market index, by definition, has no nonsystematic risk, the account's performance will look weaker relative to the market index under the Sharpe ratio than under the Treynor measure (and Jensen's alpha).

Information Ratio   The Sharpe ratio can be used to incorporate both risk-adjusted returns and a benchmark appropriate for the manager of the account under evaluation. In its traditional form, the numerator of the Sharpe ratio is expressed as the returns on the account in excess of the risk-free rate. Similarly, the denominator is expressed as the standard deviation of the difference in returns between the account and the risk-free return. However, by definition, in a single-period context the risk-free rate has no variability, and hence, the denominator can be stated as the variability in the account's returns.

Because the Sharpe ratio is based on a differential return, it represents the results of a self-financing strategy. A certain dollar amount can be viewed as being invested in the account, with this long position funded by short-selling the risk-free asset; that is, borrowing at the risk-free rate is assumed to fund the investment in the account. In order to provide a relevant context for performance appraisal using the traditional form, we must identify an appropriate benchmark and compute the Sharpe ratio for that benchmark as well as the account. A higher Sharpe ratio for the account than for the benchmark indicates superior performance.

There is no reason, however, for insisting on appraising performance in the context of borrowing at the risk-free rate to fund the investment in the account. Instead, the Sharpe ratio can be generalized to directly incorporate a benchmark appropriate to the account manager's particular investment style. Equation 20 can be rewritten to show the long position in the account is funded by a short position in the benchmark:

$$\text{IR}_A = \frac{\overline{R}_A - \overline{R}_B}{\hat{\sigma}_{A-B}} \qquad (22)$$

where $\hat{\sigma}_{A-B}$ is the standard deviation of the difference between the returns on the account and the returns on the benchmark. The Sharpe ratio in this form is commonly referred to as the **information ratio**, defined as the excess return of the account over the benchmark relative to the variability of that excess return. The numerator is often referred to as the **active return** on the account, and the denominator is referred to as the account's **active risk**. Thus, from this perspective, the information ratio measures the reward earned by the account manager per incremental unit of risk created by deviating from the benchmark's holdings.

Criticisms of Risk-Adjusted Performance Appraisal Methods   A number of criticisms of risk-adjusted performance measures have surfaced over the years, and we will return to some of those arguments later in the discussion. Perhaps the most prominent criticisms have involved the reliance of the *ex post* alpha and the Treynor measure on the validity of the CAPM. The CAPM has come under attack for a variety of reasons, most notably the appropriateness of its underlying assumptions and the single-index nature of the model. If assets are valued according to some other equilibrium pricing model, then beta-based performance measures may give inaccurate appraisals.

Critics (for example, Roll 1978) have also pointed to problems raised by the use of surrogates (such as the S&P 500) for the true market portfolio. Roll showed that slight changes in the market portfolio surrogate can yield significantly different performance appraisal answers.

Even those appraisal methods not tied to the CAPM face implementation problems. For example, the use of a market index or custom benchmark in the appraisal of investment performance is open to criticism in that it is difficult in most cases for the account manager to replicate precisely the benchmark's return over time (see French and Henderson 1985). Transaction costs associated with initially creating and then later rebalancing the benchmark, as well as the costs of reinvesting income flows, mean that the benchmark's reported returns overstate the performance that a passive investor in the benchmark could earn.

Stability of the parameters and the estimation error involved in the risk-adjusted appraisal measures is also an issue. Even if the assumptions underlying the appraisal measures hold true, the *ex post* calculations are merely estimates of the true parameters of the actual risk–return relationships. If the estimates are recalculated over another period, they may well show conclusions that conflict with the earlier estimates, even if those relationships are stable over time. Further, that stability cannot be taken for granted; the aggressiveness of the account manager may change rapidly over time in ways that cannot be captured by the estimation procedures.

7.2 Quality Control Charts

Conveying the essence of performance appraisal to decision makers is a difficult task. A vast quantity of data needs to be synthesized into a relatively few graphs and tables if information overload is to be avoided. Yet this summary process should not come at the expense of sound data analysis. In particular, it should not preclude a consideration of the statistical and economic significance of the performance results. One effective means of presenting performance appraisal data is through the use of **quality control charts**.

Exhibit 15 presents an example of a quality control chart. It illustrates the performance of an actively managed account versus a selected benchmark. The straight horizontal line emanating from the vertical axis at zero represents the performance of the benchmark. The jagged line is the portfolio's cumulative annualized performance relative to the benchmark (that is, the manager's value-added return). The funnel-shaped lines surrounding the horizontal lines form a confidence band, a statistical concept about which we will have more to say shortly. The confidence band offers a means to evaluate the statistical significance of the account's performance relative to the benchmark.

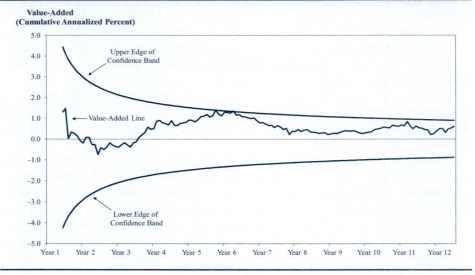

Exhibit 15   Quality Control Chart: Cumulative Annualized Value-Added Illustrating Manager Performance within Expectations

Underlying the quality control chart's construction are three assumptions concerning the likely distribution of the manager's value-added returns. The primary assumption (and one that we will subsequently test) is referred to as the null hypothesis. The null hypothesis of the quality control chart is that the manager has no investment skill; thus, the expected value-added return is zero. With respect to Exhibit 15, we expect that the manager's value-added return line will coincide with the benchmark line.

Of course, at the end of an evaluation period it is highly unlikely that the account's return will precisely equal that of the benchmark. The account's actual return will be either above or below the benchmark's return. The null hypothesis, however, suggests that those *ex post* differences have no directional biases and are entirely due to random chance.

Our second assumption states that the manager's value-added returns are independent from period to period and normally distributed around the expected value of zero. The third assumption is that the manager's investment process does not change from period to period. Among other things, this third assumption implies that the variability of the manager's value-added returns remains constant over time.

Now consider the manager whose investment results are shown in Exhibit 15. Employing the three assumptions described above, we can completely describe the expected distribution of the manager's value-added returns, as illustrated in Exhibit 16. Corresponding to our second assumption of normally distributed value-added returns, the shape of the distribution is the familiar bell-shaped curve. Under our first assumption of no skill (the null hypothesis), the center (or mean) of the distribution is located at 0 percent. Finally, given our third assumption that the manager does not alter his or her investment process over time, we can use the manager's past performance to estimate the dispersion of the value-added return distribution. That dispersion is measured by the standard deviation of the value-added returns, which in this case is an annualized 4.1 percent. We therefore expect that two-thirds of the time, the manager's annual value-added return results will be within ±4.1 percentage points of the zero mean.

Exhibit 16	Expected Distribution of the Manager's Value-Added Returns

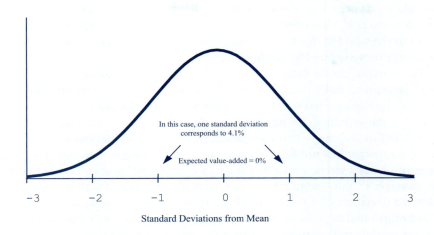

In this case, one standard deviation corresponds to 4.1%

Expected value-added = 0%

−3   −2   −1   0   1   2   3

Standard Deviations from Mean

Given this information, we can compute a confidence band associated with the expected distribution of the manager's value-added returns. Based on our three assumptions, the **confidence band** indicates the range in which we anticipate that the manager's value-added returns will fall a specified percentage of the time.

In our example, suppose that we wished to determine a confidence band designed to capture 80 percent of the manager's value-added return results. Based on the properties of a normal distribution, we know that 1.28 standard deviations around the mean will capture *ex ante* 80 percent of the possible outcomes associated with a normally distributed random variable. With a 4.1 percent annual standard deviation of value-added returns, the 80 percent confidence band in our example therefore covers a range from approximately −5.2 percent to approximately +5.2 percent around the manager's expected value-added return of zero.

This range, however, corresponds to only one time period: one year from the start of the analysis. To create the confidence band at other points in time, we must transform the standard deviation of the manager's value-added returns to address annualized cumulative value-added returns. This transformation produces the funnel-shaped lines shown in Exhibit 15.

The standard deviation of annualized cumulative value-added returns decreases at a rate equal to the square root of time. As a result, the standard deviation of annualized cumulative value-added returns at two years is $1/\sqrt{2}$ of the one-year value, at three years it is $1/\sqrt{3}$ of the one-year value, and so on. Because the width of the confidence band depends on the standard deviation of value-added returns, as time passes, the confidence band will narrow, converging on the benchmark line.

Intuitively, that convergence means that as we collect more observations on the manager's value-added returns, the cumulative annualized results should lie closer to our expected value of zero. That is, as time passes, it becomes increasingly likely that the manager's random positive and negative value-added returns will offset one another. Therefore, the chances that the manager will produce a "large" cumulative annualized value-added return, on either side of the mean, declines over time.

7.3 Interpreting the Quality Control Chart

Statistical inference by its nature can be a baffling exercise in double negatives. For example, we do not *accept* the null hypothesis. Rather, lacking evidence to the contrary, we *fail to reject* it. Nevertheless, the equivocal nature of this type of analysis is well suited to the world of investments, where luck often masquerades as skill and skill is frequently overwhelmed by random events.

For example, do the data presented in Exhibit 15 tell us anything about the manager's investment skill? The answer in this case is inconclusive. Over the full period of analysis, the manager has outperformed the benchmark by about 1.0 percent per year. Based on this outcome, we might be tempted to certify the manager as being truly skillful. Before leaping to that conclusion, however, recall that our null hypothesis is that the manager has no skill. What we are really asking is, "Do the manager's performance results warrant rejecting the null hypothesis?" Remember that we assume the manager's value-added returns are normally distributed with a constant annual standard deviation of 4.1 percent. Given those assumptions, under the zero-value-added return null hypothesis, there exists a strong possibility that the manager could possess no skill and yet produce the results shown in Exhibit 15.

The quality control chart analysis provides a likely range of value-added return results for a manager who possesses no skill and who displays a specified level of value-added return variability. For a manager whose investment results are within that range (confidence band), we have no strong statistical evidence to indicate that our initial assumption of no skill is incorrect. Thus we are left with the rather unsatisfying statement, "We cannot reject the null hypothesis that the manager has no skill."

It may be true that the manager in Exhibit 15 has skill and that the 1 percent value-added return was no fluke. Unfortunately, over the limited time that we have to observe the manager, and given the variability of the manager's value-added returns, we cannot classify the manager as unambiguously skillful. Even if the manager could actually produce a 1 percent value-added return over the long run, his or her talents are obscured by the variability of his or her short-run results. That performance "noise" makes it difficult to distinguish his or her talents from those of an unskillful manager.

Now let us consider another manager who generates the value-added return series shown in Exhibit 17. The confidence interval is again designed to capture 80 percent of the potential value-added return outcomes for a zero-value-added return manager with a specified level of value-added return variability. In this case, the manager has breached the confidence band on the upside, outperforming the benchmark by about 5 percent per year over the evaluation period. How should we interpret this situation? One view is that the manager has no skill and was simply lucky. After all, there is a 2-in-10 chance that a zero-value-added return manager might produce results that lie somewhere outside the confidence band (actually, a 1-in-10 chance of lying above and a 1-in-10 chance of lying below the confidence band).

On the other hand, we could reject the null hypothesis. That is, there is only a 20 percent chance that a zero-value-added return manager would produce results that lie outside the confidence band. Therefore, the occurrence of such an event might indicate that our initial assumption that the manager has no skill is incorrect. Note that our statement would then be, "We reject the null hypothesis that the manager's expected value-added return is zero." By implication, then, we accept a strategy hypothesis that the manager's expected value-added return is not zero.[32]

---

[32] Of course, the assumptions underlying the statistical test may not hold. For example, the manager's investment process may have become more aggressive, and hence, the variability of his value-added returns may have increased.

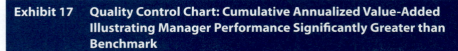

Exhibit 17   Quality Control Chart: Cumulative Annualized Value-Added Illustrating Manager Performance Significantly Greater than Benchmark

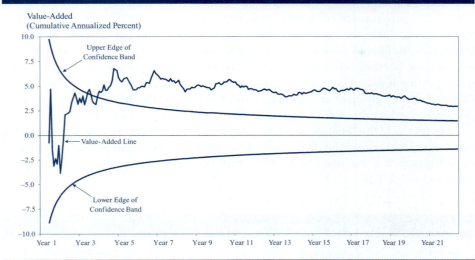

The quality control chart analysis is similar on the downside. That is, suppose that the manager produces a cumulative negative value-added return yet lies above the lower edge of the confidence band. In that situation, we should not reject the null hypothesis that the manager's expected value-added return is zero. The manager might be a negative value-added return investor (that is, be unable to earn back his or her management fees and trading costs). On the other hand, the manager might be skillful and simply be having a poor run of investment luck. In such a case, the relatively small negative value-added return compared to the variability of that value-added return would make it difficult to reject the null hypothesis.

Conversely, piercing the confidence interval on the downside might lead us to reject the null hypothesis that the manager's expected value-added return is zero. The unstated implication is that the manager is systematically incapable of recapturing the costs of doing business and should be classified as an "underperformer."

THE PRACTICE OF PERFORMANCE EVALUATION   8

The three components of performance evaluation provide the quantitative inputs required to evaluate the investment skill of an account's manager. However, regardless of the amount of performance data compiled, the process of performance evaluation is fraught with imprecision. Performance evaluation is ultimately a forward-looking decision, and the connection between past performance and future performance is tenuous at best.[33] Indiscriminate use of quantitative data can lead to counterproductive decisions.

As a result, in evaluating investment managers, most fund sponsors follow a procedure that incorporates both quantitative and qualitative elements, with the latter typically receiving more weight than the former. For example, in selecting investment managers, many fund sponsors follow a relatively standard set of procedures. For the sake of exposition, we consider a "typical" fund sponsor. The fund sponsor has

---

33 See Carhart (1997).

a several-person staff that carries out the fund's day-to-day operations. The fund sponsor may retain a consultant to assist in the search for new managers. The staff continually scans the marketplace for promising investment managers. The staff may become aware of a manager through such means as visits from the manager to the staff's office, attendance at various conferences, discussions with peers at other fund sponsor organizations, meetings with consulting firms, and the financial press. The staff maintains files on those managers who have attracted interest, collecting historical return data, portfolio compositions, manager investment process descriptions, and other pertinent data. Upon deciding to hire a new manager, the staff will research its files and select a group of managers for extensive review. This initial cut is an informal decision based on the staff's ongoing survey of the manager marketplace.

The review of the "finalist" group is a much more formal and extensive process. The staff requests that each finalist submit detailed data concerning virtually all aspects of its organization and operations. We broadly group this data into six categories, as shown in Exhibit 18.

Exhibit 18 Criteria for Manager Selection	
Criteria	**Importance (%)**
Physical	5
Organizational structure, size, experience, other resources	
People	25
Investment professionals, compensation	
Process	30
Investment philosophy, style, decision making	
Procedures	15
Benchmarks, trading, quality control	
Performance	20
Results relative to an appropriate benchmark	
Price	5
Investment management fees	

The staff assigns weights or relative importance to each of these criteria. Exhibit 18 shows one possible set of weights. The staff does not apply these criteria and weights in a mechanical manner. Its ultimate decisions are actually quite subjective. The important point is that the staff considers a broad range of quantitative and qualitative factors in arriving at a selection recommendation. No single factor dominates the decision: performance data are only one component in the ultimate evaluation decision.

In addition to collecting written information, the staff meets personally with the key decision makers from each of the finalist managers. In those meetings the staff engages in a broad discussion, the purpose of which is to focus on specific aspects of the managers' operations as highlighted by the selection criteria.

After meeting with all of the finalists, the staff compares notes and selects a manager (or managers) to recommend to the fund sponsor's investment committee, which makes the final decision. The committee members are much more performance-oriented than the staff. Nevertheless, they usually support the staff's well-researched recommendations.

8.1 Noisiness of Performance Data

The goal of evaluating prospective or existing managers is to hire or keep the best managers and to eliminate managers likely to produce inferior future results. If past performance were closely tied to future performance, then it would be desirable to rely heavily on past performance in evaluating managers. The problem is that empirical evidence generally does not support such a relationship.

The confusion results from the uncertain, or stochastic, nature of active management. Active managers are highly fallible. While we may expect a superior manager to perform well over any given time period, we will observe that the superior manager's actual performance is quite variable. Even sophisticated investors tend to focus on expected returns and ignore this risk element.

EXAMPLE 17

The Influence of Noise on Performance Appraisal

Suppose that we know in advance that a manager is superior and will produce an annual value-added return of 2 percent, on average. The variability of that superior performance is 5 percent per year. Our hypothetical manager has an information ratio of 0.40 (2% ÷ 5%), which by our experience is a high figure. (Hence our assertion that this manager is a superior manager.) Exhibit 19 shows the probability of managers outperforming their benchmarks over various evaluation periods, given the information ratios.

Exhibit 19   Probability of a Manager Outperforming a Benchmark Given Various Levels of Investment Skill

	Information Ratio					
Years	0.20	0.30	0.40	0.67	0.80	1.00
0.5	55.63%	58.40%	61.14%	68.13%	71.42%	76.02%
1.0	57.93	61.79	65.54	74.75	78.81	84.03
3.0	63.81	69.83	75.58	87.59	91.71	95.84
5.0	67.26	74.88	81.45	93.20	96.32	98.73
10.0	73.65	82.86	89.70	98.25	99.43	99.92
20.0	81.70	91.01	96.32	99.86	99.98	99.99

Perhaps surprisingly, Exhibit 19 shows that the manager has a 1-in-4 chance of underperforming the benchmark over a period as long as three years, as seen by the boxed cell in the exhibit. Remember, we have defined this manager in advance to be a superior manager. Other value-added managers with less skill than this one have a greater chance of underperforming their benchmarks over typical evaluation periods.

Most fund sponsors hire more than one manager. Consider a group of ten superior managers whose investment skills equal those of the manager in Example 17 (who has an information ratio of 0.40) and assume independence of decision-making processes. Exhibit 20 shows the probability of a given number of this group simultaneously underperforming their benchmarks over a three-year period. As we can see, a fund sponsor using a simple decision rule of firing any manager who underperforms his or her benchmark over a three-year period can expect to follow a busy manager search schedule. Moreover, these probabilities are conservatively low. Few of the fund sponsor's managers will have the investment skill with which we have endowed our hypothetical managers.

Exhibit 20	Probability of Superior Managers Jointly Underperforming Their Benchmarks over a Three-Year Period
Managers below Benchmark	**Probability**
0	6.10%
1	19.68
2	28.59
3	24.60
4	13.90
5	5.38
6	1.45
7	0.27
8	0.03
9	0.00
10	0.00

In summary, using past performance to evaluate existing managers is statistically problematic. In the long run, superior managers will outperform inferior managers. However, due to the inherent uncertainty of investment management, over typical evaluation periods (3–5 years) the odds that superior managers will underperform their benchmarks (and, conversely, that inferior managers will outperform their benchmarks) are disturbingly high. Expensive, incorrect decisions may frequently result from relying on past performance to evaluate investment managers.

8.2 Manager Continuation Policy

Frequent manager firings based on recent performance might seem to be merely a waste of a fund sponsor's time if not for the expenses associated with manager transitions. Fired managers' portfolios must be converted to the hired managers' portfolios. This conversion requires buying and selling securities, which in turn involves trading costs. Making assumptions about the cost of trading securities is a tenuous business at best, because many factors influence that cost. For US large-capitalization common stocks, it is reasonable to assume transaction costs of 0.50 percent (one way), and for small company stocks and stocks of companies traded in less liquid markets, those costs can be much higher. A substantial percentage of the fired manager's portfolio may need to be liquidated in the process of moving the assets to a new manager, particularly when the managers' styles are not closely similar. Moreover, this tally of the expenses of converting a manager's portfolio considers only direct monetary costs. For most fund sponsors, replacing managers involves significant time and effort.[34]

---

[34] The costs associated with manager hiring and firing decisions are discussed in Goyal and Wahal (2005).

In an attempt to reduce the costs of manager turnover yet systematically act on indications of future poor performance, some fund sponsors have adopted formal, written **manager continuation policies** (MCP) to guide their manager evaluations. The purpose of an MCP is severalfold:

- to retain superior managers and to remove inferior managers, preferably before the latter can produce adverse results;
- to ensure that relevant nonperformance information is given significant weight in the evaluation process;
- to minimize manager turnover; and
- to develop procedures that will be consistently applied regardless of investment committee and staff changes.

An MCP can be viewed as a two-part process. The first part we refer to as **manager monitoring**, while the second part we call **manager review**. Exhibit 21 displays a flow chart description of an MCP.

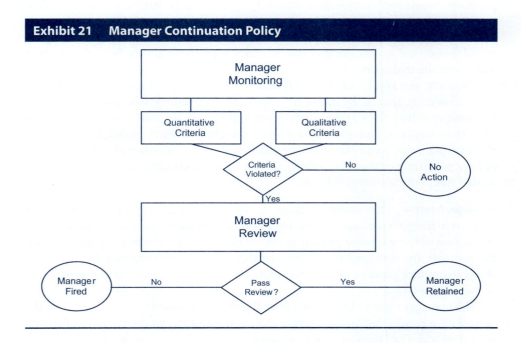

Exhibit 21   Manager Continuation Policy

Manager Monitoring   The ongoing phase of an MCP is manager monitoring. The goal of MCP manager monitoring is to identify warning signs of adverse changes in existing managers' organizations. It is a formal, documented procedure that assists fund sponsors in consistently collecting information relevant to evaluating the state of their managers' operations. The key is that the fund sponsor regularly asks the same important questions, both in written correspondence and in face-to-face meetings.

There is no firm set of appropriate manager monitoring criteria. Each fund sponsor must determine for itself the issues that are relevant to its own particular circumstances. Monitoring criteria may even vary from manager to manager. Regardless, the fund sponsor should clearly articulate its established criteria at the time a manager is hired, rather than formulate them later in a haphazard manner.

As part of the manager monitoring process, the fund sponsor periodically receives information from the managers, either in written form or through face-to-face meetings. This information is divided into two parts. The first part covers operational matters, such as personnel changes, account growth, litigation, and so on. The staff should flag significant items and discuss them in a timely manner with the respective managers.

The second part of the responses contains a discussion of the managers' investment strategies, on both a retrospective and a prospective basis. The fund sponsor should instruct the managers to explain their recent investment strategies relative to their respective benchmarks and how those strategies performed. The managers should follow this review with a discussion of their current strategies relative to the benchmark and why they believe that those strategies are appropriate. The goal of these discussions is to assure the fund sponsor that the manager is continuing to pursue a coherent, consistent investment approach. Unsatisfactory manager responses may be interpreted as warning signs that the manager's investment approach may be less well-defined or less consistently implemented than the staff had previously believed.

As part of the manager monitoring process, the staff should regularly collect portfolio return and composition data for a performance attribution analysis. The purpose of such a periodic analysis is to evaluate not how well the managers have performed, but whether that performance has been consistent with the managers' stated investment styles. The staff should address questions arising from this analysis directly to the managers.

Typically, the results of the MCP manager monitoring stage reveal nothing of serious concern. That is, the managers' organizations remain stable, and the managers continue to follow their stated investment approaches regardless of the near-term success or failure of their particular active strategies. While the managers should be able to explain why particular strategies failed, the mere occurrence of isolated periods of poor performance should typically not be a cause for concern, unless the staff finds related nonperformance problems.

Manager Review   Occasionally, manager monitoring may identify an item of sufficient concern to trigger a manager review. For example, a recently successful small manager might experience excessive growth in accounts and assets. Despite discussions with the manager, the staff might be convinced that such growth threatens the manager's ability to produce superior returns in the future. At this point, a formal manager review becomes necessary.

The manager review closely resembles the manager selection process, in both the information considered and the comprehensiveness of the analysis. The staff should review all phases of the manager's operations, just as if the manager were being initially hired. We can view this manager review as a zero-based budgeting process (a budgeting process in which all expenditures must be justified each new period). We want to answer the question, "Would we hire the manager again today?"

As with the initial selection of a manager, the fund sponsor should collect the same comprehensive data and meet face-to-face with the manager in a formal interview setting. The manager's key personnel should attend, with the advance understanding that they must persuade the staff to "rehire" them. On conclusion of the interview, the staff should meet to compare observations, weighing the evaluation criteria in the same manner that it would if it were initially considering the manager. As part of these deliberations, the fund sponsor should also review the information that led to the manager's hiring in the first place.

The primary differences between hiring a new manager and retaining a manager under review are that the fund sponsor once had enough confidence in the manager to entrust a large sum of money to the manager's judgment and that there is a sizable cost associated with firing the manager. Thus, the fund sponsor should address the following questions:

- What has fundamentally changed in the manager's operation?
- Is the change significant?
- What are the likely ramifications of the change?
- Are the costs of firing the manager outweighed by the potential benefits?

8.3 Manager Continuation Policy as a Filter

For many reasons, investment skill does not readily lend itself to rigid "good" or "bad" interpretations. For discussion purposes, however, we will arbitrarily divide the investment manager community into three categories: positive-, zero-, and negative-value-added managers. Assume that positive-value-added managers beat their benchmarks (after all fees and expenses) by 2 percent per year, on average. Zero-value-added managers exhibit just enough skill to cover their fees and expenses and thereby match the performance of their benchmarks. Finally, negative-value-added managers lose to their benchmarks by 1 percent per year, on average, due primarily to the impact of fees and expenses.

We have no firm evidence as to how the manager community is apportioned among these three categories, although if we follow the logic of Grossman and Stiglitz (1980) and Sharpe (1994), the zero- and negative-value-added managers must predominate, with the former outnumbering the latter. Nevertheless, we speculate that out of five managers hired, a fund sponsor would be fortunate to hire two positive-value-added managers, two zero-value-added managers, and one negative-value-added manager. Therefore, in aggregate, this successful fund sponsor's managers are expected to outperform their benchmarks by 60 basis points per year, net of all costs [0.6% = (2% × 0.4) + (0% × 0.4) + (−1% × 0.2)].

We can view a MCP as a statistical filter designed to remove negative-value-added managers and retain positive-value-added managers. Zero-value-added managers, much to the consternation of fund sponsors, always present a problem for a MCP, because they are so numerous and because they are statistically difficult to distinguish from positive- and negative-value-added managers.

We begin our MCP analysis with the null hypothesis that the managers under evaluation are at best zero-value-added managers. Then, as with any filter, two types of decision errors may occur:

- **Type I error**—keeping (or hiring) managers with zero value-added. (Rejecting the null hypothesis when it is correct.)
- **Type II error**—firing (or not hiring) managers with positive value-added. (Not rejecting the null hypothesis when it is incorrect.)

In implementing a MCP, the fund sponsor must determine how fine a filter to construct. A coarse filter will be conducive to Type I errors. For example, a fund sponsor may choose to overlook many violations of its manager monitoring guidelines, with the expectation that most problems experienced by managers are temporary and that they will eventually work themselves out. While this policy will avoid firing some positive-value-added managers, the fund sponsor could have identified in advance some managers who will provide mediocre long-term performance.

Conversely, a fine filter will lead the sponsor to commit more Type II errors. For example, a fund sponsor might apply its manager monitoring guidelines rigidly and automatically fire any manager who loses a key decision maker. While this policy will remove some managers whose operations will be disrupted by personnel turnover, it will also eliminate some managers possibly anticipated to recover from that turnover and to continue with superior results.

Exhibit 22 presents the four possible results from testing the null hypothesis that a manager has no investment skill. Referring back to the quality control chart, if in truth the manager has no skill and we reject the null hypothesis because the manager's value-added returns fall outside of the confidence band (particularly, in this case, on the upside), then we have committed a Type I error. Conversely, if the manager is indeed skillful yet we fail to reject the null hypothesis because the manager's value-added returns fall inside the confidence band, then we have committed a Type II error.

Exhibit 22   Null Hypothesis: Manager Has No Skill; Alternative Hypothesis: Manager Is Skillful

	Reality	
	Value-Added = 0	Value-Added > 0
Reject	Type I	Correct
Do Not Reject	Correct	Type II

Both Type I and Type II errors are expensive. The art of a MCP is to strike a cost-effective balance between the two that avoids excessive manager turnover yet eliminates managers likely to produce inferior performance in the future. We can control the probabilities of committing Type I and Type II errors by adjusting the width of the confidence band within the quality control chart. For example, suppose that we widened the confidence band to encompass 95% of a manager's possible value-added return outcomes. Now it will be less likely than in our earlier examples that a zero-value-added return manager will generate returns that lie outside the confidence band. We thus reduce the chances of a Type I error. However, it will also now be less likely that a truly skillful manager will come to our attention by generating returns that fall outside that manager's confidence band. By continuing not to reject the null hypothesis for such a manager, we commit a Type II error.

Due to the high costs and uncertain benefits of replacing managers, it would seem advisable for fund sponsors to develop manager evaluation procedures that are tolerant toward Type I errors in order to reduce the probability of Type II errors. That is, it may be preferable to endure the discomfort of keeping several unskillful managers to avoid the expense of firing a truly superior manager. However, there is no right answer to this dilemma, and fund sponsors must undertake their own cost–benefit analyses, weighing the chances of committing one type of error versus the other. The quality control chart approach, however, provides fund sponsors with an objective framework with which to address this issue.

SUMMARY

Performance evaluation is as important as it is challenging. Decisions reached concerning manager skill can affect the attainment of investment objectives. It therefore benefits investors and their advisors to be up-to-date in their knowledge of this field.

- From the fund sponsor's perspective, performance evaluation serves as a feedback mechanism to a fund's investment policy. It identifies strengths and weaknesses, attributes results to key decisions, and focuses attention on poor performance. It provides evidence to fund trustees on whether the investment program is being conducted effectively. From the investment manager's perspective, performance evaluation permits an investigation of the effectiveness of various elements of the investment process and the contributions of those elements to investment results.

- Performance evaluation is composed of three parts: 1) performance measurement, 2) performance attribution, and 3) performance appraisal.

- The rate of return on an asset is typically defined as the investment-related growth in the asset's value over the evaluation period. When there are intraperiod cash flows, the rate of return can be measured as the growth rate applied to a single dollar invested at the start of the period (time-weighted rate of return, or TWR) or to an "average" amount of dollars invested over the evaluation period (money-weighted rate of return, or MWR). The MWR is sensitive to the size and timing of cash flows, but the TWR is not. Because investment managers rarely have control over the size or timing of cash flows, the TWR is the most commonly used performance measure.

- When the investment manager has control over the size and timing of cash flows into an account, the MWR may be an appropriate performance measure.

- When the MWR is calculated over reasonably frequent time periods and those returns are chain-linked over the entire evaluation period, which could be of any length, an approximation of the TWR for the period, called the Linked Internal Rate of Return (LIRR), is obtained.

- If external funds are added to an account prior to a period of strong performance, the MWR will give a higher rate of return than the TWR. If a large amount is withdrawn prior to a period of strong performance, the MWR will yield a lower rate of return than the TWR. The opposite effect is experienced during periods of weak performance.

- Data quality is important in determining the accuracy of rates of return. Rates of return for large-capitalization securities are likely to be more accurate than those for illiquid and infrequently priced assets.

- A valid benchmark should meet the following criteria: It should be unambiguous, investable, measurable, and appropriate for the manager's style and area of expertise; reflect current investment opinions; be specified in advance; and exhibit ownership by the investment manager.

- The types of benchmarks in common use are: absolute return, manager universes, broad market indexes, style indexes, factor-model-based, returns-based, and custom security-based. A custom security-based benchmark meets all fundamental and quality-based benchmark criteria, making it the most appropriate benchmark to use.

- The median manager or median fund, though intuitively appealing, lacks the following desirable benchmark properties: It is not specified in advance, it is not investable, and it cannot serve as a passive investment.

- Steps in creating a custom security-based benchmark are: Identify prominent aspects of the manager's investment process; select securities consistent with that investment process; devise a weighting scheme for the benchmark securities, including a cash position; review the preliminary benchmark and make modifications; rebalance the benchmark portfolio on a predetermined schedule.

- Good benchmarks should generally display the following characteristics: minimal systematic bias between the account and the benchmark, less tracking error of the account relative to the benchmark when compared to alternative benchmarks, strong correspondence between the manager's universe of potential securities and the benchmark, and low turnover.

- When a factor model is used as a benchmark, an analysis of past portfolios gives a sense of typical exposures (betas) to various systematic sources of return. A "normal" portfolio is one where the factor sensitivities are set to these "normal" betas.

- Performance attribution compares account and benchmark performance and identifies and quantifies sources of differential returns. It requires an appropriate framework for decomposing an account's returns relative to those of the benchmark.

- A manager has two basic avenues for superior performance relative to the benchmark: 1) selecting superior (or avoiding inferior) performing assets and 2) owning the superior (inferior) assets in greater (lesser) proportions than are held in the benchmark.

- Performance attribution conducted at the fund sponsor level is called macro attribution. It has three sets of inputs: 1) policy allocations to asset categories within the fund and to individual managers within asset categories; 2) benchmark portfolio returns; and 3) account returns, valuations, and external cash flows.

- Several decision-making levels can be of interest when evaluating a fund sponsor's decision-making process. These decision levels include: net contributions, the risk-free asset, asset categories, investment style, investment managers, and allocation effects.

- Micro attribution is concerned with the investment results of individual portfolios rather than the entire fund. Over a given period, the difference between the portfolio return and the benchmark return is the manager's value-added return, or active return. Because security-by-security micro attribution is unwieldy, a more productive method uses a factor model of returns to assign value-added return to sources of systematic returns.

- The common stock manager's value-added can be expressed as the difference between the weighted average return on the economic/industry sectors in the portfolio and the benchmark. This value-added return can be further divided into 1) a pure sector allocation component, 2) a within-sector selection component, and 3) an allocation/selection interaction.

- For common stocks, fundamental factors such as company size, industry, and growth characteristics seem to have a systematic impact on account performance. These factors can be combined with economic sector factors to conduct micro attribution.

- Fixed-income portfolio returns may be decomposed to show the contributions from the external interest rate environment, on one hand, and the management effect, on the other.

- The widely accepted tenet that investors are risk averse leads to risk-adjusted performance appraisal methods which compare returns with an account's corresponding risk. Two types of risk measures are typically used: the account's systematic risk (beta) and the account's standard deviation of returns.

- There are several measures of the return relative to the risk of a portfolio. The *ex post* alpha measures the account's excess return over the risk-free rate relative to the excess return of the market proxy over the risk-free rate scaled by the account's beta. The intercept, or alpha, from the estimating regression is a measure of the manager's skill. The Treynor measure is similar to the *ex post* alpha measure and will always give the same assessment of investment skill. It is the account's average return less the average risk-free rate divided by the account's beta. Unlike the *ex post* alpha and Treynor measures, which compare returns on an account relative to its systematic risk, the Sharpe ratio measures returns relative to the account's standard deviation of returns. The Sharpe ratio is an account's average return less the average risk-free rate divided by the account's standard deviation. The M^2 measure is equal to the Sharpe measure multiplied by the standard deviation of the market index and then added to the average risk-free rate.

- The Sharpe ratio can be generalized to directly compare the performance of an account to that of a specific benchmark. In this general form, the Sharpe ratio is called the information ratio and is defined as the excess return of the account over the benchmark, divided by the standard deviation of the excess returns.

- Roll's critique is a major issue when using methods based on the CAPM to evaluate performance. Slight changes in the market portfolio surrogate can yield significantly different performance appraisal answers.

- Quality control charts are an effective way of illustrating performance appraisal data. In simple terms, a quality control chart plots a portfolio manager's performance over time and relative to a benchmark within a statistically derived confidence band. The confidence band indicates whether the manager's performance was statistically different from that of the benchmark.

- Fund sponsors adopt manager continuation policies (MCPs) to guide their manager evaluations. A MCP seeks to develop consistent procedures designed to retain good managers and remove inferior ones based on both quantitative and qualitative information.

- If we begin with the null hypothesis that all managers under evaluation are zero-value-added managers (have no investment skill) and our goal is to identify and separate positive-value-added managers from those without skill, then two types of error can occur. A Type I error results when we keep or hire managers because we believe they are superior when in fact they are not. A Type II error causes us to not reject the null hypothesis when it is incorrect, thus firing or not hiring skillful managers.

PRACTICE PROBLEMS

1   Paul Joubert retired from his firm. He has continued to hold his private retirement investments in a portfolio of common stocks and bonds. At the beginning of 2002, when he retired, his account was valued at €453,000. By the end of 2002, the value of his account was €523,500. Joubert made no contributions to or withdrawals from the portfolio during 2002. What rate of return did Joubert earn on his portfolio during 2002?

2   Frederic Smith works for the Swanson Manufacturing Company and participates in the savings plan at work. He began the month with a balance in his account of £42,000. When he got paid on the last day of the month, the company deposited 10% of his gross salary into his savings plan account (£5,000 gross salary). The ending balance in his account at the end of the month was £42,300.

   A   What was the rate of return for the month in Smith's savings plan?

   B   What would be the rate of return for the month if Swanson had paid Smith and deposited 10% of his salary on the first rather than the last day of the month, holding all else constant?

3   Mary Nesbitt has an investment account with a local firm, and she makes contributions to her account as funds become available. Self-employed, Mary receives money from her clients on an irregular basis. She began the month of September with a balance in her account of $100,000. She received funds in the amount of $3,000 and made a deposit into her account on September 14th. Next, she received a payment of $2,500 on September 21st and made another contribution. The value of her account after the first contribution was $105,000, and the account value was $108,000 after the second contribution. The account was valued at $110,000 at the end of the month. Mary believes that it will be difficult, if not impossible, to determine an accurate rate of return for her account, since her cash flows do not occur on a regular basis.

   A   State and justify whether an accurate rate of return can be calculated.

   B   If an accurate rate of return can be calculated, determine that rate of return.

4   An investment manager has time-weighted returns for the first six months of the year as follows:

January	1.25%
February	3.47%
March	−2.36%
April	1.89%
May	−2.67%
June	2.57%

   A   Calculate a time-weighted rate of return for the investment manager by chain-linking the monthly time-weighted returns.

   B   Compare and contrast the time-weighted rate of return with a calculation involving adding the monthly rates of return.

Practice Problems and Solutions: *Managing Investment Portfolios: A Dynamic Process*, Third Edition, John L. Maginn, CFA, Donald L. Tuttle, CFA, Jerald E. Pinto, CFA, and Dennis W. McLeavey, CFA, editors. Copyright © 2007 by CFA Institute.

5 Compare and contrast the time-weighted rate of return with the money-weighted rate of return. In general terms, how is each calculated? Are there certain situations that would cause the two methods to have drastic differences in the calculated rates of return?

6 A pension portfolio manager is about to upgrade his performance calculation software. Currently, his performance software will only calculate his performance on a quarterly basis. For the year 2005, the quarterly performance numbers are as shown below:

Quarter 1	5.35%
Quarter 2	−2.34%
Quarter 3	4.62%
Quarter 4	1.25%

These values were calculated on a money-weighted rate-of-return basis.

A Explain how you would approximate a time-weighted rate of return for the entire year (2005).

B Determine the approximate time-weighted rate of return.

7 Swennson, who manages a domestic equities portfolio of Swedish shares, has had fairly volatile returns for the last five years. Nevertheless, Swennson claims that his returns over the long run are good. Another Swedish equity manager, Mattsson, has had less volatile returns. Their records are as follows:

Year	Swennson	Mattsson
1	27.5%	5.7%
2	−18.9%	4.9%
3	14.6%	7.8%
4	−32.4%	−6.7%
5	12.3%	5.3%

Assume no interim cash flows.

A Calculate the annualized rates of return for Swennson and Mattsson.

B State which manager achieved a higher return over the five-year period.

8 A US large-cap value portfolio run by Anderson Investment Management returned 18.9% during the first three quarters of 2003. During the same time period, the Russell 1000 Value Index had returns of 21.7% and the Wilshire 5000 returned 25.2%.

A What is the return due to style?

B What is the return due to active management?

C Discuss the implications of your answers to Parts A and B for assessing Anderson's performance relative to the benchmark and relative to the market.

9 You have selected a US domestic equity manager for a small-cap mandate. Your consultant has suggested that you use the Russell 2000® Index as a benchmark. You find the following information on the Russell website:

Russell 3000® Index

The Russell 3000 Index offers investors access to the broad US equity universe representing approximately 98% of the US market. The Russell 3000 is constructed to provide a comprehensive, unbiased, and stable barometer of the broad market and is completely reconstituted annually to ensure new and growing equities are reflected.

Russell 2000® Index

The Russell 2000 Index offers investors access to the small-cap segment of the US equity universe. The Russell 2000 is constructed to provide a comprehensive and unbiased small-cap barometer and is completely reconstituted annually to ensure larger stocks do not distort the performance and characteristics of the true small-cap opportunity set. The Russell 2000 includes the smallest 2000 securities in the Russell 3000.

As of the latest reconstitution, the average market capitalization was approximately $607.1 million; the median market capitalization was approximately $496 million. The index had a total market-capitalization range of approximately $1.6 billion to $175.8 million.

What analysis could you conduct to verify that the Russell 2000® Index is appropriate for the small-cap manager?

10 The information in the table below pertains to a New Zealand pension plan sponsor.

New Zealand Pension Plan Sponsor Account Returns Year of 2002		
Asset Category	**Actual Return**	**Benchmark Return**
Domestic equities	4.54%	4.04%
Equity Mgr A	4.76	4.61
Equity Mgr B	4.13	4.31
International equities	6.39	5.96
Int'l Equity Mgr A	6.54	5.82
Int'l Equity Mgr B	6.20	6.02
Domestic fixed income	1.94	2.56
Fixed-Income Mgr A	1.60	1.99
Fixed-Income Mgr B	2.41	2.55
Total fund	4.33	4.22

Based on the information given in the table, address the following:

A Which asset classes and managers have done relatively well and which have done relatively poorly as judged by returns alone?

B Characterize the overall performance of the pension plan sponsor.

C Assuming that relative outperformance or underperformance as indicated in the table is representative of performance over a substantial time period, would you recommend any changes? If so, what changes would you consider?

11 Briefly discuss the properties that a valid benchmark should have.

12 Kim Lee Ltd., an investment management firm in Singapore managing portfolios of Pacific Rim equities, tells you that its benchmark for performance is to be in the top quartile of its peer group (Singapore managers running portfolios of Pacific Rim equities) over the previous calendar year. Is this a valid benchmark? Why or why not?

13 Susan Jones is a US domestic equities investor. Her portfolio has a zero-factor value of 0.5 and a beta of 1.15 at the beginning of the investment period. During the first quarter of 2003, the return on the Wilshire 5000, a broad US equity market index, was 5.9%.

Jones has just been hired by a large plan sponsor. The sponsor is sophisticated in its use of benchmarks. It has developed a custom benchmark for her portfolio. This benchmark has a zero-factor value of 1.5 and a beta of 0.95.

Calculate the expected return on the portfolio and the benchmark. What is the incremental expected return of the portfolio versus the benchmark? If the portfolio actually returned 8.13% during the period, what is the total differential return, and how much of this can be attributed to the value-added investment skill of Jones?

14 A plan sponsor is considering two UK investment managers, Manchester Asset Management and Oakleaf Equities, for the same mandate. Manchester will produce on average an annual value-added return of 1.5% over the benchmark, with variability of the excess returns of 2.24%. Oakleaf is expected to produce a higher annual value-added return of 4%, but with variability of excess returns around 10%. Using the information in the following table, determine which manager has a larger chance of underperforming the benchmark over periods of 1, 5, and 10 years. Explain the factor(s) causing the manager you identify to have a larger chance of underperforming for a given time period.

Probability of a Manager Outperforming a Benchmark Given Various Levels of Investment Skill

Years	Information Ratio					
	0.20	0.30	0.40	0.67	0.80	1.00
1.0	57.93	61.79	65.54	74.75	78.81	84.03
5.0	67.26	74.88	81.45	93.20	96.32	98.73
10.0	73.65	82.86	89.70	98.25	99.43	99.92
20.0	81.70	91.01	96.32	99.86	99.98	99.99

15 You are a plan sponsor trying to decide between two equity portfolio managers. As you review the information you have gathered during your search, you notice that the two managers have similar investment styles and similar returns for the equity portion of their portfolios. However, the first manager, Acorn Asset Management, keeps its cash level very low, typically around 1% of assets. But the second manager, Zebra Investments, has much more cash in the portfolio and usually keeps approximately 10% in cash for clients' accounts.

Contrast Zebra and Acorn in terms of cash level in the accounts relative to overall portfolio performance. Are there time periods when higher or lower cash levels could be beneficial to an equity portfolio?

16 Briefly explain the challenges inherent in performance measurement and performance evaluation for a long–short hedge fund. If traditional performance measurement and evaluation are not appropriate in a long–short environment, are there other options that may be useful?

17 Compare and contrast macro attribution with micro attribution. What is the difference between using a return metric and using a dollar metric? Briefly discuss the inputs and methodology that could be used with a macro analysis.

Questions 18 through 25 relate to William Denker College[1]

William Denker College (Denker) is a small, liberal arts college in southwestern Pennsylvania with an endowment of $1 billion. Denker outsources the management of their endowment and brought in DBC Advisors (DBCA) to manage a portion of their domestic equity allocation.

DBCA is a small boutique investment firm that specializes in US equities. Denker is their largest client. Denker utilizes DBCA specifically for the large cap value segment of their US equity allocation. On April 1, the account had a market value of $25,000,000.

Chad Driver, CFA, is a recently hired portfolio manager for DBCA. DBCA asks Driver to take over the Denker account from the previous manager, Erik Tarler, who was fired for consistently underperforming his benchmark.

Driver assumes management of the Denker account on April 1 and immediately discovers that Tarler had been using an inappropriate benchmark. Had Tarler been using an appropriate benchmark, DBA would have seen that he had actually been adding value rather than underperforming.

As a result, Driver's first order of business is to develop a new, more appropriate benchmark portfolio. He considers one of the following three options for the benchmark:

Option 1   Absolute return based on a minimum return target of 9.5%

Option 2   Manager universe based on the median of the US Large Cap Core Equity universe

Option 3   Custom security-based

After selecting the benchmark, Driver implements the portfolio. The account activity for his first month is shown in Exhibit 1.

Exhibit 1   Denker's Large Cap Value Account Activity for April

Date	Beginning Market Value	Contribution/ (Withdrawal)	Ending Market Value
April 1	$25,000,000		
April 10		$1,000,000	$25,800,000
April 20		$(500,000)	$25,600,000
April 30			$26,000,000

1 This item set was developed by Danny Hassett, CFA (Cedar Hill, TX, USA)

Statistical measures related to the account and benchmark portfolio for May are displayed in Exhibit 2.

Exhibit 2   Statistical Measures for Denker's Account and the Benchmark Portfolio for the Month of May

	Denker Account	Benchmark Portfolio	Market Index
Return (%)	2.0	2.1	2.5
Beta (β)	0.8	0.8	1.00
Standard Deviation (%)	1.1	1.3	1.4
30-Day US T-bill (%)	0.2	0.2	0.2

In July, Denker requested an update on the performance of their account. As a result, DBCA asked Driver to prepare a micro performance attribution analysis only for the month June. The June return figures by sector for the portfolio and the benchmark are shown in Exhibit 3.

Exhibit 3   Denker's Large Cap Value Portfolio—Return by Sector for the Month of June

Market Value of Portfolio on June 1: $26,520,000

Economic Sectors	Portfolio Weight (%)	Sector Benchmark Weight (%)	Portfolio Return (%)	Sector Benchmark Return (%)
Basic Materials	3.56	6.03	-2.40	-1.61
Communication	1.53	2.33	-0.13	-0.13
Consumer Cyclical	8.69	5.97	4.10	4.62
Consumer Defensive	13.92	18.80	3.08	3.03
Energy	8.46	6.69	4.42	4.05
Financial Services	14.52	18.36	-0.05	-1.43
Healthcare	15.55	12.59	3.65	4.49
Industrials	3.71	2.40	0.12	0.10
Real Estate	6.76	5.44	-1.84	0.13
Technology	15.72	13.52	3.55	3.57
Utilities	4.96	7.87	0.10	0.07
Cash and Equivalents	2.62	0.00	0.12	
Buy/hold + cash	**100.00**	**100.00**	**2.08**	**1.82**
Trading and other			-0.12	
Total Portfolio			**1.96**	**1.82**

18 The DBCA's employment decision related to Tarler and the Denker account represents which type of error?

   A   Type I error.

B Type II error.

C No error was made.

19 Which of the following properties of a valid benchmark do benchmark Option 1 and Option 2 possess?

A Investible

B Measurable

C Unambiguous

20 Based upon Exhibit 1, the time-weighted return for Driver's portfolio from April 1 to April 30 is *closest* to:

A 1.92%.

B 1.96%.

C 2.00%.

21 Based upon the data shown in Exhibit 2, the return due to the portfolio manager's style is *closest* to:

A −0.5%.

B −0.4%.

C −0.1%.

22 Based on the data in Exhibit 2, the Sharpe ratio and Treynor measure for the Denker portfolio and benchmark portfolio *most likely* indicate that, in comparison to the benchmark portfolio, the Denker portfolio had:

A inferior risk-adjusted performance.

B superior risk-adjusted performance.

C risk-adjusted performance that was not clearly inferior or superior.

23 The data in Exhibit 3 shows Driver *most likely* achieved a positive Pure Sector Allocation return for the month of June from the economic sector in:

A Real Estate.

B Consumer Cyclical.

C Consumer Defensive.

24 The data in Exhibit 3 shows Driver *most likely* achieved the highest Within-Sector Selection return during June from the economic sector in:

A Basic Materials.

B Communication.

C Financial Services.

25 The data in Exhibit 3 shows the total value added (in dollar terms) that Driver contributed to the Denker account for the month of June is *closest* to:

A $31,824.

B $37,128.

C $68,952.

SOLUTIONS

1   In this simplest rate-of-return calculation, the portfolio experiences no external cash flows. In this situation, the account's rate of return during evaluation period t equals the market value (MV_1) at the end of the period less the market value at the beginning of the period (MV_0), divided by the beginning market value:

$$r_t = \frac{MV_1 - MV_0}{MV_0}$$

or (€523,500 − €453,000)/€453,000 = 0.1556 = 15.56%

Joubert earned a 15.56% rate of return on his portfolio during the year 2002.

2   **A**   The contribution was received at the end of the evaluation period, and it should be subtracted from the account's ending value. The external cash flow had no opportunity to affect the investment-related value of the account, and hence, it should be ignored.

$$r_t = \frac{(MV_1 - CF) - MV_0}{MV_0} \quad \text{or}$$

$$r_t = \frac{(42,300 - 500) - 42,000}{42,000} = -0.48\%$$

Even though Smith actually ended up with a larger amount in his account at the end of the period as compared to the beginning of the period (£42,300 versus £42,000), he actually lost money on his investments. His rate of return was −0.48%. The slight increase in his account balance was due to the contribution at the end of the month rather than to a positive return.

   B   In this case, the contribution was received at the beginning of the evaluation period, and it should be added to the account's beginning value. This sum is then subtracted from the ending value of the account, and the result is divided by the same sum (see formula below). In this case, the external cash flow did have an opportunity to affect the investment-related value of the account and it should be included in the calculation.

$$r_t = \frac{MV_1 - (MV_0 + CF)}{MV_0 + CF}$$

$$r_t = \frac{42,300 - (42,000 + 500)}{(42,000 + 500)} = -0.47\%$$

This rate of return is slightly higher (a smaller negative number) than the −0.48% return calculated in Part A. The slight increase in investment performance was due to the contribution made at the beginning of the month. In this case, the numerator of the formula yields an identical answer to that of Part A (−£200). But the denominator is larger (£42,500 vs. £42,000), giving a slightly higher return than in Part A.

3   **A**   Yes, an accurate rate of return can be calculated. The appropriate calculation is the time-weighted rate of return. The time-weighted rate of return (TWR) reflects the investment growth in the account as if the account began with one dollar. Its calculation requires that the account be valued every time an external cash flow occurs. If no cash flows take place, then the calculation of the TWR is simple; the change in the account's value is expressed relative to

its beginning value. If external cash flows do occur, then the TWR requires computing a set of subperiod returns. These subperiod returns must then be linked together to compute the TWR for the entire evaluation period.

B   First, we determine the appropriate subperiods by reviewing the dates of the contributions to the account. Contributions were made on September 14th and 21st. The appropriate subperiods are as shown:

Subperiod 1 = Days 1 through 14

Subperiod 2 = Days 15 through 21

Subperiod 3 = Days 22 through 30

Next, we calculate the rate of return for each subperiod:

For subperiod 1:

$$r_{t,1} = \left[(\$105,000 - \$3,000) - \$100,000\right]/\$100,000$$

$$= 0.02 \text{ or } 2.00\%$$

For subperiod 2:

$$r_{t,2} = \left[(\$108,000 - \$2,500) - \$105,000\right]/\$105,000$$

$$= 0.0048 \text{ or } 0.48\%$$

For subperiod 3:

$$r_{t,3} = (\$110,000 - \$108,000)/\$108,000$$

$$= 0.0185 \text{ or } 1.85\%$$

Converting the subperiod returns into decimal form, we use the following expression to compute the time-weighted rate of return:

$$r_{twr} = (1 + r_{t,1}) \times (1 + r_{t,2}) \times ... \times (1 + r_{t,n}) - 1$$

In the case of Mary's portfolio:

$$r_{twr} = (1 + 0.02) \times (1 + 0.0048) \times (1 + 0.0185) - 1$$

$$= 0.0439 \text{ or } 4.39\%$$

4   A   The time-weighted rate of return for the investment manager is

$$r_{twr} = (1 + 0.0125)(1 + 0.0347)(1 + [-0.0236])(1 + 0.0189)$$

$$(1 + [-0.0267])(1 + 0.0257) - 1$$

$$= 0.0405 \text{ or } 4.05\%$$

B   Adding the subperiod rates of return gives 0.0125 + 0.0347 + (−0.0236) + 0.0189 + (−0.0267) + 0.0257 = 0.0415 or 4.15%.

Characteristically, the additive calculation gives a higher return number (4.15%) than the time-weighted calculation (4.05%). In general, the time-weighted rate of return is a better indicator of long-term performance because it takes account of the effects of compounding.

5   The time-weighted rate of return (TWR) reflects the investment growth of one unit of money initially invested in the account. If external cash flows occur, then the account must be valued as of the date of each of these cash flows; the calculation of the TWR then requires computing a series of subperiod returns for the subperiods defined by the external cash flows. The subperiod returns are then combined by chain-linking, and 1 is subtracted from the result to arrive at the TWR.

The money-weighted rate of return (MWR) measures the compound growth rate in the value of all funds invested in the account over the evaluation period. The MWR also goes by the name Internal Rate of Return, or IRR. The MWR is the growth rate that will link the ending value of the account to its beginning value plus all external cash flows. The MWR is computed using an iterative procedure.

The MWR represents the average growth rate of all dollars invested in an account, while the TWR represents the growth of a single unit of money invested in the account. Consequently, the MWR is sensitive to the size and timing of external cash flows contributed to and withdrawn from the account, while the TWR is not affected by the cash flows. Under "normal" conditions, these two return measures will produce similar results. However, when external cash flows occur that are large relative to the account's value (rule of thumb: greater than 10%) and the account's performance fluctuates significantly, then the MWR and the TWR can differ substantially.

6   A   The correct methodology for approximating a time-weighted rate of return for the entire year of 2005 is to use a Linked Internal Rate of Return (LIRR) approach. This approach takes the money-weighted rate-of-return values and then chain-links the returns over the entire evaluation period.

   B   The calculation is

$$r_{LIRR} = (1 + 0.0535) \times (1 + [-0.0234]) \times (1 + 0.0462)$$
$$\times (1 + 0.0125) - 1$$
$$= 0.0898 \text{ or } 8.98\%$$

7   A   For Swennson, the annualized rate of return is:

$$r_a = \left[(1 + 0.275)(1 - 0.189)(1 + 0.146)(1 - 0.324) \right.$$
$$\left. (1 + 0.123) \right]^{1/5} - 1$$
$$= -0.0209 = -2.09\%$$

   For Mattsson, the annualized rate of return is:

$$r_a = \left[(1 + 0.057)(1 + 0.049)(1 + 0.078)(1 - 0.067) \right.$$
$$\left. (1 + 0.053) \right]^{1/5} - 1$$
$$= 0.0327 \text{ or } 3.27\%$$

   B   Mattsson's annualized rate of return of 3.27% was higher than Swennson's at −2.09%.

8   In this problem, the Wilshire 5000 represents the market index for US equities, the Russell 1000 Value Index represents the portfolio benchmark, and Anderson's account is the portfolio.

   A   The return due to style is the difference between the benchmark and the market index, or S = (B − M) = (21.7% − 25.2%) = −3.5%.

   B   The return due to active management is the difference between the portfolio and the benchmark, or A = (P − B) = (18.9% − 21.7%) = −2.8%.

   C   The implication of the style calculation is that large-cap value is out of favor: i.e., the Russell 1000 Value Index underperformed the Wilshire 5000 by 3.5%. In and of itself, this should not be a large concern for an investor with a properly diversified portfolio. Certain styles will periodically outperform and underperform the market index.

The implication of the active management calculation is that Anderson is not adding value as compared to the benchmark, since its portfolio underperformed the portfolio benchmark. If Anderson is indeed a large-cap value manager and the Russell 1000 Value Index is an appropriate benchmark, then the client may be better off investing in the passive alternative. Of course, one period is not enough to make a judgment such as this. However, sustained underperformance of an active manager as compared to an appropriate benchmark should be cause for concern.

9   To verify the choice of the benchmark, a potential client could compare the market capitalization (median, average, weighted average) of the subject portfolio with the respective benchmark index. This can help identify a good match (or mismatch) based on the size (market capitalization) of the stocks in the portfolio versus the index. In addition, the historical beta of the portfolio can be calculated relative to the potential benchmark. On average, it should be close to 1.0. If the beta is significantly larger (smaller) than the benchmark, it would indicate that the portfolio is substantially riskier (less risky) than the benchmark.

10 **A**   Overall, the domestic equities asset class has performed well relative to the benchmark (4.54% vs. 4.04%). However, only one of the two domestic equities managers has outperformed his respective benchmark. Equity manager A has outperformed by 15 basis points, while equity manager B has underperformed by 18 basis points.

   The international equity asset class as a whole has outperformed its benchmark. In addition, both international equity managers have also outperformed their respective benchmarks.

   The fixed-income asset class underperformed its benchmark. Both fixed-income managers have underperformed their respective benchmarks as well.

   B   Overall, the total fund has outperformed its benchmark by 11 basis points. Nevertheless, the fund may be able to improve its relative performance by considering some changes to the manager lineup.

   C   For each manager that underperformed his or her assigned benchmark (equity manager B and both fixed-income managers), the plan sponsor should first verify that the benchmarks in place are appropriate for the particular managers' investment styles. If the benchmarks are appropriate, and if performance is not expected to improve (based on many factors, including quality of people, organizational issues, etc.), then the plan sponsor may consider replacing these managers with other active managers following similar investment disciplines, or perhaps replacing them with passive investment alternatives corresponding to the benchmarks those managers are being measured against.

11 In practice, an acceptable benchmark is one that both the investment manager and the plan sponsor agree represents the manager's investment process. However, in order to function effectively in performance evaluation, a benchmark should possess certain basic properties. It should be

   ● **Unambiguous**. The names of securities and their corresponding weights in the benchmark should be clearly noted.

   ● **Investable**. The benchmark should be available as a passive option.

   ● **Measurable**. It should be possible to calculate the benchmark's return on a timely basis, for various time periods (e.g., monthly, quarterly, annually).

- **Appropriate**. The benchmark should be consistent with the manager's investment style or area of expertise.
- **Reflective of current investment opinions**. The manager should have opinions and investment knowledge of the individual securities within the benchmark.
- **Specified in advance**. The benchmark should be specified prior to the beginning of an evaluation period and known to both the investment manager and the fund sponsor.
- **Owned**. The investment manager should be aware of and accept accountability for the constituents and performance of the benchmark.

12 Kim Lee Ltd.'s benchmark is not valid. The chief criticism of this type of benchmark is that it is not, and cannot be, specified in advance. Furthermore, since no one knows who the top-quartile managers will be at the beginning of an evaluation period, the benchmark is not investable; i.e., there is no passive option for investment. Kim Lee Ltd. can inform existing and prospective clients where the firm's past performance has ranked in its peer group, but the universe should not be used *ex ante* as a performance benchmark. Furthermore, the firm should disclose sufficient information about the composition of the peer group for recipients to evaluate the meaningfulness of the firm's *ex post* ranking.

13 A one-factor model can be used to predict the return on Jones' portfolio and the benchmark. In this case, the returns can be expressed as a linear function of the return on the entire US equity market (as represented in the problem statement by the Wilshire 5000), as shown below:

$$R_p = a_p + \beta_p R_I + \varepsilon_p$$

where R_p is the return on the portfolio and R_I is the return on US equities. The term ε_p is the residual, or nonsystematic, element of the relationship. Finally, the term β_p measures the sensitivity of the portfolio to the return on the US equities market.

Calculating the expected return on Jones' portfolio gives:

$$R_{Jones} = 0.5 + 1.15(5.9) = 7.29\%$$

Calculating the expected return on the custom benchmark gives:

$$R_{Benchmark} = 1.5 + 0.95(5.9) = 7.11\%$$

The incremental expected return of the portfolio versus the benchmark is 0.18%. This can be calculated by computing the difference between the two expected returns. It can also be calculated by combining the two formulas as shown below:

$$R_{Difference} = (0.5 - 1.5) + (1.15 - 0.95)(5.9) = 0.18\%$$

Since the portfolio actually returned 8.13% during the period, the total differential return is 1.02% (the difference between the actual return of 8.13% and the expected benchmark return of 7.11%). However, based on the one-factor model, an outperformance of 0.18% was expected. The difference between the 1.02% and the 0.18% (or 0.84%) can be attributed to the value-added investment skill of Susan Jones.

14 We begin by calculating the information ratio for each of the two managers. The formula for the information ratio is:

$$IR_A = \frac{\bar{R}_A - \bar{R}_B}{\hat{\sigma}_{A-B}}$$

In our problem statement, the value-added for Manchester (1.5%) is the numerator in this formula, and the variability of excess returns (2.24%) is the denominator. Thus, for Manchester we can calculate an information ratio of 0.67.

Similarly, for Oakleaf we can calculate an information ratio of 0.4 (4% excess returns divided by 10% variability).

When we review our table, it gives the probability of outperformance. Since the question refers to underperformance, we must subtract the values in the table from 1 to determine the probability of underperformance.

Year	Manchester Outperformance	Manchester Underperformance	Oakleaf Outperformance	Oakleaf Underperformance
1	74.75%	25.25%	65.54%	34.46%
5	93.20	6.80	81.45	18.55
10	98.25	1.75	89.70	10.30

In this case, Oakleaf has a larger chance of underperforming the benchmark at all three time periods: 1, 5, and 10 years. This is interesting, since Oakleaf has a much larger expected value-added return (4% annually versus 1.5% for Manchester). However, the much larger variability of excess returns (10% for Oakleaf versus 2.24% for Manchester) clearly is an important factor in this situation.

15 In general terms, equity will earn higher returns than cash on average over the long term. However, there are periods of declining equity performance when cash may outperform equities.

In the case of Acorn and Zebra, Acorn would be preferable over Zebra, all else but the cash levels being equal. During most time periods when equities are outperforming cash, it would be better to have less cash and more equities in the portfolio. But during the time periods when equities are declining, it may be preferable to have more cash. Unfortunately, it is extremely difficult to forecast ahead of time when these time periods of declining equity performance will occur.

16 There are performance measurement issues that are created when there are short positions in a portfolio. The basic equation for the return on an account is

$$r_t = \frac{MV_1 - MV_0}{MV_0}$$

In theory, the net assets of a long-short portfolio could be zero. If the value of the portfolio's long positions is equal to the value of the portfolio's short positions, then the beginning market value, MV_0, would be zero and the account's rate of return would be either positive infinity or negative infinity.

To address this problem, we need to revise our performance measurement methodology. One approach would be to determine returns by summing the performance impacts of the individual security positions (both long and short). A return could be calculated for the period that the individual security positions were maintained. Once an individual security position changed, the return period would end and a new return period would start.

Regarding performance evaluation, if we have information regarding the historical returns and holdings of a long–short equity manager's long and short portfolios, we could use either returns-based or security-based benchmark building approaches to construct separate long and short benchmarks for the manager. These benchmarks could then be combined in appropriate proportions to create an appropriate benchmark for the manager.

Another possible option for performance evaluation is the use of the Sharpe ratio to evaluate hedge fund manager performance. It can be calculated without reference to the manager's underlying investment universe. Typically, a hedge fund manager's Sharpe ratio is compared to that of a universe of other hedge fund managers whose investment mandates are similar to those of the manager under evaluation.

17 Both macro attribution and micro attribution are different facets of performance attribution. The basic tenet behind performance attribution is that an account's performance is compared to a designated benchmark, then the sources of differential returns are identified and quantified. The main difference between macro and micro attribution is the definition of which "account's" performance we are analyzing. Macro attribution is done at the fund sponsor level; that is, analysis is typically done for a grouping of investment managers or investment accounts. Micro attribution is carried out at the level of the individual investment manager.

There are three main inputs to the macro attribution approach:

1 policy allocations;

2 benchmark portfolio returns; and

3 fund returns, valuations, and external cash flows.

Fund sponsors determine policy allocations, or "normal" weightings, for each asset class and individual manager. These are typically determined after some sort of asset liability analysis and/or determination of the risk tolerance of the governing body of the fund.

Benchmark portfolio returns are an important factor in determining the value added by the fund. If the benchmarks do not adequately match the managers' investment styles, the performance attribution will have little value. Fund sponsors may use broad market indexes as the benchmarks for asset categories (the Wilshire 5000 as the benchmark for overall US domestic equities, for example) and may use more focused indexes to represent managers' investment styles (such as the Russell 2000 Value Index for a small-cap value manager).

Fund returns, valuations, and external cash flows are all critical elements for determining the relevant performance for the portfolio as a whole and for each individual investment manager's account.

A return metric implies that fund returns are used at the level of the individual management account to allow an analysis of the fund sponsor's decisions regarding manager selection. A dollar-metric approach uses account valuation and external cash flow data to calculate rates of return and also to compute the dollar impacts of the fund sponsor's investment policy decision making.

18 B is correct. Tarler was fired for underperformance but actually had outperformed the benchmark, and a Type II error is defined as firing (or not hiring) managers with positive value-added.

19 B is correct. The return for benchmark Option 2 is measurable.

20 A is correct. TWR is equal to the linked returns for each period between cash flows into/out of the fund, where each period return is equal to [(ending value − beginning value)/beginning value − 1]

$$TWR = (1 + \text{April 1-10 return}) \times (1 + \text{April 11-20 return}) \times (1 + \text{April 21-30 return})$$

$$\text{April 1-10 TWR} = \left[(25{,}800{,}000 - 1{,}000{,}000 - 25{,}000{,}000)\,/\,25{,}000{,}000\right] = -0.00800$$

$$\text{April 11-20 TWR} = \left[(25{,}600{,}000 + 500{,}000 - 25{,}800{,}000)\,/\,25{,}800{,}000\right] = 0.01163$$

$$\text{April 21-30 TWR} = \left[(26{,}000{,}000 - 25{,}600{,}000)\,/\,25{,}600{,}000\right] = 0.01563$$

$$\text{TWR} = (1 + -0.008)(1 + 0.01163)(1 + 0.01563) - 1 = 0.01922 \text{ or } 1.922\%$$

21 B is correct. The return due to the portfolio manager's style is Benchmark return − Market index return:

2.1% − 2.5% = −0.4%.

22 C is correct. The Sharpe Ratio = $(R_A - r_f)/\sigma_A$

Denker Sharpe Ratio = (2.0 − 0.2)/1.1 = 1.636

Benchmark Sharpe Ratio = (2.1 − 0.2)/1.3 = 1.462

Thus, the Denker portfolio has a higher Sharpe Ratio, which indicates *superior* risk-adjusted performance relative to the benchmark portfolio.

The Treynor Measure = $(R_A - r_f)/\beta_A$

Denker Treynor Measure = (2.0 − 0.2)/0.8 = 2.250

Benchmark Treynor Measure = (2.1 − 0.2)/0.8 = 2.375

Thus, the Denker portfolio has a lower Treynor Measure, which indicates *inferior* risk-adjusted performance by the benchmark portfolio.

Thus, the Sharpe ratio and the Treynor ratio offer conflicting conclusions about the performance of the Denker portfolio relative to the benchmark portfolio.

23 B is correct. The Pure Sector Allocation return equals the difference between the allocation (weight) of the Portfolio to a given sector and the Portfolio's benchmark weight for that sector, times the difference between the sector benchmark's return and the overall Portfolio's benchmark return.

$$r_{pj} = \left(w_{pj} - w_{Bj}\right) \times \left(r_{Bj} - r_B\right)$$

As a result, the return for the Consumer Cyclical sector

$$= (8.69\% - 5.97\%)(4.62\% - 1.82\%)$$
$$= (2.72\%)(2.80\%)$$
$$= 0.076\% \text{ which is } positive$$

24 C is correct because Within-Sector Selection Return for sector j is given by $r_{pj} = w_{Bj} \times \left(r_{pj} - r_{Bj}\right)$

As a result, the return for the Financial Services sector

$$= (18.36\%)\left(-0.05\% - (-1.43\%)\right)$$
$$= (18.36\%)(1.38\%)$$
$$= 0.253\% \text{ which is highest among the three}$$

25 B is correct.

$$\text{Total value added} = \text{Beginning Portfolio Value} \times (\text{Portfolio Return} - \text{Benchmark Return})$$
$$= \$26{,}520{,}000 \times (1.96\% - 1.82\%) = \$37{,}128$$

Global Investment Performance Standards

The Global Investment Performance Standards (GIPS®) contain ethical and professional standards for presenting investment performance to prospective clients. These guidelines provide for standardized performance calculation and presentation among investment managers, enabling investors to objectively compare manager return histories and clearly evaluate performance. This study session consists of a single reading that provides grounding in the requirements and recommendations of GIPS.

READING ASSIGNMENTS

33

Overview of the Global Investment Performance Standards

by Philip Lawton, CFA, CIPM

LEARNING OUTCOMES

Mastery	The candidate should be able to:
☐	a. discuss the objectives, key characteristics, and scope of the GIPS standards and their benefits to prospective clients and investment managers;
☐	b. explain the fundamentals of compliance with the GIPS standards, including the definition of the firm and the firm's definition of discretion;
☐	c. explain the requirements and recommendations of the GIPS standards with respect to input data, including accounting policies related to valuation and performance measurement;
☐	d. discuss the requirements of the GIPS standards with respect to return calculation methodologies, including the treatment of external cash flows, cash and cash equivalents, and expenses and fees;
☐	e. explain the requirements and recommendations of the GIPS standards with respect to composite return calculations, including methods for asset-weighting portfolio returns;
☐	f. explain the meaning of "discretionary" in the context of composite construction and, given a description of the relevant facts, determine whether a portfolio is likely to be considered discretionary;
☐	g. explain the role of investment mandates, objectives, or strategies in the construction of composites;
☐	h. explain the requirements and recommendations of the GIPS standards with respect to composite construction, including switching portfolios among composites, the timing of the inclusion of new portfolios in composites, and the timing of the exclusion of terminated portfolios from composites;

(continued)

CFA Institute gratefully acknowledges the contributions of W. Bruce Remington, CFA, as co-author of the original (2005) version of this reading. This version was updated July 2012 by Kenneth Robinson, CFA, CIPM. Copyright © 2012 by CFA Institute.

LEARNING OUTCOMES

Mastery	The candidate should be able to:
☐	i. explain the requirements of the GIPS standards for asset class segments carved out of multi-class portfolios;
☐	j. explain the requirements and recommendations of the GIPS standards with respect to disclosure, including fees, the use of leverage and derivatives, conformity with laws and regulations that conflict with the GIPS standards, and noncompliant performance periods;
☐	k. explain the requirements and recommendations of the GIPS standards with respect to presentation and reporting, including the required timeframe of compliant performance periods, annual returns, composite assets, and benchmarks;
☐	l. explain the conditions under which the performance of a past firm or affiliation must be linked to or used to represent the historical performance of a new or acquiring firm;
☐	m. evaluate the relative merits of high/low, range, interquartile range, and equal-weighted or asset-weighted standard deviation as measures of the internal dispersion of portfolio returns within a composite for annual periods;
☐	n. identify the types of investments that are subject to the GIPS standards for real estate and private equity;
☐	o. explain the provisions of the GIPS standards for real estate and private equity;
☐	p. explain the provisions of the GIPS standards for Wrap fee/ Separately Managed Accounts;
☐	q. explain the requirements and recommended valuation hierarchy of the GIPS Valuation Principles;
☐	r. determine whether advertisements comply with the GIPS Advertising Guidelines;
☐	s. discuss the purpose, scope, and process of verification;
☐	t. discuss challenges related to the calculation of after-tax returns;
☐	u. identify and explain errors and omissions in given performance presentations and recommend changes that would bring them into compliance with GIPS standards.

1   INTRODUCTION

The Global Investment Performance Standards (the GIPS® standards) fulfill an essential role in investment management around the world. They meet the need for globally accepted standards for investment management firms in calculating and presenting their results to potential clients.

The GIPS standards are based on the ideals of fair representation and full disclosure of an investment management firm's performance history. Firms that claim compliance with the GIPS standards must adhere to rules governing not only rate-of-return calculations but also the way in which returns are displayed in a performance presentation. They are further required to make certain disclosures and are encouraged to make others in a performance presentation, thereby assisting the user in interpreting and evaluating the reported returns. Potential and existing clients are assured that the information shown in a GIPS-compliant performance presentation reflects the results of the presenting firm's past investment decisions. They are also assured that the returns are calculated and presented on a consistent basis and that they are objectively comparable for a given strategy to those reported by other firms claiming compliance with the GIPS standards.

This reading comprehensively presents the requirements and recommendations of the 2010 version of the GIPS standards. In addition to presenting the GIPS standards, the reading explains the rationale and application of specific provisions, with particular attention to implementation issues. Section 2 of this reading provides background information on the need for the GIPS standards, their history, their governance, and the objectives and key characteristics of the GIPS standards. Section 3 covers the provisions of the GIPS standards. Section 4 explains the GIPS Valuation Principles, Section 5 reviews the GIPS Advertising Guidelines enabling firms to claim compliance with the GIPS standards in advertisements, and Section 6 describes verification. Section 7 considers other issues relevant to the GIPS standards, and Section 8 summarizes the reading's main points.

BACKGROUND OF THE GIPS STANDARDS

2

The GIPS standards, which offer significant advantages to investors and investment management firms, evolved from earlier efforts to improve the reliability of investment performance information and to standardize calculation methodologies. In this part of the reading, we will explain the benefits of the GIPS standards, recount their historical development, and introduce the governance body responsible for developing and interpreting the GIPS standards. We will also provide an overview of the GIPS standards.

2.1 The Need for Global Investment Performance Standards

In their current state, the GIPS standards are so broadly accepted and endorsed in the investment industry that it is worthwhile to recall the reasons they were developed in the first place. The total economic cost of defining, promulgating, interpreting, implementing, updating, monitoring, and validating claims of compliance with these voluntary ethical standards can be substantial. Why have investment industry participants seen fit to incur such costs? What are the benefits?

To appreciate the value of industry-wide performance presentation standards, consider some of the many ways in which unscrupulous employees might attempt to gather and retain assets by misrepresenting a firm's historical record in the GIPS standards' absence. In communicating with a prospective client, they could

- present returns only for the best-performing portfolios as though those returns were fully representative of the firm's expertise in a given strategy or style;
- base portfolio values on their own unsubstantiated estimates of asset prices;
- inflate returns by annualizing partial-period results;
- select the most favorable measurement period, calculating returns from a low point to a high point;
- present simulated returns as though they had actually been earned;

- choose as a benchmark the particular index the selected portfolios have outperformed by the greatest margin during the preferred measurement period;

- portray the growth of assets in the style or strategy of interest so as to mask the difference between investment returns and client contributions; or

- use the marketing department's expertise in graphic design to underplay unfavorable performance data and direct the prospect's attention to the most persuasive elements of the sales presentation.

Some of the foregoing examples are admittedly egregious abuses. They are not, however, farfetched. In the late 1980s, before performance presentation standards became widely accepted, a groundbreaking committee of the Financial Analysts Federation (a predecessor organization of CFA Institute) reported that investment advisors were "left to their own standards, which have been varied, uneven, and, in many instances, outright irresponsible and dishonest."[1] The investment management industry remains highly competitive, and people whose careers and livelihoods depend on winning new business want to communicate their firm's performance in the most favorable light (as they certainly should). The GIPS standards are ethical criteria designed simply to ensure that the firm's performance history is fairly represented and adequately disclosed. Indeed, employees who are pressured to misrepresent their firm's investment results can and should cite the GIPS standards.

Without established, well formulated standards for investment performance measurement and presentation, the prospective client's ability to make sound decisions in selecting investment managers would be impaired. Individual investors and their advisors, as well as pension plan sponsors, foundation trustees, and other institutional investors with fiduciary responsibility for asset pools, need reliable information. The GIPS standards give them greater confidence that the returns they are shown fairly represent an investment firm's historical record. The GIPS standards also enable them to make reasonable comparisons among different investment management firms before hiring one of them. Evaluating past returns is only one dimension of the manager selection process, but it is an important one, and the due diligence legally and ethically expected of fiduciaries cannot be satisfied without it.

Global standards for performance presentation, including the requirement that a firm show each composite's[2] investment returns alongside the returns of an appropriate benchmark, can lead to an informative discussion about the firm's investment decision-making process. The prospective client might ask, for instance, why the composite outperformed the benchmark in some periods and not in others, inviting the firm's spokespersons to explain past returns and to describe how the investment product is positioned for the future.

It must be stressed in this context that reviewing properly calculated, fully disclosed historical results does not exempt the prospective client from a thorough investigation of the candidate firm's background, resources, and capabilities for the mandate under consideration. Due diligence in selecting an investment manager includes, among many other important elements, examining a firm's regulatory history, the experience and professional credentials of its decision makers, the soundness of its investment philosophy, the nature of its investment and operational risk controls, and the independence of its service providers. At a minimum, however, the firm's representatives should be able to explain the sources of its past returns reasonably, credibly, and insightfully in light of the firm's investment philosophy and investment decision-making process as well as the then-prevailing capital market environment.

---

1 The Committee for Performance Presentation Standards (1987, p. 8).
2 A "composite" is formally defined as an "aggregation of one or more portfolios managed according to a similar investment mandate, objective, or strategy." The construction of composites is discussed in detail later.

The GIPS standards' benefits to prospective and existing clients are clear. What, if any, are the benefits to the investment management firms incurring the expenses required to achieve and maintain compliance with the GIPS standards?

There is, first, an incalculable benefit to the investment management industry as a whole. The development of well founded, thoughtfully defined performance presentation standards is a great credit not only to the vision of certain professionals and organizations but, above all, to the leadership of the investment management firms that were the early adopters. At present, widespread adherence to the GIPS standards may help restore the industry's credibility, which was severely damaged by the discovery of numerous fraudulent investment schemes in the aftermath of the financial crisis that followed the collapse of the subprime mortgage loan and credit default swap markets in 2008. The GIPS standards may reassure investors about compliant firms' veracity in the area of investment performance reporting, especially if they have been verified. Verification, discussed later in this reading, refers to an investment firm's voluntarily engaging an independent third party to test the firm's performance measurement and composite construction procedures in order to bring additional credibility to the firm's claim of compliance with the GIPS standards.

The practical benefits to individual firms facing the initial and ongoing expenses of GIPS compliance have increased over time. In some markets, the GIPS standards are so well accepted by plan sponsors and consultants that non-compliance is a serious competitive impediment to a firm's winning new institutional business. Requests for proposals (RFPs) in manager searches routinely ask if the responding firm is in compliance with the GIPS standards and if the firm has been independently verified.[3] In addition, the global recognition the GIPS standards have gained helps the compliant firm to compete in international markets because prospective clients should value the ability to equitably compare its investment performance to that of local GIPS-compliant firms. Compliance with the GIPS standards has appropriately been characterized as the investment management firm's passport to the international marketplace.

Because the GIPS standards reflect best practices in the calculation and presentation of investment performance, firms may also realize internal benefits. In the course of implementing the GIPS standards, they might identify opportunities to strengthen managerial controls. The discipline of reviewing portfolio guidelines and defining, documenting, and adhering to internal policies in support of compliance with the GIPS standards typically improves the firm's oversight of investment operations and provides management with additional comfort in the accuracy of the firm's composite performance and the quality of the composite presentations provided to prospective investors. Similarly, technological enhancements designed to provide valid calculation input data and presentation elements, such as dispersion statistics, may improve the quality of information available to the firm.

Only investment management **firms** may claim compliance with the GIPS standards.[4] Consultants, software houses, or third-party performance measurement providers such as custodians may not claim to be GIPS-compliant. Moreover, investment firms may claim to be compliant only on a firm-wide basis (I.0.A.4).[5] GIPS compliance cannot be claimed only for some of an investment firm's products, nor for specific composites or portfolios. A firm's claim of compliance signifies, among other things,

---

3 Competence in evaluating compliance with the GIPS standards is a curriculum element in the Certificate in Investment Performance Measurement (CIPM®) program.

4 The GIPS standards refer to the investment management firm claiming compliance as the FIRM. This reading uses boldface type for terms that are defined in the GIPS Glossary (Section V of the Global Investment Performance Standards).

5 Following a Preface and an Introduction, the GIPS standards have four chapters: I. Provisions of the Global Investment Performance Standards; II. Valuation Principles; III. Advertising Guidelines; and IV. Verification. (See Exhibit 1.) This reading cites the GIPS standards by giving the chapter followed by section and provision identifiers.

that the firm's performance measurement data inputs, processes, and return calculation methodology conform to the prescribed guidelines and that all of the firm's fee-paying discretionary **portfolios** have been assigned to at least one **composite**.

2.2 The Development of Performance Presentation Standards

Investors have been keeping track of their wealth for as long as capital markets have existed. The industry standards for performance measurement and presentation as we know them today, however, have resulted from developments that began in the late 1960s and gathered speed in the 1990s.

Peter O. Dietz published his seminal work, *Pension Funds: Measuring Investment Performance*, in 1966. The Bank Administration Institute (BAI), a US-based organization serving the financial services industry, subsequently formulated rate-of-return calculation guidelines based on Dietz's work.

In 1980, Wilshire Associates joined with a number of custodial banks to establish the Trust Universe Comparison Service (TUCS), a database of portfolio returns organized for use in peer group comparisons, and the members established standards for computing returns in order to ensure comparability.

The direct lineage of the current Global Investment Performance Standards starts with the voluntary guidelines for the North American marketplace defined by a committee of the Financial Analysts Federation. The Committee for Performance Presentation Standards (CPPS) published a report in the September/October 1987 issue of the *Financial Analysts Journal*. The committee's recommendations notably included using a time-weighted total return calculation; reporting performance before the effects of investment management fees; including cash in portfolio return calculations; reaching agreement with the client in advance on the starting date for performance measurement; selecting a risk- or style-appropriate benchmark for performance comparisons; and constructing and presenting accurate, asset-weighted composites of investment performance. The committee strongly recommended that the Financial Analysts Federation disseminate and attempt to impose performance presentation standards for investment management organizations.[6]

Another milestone was the development of the Association for Investment Management and Research (AIMR) Performance Presentation Standards (AIMR-PPS®). AIMR, founded in January 1990 when the Financial Analysts Federation merged with the Institute of Chartered Financial Analysts, subsequently became CFA Institute. In 1990, as one of its first actions, the AIMR Board of Governors endorsed the AIMR-PPS standards. The Board also established the AIMR Performance Presentation Standards Implementation Committee to review the proposed Standards and to seek industry input prior to formal implementation. The AIMR-PPS standards were implemented, and the first edition of the *AIMR Performance Presentation Standards Handbook* was published in 1993.

Acting independently, the Investment Management Consultants Association (IMCA) also issued performance measurement guidelines in 1993. IMCA endorses the GIPS standards, which apply to investment firms. The IMCA standards complement the GIPS standards with guidelines for investment consultants in analyzing data obtained from investment managers in the course of manager searches as well as in reporting, monitoring, and analyzing performance results for clients.[7]

---

6 CPPS (1987, pp. 8–11).
7 For further information, see the IMCA Performance Reporting Guidelines (2010) on the Investment Management Consultants Association website at www.imca.org.

In 1995, AIMR formed the Global Performance Presentation Standards Subcommittee, reporting to the Implementation Committee, to address international performance issues and to develop global standards for presenting investment performance. The following year, AIMR revised the AIMR-PPS standards, stipulating new requirements, such as the inclusion of accrued income in bond market values in both the numerator and the denominator of return calculations, and presenting new recommendations, such as the use of temporary accounts for significant cash flows. In 1997, AIMR released the second edition of the *AIMR Performance Presentation Standards Handbook* incorporating these and other changes.

In 1998, after circulating several preliminary drafts among industry participants, the Global PPS Subcommittee released the Global Investment Performance Standards for public comment. The AIMR Board of Governors formally endorsed the GIPS standards early in 1999 and established the Investment Performance Council (IPC) later that year to manage the further development and promulgation of the GIPS standards.

The IPC consisted of approximately 36 members from a variety of fields within the global investment industry representing 15 countries. From 1999 to 2006, the IPC focused on its principle goal: to have all countries adopt the GIPS standards as the standard for investment firms seeking to present historical investment performance.

The IPC strongly encouraged countries without an investment performance standard in place to accept the GIPS standards as the local norms, either in English or in a Translation of GIPS (TG).

Due to local regulation or to well-accepted practice, some countries have additional requirements over and above those set forth in the GIPS standards. In these cases, the IPC promoted an approach designated as a "Country Version of GIPS" (CVG). The country would adopt the GIPS standards as their core standards, supplemented by additional provisions as necessary to meet local requirements. If the CVG included any differences that could not be justified on the basis of regulatory stipulations or widely recognized practice, the local sponsor (typically a professional association) was required to provide a transition plan for eliminating the differences within a specified period. In 2001, the AIMR-PPS standards were adopted by the AIMR Board of Governors and the IPC as the US and Canadian version of GIPS. The first edition of *The Global Investment Performance Standards (GIPS) Handbook* was published in 2002 in a loose-leaf format to accommodate changes and additions to the GIPS standards with the passage of time.

In February 2005, the IPC revised the GIPS standards and created a single global standard for investment performance reporting. The revised GIPS standards granted all CVG-compliant firms reciprocity for periods prior to 1 January 2006, such that their CVG-compliant history will satisfy the GIPS requirement, discussed later in this reading, to show at least a five-year track record in performance presentations.

The IPC was superseded by the GIPS Executive Committee (EC) and the GIPS Council in 2005. (We discuss the governance of the GIPS standards below.)

The second edition of *The Global Investment Performance Standards (GIPS) Handbook* was published in 2006.

Working in close collaboration with its technical subcommittees, ad hoc working groups, and representatives of the GIPS country sponsors, the EC undertook a comprehensive review of the GIPS standards' requirements, recommendations, and guidance that led, with substantial industry input, to the 2010 edition of the GIPS standards.

The present reading is based on the 2010 edition of the GIPS standards, which notably includes new risk-related provisions intended to provide investors with a more comprehensive view of a firm's performance. The effective date for the 2010 GIPS standards is 1 January 2011.

Please note that in 2010 many of the GIPS Guidance Statements were updated to reflect the 2010 edition of the GIPS standards. These updates were also effective 1 January 2011.

2.3 Governance of the GIPS Standards

The GIPS Executive Committee (EC), a standing committee of the CFA Institute, is the decision-making body responsible for developing and implementing the provisions of the Global Investment Performance Standards. The EC has nine members, including its Executive Director and the chairs of four technical subcommittees, the GIPS Council, and three regional investment performance subcommittees.

The Interpretations Subcommittee, which seeks to clarify the GIPS standards through interpretations that effectively respond to new issues presented by the global investment industry, is responsible for ensuring the integrity, consistency and applicability of the GIPS standards. Firms claiming compliance with the GIPS standards must also comply with all applicable interpretations and guidance.

The Investment Manager Subcommittee, Investor/Consultant Subcommittee, and Verification/Practitioner Subcommittee are forums for understanding GIPS-related issues faced by investment management firms, investors and their representatives, and verifiers and third-party service providers, respectively. Their perspectives are shared with the Executive Committee, the Interpretations Subcommittee, and other EC Subcommittees in order to ensure a consistent understanding and to improve the quality of the GIPS standards. The EC established the GIPS Council to facilitate the involvement of all country sponsors in the ongoing development and promotion of the GIPS standards. (As of this writing, there are 35 endorsed GIPS country sponsors.) In addition, the EC established Regional Investment Performance Subcommittees (RIPS) under the GIPS Council to represent the interests of the countries within regions and encourage national and regional support in the development, promulgation, and maintenance of the GIPS standards. There are RIPS for the Americas; Europe, the Middle East, and Africa (EMEA); and Asia Pacific.

The EC also has a Nominations Committee that is responsible for developing a fair and objective selection process for the electable members of the EC and its standing subcommittees, and a Promotion and Awareness Subcommittee charged with formulating clear, consistent messages to educate key stakeholders about the benefits of the GIPS standards.

In addition, temporary working groups are also formed as deemed necessary by the EC to address specific subject matters.

The GIPS EC is supported by a dedicated team of CFA Institute staff members under the leadership of the Executive Director.

2.4 Overview of the GIPS Standards

To orient the reader, we present the Table of Contents of the Global Investment Performance Standards in Exhibit 1. The Preface recapitulates the historical development of the GIPS standards, which we presented somewhat more extensively earlier. The Introduction, to which we now turn, provides extensive information about the GIPS standards. Rather than paraphrasing and commenting on every point made in the Introduction, we will highlight certain concepts in the following paragraphs.

Exhibit 1	Table of Contents
	GLOBAL INVESTMENT PERFORMANCE STANDARDS (GIPS®)
	As Adopted by the GIPS Executive Committee

PREFACE

INTRODUCTION

PROVISIONS OF THE GLOBAL INVESTMENT PERFORMANCE STANDARDS

0   Fundamentals of Compliance

1   Input Data

2   Calculation Methodology

3   Composite Construction

4   Disclosure

5   Presentation and Reporting

6   Real Estate

7   Private Equity

8   Wrap Fee/Separately Managed Account (SMA) Portfolios

VALUATION PRINCIPLES

ADVERTISING GUIDELINES

VERIFICATION

GLOSSARY

Appendix A: Sample Compliant Presentations

Appendix B: Sample Advertisements

Appendix C: Sample List of Composite Descriptions

The Introduction to the GIPS standards articulates the Standards' objectives: "The establishment of a voluntary global investment performance standard leads to an accepted set of best practices for calculating and presenting investment performance that is readily comparable among investment firms, regardless of geographic location. These standards also facilitate a dialogue between investment firms and their existing and prospective clients regarding investment performance." Because the GIPS standards are global, **prospective clients** engaged in an evaluation of competing investment firms' historical performance know that rates of return have been calculated in accordance with a common set of valuation principles and methodological guidelines. In addition, because they presumably understand the firms' GIPS-compliant basis for valuing assets and calculating returns, prospective clients can proceed directly to a discussion of how the historical results were achieved. This dialogue can help them assess the quality of the asset managers' thinking and the consistency of their investment process in past market conditions.

The Introduction additionally sets forth the goals of the GIPS Executive Committee. They are to establish industry-wide best practices for calculating and presenting performance information; to obtain worldwide acceptance of a common performance measurement and presentation standard based on the principles of fair representation and full disclosure; to promote the use of accurate and consistent performance data; to encourage fair, global competition for all markets without creating barriers to entry for new investment management firms; and to foster the notion of industry self-regulation on a global basis. Performance presentation standards thoughtfully and carefully designed by well-informed industry participants who are committed to the ethical principles of fairness and full disclosure may serve to moderate the need for expanded regulatory intervention in this area.

The Introduction also has an Overview section that states certain key characteristics of the GIPS standards. Among them is the proposition that the Global Investment Performance Standards are *ethical* standards intended to ensure fair representation and full disclosure of an investment firm's performance. As ethical standards, they are voluntary. Meeting the objectives of fair representation and full disclosure is likely to require more than simply adhering to the minimum requirements of the GIPS standards. For instance, when appropriate, firms have the responsibility to include information not addressed by the GIPS standards in the GIPS-compliant presentation.

The GIPS standards apply to investment management firms, not to individuals. (We will return to the definition of the firm for the purpose of compliance with the GIPS standards.) In order to promote fair representations of performance, the GIPS standards require firms to include *all* actual fee-paying, discretionary portfolio composites that are defined by investment mandate, objective, or strategy. Relying on the integrity of input data, the GIPS standards require firms to use certain calculation methods and to make certain disclosures along with the firm's performance. When the GIPS standards conflict with law and/or regulations regarding the calculation and presentation of performance, the GIPS standards obligate firms to comply with the local requirements and to disclose the conflict in the performance presentation.

The GIPS standards consist of **requirements**, which **must** be followed in order for a firm to claim compliance, and **recommendations**, which are optional but **should** be followed because they represent best practice in performance presentation. Firms must comply with all requirements of the GIPS standards, including not only the provisions of the GIPS standards but also any updates, Guidance Statements, interpretations, Questions & Answers, and clarifications published by CFA Institute and the GIPS Executive Committee which are available on the GIPS website (www.gipsstandards.org) and in the *GIPS Handbook*. The GIPS standards will continue to evolve as the industry tackles additional areas of performance measurement and recognizes the implications of new investment strategies, instruments, and technologies.

The Introduction comments as well on the extent of the historical performance record to be minimally included in compliant presentations. The GIPS standards require firms to show investment performance for a minimum of five years, or since the inception of the firm or composite if either has existed for less than five years. After presenting at least five years of GIPS-compliant history, the firm must add annual performance each subsequent year building to a minimum of 10 years. In general, firms may link non-GIPS-compliant performance to their GIPS-compliant performance so long as only GIPS-compliant returns are presented for periods after 1 January 2000 and the firm discloses the periods of non-compliance. In the case of private equity and real estate, firms must also comply with Sections 6 and 7, respectively, of Chapter I in the GIPS standards. We will consider them later in this reading.

We have remarked that firms must meet *all* the requirements set forth in the GIPS standards. There can be no exceptions. As stated in the part of the Introduction headed "Compliance," firms must accordingly take all steps necessary to ensure that they have satisfied all the requirements before claiming compliance with the GIPS standards. Moreover, firms are strongly encouraged to perform periodic internal compliance checks to confirm the validity of compliance claims. Implementing adequate internal controls during all stages of the investment performance process will instill confidence in the performance presented and in the claim of compliance. The GIPS Executive Committee strongly recommends that firms be verified.

As previously mentioned, the effective date for the 2010 GIPS standards is 1 January 2011. In other words, GIPS-compliant presentations that include performance for periods that begin on or after 1 January 2011 must be prepared in accordance with the 2010 edition of the GIPS standards.

The Introduction includes a section subtitled, "Implementing a Global Standard," which recognizes the vital part that local sponsoring organizations play in the effective implementation and ongoing administration of the GIPS standards within their countries. Country sponsors link the GIPS EC and the local markets in which investment managers conduct their business. In addition to supporting the adoption of the GIPS standards, country sponsors will ensure that their country's interests are taken into account as the governing body continues to develop the GIPS standards. The GIPS standards also encourage regulators to recognize the benefit of investment management firms' voluntary compliance with standards representing global best practices, to consider taking enforcement action on firms that falsely claim compliance with the GIPS standards, and to encourage independent third-party verification.

Finally, the Introduction closes by restating the vitally important role of country sponsors and identifying the endorsed GIPS country sponsors as of 31 December 2010. As of 1 July 2012, there are 35 country sponsors including organizations from Luxembourg, Korea, Mexico, and Peru.

IMPLEMENTATION (1)

Management Commitment. Senior management's stated commitment to the spirit and objectives of the GIPS standards and steadfast willingness to invest the necessary time and resources are essential for a firm to achieve compliance with the GIPS standards. The implementation effort is most likely to succeed if senior management makes achieving compliance a high priority; clearly communicates the importance of the initiative throughout the firm; oversees the preparation of a comprehensive project plan; and establishes an adequate budget, with particular attention to consulting and information systems requirements.

Some firms may wrongly assume that implementation of the GIPS standards involves "re-crunching" a few numbers and reformatting performance presentation tables. In fact, achieving compliance can be a complex, challenging, and potentially expensive undertaking. Merely adopting the GIPS standards as a means of passing the initial screening in RFP competitions may lead to shortcuts that ultimately compromise the firm's application of the GIPS standards, deprive it of valuable internal benefits, and needlessly expose it to reputational and regulatory risk.

A firm must also have a high level of commitment from its compliance, investment management, operating, and marketing staff. Achieving and maintaining compliance with the GIPS standards typically involves an investment firm's portfolio accounting, market data services, information technology, portfolio management, marketing, and compliance groups, as well as the performance measurement team. It is a complex process for investment management organizations to define and document policies, gather and validate input data, calculate rates of return, construct and maintain meaningful composites, and present investment results in accordance with the GIPS standards. Careful planning with the active participation of diverse organizational units is a critical element of the implementation project.

PROVISIONS OF THE GIPS STANDARDS

3

We turn now to the specific provisions of the GIPS standards. Chapter I, Provisions of the Global Investment Performance Standards, presents firm-wide requirements and recommendations in subsections addressing the fundamentals of compliance, input data, calculation methodology, composite construction, disclosures, and presentation and reporting. In addition, the GIPS standards include particular provisions for real estate and private equity. Exhibit 2 contains an excerpt from the GIPS standards introducing each of these topics.

Exhibit 2	CONTENT OF THE GLOBAL INVESTMENT PERFORMANCE STANDARDS

0   **Fundamentals of Compliance:** Several core principles create the foundation for the GIPS standards, including properly defining the firm, providing compliant presentations to all prospective clients, adhering to applicable laws and regulations, and ensuring that information presented is not false or misleading. Two important issues that a firm must consider when becoming compliant with the GIPS standards are the definition of the firm and the firm's definition of discretion. The definition of the firm is the foundation for firm-wide compliance and creates defined boundaries whereby total firm assets can be determined. The firm's definition of discretion establishes criteria to judge which portfolios must be included in a composite and is based on the firm's ability to implement its investment strategy.

1   **Input Data:** Consistency of input data used to calculate performance is critical to effective compliance with the GIPS standards and establishes the foundation for full, fair, and comparable investment performance presentations. For periods beginning on or after 1 January 2011, all portfolios must be valued in accordance with the definition of fair value and the GIPS Valuation Principles in Chapter II.

2   **Calculation Methodology:** Achieving comparability among investment management firms' performance presentations requires uniformity in methods used to calculate returns. The GIPS standards mandate the use of certain calculation methodologies to facilitate comparability.

3   **Composite Construction:** A composite is an aggregation of one or more portfolios managed according to a similar investment mandate, objective, or strategy. The composite return is the asset-weighted average of the performance of all portfolios in the composite. Creating meaningful composites is essential to the fair presentation, consistency, and comparability of performance over time and among firms.

4   **Disclosure:** Disclosures allow firms to elaborate on the data provided in the presentation and give the reader the proper context in which to understand the performance. To comply with the GIPS standards, firms must disclose certain information in all compliant presentations regarding their performance and the policies adopted by the firm. Although some disclosures are required for all firms, others are specific to certain circumstances and may not be applicable in all situations. Firms are not required to make negative assurance disclosures (e.g., if the firm does not use leverage in a particular composite strategy, no disclosure of the use of leverage is required). One of the essential disclosures for every firm is the claim of compliance. Once a firm meets all the requirements of the GIPS standards, it must appropriately use the claim of compliance to indicate compliance with the GIPS standards. The 2010 edition of the GIPS standards includes a revised compliance statement that indicates if the firm has or has not been verified.

5   **Presentation and Reporting:** After constructing the composites, gathering the input data, calculating returns, and determining the necessary disclosures, the firm must incorporate this information in presentations based on the requirements in the GIPS standards for presenting investment performance. No finite set of requirements can cover all potential situations or anticipate future developments in investment industry

Exhibit 2 (Continued)

structure, technology, products, or practices. When appropriate, firms have the responsibility to include in GIPS-compliant presentations information not addressed by the GIPS standards.

6 **Real Estate:** Unless otherwise noted, this section supplements all of the required and recommended provisions in Sections 0–5 in Chapter I of the GIPS standards. Real estate provisions were first included in the 2005 edition of the GIPS standards and became effective 1 January 2006. The 2010 edition of the GIPS standards includes new provisions for closed-end real estate funds. Firms should note that certain provisions of Sections 0–5 in Chapter I of the GIPS standards do not apply to real estate investments or are superseded by provisions within Section 6 in Chapter I. The provisions that do not apply have been noted within Section 6 in Chapter I.

7 **Private Equity:** Unless otherwise noted, this section supplements all of the required and recommended provisions in Sections 0–5 in Chapter I of the GIPS standards. Private equity provisions were first included in the 2005 edition of the GIPS standards and became effective 1 January 2006. Firms should note that certain provisions in Sections 0–5 in Chapter I of the GIPS standards do not apply to private equity investments or are superseded by provisions within Section 7 in Chapter I. The provisions that do not apply have been noted within Section 7 in Chapter I.

8 **Wrap Fee/Separately Managed Account (SMA) Portfolios:** Unless otherwise noted, this section supplements all of the required and recommended provisions in Sections 0–5 in Chapter I of the GIPS standards. The provisions that do not apply have been noted within Section 8 in Chapter I. All wrap fee/SMA compliant presentations that include performance results for periods beginning on or after 1 January 2006 must meet all the requirements of the wrap fee/SMA provisions.

3.1 Fundamentals of Compliance

Section I.0, "Fundamentals of Compliance," indicates that firms must comply with all the requirements of the GIPS standards[8] as well as all applicable laws and regulations regarding the calculation and presentation of performance, and—tacitly recognizing that firms which are arguably in technical compliance might still find ways to misrepresent investment results—they must not present performance or performance-related information that is false or misleading. (I.0.A.1–3.) Furthermore, the GIPS standards must be applied on a firm-wide basis (I.0.A.4); firms cannot claim to be in compliance with the GIPS standards with regard only to certain of the asset classes, investment strategies, products, or composites that fall within the definition of the firm.

Provision I.0.A.5 stipulates that firms must document the policies and procedures used in establishing and maintaining compliance with the GIPS standards and that the stated policies and procedures must be applied consistently including ensuring the existence and ownership of client's assets. We will see that the policies and procedures to be documented notably include, but are not limited to, the firm's definition of discretion; the criteria for including portfolios in specific composites; the timing of the inclusion and exclusion of new and terminated portfolios, respectively; the

---

8 This includes any updates, Guidance Statements, interpretations, Questions & Answers (Q&As), and clarifications published by CFA Institute and the GIPS Executive Committee, which are available on the GIPS standards website (www.gipsstandards.org) as well as in the *GIPS Handbook*.

treatment of cash flows; and the firm's policies, procedures, and methodologies for valuing investments. The firm's error correction policies and procedures must also be documented.

Completing and updating the firm's documentation of performance-related policies and procedures may prove to be one of the biggest contributions the GIPS implementation project makes to effective operations management. Because preparing proper documentation is typically less urgent than other business matters, it is not uncommon for refinements in policies and, especially, changes in the way tasks are accomplished to be explained, if at all, only in e-mails and memoranda that are not integrated into manuals or handbooks. Over time, the existing documentation can become inadequate or inaccurate. Implementing the GIPS standards may help managers assemble resources and allocate time to upgrading their existing documentation. Oftentimes, too, the effort to document longstanding policies and procedures leads to actions taken which improve internal controls and/or achieve operational efficiencies.

As we have already indicated, no exceptions to the GIPS standards are permitted; the firm cannot represent that it is in compliance with the GIPS standards "except for" anything, or make any other statements that might indicate partial compliance. Moreover, statements characterizing the calculation methodology used in a composite presentation as being in accordance with, in compliance with, or consistent with the GIPS standards, or similar statements, are prohibited.[9] Statements referring to the performance of a single, existing client as being "calculated in accordance with the Global Investment Performance Standards" are also prohibited except when a GIPS-compliant firm reports the performance of an individual client's portfolio to that client. (I.0.A.6–8)

Provisions I.0.A.9–11 of the GIPS standards describe other fundamental responsibilities of GIPS-compliant firms. First, firms are expected to "make every reasonable effort" to provide all prospective clients with a compliant presentation. In other words, firms cannot choose to whom they want to present GIPS-compliant performance. (The GIPS standards clarify that a firm will have met this requirement if a prospect has received a compliant presentation within the previous 12 months.) In addition, firms must provide a list of composite descriptions to any prospective client asking for such information, and they must provide upon request a compliant presentation for any composite listed. Discontinued composites must remain on the list for at least five years after their termination date.

To comply with the GIPS standards, a firm must be an investment firm, subsidiary, or division *held out to clients or potential clients as a distinct business entity* (I.0.A.12; emphasis added). The GIPS Glossary entry defines a **distinct business entity** as a "unit, division, department, or office that is organizationally and functionally segregated from other units, divisions, departments, or offices and that retains discretion over the assets it manages and that should have autonomy over the investment decision-making process." Possible criteria for identifying a distinct business entity are the organization being a legal entity, having a distinct market or client type, or using a separate and distinct investment process.

The way in which the investment management organization is held out to the public is a key factor in defining the firm. For example, if a unit of a larger company specializes in providing investment management services to private clients, and is marketed as a specialist in meeting the investment needs of high-net-worth individuals and family offices, then that organizational unit might qualify as a "firm" for the purpose of compliance with the GIPS standards. Certainly, however, the unit's

---

9 It merits emphasis that only investment management firms can claim to be in compliance with the GIPS standards, and such claims are legitimate only if *all* the requirements have been met. Accordingly, software developers and third-party performance measurement providers may not claim compliance with the GIPS standards.

entitlement to be considered a firm under the GIPS standards could be justified if it additionally were incorporated as a subsidiary and had its own dedicated financial analysts, portfolio managers, and traders located in a separate building or area of the company and reporting through a separate chain of command to the parent organization's senior management.

IMPLEMENTATION (2)

Defining the Firm. For small investment management boutiques, defining the firm may be a relatively easy task, but it can prove challenging for large firms or subsidiary companies.

Consider the case of a super-regional bank whose trust department consists of two separate and distinct divisions, Personal Trust and Institutional Trust. The personal trust division, called Eastern National Bank Personal Trust Services, offers investment management to private individuals and families. The institutional trust division, called Eastern Institutional Asset Advisors, serves tax-exempt non-profit organizations including pension funds and charitable foundations; it does not solicit or handle non-institutional business. Each division has its own investment management team, traders, marketing department, administrative personnel, and accounting department. After a few years of operating in this manner, the institutional investment unit decides to achieve compliance with the GIPS standards, but the personal trust department makes a business decision not to implement the GIPS standards. The institutional investment division may nonetheless be in position to become GIPS-compliant because it holds itself out to customers as a distinct business unit, with its own autonomous investment management, research, trading, and administrative team.

Based on the information provided, the institutional trust division appears to satisfy the conditions for defining itself as a firm for the purpose of compliance with the GIPS standards. Sample language might be, "The firm is defined as Eastern Institutional Asset Advisors, the institutional asset management division of Eastern National Bank."

On the other hand, if both divisions were to use the same investment process, approved security list, style models, etc., and merely divided assets between personal and institutional portfolios, then neither division alone could compellingly claim compliance. If the senior investment personnel of the personal trust division had authority to dictate the institutional trust division's investment strategy or tactical asset allocations, or to mandate the investment of institutional clients' funds in specific securities, then the institutional trust division would likely not qualify as a distinct business unit having autonomy over the investment decision-making process and discretion over the assets it manages. If the two divisions were organizationally segregated but shared the same trading desk, the institutional trust division would have to determine whether its decision-making autonomy is compromised by the trading arrangement—if the traders merely fill the portfolio manager's orders, then the institutional trust division arguably remains autonomous, but if the traders actively participate in the identification of misvalued securities, a greater impediment to the autonomy argument would exist.

Defining the firm in such a situation calls for the scrupulous exercise of professional judgment, with due attention to the ethical objectives of the Global Investment Performance Standards.

In view of the complexity of modern organizational structures, it may require judgment to determine if a given unit properly meets the definition of a firm. The decision has immediate and lasting practical consequences, however. Because the GIPS standards apply firm-wide, the definition of the firm will determine the extent of the initial implementation and ongoing compliance activities. It also establishes the boundaries for determining total firm assets. (As we will see, the presentation and reporting requirements of the GIPS standards include displaying the percentage of total firm assets represented by a composite or the amount of total firm assets at the end of each annual period). The phrase **total firm assets** refers to the aggregate fair value[10] of all assets (whether or not discretionary or fee-paying) for which a firm has investment management responsibility. Total firm assets include assets managed by subadvisors that the firm has authority to select, and the performance of assets assigned to a subadvisor must be reflected in a composite provided the firm has discretion over the selection of the subadvisor. (I.0.A.13–14)

The fundamentals of compliance include two further requirements. First, a firm that has been defined for the purposes of the GIPS standards may very well undergo subsequent changes in its corporate structure or organizational design. However, changes in a firm's organization are not permitted to lead to alteration of historical composite results. Indeed, we may put it down as a general rule that, apart from correcting errors, historical composite results are not to be altered. Second, when a GIPS-compliant firm engages in joint marketing activities with other firms, the compliant firm must be distinguished from the other firms, and the marketing communication must make clear which firm is claiming compliance. (I.0.A.15–16)

Recall that the GIPS standards consist of requirements, which must be followed without exception in order for a firm to claim compliance, and recommendations, which are optional but represent best practice in performance presentation. The requirements described earlier are accompanied by four recommendations (I.0.B.1–4), the first of which is simply that firms should comply with the recommendations of the GIPS standards.

The second recommendation is that firms should be verified.

Third, firms should adopt the broadest, most meaningful definition of the firm. The GIPS standards recommend that the scope of the definition should include all offices operating under the same brand regardless of their geographical location and the actual name of the individual investment management companies. We may observe that defining the firm as broadly as possible reduces the likelihood of confusion among investors and regulators over the intended applicability of a claim of compliance.

Fourth, firms should annually provide each *existing* client a GIPS-compliant presentation for any composite in which the client's portfolio is included. Firms that act upon this recommendation will have to be prepared to explain to some clients why their portfolio's return falls below the composite's return; while this may be a difficult conversation, their explanation may lead the client to a better understanding of the firm's investment process and, perhaps, the impact of the client's constraints. (See the discussion of investment discretion later in this reading.)

3.2 Input Data

Before turning to time-weighted total return calculations, we will discuss the necessary input data. We observed earlier in this reading that accurate input data are a key characteristic of the GIPS standards. In fact, the GIPS standards rely on the integrity of input data, because correct rates of return obviously cannot be computed from incorrect asset values and transaction records. Accurately calculated results assume accurate inputs.

The provisions for input data are laid out in Provisions I.1.A.1–7 (requirements) and I.1.B.1–4 (recommendations). The first requirement is basic: All data and information necessary to support all items included in a compliant presentation must be captured and maintained. The need for a firm to obtain the inputs required for rate-of-return calculations and performance presentations is self-evident, although not always easily accomplished. "Maintaining" or storing the data and information, as

---

10 For periods prior to 1 January 2011, total firm assets must be the aggregate of the market value of all discretionary and non-discretionary assets under management within the defined firm. We address the difference between "market value" and "fair value" in Section 4.

required by the GIPS standards, is sound business practice, similar to documenting the firm's performance-related policies and procedures. Only if the historical input data have been kept, and are retrievable, can return calculations be replicated for clients, regulators, verifiers, and other parties in the event that questions arise.

There are three central input data concepts having to do with asset valuations. First, for periods beginning on or after 1 January 2011, portfolios must be valued in accordance with the definition of **fair value** and the GIPS Valuation Principles (I.1.A.2), not cost or book values. Second, **trade date accounting** is required for periods beginning on or after 1 January 2005 (I.1.A.5). Third, **accrual accounting** must be used for fixed-income securities and all other assets that earn interest income (I.1.A.6). Let us now consider each of these provisions.

Fair value supersedes **market value**, a subtly narrower concept that was contained in earlier editions of the GIPS standards.[11] We will briefly discuss fair value in this section and return to this concept in greater detail when we review the GIPS Valuation Principles later in this reading. Fair value reflects the amount at which an investment could be exchanged in a current arm's length transaction between willing parties acting knowledgeably and prudently. Accordingly, fair value must include earned income. Under the GIPS standards, valuations must represent the objective, observable, unadjusted quoted market prices for identical investments in active markets on the measurement date, if available; in the absence of prices that satisfy those criteria, valuations must represent the firm's best estimate of the market value, determined in accordance with the GIPS Valuation Principles.

In this context, it merits mention that cost is pertinent to performance measurement only insofar as it reflects an investment's beginning value. Book value, an accounting convention, is also irrelevant. (Roughly speaking, a financial asset's book value is its cost adjusted for the accretion of income and the amortization of any discount or premium.) For performance measurement, as opposed to financial or tax accounting, it does not matter whether gains and losses are realized or unrealized.[12] Along with investment income, the significant factors are the magnitude and direction of change in the assets' aggregate fair value over the measurement period.

The GIPS standards require that firms use trade-date accounting for the purpose of performance measurement for periods beginning on or after 1 January 2005 (I.1.A.5). This requirement is related to the mandatory use of fair value. A portfolio manager makes purchase and sale decisions based on current market conditions. (Even holding a security may be considered an investment decision, continuously renewed, to "buy" the security, or equivalently not to sell it and reinvest the proceeds in another security, at the current value.)

For the purposes of the GIPS standards, under trade-date accounting the "transaction is reflected in the portfolio on the date of the purchase or sale, and not on the settlement date." Settlement—the actual exchange of a security for cash at the price agreed on when the trade was executed—may take place days later. **Settlement-date accounting** is defined as "recognizing the asset or liability on the date when the exchange of cash and investments is completed." If the trade and settlement dates straddle the end date of a performance measurement period, then return comparisons between portfolios that use settlement-date accounting, on one hand, and benchmarks or portfolios that use trade-date accounting, on the other, may be invalid. Thus, the principle behind requiring trade-date accounting is to ensure that no significant lag occurs between a trade's execution and its reflection in the portfolio's performance.

---

11 Portfolio valuations must be based on market values (not cost basis or book values) for periods prior to 1 January 2011. The GIPS Glossary defines market value as the price at which investors can buy or sell an investment at a given time multiplied by the quantity held, plus any accrued income.

12 Note, however, that cost or book values and realized gains and losses are pertinent for after-tax performance calculations, discussed later.

For compliance with the GIPS standards, the trade-date accounting requirement is considered to be satisfied if assets and liabilities are recognized within three days of entering into the transaction.

The GIPS standards also stipulate that accrual accounting must be used for fixed-income securities and all other assets that earn interest income (I.1.A.6). This provision is also related to the fair valuation of assets. When a conventional bond is sold, it will be exchanged for cash in an amount that reflects not only the agreed-upon price of the instrument but also the seller's entitlement to interest earned but not yet paid. Similarly, for GIPS-compliant performance, interest income on an asset that is held in a portfolio must be recognized as it is earned versus when it is received. Accordingly, interest income earned but not yet received must be included in the value of fixed-income securities and all other assets that accrue interest income. With respect to dividend-paying equities, the GIPS standards recommend that dividends be accrued as of the ex-dividend date (I.1.B.3).

In addition to the key valuation-related provisions explained earlier, the input data requirements of the GIPS standards specify the frequency and timing of portfolio valuations (II.1.A.3–4). Exhibit 3 presents the pertinent requirements. Note that the requirements changed as of 1 January 2010 (not 2011). These changes were included in the 2005 edition of the GIPS standards, but their effective date was deferred until 1 January 2010 so as to provide firms enough time to accommodate them.

Exhibit 3	Frequency and Timing of Portfolio Valuations
For Periods...	**Portfolios Must Be Valued...**
Prior to 1 January 2001	At least quarterly
Beginning on or after 1 January 2001	At least monthly
Beginning on or after 1 January 2010	▪ On the date of all large cash flows as defined by the firm for each composite; and
	▪ As of each calendar month-end or the last business day of each month

An **external cash flow** is capital (cash or investments) that enters or exits a portfolio. The GIPS standards do not specify the level of **large cash flows**; firms are required to define portfolio- or composite-specific amounts or percentages that constitute large external cash flows. Later in this reading, we examine the potentially distorting effect of large cash flows on rate-of-return calculations.

Provision 1.A.3.c further specifies that portfolios must be valued no more frequently than required by the valuation policy. The objective of this provision is to prohibit firms from opportunistically valuing a portfolio by selecting the most advantageous sub-periods over which to calculate their performance. Firms must adhere to their composite-specific valuation policy consistently and not "cherry pick" when to value portfolios.

The GIPS standards additionally require that, for periods beginning on or after 1 January 2006, the firm's composites, and necessarily the portfolios within the composites, must have consistent beginning and ending *annual* valuation dates. Unless the composite is reported on a non-calendar fiscal year, the beginning and ending valuation dates must be at calendar year-end or on the last business day of the year (I.1.A.7).

The GIPS standards governing input data also include three recommendations that we have not previously mentioned. First, the GIPS standards recommend that firms adopt a policy to value portfolios, not merely when large cash flows occur, but on the date of all external cash flows (I.1.B.1).

Second, valuations should be obtained from a qualified independent third party (I.1.B.2). Certainly, a firm's judicious selection of asset-pricing sources is a key element in achieving the fair representation of investment performance. Obtaining valuations from an independent third-party in most instances is considered to be best practice and the firm must insure that the valuations obtained satisfy the requirements of the GIPS standards. In addition, switching from one source to another so as to improve stated performance at the end of a reporting period is ethically indefensible.

Third, the GIPS standards related to input data also recommend that, when presenting net-of-fees returns, firms should accrue investment management fees (I.1.B.4). We discuss net-of-fees return calculations below. As a practical matter, the GIPS standards' input data requirements and recommendations have important implications for the design of a firm's performance measurement system, including its interface with the firm's portfolio accounting system. Management must ensure that portfolio valuations are performed properly and that all the data needed to substantiate the information contained in GIPS-compliant performance presentations are captured and maintained.

IMPLEMENTATION (3)

Input Data. Typically, the firm's portfolio accounting system is the primary source of data inputs to the performance measurement system. (The accounting system may itself have automated feeds from other sources, including the trading system for security transactions and external data services for market prices.) What we may call "performance accounting"—the compilation of data inputs for rate-of-return calculations—may differ from financial accounting, however, and any differences must be recognized when designing an interface between the portfolio accounting system and the performance measurement system. For instance, book values and the distinction between realized and unrealized capital gains and losses are necessary for financial accounting but might be inappropriate or irrelevant for before-tax performance measurement. Investment management fees may also require special treatment. A net-of-fees return is defined as the gross-of-fees return reduced by **investment management fees**, including performance-based fees and carried interest (the general partners' portion of the profits earned on the investments made by an investment vehicle). The portfolio accounting system may treat the performance-based fees and carried interest differently than the way they need to be treated for investment performance purposes. In order to meet the requirements—and, optimally, the recommendations—of the GIPS standards for input data, calculation methodology, composite construction, and performance presentation and reporting, the firm must comprehensively address these and many other accounting- and system-related issues.

3.3 Calculation Methodology: Time-Weighted Total Return

The GIPS standards mandate the use of a total rate of return, called total return for short (I.2.A.1). Total return is the most comprehensive and accurate expression of investment results because it reflects the change in portfolio value during the measurement period, taking into account not only income but also realized and unrealized gains and losses. (Recall from our discussion of input data that, for performance measurement, it does not matter whether gains and losses are transactionally realized. What matters is the change in fair value.) In other words, total return captures both the return from investment income and the return from capital gains and losses.

In the simplest case, when no external cash flows (i.e., client-initiated additions to or withdrawals from invested assets) occur during the period, calculating total return is straightforward:

$$r_t = \frac{V_1 - V_0}{V_0}$$ (1)

where r_t is the total return for period t, V_1 is the ending value of the portfolio, including cash and accrued income, at the end of the period; and V_0 is the portfolio's beginning value, including cash and accrued income, at the beginning of the specified period. (Recall that the requirement to include accrued interest income in the values of fixed-income securities appears in Provision I.1.A.6, and the recommendation that accrual accounting should be used for dividends as of the ex-dividend date appears in Provision I.1.B.3. We discuss the requirement to include cash, and cash equivalents, later.) Equation 1 assumes that income received remains in the portfolio, and expresses return as the ratio of the change in value during the period to the value at the start of the period. Despite its simplicity, the total return equation shown above produces an accurate representation of investment results in a single period with no external cash flows. As we will see, this equation is also used to calculate subperiod results under the intraperiod valuation method when external cash flows occur.

Most portfolios, of course, do have external cash flows. A separate account for an institutional investor, for example, may routinely have contributions and withdrawals based on the needs of the institution. In evaluating an investment firm, the effect of such contributions and withdrawals should be removed from the return calculation because the timing and amount of external cash flows are typically controlled not by the investment management firm but by the client (in this case, an institutional investor). Because performance measurement attempts to quantify the value added by investment decisions, the GIPS standards require the use of **time-weighted rates of return**, or approximations to time-weighted rates of return, to eliminate the impact of external cash flows on the return calculation.

Provision I.2.A.2 specifies the use of time-weighted rates of return that adjust for external cash flows. For periods beginning on or after 1 January 2005, firms must approximate rates of return that adjust for daily weighted external cash flows, and we have seen that for periods beginning on or after 1 January 2010, firms must value portfolios on the date of all large external cash flows. (We will return to the definition of "large" external cash flows below.) Provision I.2.A.2 also holds that, for periods beginning on or after 1 January 2001, firms must calculate portfolio returns at least monthly; for earlier periods, firms may calculate portfolio returns quarterly.

The most accurate way to calculate a total return while eliminating the impact of external cash flows is to value the portfolio whenever an external cash flow occurs, compute a subperiod return, and geometrically chain-link subperiod returns expressed in relative form according to the following equation:

$$r_{twr} = (1 + r_{t,1}) \times (1 + r_{t,2}) \times \ldots \times (1 + r_{t,n}) - 1$$ (2)

where r_{twr} is the time-weighted total return for the entire period and $r_{t,1}$ through $r_{t,n}$ are the subperiod returns. We explicitly point out that Provision I.2.A.2 requires periodic returns to be geometrically **linked**—that is, converted to relative form $(1 + r)$ and multiplied—according to the firm's composite-specific policy.

For example, consider a portfolio with a beginning value of $100,000 as of 31 May, a value of $109,000 on 5 June (including a cash contribution of $10,000 received that day), and an ending value of $110,550 on 30 June. Consider that the first subperiod ends and the second begins on the cash flow date, such that the ending value for subperiod 1 is $99,000 ($109,000 less the contribution of $10,000) and the beginning value for Subperiod 2, including the $10,000 contribution, is $109,000. The portfolio's true time-weighted return using the intraperiod valuation method is 0.41 percent, computed as follows:

$$r_{t,1} = \frac{V_1 - V_0}{V_0} = \frac{(109,000 - 10,000) - 100,000}{100,000} = \frac{99,000 - 100,000}{100,000} = -0.01$$

$$r_{t,2} = \frac{V_1 - V_0}{V_0} = \frac{110,550 - 109,000}{109,000} = 0.0142$$

$$r_{twr} = \left(1 + r_{t,1}\right) \times \left(1 + r_{t,2}\right) - 1 = \left[1 + (-0.01)\right] \times \left(1 + 0.0142\right) - 1$$
$$= 1.0041 - 1 = 0.0041 = 0.41\%$$

Geometric linking, as shown here, is correct (and required by the GIPS standards) because returns are compounded and so are not additive but multiplicative.

Assuming the input data are valid, the intraperiod valuation method illustrated above gives truly accurate total returns. Accordingly, for periods beginning on or after 1 January 2010, the GIPS standards *require* firms to calculate returns by geometrically linking periodic returns before and after *large* cash flows and, as we saw when reviewing the provisions related to input data, the GIPS standards *recommend* that portfolios be valued on the date of *all* external cash flows. For earlier periods, however, estimation methods can be used.

For periods prior to 1 January 2005, cash flows can be assumed to occur at the midpoint of the measurement period. The Original Dietz method reflects this midpoint assumption:

$$r_{Dietz} = \frac{V_1 - V_0 - CF}{V_0 + (CF \times 0.5)} \tag{3}$$

where CF is the net external cash flow for the period.

Using the same example, the Original Dietz formula gives a return of 0.52 percent:

$$r_{Dietz} = \frac{V_1 - V_0 - CF}{V_0 + (CF \times 0.5)} = \frac{110,550 - 100,000 - 10,000}{100,000 + (10,000 \times 0.5)} = 0.0052 = 0.52\%$$

A time-weighted total return calculation that adjusts for *daily* weighted cash flows is required for periods beginning on or after 1 January 2005. Examples of acceptable approaches are the Modified Dietz method and the Modified Internal Rate of Return (Modified IRR) method, both of which weight each cash flow by the proportion of the measurement period it is held in the portfolio.

The formula for estimating the time-weighted rate of return using the Modified Dietz method is

$$r_{ModDietz} = \frac{V_1 - V_0 - CF}{V_0 + \sum_{i=1}^{n}(CF_i \times w_i)} \tag{4}$$

where $\sum_{i=1}^{n}(CF_i \times w_i)$ is the sum of each cash flow multiplied by its weight and $CF = \sum CF_i$.

The weight (w_i) is simply the proportion of the measurement period, in days, that each cash flow has been in the portfolio:

$$w_i = \frac{CD - D_i}{CD} \tag{5}$$

where CD is the total number of calendar days in the period and D_i is the number of calendar days from the beginning of the period to the time cash flow CF_i occurs. (Note that this formula assumes that cash flows occur at the end of the day.)[13] In our example, there is a $10,000 contribution on 5 June so $D_i = 5$, and there are 30 days in June, so $CD = 30$. The proportion of the measurement period that the $10,000 is in the portfolio is thus

$$w_i = \frac{CD - D_i}{CD} = \frac{30 - 5}{30} = \frac{25}{30} = 0.83$$

Applying the Modified Dietz formula to the same example gives a return of 0.51 percent:

$$r_{ModDietz} = \frac{V_1 - V_0 - CF}{V_0 + \sum_{i=1}^{n}(CF_i \times w_i)} = \frac{110,550 - 100,000 - 10,000}{100,000 + [10,000 \times (25 / 30)]} = 0.0051 = 0.51\%$$

The Modified IRR method is another estimation approach. This method determines the internal rate of return (IRR) for the period, adjusted to take into effect the timing of cash flows. The Modified IRR is the value of r that satisfies the following equation:

$$\text{Ending Value} = V_1 = \sum_{i=1}^{n}\left[CF_i \times (1 + r)^{w_i}\right] + V_0(1 + r) \qquad \textbf{(6)}$$

where the exponent, w_i, is as previously defined the ratio of the amount of time CF_i is in the portfolio to the total time in the measurement period. The equation is solved iteratively by a trial-and-error procedure, settling on the value of r that makes the series of cash flows equal to the ending fair value.[14] The Modified IRR method is computationally intensive, but programs are available for solving the equation efficiently. (Some Modified IRR programs use the Modified Dietz return as an initial estimate or seed value.) Applying the Modified IRR method to the simple example used earlier in this section gives a result of 0.51 percent, the same as the rate of return found with the Modified Dietz method.

3.4 Return Calculations: External Cash Flows

In the previous section, different methodologies for calculating a rate of return from a single set of input data gave different answers. To recapitulate:

Inputs:

Fair value on 31 May: $100,000

Cash flow on 5 June: + $10,000

Fair value on 5 June: $109,000 (after the cash flow)

Fair value on 30 June: $110,550

Solutions:

True time-weighted return: 0.41 percent

Original Dietz method: 0.52 percent

Modified Dietz method: 0.51 percent

Modified IRR method: 0.51 percent

---

13 Cash flows can also be assumed to occur at the beginning of the day. In that case, the weight factor is adjusted to add another day to the period of time the cash flow is in the portfolio: $w_i = (CD - D_i + 1)/CD$. It is incumbent upon the firm to establish a policy to weight external cash flows consistently.
14 The Modified IRR method differs from the original internal rate of return method in that the exponent is the proportion of the measurement period that each cash flow is in the portfolio. Therefore, while the original IRR is a money-weighted return, the Modified IRR approximates a time-weighted return.

In this particular example, the estimated rates of return given by the Modified Dietz and Modified IRR methods are nearly the same as the estimated return calculated by the Original Dietz method, which assumes that the external cash flow occurred at mid-month. However, the external cash flow causes the day-weighted estimates (0.51 percent) to vary by 10 basis points from the true time-weighted return (0.41 percent).

To appreciate the potentially distorting impact of external cash flows on estimated time-weighted rates of return, consider Exhibits 4 through 6. The exhibits depict a "market index" with a value of 100 as of 31 May, and the data below each exhibit represent portfolios with a value of $100,000 on 31 May and contributions of $10,000 received on 5 June (on the left-hand side) and 15 June (on the right-hand side). In flat and steadily rising or falling markets (illustrated in Exhibit 4 and Exhibit 5), the timing of the cash flows has a relatively modest impact on the accuracy of the estimates. We can observe this phenomenon by comparing the true time-weighted returns with those calculated using the Modified Dietz method. (Note that the Modified Dietz method is mathematically equivalent to the Original Dietz method when the cash flow occurs at the midpoint of the measurement period.) When markets are volatile, however, as illustrated in Exhibit 6, large external cash flows may have a material impact on the accuracy of the estimated return. The reader should work through these examples using the formulas for the true time-weighted return and the Modified Dietz method. The calculations for the first example, on the left-hand side of Exhibit 4, were shown above.

Exhibit 4   Impact of Cash Flows in a Flat Market

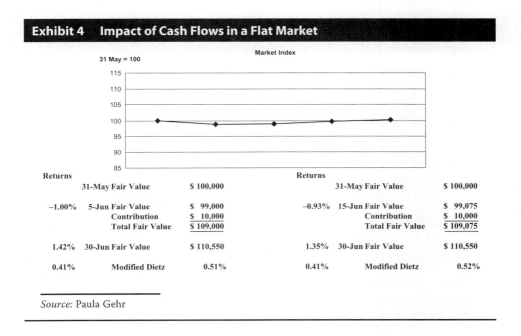

Returns				Returns		
	31-May Fair Value	$ 100,000			31-May Fair Value	$ 100,000
−1.00%	5-Jun Fair Value	$ 99,000		−0.93%	15-Jun Fair Value	$ 99,075
	Contribution	$ 10,000			Contribution	$ 10,000
	Total Fair Value	$ 109,000			Total Fair Value	$ 109,075
1.42%	30-Jun Fair Value	$ 110,550		1.35%	30-Jun Fair Value	$ 110,550
0.41%	Modified Dietz	0.51%		0.41%	Modified Dietz	0.52%

Source: Paula Gehr

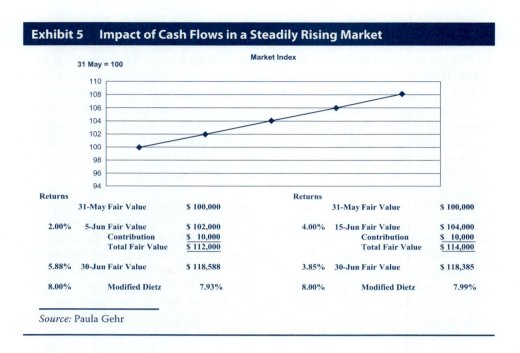

Exhibit 5   Impact of Cash Flows in a Steadily Rising Market

Returns			Returns		
	31-May Fair Value	$ 100,000		31-May Fair Value	$ 100,000
2.00%	5-Jun Fair Value	$ 102,000	4.00%	15-Jun Fair Value	$ 104,000
	Contribution	$ 10,000		Contribution	$ 10,000
	Total Fair Value	$ 112,000		Total Fair Value	$ 114,000
5.88%	30-Jun Fair Value	$ 118,588	3.85%	30-Jun Fair Value	$ 118,385
8.00%	Modified Dietz	7.93%	8.00%	Modified Dietz	7.99%

Source: Paula Gehr

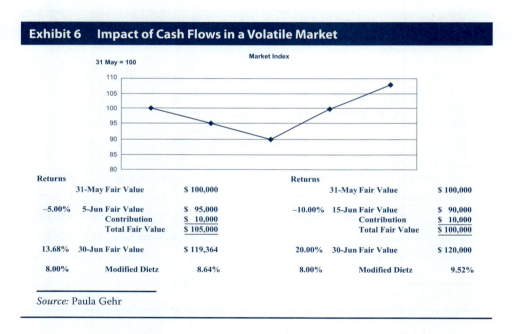

Exhibit 6   Impact of Cash Flows in a Volatile Market

Returns			Returns		
	31-May Fair Value	$ 100,000		31-May Fair Value	$ 100,000
−5.00%	5-Jun Fair Value	$ 95,000	−10.00%	15-Jun Fair Value	$ 90,000
	Contribution	$ 10,000		Contribution	$ 10,000
	Total Fair Value	$ 105,000		Total Fair Value	$ 100,000
13.68%	30-Jun Fair Value	$ 119,364	20.00%	30-Jun Fair Value	$ 120,000
8.00%	Modified Dietz	8.64%	8.00%	Modified Dietz	9.52%

Source: Paula Gehr

The GIPS standards require firms to formulate and document composite-specific policies for the treatment of external cash flows and to adhere to those policies consistently. (Provision I.2.A.2 reads in pertinent part, "External cash flows must be treated according to the firm's composite-specific policy.") Each policy should describe the firm's methodology for computing time-weighted returns and the firm's assumptions about the timing of capital inflows and outflows. If it is the firm's rule to value portfolios on the date of all external cash flows, as the GIPS standards recommend, then the firm should also state that policy.

As we have previously remarked, the GIPS standards do not specify a quantitative definition of large external cash flows. Taking into account the liquidity of the market segments or asset classes and the nature of the investment strategy, firms must make their own determinations for each composite. For example, a relatively high percentage of portfolio value might be easily deployed in a developed equity market, while a lower percentage of portfolio value might be deemed the appropriate criterion for a large external cash flow in a comparatively illiquid emerging debt market.

A composite-specific policy may define a "large" external cash flow in terms of the value of cash/asset flow or in terms of a percentage of the portfolio assets or the composite assets. Whatever definition a firm adopts, it must document the policy and follow it without exception. If a portfolio receives a large external cash flow, as defined for the composite in which the portfolio is included, the firm is not at liberty to omit the valuation on the grounds that the market was not especially volatile during the measurement period. Inconsistent applications of firm policies constitute a breach of the GIPS standards.

IMPLEMENTATION (4)

Return Calculation Policies. The GIPS standards state, "Firms must calculate time-weighted rates of return that adjust for external cash flows. Both periodic and sub-period returns must be geometrically linked. External cash flows must be treated according to the firm's composite –specific policy." (Excerpted from Provision I.2.A.2). The GIPS standards also state that, for periods beginning on or after 1 January 2010, portfolios must be valued on the date of all large cash flows, and that firms must define large cash flow for each composite to determine when the portfolios in that composite must be valued. (Excerpted from Provision I.1.A.3). Here are examples of internal policy statements addressing these elements:

Portfolio return calculation methodology: "Eastern Institutional Asset Advisors calculates each portfolio's time-weighted rate of return on a monthly basis. For periods beginning on or after 1 January 2010, portfolios are valued when large cash flows occur; in earlier periods, monthly returns are calculated using the Modified Dietz method. Returns for longer measurement periods are computed by geometrically linking the monthly returns."

Large external cash flows: "Eastern Institutional Asset Advisors revalues portfolios that belong to the Large-Cap Domestic Equity composite when capital equal to 10 percent or more of fair value as of the end of the most recent measurement period is contributed or withdrawn."

3.5 Additional Portfolio Return Calculation Provisions

The GIPS standards for calculation methodology include further provisions directly affecting portfolio returns. (We will discuss the calculation-related guidelines for composites in a later section.)

One requirement is that returns from cash and cash equivalents held in portfolios must be included in all total return calculations (I.2.A.3). A primary purpose of performance measurement is to enable prospective clients and, by extension, their consultants to evaluate an investment management firm's results. Within the constraints established by a client's investment policy statement (IPS), active managers often have discretion to decide what portion of a portfolio's assets to hold in cash or cash equivalents. In other words, the cash allocation decision may be at least partially under the manager's control, and thus return calculations must reflect the contribution of the cash and cash equivalents to investment results.

Consider the case of an institutional investor such as a defined-benefit pension plan sponsor. The structure of the sponsor's investment program is, generally, based on an asset allocation study or, preferably, an asset/liability study identifying the optimal mix of asset classes to meet the fund's financial objectives at an acceptable level of risk. The sponsor retains investment management firms to invest the fund's assets in specific markets in accordance with the study results. For example, within the domestic equity allocation, the sponsor might hire one firm to invest a certain portion of the fund's assets in small-cap growth stocks and another firm to invest a portion in large-cap value stocks. The sponsor expects the managers to remain fully invested in their mandated market sectors at all times. The sponsor's IPS may, however, allow the managers to hold some amount (e.g., up to 5 percent of portfolio assets) in cash and cash equivalents, if only to accommodate the cash thrown off in the process of buying and selling securities. (The client will usually define "cash equivalents," for example, as money market instruments and fixed income securities with less than one year to maturity.) In this case, it is up to the manager to decide how much cash to hold, up to 5 percent of assets.

The total portfolio return will be higher or lower depending on how much cash the manager holds and how the domestic equity and money markets perform relative to one another during the measurement period. A few simple scenarios based on actual historical US market returns will illustrate these points. First, in a rising equity market, cash positions reduce overall portfolio returns; the higher the cash position, the lower the portfolio return. This relationship is illustrated in Exhibit 7, in which increasing the cash position (represented here by US Treasury bills) from 1 percent to 5 percent of portfolio assets reduces the portfolio return for a three-month period by 26 basis points (0.26 percent).

Exhibit 7	Illustration of the Effect of Cash Holdings in Rising Markets			
	1% Held in Cash		5% Held in Cash	
	Weight	Return	Weight	Return
Broad US equity market index	99%	6.57%	95%	6.57%
US Treasury bills	1%	0.26%	5%	0.26%
Total portfolio	100%	6.51%	100%	6.25%

In contrast, a higher cash position improves the portfolio return in a falling market. Exhibit 8 illustrates this result, whereby increasing the percentage of the portfolio held in cash from 1 percent to 5 percent boosts the three-month portfolio return by 11 basis points (0.11 percent).

Exhibit 8	Illustration of the Effect of Cash Holdings in Declining Markets			
	1% Held in Cash		5% Held in Cash	
	Weight	Return	Weight	Return
Broad US equity market index	99%	−2.39%	95%	−2.39%
US Treasury bills	1%	0.45%	5%	0.45%
Total portfolio	100%	−2.36%	100%	−2.25%

Note that cash and cash equivalents must be included in the total return calculation even if the cash is not actually invested by the same person or group. The amount of cash available for short-term investment is more important to overall portfolio results than the money market manager's success in outperforming the short-term market. For the rising and falling equity markets described above, Exhibit 9 illustrates the relative impact of the portfolio manager's increasing the cash allocation from 1 percent to 5 percent and the money market trader's simultaneously achieving excess returns 50 basis points (0.5 percent) higher than Treasury bill returns. The portfolio manager's cash allocation decision has a substantially greater effect on overall portfolio returns than does the money market trader's proficiency in selecting attractive short-term investments.

Exhibit 9   Impact of Cash on Portfolio Returns

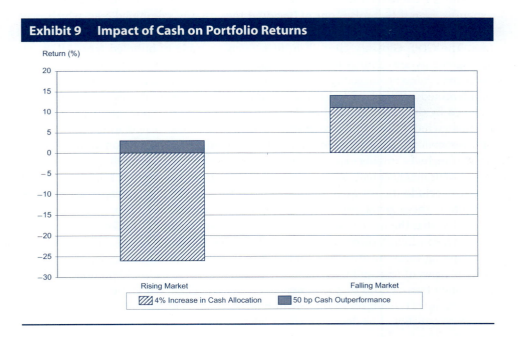

The GIPS standards further require that returns be calculated after the deduction of actual—not estimated—trading expenses (I.2.A.4). Trading expenses are costs incurred in the purchase or sale of investments, and the performance calculation must include them because these expenses must be paid in order to execute the investment strategy. The GIPS Glossary defines **trading expenses** as the actual costs of buying or selling investments and notes that these costs typically take the form of brokerage commissions, exchange fees and/or taxes, or spreads from either internal or external brokers. Commissions are explicit costs, generally a negotiated amount per share of common stock bought or sold, intended to compensate the broker, as the investor's agent, for arranging and settling trades. Bid–ask spreads are the difference between the price at which a dealer, acting for his firm's account, is willing to buy a security from a seller and the price at which he is willing to sell the security to a buyer. From the investor's perspective, the spread is the cost of immediacy or liquidity, and it compensates the dealer for both the cost of operations and the risk of adverse selection (the possibility that a well-informed trader has better information than the dealer has about the fundamental value of a security in the dealer's inventory).[15] Actual trading expenses are necessary input data for GIPS-compliant rate-of-return calculations.

It merits mention in this context that, as the GIPS Glossary makes clear, **custody fees** should not be considered direct trading expenses, even when they are charged on a per-transaction basis. From a performance measurement perspective, although trading costs are unavoidably part of executing an investment strategy, they will typically be higher in a portfolio with relatively greater turnover. External cash flows, whether inflows or outflows, will typically result in a higher-than-normal volume of security transactions, but on an ongoing basis, a manager generally has control over portfolio turnover. A firm's trading capabilities will also affect its level of execution

---

15 For a comprehensive treatment of these topics, the interested reader is referred to Larry Harris (2003).

costs. Although it is not a matter of compliance with the GIPS standards, the investment manager has an ethical and fiduciary responsibility to achieve best execution on behalf of clients. If a client's directed brokerage program requires the firm to channel trades through approved brokers, regular communication with the client is in order.[16]

With respect to the GIPS standards, there are additional requirements when trading expenses cannot be broken out of **bundled fees**, that is, combined fees, which may include any combination of management, trading, custody, and/or administrative fees. The GIPS Glossary cites all-in fees as an example of bundled fees. All-in fee arrangements are common when a single company offers diverse services such as asset management, brokerage, and custody. When actual trading expenses cannot be identified and segregated from a bundle fee, the gross-of-fees return must be reduced by the entire amount of the bundled fee or by that portion of the bundled fee that includes the trading expenses. In other words, when calculating returns gross of investment management fees, the entire bundled fee or the portion of the bundled fee that includes trading expenses must be deducted. When calculating returns net of investment management fees, the entire bundled fee or the portion(s) of the bundled fee that include the investment management fee and the trading expenses must be deducted. These requirements are presented in Provisions I.2.A.5.a–b, where it is reiterated that the use of estimated trading expenses is not permitted.

Provision I.2.B.1 recommends that returns be calculated net of non-reclaimable withholding taxes on dividends, interest, and capital gains. Some countries allow certain types of foreign investors to recoup a portion of withholding taxes that are paid when transactions or payments occur by filing claims. It is recommended that withholding taxes subject to reclamation be accrued. Withholding taxes that cannot be recovered should be deducted when calculating returns.

3.6 Composite Return Calculation Provisions

The notion of a composite is central to the GIPS standards. Because composite returns convey the firm's investment results for a given investment mandate, objective, or strategy, proper composite construction is essential to achieving the ethical aims of the GIPS standards, the fair representation and full disclosure of the firm's performance.

A composite may be thought of as a combined portfolio composed of similar portfolios in proportion to their weights as a percent of the composite's total assets. Accordingly, the composite return is the asset-weighted average of the returns of all the individual constituent portfolios. The GIPS standards prescribe an asset-weighting method for composite return calculations as described further below.

Standard I.2.A.6 reads, "Composite returns must be calculated by asset-weighting the individual portfolio returns using beginning-of-period values or a method that reflects both beginning-of-period values and external cash flows." Let us explore these methods in an example. Exhibit 10 displays the beginning asset values of four portfolios that, taken together, constitute a composite. The exhibit also shows the external cash flows experienced by each portfolio during the month of June. (We have seen Portfolio A before.) For completeness, the exhibit also shows each portfolio's ending fair value.

---

16 CFA Institute addresses this and many related issues in its "Trade Management Guidelines" and "Soft Dollar Standards," available on the CFA Institute website.

Exhibit 10	A Composite Including Four Portfolios: Weighted External Cash Flows					
	Cash Flow Weighting Factor	Portfolio ($ Thousands)				
		A	B	C	D	Total
Beginning assets (31 May)		100.00	97.40	112.94	124.47	434.81
External cash flows:						
5 June	0.83	10.00	15.00			25.00
8 June	0.73				−15.00	−15.00
17 June	0.43		−5.00			−5.00
24 June	0.20				−6.50	−6.50
29 June	0.03		−2.50		−4.00	−6.50
Ending assets (30 June)		110.55	105.20	113.30	100.50	429.55
Beginning assets + Weighted cash flows		108.30	107.63	112.94	112.10	440.97
Percent of total beginning assets		23.00%	22.40%	25.97%	28.63%	100.00%
Percent of total beginning assets + Weighted cash flows		24.56%	24.41%	25.61%	25.42%	100.00%

Note: Weighted cash flows reflect two-decimal-place precision in the weighting factors.

Determining the percentage of total composite assets held in each portfolio at the beginning of the measurement period is straightforward. Portfolio A had a beginning fair value of $100,000, and all four portfolios combined had a beginning fair value of approximately $435,000, so the percentage held by Portfolio A is 100/434.81 = 0.23 = 23%. As we will show in a moment, under a method reflecting only beginning-of-period values, we can calculate the composite return by multiplying the individual portfolio returns by the percentage of beginning composite assets held in each portfolio and summing the products.

Determining the return impact of portfolios based on beginning assets and weighted external cash flows is a little more complex. The weighting factor, however, is already familiar from our discussion of the Modified Dietz rate-of-return calculation. Each external cash flow is weighted in proportion to percentage of the time it is held in the portfolio during the measurement period. Recall Equation 5:

$$w_i = \frac{CD - D_i}{CD}$$

where CD is the total number of calendar days in the period and D_i is the number of calendar days since the beginning of the period to the time cash flow CF_i occurs. Exhibit 10 showed the weighting factor computed to two decimal places with this formula for each of the days in the measurement period (the month of June) on which external cash flows occur that affect any of the portfolios in the composite. The exhibit also showed the weighted external cash flows under the two methods discussed. For the method incorporating weighted external cash flows, the sum of beginning assets and weighted external cash flows, V_p, is calculated as:

$$V_p = V_0 + \sum_{i=1}^{n}(CF_i \times w_i) \tag{7}$$

where V_0 is the portfolio's beginning value and $\sum_{i=1}^{n}(CF_i \times w_i)$ is the sum of each portfolio's weighted external cash inflows and outflows. Note that the right-hand side in Equation 7 is the denominator of the Modified Dietz formula (see Equation 4).

The composite return is the weighted-average return of the individual portfolios that belong to that composite. Under the "beginning assets" weighting method, the composite return calculation is

$$r_C = \sum \left[r_{pi} \times \frac{V_{0,pi}}{\sum_{pi=1}^{n} V_{0,pi}} \right]$$ (8)

where r_C is the composite return, r_{pi} is the return of an individual portfolio i, $V_{0,pi}$ is the beginning value of portfolio i, and $\sum_{pi=1}^{n} V_{0,pi}$ is the total beginning fair value of all the individual portfolios in the composite. In other words, the composite return is the sum of the individual portfolio returns weighted in proportion to their respective percentages of aggregate beginning assets.

Under the alternate "beginning assets plus weighted cash flows" method, the return calculation uses the individual portfolios' V_P, computed above, in place of $V_{0,p}$:

$$r_C = \sum \left(r_{pi} \times \frac{V_{pi}}{\sum V_{pi}} \right)$$ (9)

Exhibit 11 supplies each individual portfolio's return for the month of June and presents the composite returns resulting from these two weighting methods.

Exhibit 11	Composite Returns		
	Percent of Beginning Assets	Percent of Beginning Assets + Weighted Cash Flows	Return for Month of June
Portfolio A	23.00%	24.56%	0.51%
Portfolio B	22.40%	24.41%	0.28%
Portfolio C	25.97%	25.61%	0.32%
Portfolio D	28.63%	25.42%	1.36%
	100.00%	100.00%	
Composite Return:			
Based on beginning assets			0.65%
Based on beginning assets plus weighted cash flows			0.62%

Under the "beginning assets" weighting method, the composite return shown in Exhibit 11 is:

$$r_C = (0.0051 \times 0.23) + (0.0028 \times 0.224) + (0.0032 \times 0.2597) + (0.0136 \times 0.2863)$$
$$= 0.0065 = 0.65\%$$

Similarly, the composite return under the "beginning assets plus weighted cash flows" method is:

$$r_C = (0.0051 \times 0.2456) + (0.0028 \times 0.2441) + (0.0032 \times 0.2561) + (0.0136 \times 0.2542) = 0.0062 = 0.62\%$$

Mathematically astute performance analysts may already have discerned another valid way to compute composite returns under a method that correctly reflects both beginning-of-period values and external cash flows. Beginning assets and intraperiod external cash flows can be summed and, treating the entire composite as though it were a single portfolio, the return can be computed directly with the Modified Dietz formula. Paying attention to the direction of the cash flows, this approach can be illustrated with data from Exhibit 10, using Equation 4:

$$r_{ModDietz} = \frac{V_1 - V_0 - CF}{V_0 + \sum_{i=1}^{n}(CF_i \times w_i)}$$

$$r_C = \frac{429.55 - 434.81 - 25 - (-15) - (-5) - (-6.5) - (-6.5)}{440.97}$$

$$= \frac{2.74}{440.97} = 0.0062 = 0.62\%$$

In the interest of ensuring that firms present composite returns with reasonable accuracy, the GIPS standards specify the required frequency of asset weighting. Provision I.2.A.7 states that for periods beginning on or after 1 January 2010 composite returns must be calculated by asset weighting the individual portfolio returns at least monthly, and Provision I.2.B.2 recommends that the same be done for earlier periods. The less frequently the asset-weighting exercise is conducted, the greater the likelihood that composite returns will inaccurately reflect the constituent portfolios' aggregate performance. We will encounter this issue again, and illustrate the potential for returns to drift away from mathematically precise computations, when we discuss custom benchmark rebalancing.

3.7 Constructing Composites I—Qualifying Portfolios

In order to prevent firms from presenting only their best-performing portfolios to prospective clients, the GIPS standards require firms to include all portfolios that meet certain criteria in at least one composite. The first requirement for composite construction reads, "All actual, fee-paying, discretionary portfolios must be included in at least one composite." It goes on to clarify that non-fee-paying portfolios may be included in a composite (with appropriate disclosure)[17] provided that they are discretionary, but non-discretionary portfolios must not be included in a firm's composites. (I.3.A.1).

IMPLEMENTATION (5)

Composite Construction: Portfolio Documentation. The GIPS standards require that all data and information necessary to support all items included in a compliant presentation must be captured and maintained (I.1.A.1). At the outset of the implementation project, it is useful to develop a complete list of the firm's portfolios. The list can then be used to check that all documentation such as investment management contracts, custody agreements, investment policy statements (IPS), and compliance documents are available and up to

---

17 See Provision I.5.A.6.

date. This exercise creates a good opportunity for managers and administrative staff to confirm that portfolios are discretionary and to verify target asset mixes, acceptable asset ranges, portfolio size, tax status, investment restrictions, and other characteristics pertinent to the portfolios' assignment to composites. It is also advisable to conduct a formal review and update of the master portfolio list annually. Doing so will help ensure that documentation is kept current and that portfolios are assigned to the correct composites, particularly if clients have modified portfolio mandates and constraints during the year. The review will also point out the need for the creation of new composites if a significant number of portfolios no longer fit into existing composites or if a new investment strategy is launched.

A key term in this requirement is "discretionary." If an actual, fee-paying portfolio is discretionary, it must be included in at least one composite; if it is not discretionary, it must not be included in any composite. A portfolio is discretionary if the manager is able to implement the intended investment strategy. For example, the manager of a fully discretionary domestic mid-cap value portfolio is free to purchase any stock issued in the investor's home country that meets the pertinent market capitalization and style criteria. The firm might define mid-cap stocks as those whose market capitalization falls within a certain range. Similarly, the firm might define value stocks in terms of their price-to-earnings multiple, price-to-book ratio, dividend yield, or other characteristics intended to distinguish them from growth stocks. In line with best practice, the firm and the client will agree in advance that the portfolio's investment objective is to outperform a specified benchmark that is an appropriate measure of success in the domestic mid-cap market. For instance, the firm might construct a custom benchmark that is acceptable to the client, or the firm and the client might agree to use a commercially available index that mirrors the domestic mid-cap market.

If the client imposes restrictions on the manager's freedom to make investment decisions to buy, hold, and sell securities so as to carry out the investment strategy and achieve the portfolio's financial objectives, then the manager must consider whether the portfolio is in fact discretionary. In general, restrictions that impede the investment process to such an extent that the strategy cannot be implemented as intended may be presumed to render the portfolio non-discretionary.

Investors commonly set forth investment restrictions in investment policy statements (IPS). In addition to articulating the investor's overall financial objectives, an IPS normally expresses a number of constraints intended to limit the investment risks to which the assets are exposed. For example, the IPS may limit an individual equity portfolio's economic sector exposure to a certain percentage of portfolio assets or a certain relationship to the comparable benchmark weight: "No portfolio shall hold more than 15 percent of assets or 125 percent of the corresponding benchmark weight, whichever is greater, in any given sector, such as consumer discretionary stocks or information technology stocks." A fixed-income portfolio may be constrained to hold no securities rated below investment grade and to maintain the portfolio's weighted-average duration within a specified range, such as 75 percent to 125 percent of the benchmark duration. These restrictions are intended to preserve the portfolios from losses in value due to inadequate sector diversification, excessive credit quality risk, or unacceptable levels of interest rate risk.

Clearly, in addition to ensuring that the benchmark is appropriate, investors must be careful to formulate constraints that achieve their intended risk-control objectives without unduly impairing the portfolio managers' ability to act on their professional judgment regarding the relative attractiveness of sectors and securities. In other words, a well-written IPS meets the client's need for risk mitigation while respecting the portfolio manager's discretion. The manager is well advised to discuss with the client any restrictions that are incompatible with the intended investment strategy. Upon accepting the investment management assignment, however, the portfolio manager is ethically bound by the client's stated policies. Moreover, investment management agreements often incorporate the IPS, so the portfolio manager may also be legally required to comply with properly communicated client-specified constraints.

In some cases, the client's investment constraints may impinge on the portfolio manager's flexibility. A personal investor might prohibit investment in securities issued by companies operating in industries he or she considers socially unacceptable, such as alcohol, tobacco, or gaming. A corporate client might prohibit the sale of company stock, or a foundation might similarly ban the sale of "sentimental holdings," securities issued by the company in which its founder made a fortune. Additionally, legal restrictions may apply. For instance, a public fund might be statutorily precluded from investing in non-domestic securities. None of these constraints automatically renders a portfolio non-discretionary. Rather, in these and other cases, the portfolio managers must determine whether or not they have scope to execute the investment strategy. It may be appropriate to classify a portfolio as discretionary despite the presence of restrictions (such as the prohibition of alcohol, tobacco, or gaming stocks cited above) and to include it in a composite with other, similarly constrained portfolios.

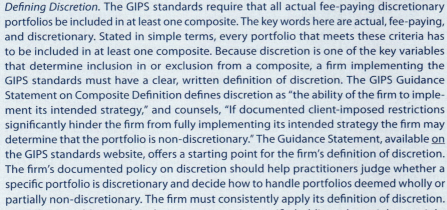

IMPLEMENTATION (6)

Defining Discretion. The GIPS standards require that all actual fee-paying discretionary portfolios be included in at least one composite. The key words here are actual, fee-paying, and discretionary. Stated in simple terms, every portfolio that meets these criteria has to be included in at least one composite. Because discretion is one of the key variables that determine inclusion in or exclusion from a composite, a firm implementing the GIPS standards must have a clear, written definition of discretion. The GIPS Guidance Statement on Composite Definition defines discretion as "the ability of the firm to implement its intended strategy," and counsels, "If documented client-imposed restrictions significantly hinder the firm from fully implementing its intended strategy the firm may determine that the portfolio is non-discretionary." The Guidance Statement, available on the GIPS standards website, offers a starting point for the firm's definition of discretion. The firm's documented policy on discretion should help practitioners judge whether a specific portfolio is discretionary and decide how to handle portfolios deemed wholly or partially non-discretionary. The firm must consistently apply its definition of discretion.

A client could insist that the manager retain specific holdings that might or might not otherwise be held in a portfolio. For example, the client could direct that legacy holdings with a low cost basis must not be sold due to the adverse tax consequences of realizing large gains. In such cases, retaining the asset in the portfolio may skew performance, and—whether the impact is favorable or unfavorable in any given measurement period—the outcome would not reflect the results of the manager's actual discretionary investment management. If holding the assets hinders the ability to implement the intended strategy, either the entire portfolio should be considered non-discretionary and removed from the firm's composites or the individual assets should be removed and the remaining assets for which the manager has full discretion should be retained in (or added to) the composite. Alternately, the firm might include a materiality threshold in its policy, enabling it to consider a portfolio discretionary if the non-discretionary assets consist of less than a certain percentage of portfolio assets.

Recognizing that degrees of discretion exist, the firm must consider the interactions among client-directed constraints, the portfolio's strategy or style, and the investment process, notably including the financial instruments employed. For example, a client's investment policy might proscribe the use of derivative securities such as futures, swaps, and options. In this case, the firm must consider whether the restriction is pertinent. To take up the example of the domestic mid-cap stock portfolio again, the fact that the client prohibits the use of derivatives may be irrelevant if the manager simply buys, holds, and sells common stocks. If the use of derivative securities is central to the firm's implementation of the investment mandate, however, then the client's policy may render the portfolio non-discretionary.

In some cases, the pattern of external cash flows might make a portfolio non-discretionary. For example, if a client frequently makes large withdrawals, perhaps on a regular schedule, the portfolio managers might have to maintain such a high level of liquidity that they cannot truly implement the investment strategy as they do for other portfolios with a similar stated investment mandate, objective, or strategy.

All actual portfolios that are fee-paying and discretionary must be included in at least one composite; no portfolios that are not actual may be included in any composite. The GIPS standards state that composites must include only actual assets managed by the firm (I.3.A.2). Firms must not link the performance of simulated or model portfolios with actual performance (I.3.A.3). In the process of developing, testing, and refining new investment strategies, firms frequently construct model portfolios and use historical security prices to simulate hypothetical performance in past measurement periods. Composites cannot include simulated, backtested, or model portfolios (The GIPS Guidance Statement on the Use of Supplemental Information states that model, hypothetical, backtested, or simulated returns can be shown as **supplemental information** but cannot be linked to actual composite returns.)

On the other hand, if the firm actually created and managed portfolios with its own assets—sometimes called seed money—it could include them from inception in appropriate composites (or, more likely, construct new composites reflecting the new strategies), subject to a presentation and reporting requirement related to the inclusion of non-fee-paying portfolios in composites (see provision I.5.A.6, discussed later). The GIPS standards recommend that firms disclose if a composite contains proprietary assets (I.4.B.8).

To summarize the criteria for including portfolios in composites: All actual, fee-paying, discretionary portfolios must be included in at least one composite. Actual, discretionary portfolios that are non-fee-paying may be included in at least one composite, but neither non-discretionary nor non-actual portfolios may be included in any composite.

3.8 Constructing Composites II—Defining Investment Strategies

Defining and constructing meaningful composites is a vital step toward achieving the ideal of fair representation and the goal of providing prospective clients with useful comparative information. Under the GIPS standards, composites must be defined according to investment mandate, objective, or strategy; composites must include all portfolios that meet the composite definition as documented in the firm's policies and procedures; and the **composite definition**, including detailed criteria that determine the assignment of portfolios to the composite, must be made available upon request (I.3.A.4). Well-defined composites will be objectively representative of the firm's products and consistent with the firm's marketing strategy. To promote comparability, it is beneficial for firms to take into account how other firms characterize similar products.

The GIPS Guidance Statement on Composite Definition suggests a hierarchy that may be helpful for the firm considering how to define composites. Firms are not required to define their composites according to each level of the suggested hierarchy.

Investment Mandate

Asset Classes

Style or Strategy

Benchmarks

Risk/Return Characteristics

A composite based on the investment mandate bears a summary product or strategy description, such as "Global Equities." This may be an entirely acceptable composite definition as long as no significant strategic differences exist among the portfolios included in the composite. It is a guiding principle of composite definition that firms are not permitted to include portfolios with different investment mandates, objectives, or strategies in the same composite.

A composite based on the constituent portfolios' asset class, such as "equity" or "fixed income," may also be acceptable; however, asset classes are broadly inclusive, and, because generic descriptions are not very informative, asset class composites should be offered only if they are legitimately and meaningfully representative of the firm's products.

In order to afford investors a better understanding of the nature of a composite, the firm may use an asset-class modifier indicating the composite's investment style or strategy. For example, equity portfolios may be restricted to a specific economic sector such as telecommunication services. Stocks issued by corporations competing in the same economic sector are presumably affected more or less the same way by exogenous factors such as changes in raw material prices, consumer demand, or the general level of interest rates.

Equity portfolios might also be actively managed to a defined style. A nine-box style matrix widely used by investment consultants in asset allocation studies and performance evaluations classifies portfolios by capitalization (large cap, midcap, and small cap) and by style (value; core, also called neutral, market oriented, or blend; and growth). In addition, some capital market index providers offer capitalization- and style-based indices. Although the construction methodologies for such indices must be carefully considered, they may serve adequately as market-based performance benchmarks for portfolios managed in conformity with these categories. Stocks assigned to one category may move more or less together, and one category may have favorable performance relative to the equity market as a whole while another category underperforms the broad market. For instance, the investment performance of portfolios managed to a small-cap growth strategy may vary considerably from the results achieved by large-cap value portfolios, depending on whether large-cap or small-cap stocks and growth or value stocks are in favor during a given measurement period.

A portfolio may be assigned to one of the style matrix categories based on the money-weighted averages of pertinent characteristics of the portfolio's holdings. For example, a portfolio holding stocks with an average market capitalization of USD 2 billion along with a relatively high price-to-earnings multiple, a relatively high price-to-book ratio, and a relatively low dividend yield, would likely be identified as a midcap growth portfolio.[18] Alternately, the portfolio's historical monthly or quarterly returns might be regressed against the returns of pertinent capital market indices to determine which style-specific benchmarks best explain the portfolio's performance. Evaluating the comparative merits of these approaches falls outside the scope of this reading. Suffice it to say that, given the widespread acceptance of these categories, a firm may meaningfully and usefully define composites with reference to the capitalization range and the style in which the constituent portfolios are managed.

---

18 For a more complete discussion, see Stephen C. Gaudette and Philip Lawton (2007).

IMPLEMENTATION (7)

Defining Composites. One of the greatest challenges in implementing the GIPS standards is devising the set of composites that will most meaningfully represent the firm's products. The GIPS standards require each actual, fee-paying, discretionary portfolio to be included in at least one composite, and composites to be defined according to similar investment criteria (i.e., mandates, objectives and/or strategies). What appears to be a straightforward exercise—defining composites and assigning portfolios to them—may prove rather difficult in practice.

A useful guideline is to build a set of composites that will accurately represent the firm's distinct investment strategies. With too few composites, a firm risks overlooking significant differences and grouping diverse portfolios together into a single, overly broad composite subject to a wide dispersion of portfolio returns. With too many composites, in addition to incurring unnecessary costs, the firm runs the risk of creating narrowly defined groupings that are too much alike in investment strategy, contain too few portfolios or assets to be useful, or compromise client confidentiality.

Assuming that the implementation team has already defined the "firm" and "discretion" and compiled a master list of portfolios, here is a common-sense strategy for reaching agreement on composite definitions.

1   Review the firm's organizational structure and investment process to see if distinctive strategies can be readily identified. For instance, an equity advisor might have units specializing in one or more active management strategies as well as index fund construction and quantitatively driven enhanced indexing.

2   Review the firm's existing marketing materials including, if possible, marketing materials from competitors and recently received requests for proposals (RFPs). The objective is to determine how the industry defines products similar to those the firm offers.

3   Referring to the hierarchy presented in the GIPS Guidance Statement on Composite Definition, construct a provisional framework using descriptive captions to identify possible composites.

4   Taking into consideration the clients' investment policies, test how well the firm's actual, fee-paying, discretionary portfolios would fit the provisional framework. The inevitable identification of exceptions—that is, the discovery that portfolios that must be included in some composite do not really fit any—will lead to the redefinition of proposed composites or the creation of new composites. Several iterations may be needed.

5   Review the proposed set of composites for compliance with the GIPS standards.

6   Document the composite definitions in detail, and circulate the definitions for final review by all affected parties within the firm.

Of course, the most effective process for defining composites may differ from one firm to another in view of variables such as organizational structure, culture, and investment strategies, among other factors. Nonetheless, composite definitions have lasting consequences, and it is highly desirable to have a plan for reaching consensus.

Firms may also define composites based on the portfolios' benchmarks, as long as the benchmarks reflect the investment strategy and the firm has no other composites with the same characteristics. This approach is particularly appropriate if the portfolios are limited to holding stocks that are held in the index.

Finally, portfolios sharing distinctive risk/return profiles may reasonably be grouped together. For example, enhanced index funds with benchmark-specific targeted excess returns and tracking error tolerances might fall into natural groups.

Fixed-income composites can likewise be meaningfully and usefully defined in many dimensions. For example, composites might conform to asset classes or market segments such as government debt, mortgage-backed securities, convertible bonds, or high-yield bonds; investment strategies such as fundamental credit analysis, sector rotation, or interest rate anticipation; or investment styles such as indexing or core-plus. However a firm chooses to define the composites representing its investment products, they must be composed of portfolios managed in accordance with similar investment strategies or objectives.

3.9 Constructing Composites III—Including and Excluding Portfolios

The GIPS standards governing composite construction hold that composites must include new portfolios on a timely and consistent basis after the portfolio comes under management (I.3.A.5). Firms are required to establish, document, and consistently apply a policy of including new portfolios in the appropriate composites on a timely basis. Preferably, new portfolios should be included as of the beginning of the next full performance measurement period after the firm receives the funds. For example, if a portfolio is funded on 20 May and the firm calculates composite returns monthly (as indeed it must for periods beginning on or after 1 January 2001)[19], optimally the composite should include the new portfolio as of the beginning of June. It may take time to invest the assets of a new portfolio in accordance with the desired investment strategy, however, particularly when the portfolio is funded in kind (that is, with securities other than cash and cash equivalents) and the assets have to be redeployed, or when the securities to be purchased are relatively illiquid (e.g., in emerging markets). Accordingly, the GIPS standards give firms some discretion to determine when to add the new portfolio to a composite. In such cases, the firm must establish a policy on a composite-by-composite basis and apply it consistently to all new portfolios.

In addition to winning new business, firms routinely lose relationships. Under the GIPS standards, a firm must include a terminated portfolio in the historical performance of the appropriate composite up to the last full measurement period that the portfolio was under management (I.3.A.6). In many cases, the firm loses its discretion over the portfolio upon being notified of a pending termination. The client may instruct the firm to stop buying securities immediately and to commence the liquidation of holdings in preparation for an outbound cash transfer on a specified date. Alternately, the client may halt trading and transfer control of the portfolio to a transition management organization to facilitate moving assets to a new firm. When the firm being terminated thus loses its discretion over the portfolio, it should include the portfolio in the composite through the last full measurement period prior to notification of termination. To use the same example, if a firm that calculates performance monthly is informed on 20 May that its management contract is being terminated effective 31 May, and is instructed to stop trading forthwith, then the firm should include the portfolio in its composite through 30 April. In any event, it is incumbent upon the GIPS-compliant firm to have defined and documented its policies governing the removal of terminated portfolios from composites and, of course, to apply those policies consistently.

IMPLEMENTATION (8)

Adding, Removing, and Switching Portfolios. GIPS-compliant firms must have written policies setting forth when portfolios may be added to or removed from composites. These policies should be composite-specific. For a firm that reports composite performance monthly, a policy statement could read as follows:

---

19 Provision I.2.A.2.a.

> "All new portfolios funded with cash or securities on or before the 15th day of the month shall be added to the appropriate composite at the beginning of the following month. All new portfolios funded with cash or securities after the 15th day of the month shall be added to the appropriate composite at the beginning of the second month after funding. All portfolios shall be deemed 'non-discretionary' on the date notice of termination is received and removed from the composite at the end of the month prior to notification. The historical performance of terminated portfolios shall remain in the appropriate composite."

Policies like the sample above allow firms a reasonable amount of time to implement the strategy without delaying inclusion of the portfolio in the appropriate composite. Each firm should develop a policy that conforms to its own investment process while meeting the GIPS standards' requirement to include portfolios in composites on a timely basis. The firm's policy for adding or removing portfolios should also include language strictly limiting the switching of portfolios from one composite to another, in accordance with Provision I.3.A.7. Here is a sample statement for a policy:

> "Portfolios shall not be moved from one composite to another unless the composite is redefined or documented changes in the client's guidelines require restructuring the portfolio in such a way that another composite becomes more appropriate. The portfolio shall be removed from the original composite at the end of the last calendar month before the event causing the removal occurred and shall be added to the appropriate new composite at the beginning of the calendar month following the date on which the portfolio is substantially invested. The historical performance of the portfolio shall remain in the appropriate composite."

The GIPS standards also stipulate that portfolios cannot be switched from one composite to another unless documented changes in the portfolio's investment mandate, objective, or strategy or the redefinition of the composite make it appropriate. The historical performance of the portfolio must remain with the original composite (I.3.A.7). This is an important provision; if the GIPS standards permitted firms to transfer portfolios from one composite to another at will, an unethical firm might identify and exploit opportunities to improve the reported performance of selected composites by re-populating them with the portfolios whose investment results were most advantageous during the measurement period.

The GIPS standards describe two conditions under which portfolios can be reassigned. First, a portfolio can be switched from one composite to another if the client revises the mandate, objective, or strategy governing the investment of portfolio assets and the guideline changes are documented. For instance, a client might decide to modify the portfolio mandate from mid-cap value to large-cap value, or from domestic equity to global equity, with a corresponding change in the benchmark, while retaining the same investment advisor to restructure and manage the "same" portfolio in accordance with the new strategy. Or perhaps a client might decide to allow the use of derivative securities, previously prohibited, triggering a change in the investment strategy and making it suitable to assign the portfolio to a composite made up of portfolios that use derivatives.

Second, a portfolio can be reassigned to another composite if the original composite is redefined in such a way that the portfolio no longer fits it. Generally, if a strategy changes over time, it is most appropriate to create a new composite; accordingly, the redefinition of an existing composite should be a highly unusual event. (See the related requirement stated in Provision I.3.A.4, where it is also asserted that the GIPS standards do not permit changes to composites to be applied retroactively.) To repeat, if a portfolio is switched from one composite to another as permitted in these two situations—a pertinent, documented change in the portfolio's investment mandate, objective, or strategy, or a redefinition of the composite—then the historical record of the portfolio must remain in the composite to which it was originally assigned.

In the event of significant[20] external cash flows, the GIPS standards recommend that firms use **temporary new accounts** rather than temporarily removing entire portfolios from composites (see Provision I.3.B.2). Firms adopting this direct approach place client initiated incoming cash and securities into a temporary account that is not included in any composite until the external cash flows have been invested in accordance with the portfolio's investment mandate, objective, or strategy, at which time it would be transferred into the main portfolio and treated as an external cash flow. Relatedly, when the client initiates a large capital withdrawal, the firm transfers cash and securities in the desired amount to a temporary account until it liquidates the securities and the funds are distributed. The transfer is treated as an external cash outflow in calculating the portfolio's time-weighted total return.

This theoretically appropriate means of handling significant external cash flows is recommended but not required, in part because current technology does not readily allow for the establishment of temporary new accounts. Firms may be compelled to temporarily remove entire portfolios from composites when significant external cash flows occur. Provision I.3.A.10 addresses this situation. It states that firms wishing to remove portfolios from composites in cases of significant cash flows must define what they mean by "significant" on an *ex ante*, composite-specific basis and must consistently follow the composite-specific significant cash flow policy. We also refer the reader to the GIPS Guidance Statement on the Treatment of Significant Cash Flows for further information and direction on this practically important topic.

The GIPS provisions for composite construction additionally address the issue of minimum asset levels. A firm might decide that a particular composite will not include any portfolios whose value is below a specified level, on the grounds, for instance, that the investment strategy can be fully implemented only for portfolios above a certain size. The GIPS standards indicate that if a firm sets a minimum asset level for portfolios to be included in a composite, the firm must not include portfolios below that asset level in that composite. In other words, the policy, once established, must be followed consistently (I.3.A.9). The same provision further states that any changes to a composite-specific minimum asset level must not be applied retroactively.

The GIPS Guidance Statement on Composite Definition notes that portfolios may drop below a composite-specific minimum asset level because of client withdrawals or depreciation in value. If a firm establishes a minimum asset level for a composite, it must document its policies regarding how portfolios will be treated if they fall below the minimum and must apply these policies consistently. The Guidance Statement requires firms to specify in their policies the basis for evaluating portfolios against a composite's minimum asset level (for instance, a firm might use beginning value, ending value, or beginning value plus cash flows, etc.). In order to curtail the movement of portfolios into and out of composites, the Guidance Statement recommends that firms consider establishing a threshold and a minimum time period for applying the policy. For example, the firm might establish a range of ±5 percent of the minimum asset level and a condition that portfolios must remain above or below the minimum asset level for at least two periods before they are added to or removed from the composite. If a portfolio is removed from a composite, its prior performance must remain

---

20 The GIPS standards distinguish between *large* and *significant* cash flows. "Large" denotes the level at which the firm determines that an external cash flow may distort performance if the portfolio is not valued. "Significant" describes the level at which the firm determines that a client-directed external cash flow may temporarily prevent the firm from implementing the composite strategy.

in the composite. The firm must determine if the portfolio that has been removed meets any other composite definition and include it in the appropriate composite in a timely and consistent manner.

As previously noted, Provision I.3.A.9 also stipulates that any adjustments to a composite-specific minimum asset level cannot be applied retroactively. This requirement can create a problem when capital market movements cause portfolios' values to fall below the stated minimum. For example, the total market value of the Dow Jones Wilshire 5000 Index was approximately USD 12.1 trillion at the end of February 2008. Over the ensuing twelve months, the index had a return of −43.3 percent, representing a loss of shareholder value in excess of USD 5 trillion. If a firm's composite had a minimum portfolio asset level of $50 million, a portfolio initially valued at $85 million that experienced a comparable decline would no longer qualify for inclusion in the composite and would have to be removed from the composite when its value fell below the minimum asset level. Although the magnitude of the drop in the broad US equity market during this period was extreme, firms are well advised to consider the risk of having to exclude all portfolios from composites with minimum asset levels. The minimum asset level can be changed prospectively, subject to disclosure (see Provision I.4.A.19), but not retroactively.

The GIPS standards also recommend that firms should not present a composite presentation to a prospective client who is known not to meet the composite's minimum asset level (I.3.B.1). It is to be presumed that the firm has sound reasons for establishing a minimum asset level for a given strategy. Accordingly, it would not be in the prospective client's best interest to be shown a compliant presentation of a composite that does not represent a strategy available to that prospective client.

3.10 Constructing Composites IV—Carve-Out Segments

The GIPS standards describe the proper treatment of asset class segments "carved out" of multiple-strategy portfolios.

In discussing the requirements surrounding the calculation methodology, we recognized that returns from cash and cash equivalents held in portfolios must be included in total return calculations (I.2.A.3), and we examined the impact of short-term investments on equity portfolio results in "up" and "down" markets. The requirement that cash and cash equivalents be taken into account in portfolio and composite return calculations is based on the fundamental principle of fair representation: A composite that did not include portfolio cash positions would not fairly represent investment performance to a prospective or existing client. This principle carries over to the inclusion of portfolio segments in composites. Provision I.3.A.8 states that, for periods beginning on or after 1 January 2010, a **carve-out** must not be included in a composite unless the carve-out is managed separately with its own cash balance.[21] For example, the stock portion alone of a portfolio consisting of stocks, bonds, and cash cannot be included in an equity composite as though it were a stand-alone discretionary portfolio.

Carve-out segments are also addressed in the provisions for disclosure and for presentation and reporting. For periods prior to 1 January 2010, if carve-outs are included in a composite, firms must disclose the policy used to allocate cash to the carve-outs (see Provision I.4.A.23). In addition, for periods beginning on or after 1

---

21 For periods prior to 1 January 2010, if carve-outs were included in a composite, cash must have been allocated to the carve-out in a timely and consistent manner. The GIPS Guidance Statement on the Treatment of Carve-Outs describes some acceptable cash allocation methodologies.

January 2006 and ending before 1 January 2011, if a composite includes carve-outs, the compliant presentation must include the percentage of the composite assets represented by carve-outs as of each annual period-end (see Provision I.5.A.5).

> **IMPLEMENTATION (9)**
>
> *Carve-Out Segments.* Equilibrium Capital Advisors, a firm specializing in balanced portfolios, maintains a number of multi-strategy composites constructed according to strategic asset mix ranges. For example, among other multi-class composites, Equilibrium Capital Advisors has a Standard Balanced Account Composite composed of portfolios with a strategic asset allocation target of 50 percent equity and 50 percent fixed income; a Conservative Balanced Account Composite composed of portfolios with a 35/65 equity/fixed income strategic mix; and an Aggressive Balanced Account Composite composed of portfolios with an 80/20 equity/fixed income strategic mix. In order to control transaction expenses by reducing the frequency of portfolio rebalancing, the target mixes are accompanied by 5 percent tolerance ranges. For instance, the Aggressive Balanced Account Composite is permitted to vary from 75/25 to 85/15 equity/fixed income mixes.
>
> The equity segments of all the balanced composites are managed in accordance with a single strategy by the Equity Markets Group under the leadership of John Boyle, and the fixed income segments of the balanced composites as well as all cash and cash equivalent positions are managed by the Fixed Income Markets Group. Boyle wants to create a new equity composite composed of the equity segments of the multi-strategy portfolios. Can such a composite be constructed in compliance with the GIPS standards?
>
> Provision I.3.A.8 states that, for periods beginning on or after 1 January 2010, a carve-out must not be included in a composite unless the carve-out is managed separately with its own cash balance. In the case of Equilibrium Capital Advisors, it appears that the cash generated in the course of equity and fixed-income investment management is pooled, and short-term investing is conducted for the balanced portfolio as a whole. The equity segments of the firm's balanced portfolios are not managed separately with their own cash balances. Accordingly, Equilibrium must not create the composite that Boyle would like to have.

3.11 Disclosure

The GIPS standards advance the ideals of fair representation and full disclosure. We will consider the presentation and reporting provisions shortly. Before doing so, however, we will cite the numerous required and recommended disclosure provisions. The reader will already be familiar with many of these topics from previous sections, so we will discuss most items here only briefly. We have grouped the disclosure provisions by subject area.

A firm may claim compliance once it has satisfied all the requirements of the GIPS standards, including those we will present later in this reading. The precise wording of the claim of compliance is laid down as a disclosure requirement in Provision I.4.A.1. The wording differs depending upon whether or not a firm has been verified. A firm that is verified must use the exact wording of the following two-paragraph compliance statement in all compliant presentations (and only in compliant presentations):

> "[Insert name of firm] claims compliance with the Global Investment Performance Standards (GIPS®) and has prepared and presented this report in compliance with the GIPS standards. [Insert name of firm] has been independently verified for the periods [insert dates]. The verification report(s) is/are available upon request.

"Verification assesses whether (1) the firm has complied with all the composite construction requirements of the GIPS standards on a firm-wide basis, and (2) the firm's policies and procedures are designed to calculate and present performance in compliance with the GIPS standards. Verification does not ensure the accuracy of any specific composite presentation."[22]

A firm that has not been verified must use the following statement, again, always and only in compliant presentations:

"[Insert name of firm] claims compliance with the Global Investment Performance Standards (GIPS®) and has prepared and presented this report in compliance with the GIPS standards. [Insert name of firm] has not been independently verified."

A firm that is verified may additionally choose to have the verifier conduct a specifically focused performance examination of a particular composite performance presentation. Provision I.4.A.1 also provides the exact wording of the two-paragraph compliance statement that must be used in compliant performance presentations of composites that have been examined:

"[Insert name of firm] claims compliance with the Global Investment Performance Standards (GIPS®) and has prepared and presented this report in compliance with the GIPS standards. [Insert name of firm] has been independently verified for the periods [insert dates].

"Verification assesses whether (1) the firm has complied with all the composite construction requirements of the GIPS standards on a firm-wide basis, and (2) the firm's processes and procedures are designed to calculate and present performance in compliance with the GIPS standards. The [insert name of composite] composite has been examined for the periods [insert dates]. The verification and examination reports are available upon request."

Several provisions concern disclosures related to the GIPS-compliant firm. The definition of the "firm" used to determine the firm's total assets and firm-wide compliance is a required disclosure (I.4.A.2). A clear explanation of the way in which the firm is defined enables the prospective client to understand precisely which investment organization (or unit of a larger entity) is presenting results, is claiming compliance, and will be responsible for managing the client's assets if hired. If a firm is redefined, it must disclose the date, describe the redefinition, and explain the reason (I.4.A.16). If a parent company contains multiple firms, the GIPS standards recommend that each firm within the parent company disclose a list of the other firms contained within the parent company (I.4.B.5).

Firms are further required to disclose all significant events that would help a prospective client interpret the compliant presentation (I.4.A.14). For example, a firm must advise the prospective client if past results in a given strategy were achieved by a portfolio manager who has left the firm, or if all key members of the research team supporting the strategy have resigned. Firms must also disclose if the performance from a past firm or affiliation is linked to the performance of the firm (I.4.A.35). For periods beginning on or after 1 January 2006, firms must disclose the use of a subadvisor and the periods a subadvisor was used (I.4.A.25), and for earlier periods they should disclose the use of a sub-advisor and the periods a sub-advisor was used (I.4.B.7).

---

22 The claims of compliance given in this section may be used only in compliant performance presentations. Different wording for compliance claims in advertisements is stipulated in the GIPS Advertising Guidelines, discussed later in this reading.

Other provisions have to do with disclosures related to composites. In a compliant performance presentation, firms must disclose the composite description,[23] which must contain sufficient information to allow a prospective client to understand the key characteristics of the composite's investment mandate, objective, or strategy (I.4.A.3). It is not enough merely to have a broadly indicative name such as "Growth and Income Composite," which might mean one thing to one user and something else to another; the provision requires that prospective clients be given a reasonably informative explanation, however concise, setting forth the composite's salient features. For example, a "Growth and Income Composite" composed of balanced portfolios or "accounts" managed on behalf of individuals might be described in these terms: "The Growth and Income Composite includes taxable balanced accounts with assets greater than $100,000. The accounts are managed to a strategic asset allocation target of 50 percent equity and 50 percent fixed income within a tactical range of 10 percent. The equity segments are invested in large-capitalization common stocks. The fixed income segments of the individual accounts are invested in investment-grade instruments including US government and agency securities, corporate bonds, and mortgage-backed securities. The benchmark for this strategy is a blended index made up of 50 percent Standard & Poor's 500 Stock Index and 50 percent Barclays Capital US Aggregate Bond Index." Appendix C of the GIPS standards includes other examples of **composite descriptions**.

The availability upon request of the firm's list of composite descriptions is a required disclosure (I.4.A.11). This information enables prospective clients to determine if the composite they have been shown is the most appropriate for their needs and to request compliant performance presentations of any other composites of interest. Recall that the list must include not only all of the firm's current composites but also any that have been discontinued within the last five years (see Provision I.0.A.10).

Firms must also disclose the **composite creation date** (I.4.A.10), the date on which the firm first grouped one or more portfolios to form the composite. This is not necessarily the earliest date for which composite performance is reported. If a firm has redefined a composite, the firm must disclose the date of, description of, and reason for the redefinition (I.4.A.17).[24] Similarly, firms must disclose any changes to a composite's name (I.4.A.18).

The preceding requirements apply to all composites. Further requirements apply in certain cases. First, firms must disclose the minimum asset level, if any, below which portfolios are not included in a composite, as well as any changes to the minimum asset level (I.4.A.19). Second, as previously noted, if in periods prior to 1 January 2010 carve-outs are included in a composite, firms must disclose the policy used to allocate cash to the carve-outs (I.4.A.23). Third, if the firm has adopted a significant cash flow policy for a specific composite, then the firm must disclose how it defines significant cash flows for that composite and the periods to which the definition applies (I.4.A.32). The GIPS standards recommend that firms disclose if a composite contains proprietary assets (I.4.B.8).

The GIPS standards include both required and recommended disclosures regarding valuations. For periods prior to 1 January 2010, firms must disclose if any portfolios were not valued as of calendar month-end or as of the last business day of the month

---

23 The GIPS standards distinguish between *definitions* and *descriptions* of composites. A composite definition sets forth detailed criteria that determine the assignment of portfolios to composites, whereas a composite description provides general information regarding the investment mandate, objective, or strategy of the composite. The GIPS Glossary entry for composite description states, "The composite description may be more abbreviated than the composite definition but must include all key features of the composite and must include enough information to allow a prospective client to understand the key characteristics of the composite's investment mandate, objective, or strategy."

24 As previously noted, the GIPS standards do not permit changes to composite definitions to be applied retroactively (I.3.A.4).

(I.4.A.26). For periods beginning on or after 1 January 2011, firms must disclose if portfolio investments are valued using subjective unobservable inputs, as described in the GIPS Valuation Principles if the portfolio investments valued using subjective, unobservable inputs are material to the composite (I.4.A.27). For periods beginning on or after 1 January 2011, firms must disclose if the composite's valuation hierarchy materially differs from the hierarchy that is recommended in the GIPS Valuation Principles (I.4.A.28). (We will discuss the GIPS Valuation Principles later in this reading.) Firms should disclose the key assumptions used to value portfolio investments (I.4.B.4), and they should disclose material changes to valuation policies and/or methodologies (I.4.B.1). For periods prior to 1 January 2011, firms should disclose the use of subjective unobservable inputs for valuing portfolio investments if the investments so valued are material to the composite (I.4.B.6).

Firms must also disclose that policies for valuing portfolios, calculating returns, and preparing compliant presentations are available upon request (I.4.A.12). To cite obvious examples, GIPS-compliant firms should be prepared to respond to prospective clients' questions about their valuation methods and sources, return calculation methodology, or treatment of large external cash flows. The GIPS standards recommend, but do not require, that firms disclose material changes to calculation policies and/or methodologies (I.4.B.2).

Firms must disclose the currency used to express performance (I.4.A.7). For periods beginning on or after 1 January 2011, firms must also disclose and describe any known material differences in the exchange rates or valuation sources used among the portfolios within a composite, and between the composite and the benchmark (I.4.A.21); for earlier periods, only differences in exchange rates (not in valuation sources) need be disclosed. When defining materiality, firms would do well to consider the ethical principles of fair representation and full disclosure. If there is internal disagreement over the significance of an item, it seems advisable to disclose the pertinent facts so as to allow prospective clients and their consultants to take them into consideration.

Firms must disclose relevant details of the treatment of withholding tax on dividends, interest income, and capital gains, if material, and, if the information is available, they must also disclose if benchmark returns are net of withholding taxes (I.4.A.20).

In view of their importance for evaluating performance, it is not surprising that benchmarks are subject to disclosure requirements. Firms must disclose the **benchmark description** (I.4.A.4) and, if a custom benchmark or a combination of multiple benchmarks is used, the firm must disclose the benchmark components, weights, and rebalancing process (I.4.A.31). For example, a firm might construct a custom security-based benchmark composed of securities that conform to the firm's investment process and the composite's strategy. Or, as another example, a firm's balanced composite might have a blended benchmark reflecting the strategic asset mix with reference to which the portfolios are managed. The benchmark in this case might be constructed by weighting well-chosen capital market indices with desirable characteristics such as asset class representativeness and investability.

IMPLEMENTATION (10)

Benchmark Presentation. Eastern Institutional Asset Advisors presents the performance of a Global Balanced Composite. The strategic asset mix of the portfolios in the composite is 50 percent US equity, 10 percent international equity, 35 percent US fixed-income securities, and 5 percent cash. The composite has a blended benchmark composed of capital market indices weighted in accordance with the strategic asset allocation. Eastern Institutional Asset Advisors places the following disclosure on the Global Balanced Composite's performance presentation:

> "The benchmark for the Global Balanced Composite is composed of 50 percent S&P 500, 10 percent MSCI EAFE Index, 35 percent Barclays Capital US Aggregate Bond Index, and 5 percent US Treasury bills. The benchmark is rebalanced monthly."

The frequency of benchmark rebalancing can affect the reported returns for an annual period. Exhibit 12 displays one calendar year's data for the Global Balanced Composite described in Implementation (10). The blended benchmark return for the year is calculated first on a monthly and then on a quarterly basis for the purpose of comparison.

Exhibit 12   Illustration of Rebalancing Policies

	Domestic Equity Index	International Equity Index	Domestic Fixed Income Index	Cash Equivalents Index	Blended Benchmark
Blended benchmark weights	50%	10%	35%	5%	
Monthly Rebalancing					
January	−1.46%	−3.96%	0.79%	0.15%	-0.84%
February	−1.93%	0.61%	0.96%	0.13%	−0.56%
March	3.76%	5.56%	−1.65%	0.15%	1.87%
April	−6.06%	0.76%	1.90%	0.16%	−2.28%
May	−0.74%	1.65%	0.85%	0.16%	0.10%
June	−7.12%	−4.41%	0.74%	0.14%	−3.74%
July	−7.79%	−9.21%	1.19%	0.15%	−4.39%
August	0.66%	0.00%	1.75%	0.14%	0.95%
September	−10.87%	−10.43%	1.59%	0.16%	−5.91%
October	8.80%	4.87%	−0.45%	0.15%	4.74%
November	5.89%	4.56%	−0.02%	0.16%	3.40%
December	−5.87%	−2.86%	2.08%	0.12%	−2.49%
Linked monthly returns	−22.09%	−13.50%	10.11%	1.78%	→ **−9.30%**
Quarterly Rebalancing					
First quarter	0.27%	2.00%	0.08%	0.43%	0.38%
Second quarter	−13.39%	−2.09%	3.53%	0.46%	−5.65%
Third quarter	−17.27%	−18.68%	4.60%	0.45%	−8.87%
Fourth quarter	8.45%	6.52%	1.60%	0.43%	5.46%
Linked quarterly returns	−22.08%	−13.49%	10.11%	1.78%	→ **−8.98%**

In this example, the monthly calculation produces a blended benchmark return of −9.30 percent for the year, while the quarterly calculation (using the same input data) produces a return of −8.98 percent for the year. There is a difference of 32 basis points (0.32 percent) between the full-year benchmark returns under the two rebalancing methods. Once established, the firm must apply its benchmark rebalancing policy consistently, without regard to the *ex post* impact on the composite's relative performance in any annual period.

If the firm determines that no appropriate benchmark for the composite exists, the firm must disclose why no benchmark is presented (I.4.A.29). If the firm changes the benchmark, the firm must describe the change, disclose the date it became effective, and explain the reason for the change (I.4.A.30). The GIPS standards recommend that firms disclose material differences between the composite investment mandate, objective, or strategy and that strategy represented by the benchmark (I.4.B.3).

Numerous provisions address the topic of fees. The GIPS Glossary defines the **gross-of-fees return** as the return on investments reduced by any trading expenses incurred during the period and the **net-of-fees return** as the gross-of-fees return reduced by the investment management fees (including performance-based fees and carried interest).[25] When presenting gross-of-fees returns, firms must disclose if they deduct any other fees in addition to the actual trading expenses (I.4.A.5). Similarly, when presenting net-of-fees returns, firms must disclose if any other fees are deducted in addition to the actual trading expenses and the investment management fee; in addition, firm must disclose if model or actual investment management fees are used and if returns are net of performance-based fees (I.4.A.6). The firm must also disclose the **fee schedule** appropriate to the compliant presentation (I.4.A.9). As explained in the GIPS Glossary, the term "fee schedule" refers to the firm's current schedule of investment management fees or bundled fees relevant to the particular compliant presentation. If a composite contains portfolios with bundled fees, firms must also disclose the various types of fees that the bundled fee includes (I.4.A.24).

As we will see when examining the provisions of the GIPS standards related to presentation and reporting, firms must report a measure of the **internal dispersion** of the returns of the individual portfolios within a composite. Because there are different ways to convey dispersion, the GIPS standards require firms to disclose which measure of internal dispersion they present (I.4.A.8).

It is an important, albeit challenging, provision that firms must disclose the presence, use, and extent of leverage, derivatives, and short positions, if material. The disclosure must include a description of the frequency of use and characteristics of the instruments sufficient to identify risks (I.4.A.13). As a practical matter, it is admittedly difficult to explain in writing the use of leverage or derivative securities and the risks of their use, especially for the benefit of prospective clients who may not have been exposed previously to complex investment strategies. A clear explanation, however, will help prospective clients interpret the historical performance and evaluate the additional risk resulting from the use of leverage or derivatives.

For example, a fixed income manager might use interest rate futures contracts as an efficient and economical means of adjusting the sensitivity of corporate bond portfolios to anticipated changes in interest rates. The firm might provide the following description of its use of derivatives: "Crystal Capital routinely uses US Treasury bond futures contracts to change the portfolios' modified duration. Because of their call features and credit risk, the corporate bonds held in the portfolio may experience price changes that do not closely match movements in the US Treasury bond futures contracts, resulting in portfolio valuations that differ from the targeted outcome."

Two disclosure provisions pertain to performance presentations. Firms must disclose if the presentation conforms with laws and/or regulations that conflict with the requirements of the GIPS standards. The manner in which any laws or regulations

---

25 Performance-based investment management fees are typically contingent upon the portfolio's exceeding a prescribed level of return, either absolutely or in comparison with a benchmark. Carried interest, commonly used in private equity and real estate investing, refers to the profits allocated to general partners from the profits made by the investment vehicle.

conflict with the GIPS standards must also be disclosed (I.4.A.22). For any performance presented for periods prior to 1 January 2000 that does not comply with the GIPS standards, firms must disclose the periods of non-compliance (I.4.A.15.)

We will see when reviewing the presentation and reporting provisions that the 2010 edition of the GIPS standards requires firms to present, for each annual period, the annualized three-year *ex post* standard deviation of monthly composite and benchmark returns and, if appropriate, another measure of risk. (See the discussion of Provision I.5.A.2 later in this reading.) There are two required disclosures having to do with this presentation requirement. First, firms must disclose if the three-year annualized ex post standard deviation for the composite and/or the benchmark is not presented because 36 monthly returns are unavailable (I.4.A.33). Second, if the firm determines that the standard deviation is not a relevant or appropriate measure, and accordingly presents an additional risk measure, then the firm must disclose this decision. Specifically, the firm must describe why *ex post* standard deviation is not relevant or appropriate, describe the additional risk measure presented, and explain why the additional measure was selected (I.4.A.34).

Meeting the objectives of fair representation and full disclosure may call for providing more information than the GIPS standards minimally require. Practitioners are well advised to prepare compliance checklists to ensure that the disclosure requirements and, where feasible, the recommendations of the GIPS standards are met for the firm as a whole and for each composite presented. We turn now to the provisions for presentation and reporting.

3.12 Presentation and Reporting Requirements

The ethical ideals of fair representation and full disclosure culminate in GIPS-compliant performance presentations. In this section, we will focus on the required elements of performance presentations prepared in accordance with the GIPS standards.

For each GIPS-compliant composite presented, the GIPS standards require that firms show at least five years of annual[26] performance (less if the firm or composite has been in existence for a shorter period), and that the GIPS-compliant performance record must then be extended each year until 10 years' results have been presented. The core elements of a GIPS-compliant performance presentation additionally include composite and benchmark annual returns for all years; the number of portfolios (if six or more); the amount of assets in the composite; either the percentage of the firm's total assets represented by the composite or the amount of total firm assets at the end of each period; and a measure of **internal dispersion** of individual portfolio returns for each annual period if the composite contains six or more portfolios for the full year. For composites with an inception date on or after 1 January 2011, when the initial period is less than a full year, firms must present returns from the composite inception date through the initial annual period-end. For example, if a composite has an inception date of 1 April 2011, the performance presentation as of 31 December 2011 will cover the nine-month period 1 April–31 December 2011. Similarly, for composites with a composite termination date of 1 January 2011 or later, firms must present returns from the last annual period-end through the composite termination date. The requirements listed in this paragraph are set forth in Provisions I.5.A.1.a–i.

We have previously remarked on the importance of selecting appropriate benchmarks in order to interpret historical results and to conduct meaningful performance evaluations. We have also made note of certain benchmark-related disclosure requirements. An important presentation and reporting requirement is set forth in Provision

---

26 Annual returns are normally presented for calendar years, but they may be presented for other annual periods if the composite is reported on a non-calendar fiscal year. See Provision I.1.A.7 described earlier.

I.5.A.1.e: The total return for the benchmark must be presented for each annual period. This provision also states that the benchmark must reflect the composite's investment mandate, objective, or strategy.

The GIPS standards require that for each annual period a measure of internal dispersion of the returns earned by individual portfolios in the composite be presented (I.5.A.1.i.). This important requirement is intended to allow users to see how consistently the firm implemented its strategy across individual portfolios. A wide range of results should prompt the recipient of the performance presentation to inquire about possible causes of the variability of returns to portfolios that are purportedly managed in accordance with the same strategy. It may suggest, among many other possibilities, that the composite is defined too broadly to provide meaningful information.

The dispersion of the annual returns of individual portfolios within a composite can be measured in various ways. The GIPS Glossary entry for internal dispersion mentions several acceptable methods. Let us refer to the data in Exhibit 13, showing the beginning values (in euros) and the annual rates of return earned by the 14 portfolios that were in a German equity composite for the full year 20XX. (Note that only those portfolios in the composite for the entire year are included in the calculation of this dispersion measure.) The portfolios presented in Exhibit 13 are arrayed in descending order of returns.

Exhibit 13	Data for Calculation of Dispersion	
Portfolio	Beginning Value	20XX Return
A	€118,493	2.66%
B	€79,854	2.64%
C	€121,562	2.53%
D	€86,973	2.49%
E	€105,491	2.47%
F	€112,075	2.42%
G	€98,667	2.38%
H	€92,518	2.33%
I	€107,768	2.28%
J	€96,572	2.21%
K	€75,400	2.17%
L	€77,384	2.07%
M	€31,264	1.96%
N	€84,535	1.93%

The GIPS Glossary defines internal dispersion as "a measure of the spread of the annual returns of individual portfolios within a composite" and indicates that acceptable measures include, but are not limited to, high/low, range, and the equal-weighted or asset-weighted standard deviation of portfolio returns. Using the data in Exhibit 13, we will consider each of these measures.

The simplest method of expressing internal dispersion for an annual period is to disclose the highest and lowest returns earned by portfolios that were in the composite for the full year. In the case of the German equity composite, the highest return was 2.66 percent and the lowest was 1.93 percent. As an alternative, the high/low range—the arithmetic difference between the highest and the lowest return—might also be presented. In this case it was 0.73 percent, or 73 basis points. In either form, the high/low disclosure is easy to understand. It has, however, a potential disadvantage. In any annual period, an outlier—that is, one portfolio with an abnormally high or low return—may be present, resulting in a measure of dispersion that is not entirely representative of the distribution of returns. Although they are more difficult to calculate and to interpret, other dispersion measures may convey better information.

The standard deviation of returns for portfolios included in the composite is another acceptable measure of internal dispersion. As applied to composites, standard deviation measures the cross-sectional dispersion of returns for portfolios included in the composite. The standard deviation for a composite in which the constituent portfolios are equally weighted is[27]

$$S_c = \sqrt{\frac{\sum_{i=1}^{n}(r_i - \bar{r}_c)^2}{n-1}} \tag{10}$$

where r_i is the return of each individual portfolio, $\bar{r}_c$ is the equal-weighted mean or arithmetic mean return to the portfolios in the composite, and n is, as before, the number of portfolios in the composite. Applying Equation 10 to the portfolio data given in Exhibit 13, assuming equal weighting, the standard deviation proves to be 23 basis points (0.23 percent). If the individual portfolio returns are normally distributed around the mean return of 2.32 percent, then approximately two-thirds of the portfolios will have returns falling between the mean plus the standard deviation (2.32% + 0.23% = 2.55%) and the mean minus the standard deviation (2.32% − 0.23% = 2.09%).

The standard deviation of portfolio returns is a valid measure of internal dispersion. Most spreadsheet programs include statistical functions to facilitate the calculation of equal-weighted standard deviations, and many prospective clients will have at least a passing acquaintance with the concept.

Some firms prefer to present the asset-weighted standard deviation rather than the equal-weighted standard deviation. The equation for the asset-weighted standard deviation of individual portfolio returns within a composite is:

$$S_{C_{aw}} = \sqrt{\sum_{i=1}^{n}\left[(r_i - \bar{r}_{proxy})^2 \times w_i\right]} \tag{11}$$

where $\bar{r}_{proxy}$ is the asset-weighted mean return of portfolios 1 through n (see Equation 12); w_i is the weight of portfolio i, calculated as the ratio of the beginning value of portfolio i to the total beginning value of the assets of portfolios 1 through n, that is, $w_i = \dfrac{V_{0,i}}{V_{0,Total}}$; and the sum of the weights w_1 through w_n is 1.

$$\bar{r}_{proxy} = \sum_{i=1}^{n}(w_i \times r_i) \tag{12}$$

Applying Equations 11 and 12 to the data given in Exhibit 13, we find that the asset-weighted standard deviation is 21 basis points (0.21 percent).

Although the GIPS Glossary does not explicitly mentioned it, the interquartile range—the difference between the returns in the first and third quartiles of the distribution—is also an acceptable measure of internal dispersion. Quartiles divide the distribution of returns into quarters, such that 25 percent of the observations fall at or above the first quartile and 25 percent fall at or below the third quartile. If the

---

27 The use of both n and $n-1$ in the denominator can be supported. If n were used in calculating the standard deviation of returns for the example presented in the text, the result would be 22 basis points (0.22%).

distribution were divided into percentiles, the first quartile would contain observations at or above the 25th percentile, and the third quartile would contain observations at or above the 75th percentile. The quartiles for the German equity composite are shown in Exhibit 14.

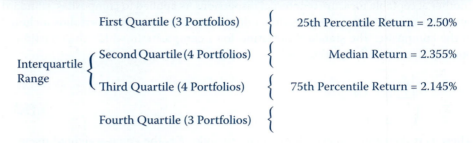

Exhibit 14   Quartile Distribution of German Equity Portfolio Returns

First Quartile (3 Portfolios)   25th Percentile Return = 2.50%

Interquartile Range

Second Quartile (4 Portfolios)   Median Return = 2.355%

Third Quartile (4 Portfolios)   75th Percentile Return = 2.145%

Fourth Quartile (3 Portfolios)

The quartile breakpoints indicated in Exhibit 14 are located by determining the returns at the 25th, 50th, and 75th percentiles (the 50th percentile is the median). The yth percentile is defined as the point above which y percent of observations lie. The location of percentiles (and thus quartile breakpoints) is approximate in small data sets. An approximation for the position of a percentile y in an array with n entries sorted in descending order is:

$$L_y = (n+1)\frac{y}{100}$$

(13)

For example, the German equity composite presented in Exhibit 13 contains 14 portfolios ($n = 14$) listed in descending order of return. Using Equation 13, the approximate location of the 25th percentile ($y = 25$) is between the third and the fourth portfolio:

$$L_{25} = (14+1)\frac{25}{100} = 3.75$$

The value of the return at the 25th percentile is found by linear interpolation. The third portfolio, identified only as Portfolio C in Exhibit 13, had a return of 2.53 percent, and the fourth, Portfolio D, had a return of 2.49 percent. Reflecting the "0.75" in "3.75," the return at the interpolated 25th percentile is below that of Portfolio C by three-quarters of the distance between the returns earned by Portfolio C and Portfolio D, respectively. Let us call r_{25} the value of the return at the 25th percentile. Then:

$$r_{25} = 0.0253 - [0.75 \times (0.0253 - 0.0249)] = 0.0253 - 0.0003 = 0.025 = 2.50\%$$

Through the same process of linear interpolation, we find that the return at the 75th percentile is 2.145 percent. With these values in hand, calculating the interquartile range is straightforward. It is the spread, or the arithmetic difference, between the returns at the 25th and the 75th percentiles. In the case of the German equity composite, the interquartile range is 2.5 percent minus 2.145 percent, or approximately 36 basis points (0.36 percent).

The interquartile range, then, represents the length of the interval containing the middle 50 percent of the data. Because it does not contain the extreme values, the interquartile range is not exposed to the risk of being skewed by outliers. However, prospective clients may be unfamiliar with the interquartile range as a measure of dispersion. When disclosing that interquartile range is the measure of internal dispersion used, as required by Provision I.4.A.8, firms might wish to include a definition of interquartile range. For instance, the disclosure might read, "The measure of internal dispersion of the returns for portfolios that were included in the composite for the full year is the interquartile range, the spread between portfolio returns at the 25th and 75th percentiles."

Note that the GIPS standards do not limit firms to using one of the measures of internal dispersion described earlier. A firm may prefer another way of expressing composite dispersion. The method chosen should, however, fairly represent the range of returns for each annual period.

The 2010 edition of the GIPS standards newly requires that firms present information about the historical variability of composite and benchmark returns. Specifically, Provision I.5.A.2.a states that, for periods ending on or after 1 January 2011, firms must present, as of each annual period end, the three-year annualized *ex post* standard deviation (using monthly returns) for the composite and the benchmark. The rationale is to give prospective clients an indication of the risk of an investment strategy as executed by the firms under consideration. Because all GIPS-compliant performance presentations include the same risk measure, and that measure is based upon historical experience rather than subjective inputs, the GIPS standards allow for some degree of comparability among firms that claim compliance.

However, standard deviation assumes that returns are normally distributed, and so it may not be the most suitable risk measure for every investment strategy. Accordingly, Provision I.5.A.2.b states that, if the firm determines that the three-year annualized *ex post* standard deviation is not relevant or appropriate, the firm must present an additional three-year *ex post* measure of risk for the composite and the benchmark. The periodicity of the composite and the benchmark must be identical; for instance, if the chosen measure of historical composite risk is calculated using monthly returns, then the equivalent measure of benchmark risk must also be based upon monthly returns.

For any performance presented for periods prior to 1 January 2000 that does not comply with the GIPS standards, the firm must disclose the periods of non-compliance (II.4.A.15). Firms may link non-compliant performance so long as only compliant returns are presented for periods beginning on or after 1 January 2000 (I.5.A.3).

The GIPS provisions for presentation and reporting state that returns for periods of less than one year must not be annualized (I.5.A.4). Extrapolating partial-year returns by annualizing them would amount to a prediction about investment results for the rest of the year.

In our discussion of composite construction (I.3.A.8) and required disclosures (I.4.A.23), we mentioned the practice of "carving out" or extracting performance data on a single segment included in a multiple-strategy portfolio for inclusion in a composite. A related presentation and reporting requirement exists. Under Provision I.5.A.5, for periods beginning on or after 1 January 2006 and ending prior to 1 January 2011, if a composite includes carve-outs, the presentation must include the percentage of composite assets that is composed of carve-outs as of the end of each annual period. The GIPS standards do not require firms to disclose what percentage of composite assets was composed of carve-outs for periods falling outside the 2006–2010 timeframe.

Another requirement of the GIPS standards for presentation and reporting addresses the inclusion of non-fee-paying portfolios in composites. We saw when discussing the requirements for composite construction that all actual, fee-paying, discretionary portfolios must be included in at least one composite. Provision I.3.A.1 goes on to state that non-fee-paying discretionary portfolios may be included in a composite (with appropriate disclosures).[28] For example, in the interest of public service or community relations, a firm might waive the investment management fee

---

[28] Non-discretionary portfolios, on the other hand, cannot be included in a firm's composites under the GIPS standards.

on a charitable organization's portfolio, or a firm might use its own or its principals' capital to implement a new investment strategy. Provision I.5.A.6 stipulates that if a composite contains any non-fee-paying portfolios, the firm must present, as of the end of each annual period, the percentage of the composite assets represented by the non-fee-paying portfolios. In addition, if a composite contains portfolios with bundled fees, firms must present as of the end of each annual period, the percentage of composite assets that are bundled-fee portfolios (I.5.A.7).

The "portability" of past performance is a complex and sometimes contentious subject, but Provision I.5.A.8 summarizes the conditions under which performance of a past firm or affiliation *must* be linked to or used to represent the historical performance of a new or acquiring firm. The conditions, which apply on a composite-specific basis, are that (1) substantially all the investment decision makers are employed by the new or acquiring firm, (2) the decision-making process remains substantially intact and independent within the new or acquiring firm, *and* (3) the new or acquiring firm has records that document and support the reported performance. If a GIPS-compliant firm acquires another firm or affiliation, the firm is given one year to bring any non-compliant assets into compliance.

Appendix A of the GIPS standards contains several sample GIPS-compliant performance presentations. We have included Sample 1 in Exhibit 15.

Exhibit 15	Sample Investment Firm Balanced Growth Composite 1 January 2002 through 31 December 2011

Year	Composite Gross Return (%)	Composite Net Return (%)	Custom Benchmark Return (%)	Composite 3-Yr Std Dev (%)	Benchmark 3-Yr Std Dev (%)	Number of Portfolios	Internal Dispersion (%)	Composite Assets ($M)	Firm Assets ($M)
2002	−10.5	−11.4	−11.8			31	4.5	165	236
2003	16.3	15.1	13.2			34	2.0	235	346
2004	7.5	6.4	8.9			38	5.7	344	529
2005	1.8	0.8	0.3			45	2.8	445	695
2006	11.2	10.1	12.2			48	3.1	520	839
2007	6.1	5.0	7.1			49	2.8	505	1,014
2008	−21.3	−22.1	−24.9			44	2.9	475	964
2009	16.5	15.3	14.7			47	3.1	493	983
2010	10.6	9.5	13.0			51	3.5	549	1,114
2011	2.7	1.7	0.4	7.1	7.4	54	2.5	575	1,236

Sample 1 Investment Firm claims compliance with the Global Investment Performance Standards (GIPS®) and has prepared and presented this report in compliance with the GIPS standards. Sample 1 Investment Firm has been independently verified for the periods 1 January 2000 through 31 December 2010. The verification report is available upon request. Verification assesses whether (1) the firm has complied with all the composite construction requirements of the GIPS standards on a firm-wide basis and (2) the firm's policies and procedures are designed to calculate and present performance in compliance with the GIPS standards. Verification does not ensure the accuracy of any specific composite presentation.

Notes:

1 Sample 1 Investment Firm is a balanced portfolio investment manager that invests solely in US-based securities. Sample 1 Investment Firm is defined as an independent investment management firm that is not affiliated with any parent organization. Policies for valuing portfolios, calculating performance, and preparing compliant presentations are available upon request.

Exhibit 15 (Continued)

2 The Balanced Growth Composite includes all institutional balanced portfolios that invest in large-cap US equities and investment-grade bonds with the goal of providing long-term capital growth and steady income from a well-diversified strategy. Although the strategy allows for equity exposure ranging between 50–70%, the typical allocation is between 55–65%. The account minimum for the composite is $5 million.

3 The custom benchmark is 60 percent YYY US Equity Index and 40 percent ZZZ US Aggregate Bond Index. The benchmark is rebalanced monthly.

4 Valuations are computed and performance is reported in US dollars.

5 Gross-of-fees returns are presented before management and custodial fees but after all trading expenses. Composite and benchmark returns are presented net of non-reclaimable withholding taxes. Net-of-fees returns are calculated by deducting the highest fee of 0.83 percent from the monthly gross composite return. The management fee schedule is as follows: 1.00 percent on the first $25 million; 0.60 percent thereafter.

6 This composite was created in February 2000. A complete list of composite descriptions is available upon request.

7 Internal dispersion is calculated using the equal-weighted standard deviation of annual gross-of-fees returns of those portfolios that were included in the composite for the entire year.

8 The three-year annualized standard deviation measures the variability of the composite and the benchmark returns over the preceding 36-month period. The standard deviation is not presented for 2002 through 2010 because monthly composite and benchmark returns were not available, and is not required for periods prior to 2011.

3.13 Presentation and Reporting Recommendations

In addition to the requirements explained earlier, the GIPS standards include recommended practices in the presentation and reporting of investment results.

Provision I.5.B.1.a recommends that firms present gross-of-fees returns; that is, the return on investments reduced by **trading expenses** incurred during the period. It is fitting to reduce returns by trading expenses so as to take into account the firm's ability to execute a strategy efficiently. More or less directly comparable to benchmark returns, gross-of-fees returns are useful for prospective clients who wish to evaluate a firm's investment skill without regard to **investment management fees**, which may be negotiable, or **administrative fees**, which may not be under the manager's control. (Administrative fees, defined as all fees other than trading expenses and the investment management fee, could include custody, accounting, auditing, consulting, performance measurement, and legal fees, among others. The GIPS standards recommend that gross-of-fees and net-of-fees returns not be reduced for administrative fees because these are typically outside the control of the firm.) Although investors only receive net-of-fees returns, gross-of-fees returns enable them to appraise a firm's investment results in comparison with an appropriate benchmark and to reach tentative conclusions about a firm's skill relative to other managers with similar strategies.

Provision I.5.B.2.a recommends that, in addition to the required annual returns, firms should present cumulative composite and benchmark returns for all periods. Cumulative returns are calculated by geometrically linking historical returns in accordance with Equation 2 (reprinted here for convenience).

$$r_{twr} = (1 + r_{t,1}) \times (1 + r_{t,2}) \times \ldots \times (1 + r_{t,n}) - 1$$

For instance, using Equation 2 and the data given in Exhibit 15, we find that the composite's cumulative gross-of-fees return was 40 percent and the cumulative benchmark return was 28.1 percent for the 2002–2011 period.

Recall that the GIPS standards require composite returns to be calculated on an asset-weighted basis (I.2.A.6). Provision I.5.B.2.b recommends that firms present equal-weighted mean and median returns for each composite. These composite returns may provide useful information to prospective clients, particularly if the required dispersion measure has been calculated on an equal-weighted basis.

The GIPS standards also recommend that performance presentations include returns for quarterly and/or monthly time periods (I.5.B.2.c). Relatedly, the GIPS standards recommend that GIPS-compliant presentations be updated quarterly (I.5.B.9).

The GIPS standards also recommend that annualized composite and benchmark returns be presented for periods longer than 12 months (I.5.B.2.d). (We have observed, of course, that returns for periods shorter than one year must *not* be annualized.) As expressed in Equation 14, annualized returns are calculated by taking the *n*th root of chain-linked returns, where *n* is the number of years in the period.

$$r_{ann} = \sqrt[n]{(1 + r_{t,1}) \times (1 + r_{t,2}) \times ... \times (1 + r_{t,N})} - 1 \qquad (14)$$

For instance, the sample GIPS-compliant presentation shown earlier in this reading covers the 10-year period 2002 through 2011. Applying Equation 14 to the cumulative returns calculated above, we find that the annualized gross-of-fees return for the composite during that 10-year period was approximately 3.42 percent, and the annualized return for the benchmark during the same period was approximately 2.5 percent.

We saw earlier that, for periods ending on or after 1 January 2011, the GIPS standards require firms to present the annualized three-year *ex post* standard deviation of composite and benchmark returns. There are four related recommendations. Provision I.5.B.3 recommends that the same measures be presented for earlier annual periods. Provisions I.5.B.4–5 state that the corresponding annualized composite and benchmark total returns should be shown for each period the standard deviation is presented, and vice-versa. Provision I.5.B.6 recommends that firms present additional relevant composite-level *ex post* risk measures. In sum, the GIPS standards strongly advocate offering prospective clients relevant quantitative information they can use to evaluate the riskiness of the investment strategy represented by a composite.

We saw when reviewing the provisions related to disclosure that, for any non-compliant performance presented for periods prior to 1 January 2000, firms are required to disclose the periods of non-compliance (I.4.A.15). The GIPS standards recommend that firms comply for all historical periods (I.5.B.8). This recommendation does not relieve firms of the requirement to add annual performance on an ongoing basis to build a ten-year compliant track record. Indeed, Provision I.5.B.7 states that firms should present more than ten years of annual performance in the compliant presentation.

3.14 Introduction to the Real Estate and Private Equity Provisions

The GIPS standards include provisions for real estate and private equity, two major asset classes with distinctive characteristics. In general, the main sections of the GIPS standards apply to real estate and private equity as well; however, the GIPS standards include certain exceptions to the main provisions and set forth separate, additional requirements and recommendations for these two asset classes as defined.

Real estate and private equity investments can be structured in many different ways. The GIPS standards specify the types of investments that are *not* considered real estate. Publicly traded real estate securities (such as real estate investment trusts, or REITs) and mortgage-backed securities are subject to the general provisions rather than to the real estate provisions of the GIPS standards. Also excluded from the real estate provisions are private debt investments, including commercial and residential loans, where the expected return is solely related to contractual interest rates without any participation in the economic performance of the underlying real estate. The GIPS Glossary complements this definition by listing the types of investments that *are* considered real estate, namely, investments in wholly or partially owned properties; commingled funds, property unit trusts, and insurance company separate accounts; unlisted, private placement securities issued by private real estate investment trusts (REITs) and real estate operating companies (REOCs); and equity-oriented debt (e.g., participating mortgage loans) or any private interest in a property where some portion of return to the investor at the time of investment is related to the performance of the underlying real estate.

Similarly, the **private equity** provisions pertain to private equity investments made by fixed life, fixed commitment vehicles, including **primary fund vehicles** (which make direct investments rather than investing in other fund vehicles), **funds of funds** (which predominately invest in **closed-end funds** and may opportunistically make direct investments), and **secondary fund vehicles** (which buy interests in existing fund investment vehicles). A closed-end fund, as defined in the GIPS Glossary for purposes of the real estate and private equity provisions, is a type of investment vehicle where the number of investors, total **committed capital**, and life are fixed; it is not open for subscriptions and/or redemptions.[29] Private equity **open-end** or **evergreen** funds, which allow for ongoing investment and redemptions, remain subject to the main provisions in Sections 0–5 in Chapter I of the GIPS standards.

The real estate and private equity provisions were first included in the GIPS standards in 2005 and became effective 1 January 2006.[30] Unless otherwise stated, the following requirements and recommendations are effective 1 January 2011. Real estate investing and private equity investing are highly specialized areas of expertise, and the GIPS standards governing them are necessarily complicated. In the following sections of this reading, we will consider the principal concepts of the real estate and private equity provisions. However, this discussion is not an exhaustive treatment of these complex topics.

3.15 Real Estate Provisions

Fair values are central to calculating returns on real estate assets, and accordingly the GIPS standards for input data[31] and disclosures[32] include provisions related to valuation procedures. For periods beginning on or after 1 January 2011, firms must value real estate investments in accordance with the definition of fair value and the GIPS Valuation Principles (I.6.A.1); for earlier periods, firms must value real estate investments at market value as defined in the 2005 edition of the GIPS standards. Firms are not required to determine the value of real estate assets as frequently as they must value portfolios composed of more-liquid (non real estate) securities in accordance with the main sections of the GIPS standards. For periods prior to 1 January 2008, real estate investments must be valued at least once every 12 months. For periods beginning on or after 1 January 2008, real estate investments must be valued at least quarterly, and for periods beginning on or after 1 January 2010 they must be valued as of each quarter end or the last business day of each quarter (I.6.A.2–3).

---

29 There are special provisions for real estate closed-end funds.

30 Firms must not link non-GIPS-compliant real estate performance for periods beginning on or after 1 January 2006 to their GIPS-compliant performance (I.6.A.15). Firms must not present non-GIPS-compliant private equity performance for periods ending on or after 1 January 2006 (I.7.A.28). Any performance presented for periods ending prior to 1 January 2006 that does not comply with the GIPS standards must be disclosed in accordance with Provisions I.6.A.11 and I.7.A.20.

31 The following input data provisions do not apply to real estate: I.1.A.3.a, I.1.A.3.b, I.1.A.4, and I.1.B.1.

32 The following disclosure provisions do not apply to real estate: I.4.A.5, I.4.A.6, I.4.A.15, I.4.A.26, I.4.A.33, and I.4.A.34.

In the absence of transactions, however, managers' internal estimates of values may be based on subjective assumptions. Accordingly, the GIPS standards require firms to have valuations conducted periodically by independent, credentialed experts. Specifically, provision I.6.A.4 states that for periods prior to 1 January 2012, real estate investments must have an external valuation at least once every 36 months. For periods beginning on or after 1 January 2012, real estate investments must have an external valuation at least once every 12 months unless client agreements stipulate otherwise; in that case, they must have an external valuation at least every 36 months (or more frequently if required by the client agreement).

Provision I.6.A.5 goes on to state that external valuations must be performed by an independent external **professionally designated, certified, or licensed commercial property valuer/appraiser**. In markets where specialists with appropriate credentials are unavailable, the firm must take steps to ensure that it uses only well-qualified, independent property valuers or appraisers. Common-sense steps might include considering the appraiser's pertinent experience in the local market with the kind of properties to be independently valued. In accordance with the real estate provisions on presentation and reporting, firms must present as of each annual period end, the percentage of composite assets valued using an external valuation during the annual period (I.6.A.16.b).

The GIPS standards also include rate-of-return calculation requirements[33] for real estate. For periods beginning on or after 1 January 2006, portfolio returns after the deduction of actual **transaction expenses** incurred during the period must be calculated at least quarterly (I.6.A.6–7). For real estate (and private equity) return calculations, the gross-of-fees return is the return on investments reduced by any transaction expenses incurred during the period. Transaction expenses include all actual legal, financial, advisory, and investment banking fees related to buying, selling, restructuring, and/or recapitalizing portfolio investments as well as any trading expenses. As with the main provisions of the GIPS standards discussed earlier in this reading, the net-of-fees return is the gross-of-fees return reduced by investment management fees. For periods beginning on or after 1 January 2011, **income returns** and **capital returns** (known as component returns) must be calculated separately using geometrically linked time-weighted rates of return (I.6.A.8). Composite and component returns must be calculated by asset-weighting the individual portfolio returns at least quarterly (I.6.A.9). Let us now discuss the concept of component returns in greater detail.

The GIPS standards require that compliant presentations for real estate composites include time-weighted component returns in addition to total returns, and component returns must be clearly identified as gross-of-fees or net-of-fees (I.6.A.14). The two components of real estate total returns are income returns and capital returns. Component returns provide information about the source of the total return. Generally, "core" real estate strategies derive most of their total return through income returns, "opportunistic" strategies derive most of their total return through capital returns, and "value-added" strategies derive their total return through both income and capital returns.

A firm may choose to present in compliant presentations total returns that are gross-of-fees, net-of-fees, or both. Likewise, a firm may choose to present in compliant presentations component returns that are gross-of-fees, net-of-fees, or both. If a firm chooses to present only gross-of-fees total returns in the compliant presentation, then the firm should also present gross-of-fees component returns. If a firm chooses to present only net-of-fees total returns in the compliant presentation, then the firm

---

33 The following calculation methodology provisions do not apply to real estate: I.2.A.2.a, I.2.A.4, and I.2.A.7.

should also present net-of-fees component returns. If a firm chooses to present both gross-of-fees and net-of-fees total returns in the compliant presentation, the firm at a minimum should present gross-of-fees component returns.

Component returns are typically calculated utilizing information from the accounting records that tracks income/expense and capital gain/loss (realized and unrealized appreciation/depreciation) amounts separately. The sum of the income and capital amounts is reflected in the numerator of the total return calculation as described below.

Real estate portfolio accounting, including valuation, is usually performed internally on a quarterly basis, and, therefore, both portfolio and composite returns are typically calculated quarterly. For any given quarter, the sum of the income and capital component returns will equal the total return, with any differences solely due to rounding. The GIPS standards require that firms must calculate real estate portfolio returns at least quarterly (I.6.A.6). However, some firms calculate portfolio returns monthly for some or all of their real estate composites. In these instances, the sum of the monthly income and capital component returns will equal the monthly total return, but this relationship will not hold for the quarterly returns calculated using three geometrically linked monthly returns. See further discussion later. The typical return formulas utilized by real estate firms to calculate component and total returns are depicted later in this section for informational purposes. The GIPS standards allow flexibility in choosing the calculation methodology, which means that firms may use alternative formulas, provided the calculation method chosen represents returns fairly, is not misleading, and is applied consistently. The calculation of component returns should be the same for all real estate portfolios within a composite.

In an earlier section of this reading, we discussed the definition of "discretion" under the main sections of the GIPS standards. The GIPS provisions for disclosure associated with real estate performance presentations require firms to provide a description of discretion (I.6.A.10.a). Real estate portfolios are considered discretionary if the firm has sole responsibility or sufficient decision-making authority for major investment decisions.

Among other disclosure requirements, performance presentations for real estate investments must include disclosures about the methods and frequency of valuations. These requirements are set forth in Provisions I.6.A.10.b–e. In each real estate compliant presentation, firms must disclose the internal valuation methodologies used to value real estate investments for the most recent period. For example, among other conventional approaches, the firm might capitalize the income generated by a property, using an income capitalization rate imputed or "extracted" from the market based on the net operating income and sale prices of similar properties; or the firm might base the valuation of the subject property directly on the reported sale prices of comparable nearby properties, with adjustments to reflect differences in the properties' location, features, or condition.[34] For periods beginning on or after 1 January 2011, firms must disclose material changes to valuation policies and/or methodologies and any material difference between an external valuation and the valuation used in performance reporting, along with the reason for the difference. Firms must also disclose the frequency of independent, external valuations by appropriately credentialed valuers or appraisers. The GIPS Valuation Principles, which are discussed later in this reading, include additional requirements and recommendations specifically related to real estate investments.

---

34 These and other appraisal techniques are explained in Shilling (2002).

For periods beginning on or after 1 January 2006, the effective date of the real estate provisions, firms must not link non-GIPS-compliant performance to their GIPS-compliant performance (I.6.A.15).[35] For any performance presented for periods prior to 1 January 2006 that does not comply with the GIPS standards, firms must disclose the periods of non-compliance (I.6.A.11).

It is important to note that GIPS Provision I.5.A.1.a–h, as discussed earlier in Section 3.12 of this reading, applies to real estate composite compliant performance presentations.

The real estate presentation and reporting provisions also stipulate that each compliant performance presentation of a composite that includes more than five portfolios must contain a specific measure of internal dispersion, namely, the high and low annual time-weighted rate of return for the individual portfolios in the composite (I.6.A.16.a).

In addition to the foregoing requirements, the GIPS standards include recommendations pertaining to real estate input data, disclosures, and presentation and reporting. For periods prior to 1 January 2012, real estate investments should be externally valued by an independent, professionally credentialed property valuer or appraiser at least once every 12 months, and external valuations should be as of the end of the annual period (I.6.B.1–2). Firms should also disclose the basis of accounting for the portfolios in the composite, for instance, US Generally Accepted Accounting Principles (GAAP) or International Financial Reporting Standards (IFRS), and they should disclose and explain material differences, as of the end of each annual period, between the valuations used in performance reporting, on one hand, and financial reporting, on the other (I.6.B.3–4). The GIPS standards further recommend that for periods prior to 1 January 2011 firms should disclose material changes to valuation policies and/or methodologies (I.6.B.5). The GIPS standards recommend that firms present both gross-of-fees and net-of-fees returns, the percentage of the total value of composite assets that are not real estate, as defined, at the end of each annual period, and component returns of the benchmark, if available (I.6.B.6–8).

The 2010 edition of the GIPS standards contain further requirements and recommendations for real estate closed-end fund composites, including provisions related to calculation methodology. In addition to time-weighted rates of return, firms must calculate annualized **since inception internal rates of return (SI-IRR)** using quarterly cash flows at a minimum (I.6.A.17–18). We will encounter SI-IRR again in connection with the private equity provisions, where it is also a required element.

An internal rate of return is the discount rate that sets an investment's net present value equal to zero; expressed another way, it is the discount rate that equates the present value of an investment's cost with the present value of its benefits. The cost is the capital the client invests; the benefits are the distributions the client receives plus the investment's value at the end of the measurement period. Mathematically, we calculate the annualized internal rate of return from the value of r that solves the following equation:

$$V_0 = \frac{CF_1}{(1+r)^1} + \frac{CF_2}{(1+r)^2} + \cdots + \frac{V_N}{(1+r)^N} \qquad (15)$$

where V_0 represents the initial investment (the beginning value), the terms CF_1, CF_2, and so on represent interim cash flows, and V_N represents the ending value. For simplicity, Equation 15 assumes equally spaced end-of-period cash flows. In this formula, r is a subperiod return; when annualized, it is the internal rate of return.

---

[35] The following presentation and reporting provisions do not apply to real estate: I.5.A.1.i, I.5.A.2, I.5.A.3, I.5.B.3, I.5.B.4, and I.5.B.5.

Of course, the investor may make more than one capital contribution. With attention to the direction (the sign) of the cash flows, we can restate the equation for the internal rate of return as follows:

$$\sum_{i=0}^{N} \frac{CF_i}{(1+r)^i} = 0 \tag{16}$$

where CF_i is the cash flow for the period i and N is the total number of periods. In Equation 16, a negative CF_i represents a net cost or outflow to the investor and a positive CF_i represents a net distribution or inflow to the investor; CF_0 and CF_N incorporate V_0 and V_N, respectively, in Equation 15. This formulation accommodates multiple contributions or capital calls (cash inflows to the portfolio) and distributions (cash outflows from the portfolio) over the entire inception-to-date timeframe. By setting the sum of the present values of cash inflows and outflows equal to zero, the equation effectively defines r as the discount rate that makes the present value of the cost equal the present value of the benefits.

An example may make the calculation more clear. Let us consider the investment from the perspective of a client who funds the real estate portfolio and receives benefits in the form of cash distributions during the measurement period and ownership of fairly valued assets as of the end of the period. For this example, Exhibit 16 shows the timing and amount of the quarterly cash flows. The portfolio's real estate assets are valued as of the end of the second year, so the since-inception performance measurement period is eight quarters.

Exhibit 16   Data for an IRR Calculation

	Date	Quarter	Amount
Initial investment	31 December Year 0	0	−$150,000
Additional investment	30 June Year 1	2	−$100,000
Distribution received	31 March Year 2	5	$12,665
Distribution received	30 September Year 2	7	$11,130
Ending value	31 December Year 2	8	$274,300

The client's experience can be expressed graphically, as in Exhibit 17, with the ending value reflected as a cash flow. Note that in some periods, no cash flows occur.

Exhibit 17

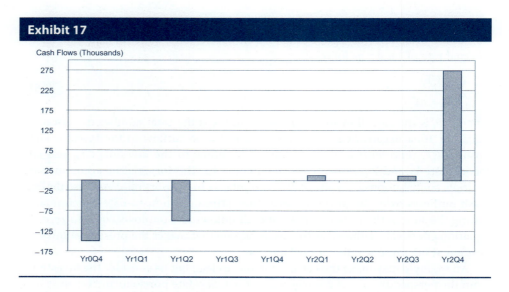

Using the data in Exhibit 16 as inputs to Equation 16, we find through an iterative trial-and-error process that the quarterly discount rate r is approximately 2.53 percent. Exhibit 15 validates this result. The present value factor applied to each cash flow is $1/(1+r)^i$, where r is the discount rate and i is the sequential number of the subperiod. For instance, the present value factor applied to the cash distribution of $12,665 paid out on 31 March of Year 2, the fifth quarter, is

$$\frac{1}{(1+0.0253)^5} = 0.88256$$

Exhibit 18 shows that 2.53 percent is the quarterly discount rate that sets the sum of the present values of the cash flows from inception through the end of the measurement period equal to zero. The GIPS real estate provisions require us to annualize the since-inception internal rate of return. To annualize a return that was computed on a quarterly basis, we calculate $(1+r)^4 - 1$, so the SI-IRR earned in this example is 10.51 percent.

Exhibit 18   Demonstration that the Computed IRR is Correct

Date	Cash Flow	Period	Present Value Factor (r = 2.53%)	Present Value
31 December Year 0	−150,000	0	1	−150,000
30 June Year 1	−100,000	2	0.95126	−95,126
31 March Year 2	12,665	5	0.88256	11,178
30 September Year 2	11,130	7	0.83954	9,344
31 December Year 2	274,300	8	0.81883	224,605
Total (does not equal zero due to rounding)				1

As noted, firms must use quarterly cash flows at a minimum in calculating the SI-IRR for closed-end real estate fund composites. In other words, CF_i must reflect the net cash flow for a period no longer than a quarter. (It is recommended in Provision I.6.B.9 that daily cash flows be used in calculating SI-IRR). Firms must disclose the frequency of cash flows used in the SI-IRR calculation (I.6.A.21).

The GIPS provisions for composite construction require closed-end real estate fund composites to be defined by **vintage year** as well as investment mandate, objective, or strategy, and to keep the composite definition consistent throughout the life of the composite (I.6.A.19). The vintage year is useful information for prospective clients who wish to establish the comparability of different composites. There is a related disclosure requirement: Firms must disclose the vintage year of the composite and how the vintage year is defined (I.6.A.22). The GIPS Glossary mentions two methods of determining the vintage year: 1) the year of the investment vehicle's first drawdown or capital call from its investors; and 2) the year when the first committed capital from outside investors is closed and legally binding.

The provisions related to presentation and reporting for real estate closed-end funds require firms to present the composite's net-of-fees SI-IRR through the end of each annual period.[36] For periods beginning on or after 1 January 2011, when the initial period is less than a full year, firms must present the net-of-fees SI-IRR through the end of the initial annual period; in this case, the SI-IRR must not be annualized. For periods ending on or after 1 January 2011, firms must present the net-of-fees SI-IRR through the composite's **final liquidation date**. (I.6.A.23.) Firms must also disclose the final liquidation date for liquidated composites (I.6.A.20).

Firms must also present the SI-IRR of the benchmark as of each annual period end. In addition to reflecting the composite's investment mandate, objective, or strategy, the benchmark must have the same vintage year and be presented for the same time period as the composite (I.6.A.26). Given that the benchmark SI-IRR must be presented, firms may also find it advantageous to present the composite's gross-of-fees SI-IRR. However, if shown, the gross-of-fees SI-IRR of the composite must be presented for the same period of time the net-of-fees SI-IRR is presented (I.6.A.24).[37]

Firms are required to present information about the financial history and status of real estate closed-end funds as of the end of each period. Specifically, they must present the composite's cumulative **committed capital** (the capital pledged to the investment vehicle), since-inception **paid-in capital** (the amount of committed capital that has been drawn down), and since-inception **distributions**. Firms must also report certain multiples or ratios for each annual period presented. One of them is the ratio of **total value** to since-inception paid-in capital (**TVPI**, also called the **investment multiple**). TVPI provides information about the value of the composite relative to its cost basis. For the purpose of the TVPI calculation, total value can be determined by adding since-inception distributions to date to the end-of-period **residual value**. Firms must also report the ratio of since-inception distributions to since-inception paid-in capital (**DPI**, also called the **realization multiple**); the ratio of since-inception paid-in capital to committed capital (the **PIC multiple**); and the ratio of residual value to since-inception paid-in capital (**RVPI**, also called the **unrealized multiple**). These requirements are set forth in Provision I.6.A.25.

Please see Appendix A of the GIPS standards for a sample real estate closed-end fund composite complaint performance presentation.

---

36 Firms must initially present at least five years of performance (or performance from the firm's inception or the composite's inception date if they have been in existence less than five years), and must present an additional year of performance each subsequent year. Please note that this requirement for real estate closed-end fund composites is in addition to the requirement to calculate time-weighted rates of return that adjust for external cash flows, and presenting such returns in a composite compliant performance presentation as required by Provision I.5.A.1.a

37 Please note that Provisions I.4.A.29-31 are not scoped out for real estate or private equity and so these disclosures are required, if applicable.

3.16 Private Equity Provisions

The GIPS provisions for private equity use technical terms that may be unfamiliar to the performance measurement generalist. Although considerably simplified for brevity, an overview of the private equity investment process may facilitate understanding of the GIPS standards' requirements and recommendations.

Let us take for an example a venture capital fund organized as a **limited partnership**, one of many investment structures used in the private equity market. A venture capital firm identifies an emerging industry, develops the fund concept, and secures commitments from investors who pledge to pay in a certain amount of capital over a certain period of time, often three to five years. In this structure, a venture capital firm will serve as **general partner**, and the investors will be **limited partners**. The general partner screens early stage companies' business plans, identifies the most promising enterprises, and conducts in-depth analysis and due diligence on the quality of their management, the legal status of their intellectual property rights, and the prospective demand for their products, among many other factors. The general partner then negotiates deals with the companies that pass scrutiny and places capital calls drawing down the limited partners' committed capital for investment in the portfolio companies. There may be multiple capital calls to meet each company's cash requirements in accordance with the terms of the deal. As the fund matures, the general partner harvests the portfolio companies (for instance, by taking them public) and distributes the proceeds to the limited partners. With this background in mind, let us turn to the GIPS provisions for private equity.

There are two provisions related to input data.[38] For periods ending on or after 1 January 2011, private equity investments must be valued in accordance with the definition of fair value and the GIPS Valuation Principles,[39] and they must be valued at least annually (I.7.A.1–2). We will discuss the GIPS Valuation Principles in a later section of this reading.

The GIPS private equity provisions related to calculation methodology[40] state that firms must calculate annualized since-inception internal rates of return (SI-IRR)[41] and that, for periods ending on or after 1 January 2011, the SI-IRR must be calculated using daily cash flows; for earlier periods, either daily or monthly cash flows may be used. Distributions of stock must be included as cash flows and valued at the time of distribution (I.7.A.3–4).

All private equity returns must be calculated after the deduction of actual **transaction expenses** incurred during the period, and net-of-fees returns must be net of actual investment management fees including **carried interest**, representing the profits on the investments of the investment vehicle that general partners are allocated (I.7.A.5–6). All private equity fund of fund returns must be net of all underlying partnership and/or fund fees and expenses, including carried interest (I.7.A.7).

The private equity provisions for composite construction[42] state that composite definitions must remain consistent throughout the life of the composite (I.7.A.8). Primary fund vehicles must be included in at least one composite defined by vintage year and investment mandate, objective, or strategy (I.7.A.9). Funds of funds must be included in at least one composite defined by vintage year of the fund of funds and/or investment mandate, objective, or strategy. (I.7.A.10).

---

38 The following input data provisions do not apply to private equity: I.1.A.3.a, I.1.A.3.b, I.1.A.4, and I.1.B.1.
39 For earlier periods, private equity investments must be valued according to either the GIPS Private Equity Valuation Principles in the 2005 edition of the GIPS standards or the GIPS Valuation Principles in the 2010 edition of the GIPS standards.
40 The following calculation methodology provisions do not apply to private equity: I.2.A.2, I.2.A.4, I.2.A.6, I.2.A.7, and I.2.B.2.
41 We explained the SI-IRR calculation in connection with the real estate provisions.
42 The following composite construction provisions do not apply to private equity: I.3.A.10 and I.3.B.2.

Specific disclosure requirements[43] also apply for private equity. Firms must disclose the vintage year of each composite, how the vintage year is determined, and, where applicable, the **final liquidation date** (I.7.A.11–12). As one might expect, there are disclosure requirements pertaining to the valuation of private equity investments. Firms must disclose their private equity valuation methodologies for the most recent period and, for periods ending on or after 1 January 2011, they must disclose any material changes to valuation policies and/or methodologies (I.7.A.13-14); disclosing such changes is recommended for earlier periods (I.7.B.4). If the firm adheres to any industry valuation guidelines in addition to the GIPS Valuation Principles, it must disclose which guidelines have been applied. (I.7.A.15). The GIPS Valuation Principles, which are explained later in this reading, set forth additional requirements and recommendations specifically related to valuing private equity investments.

There are also disclosure requirements related to calculations of private equity composite returns. If daily cash flows are not used in the SI-IRR calculation for periods prior to 1 January 2011, then firms must disclose the frequency of the cash flows that are used (I.7.A.17); recall that the SI-IRR must be calculated using either daily or monthly cash flows for periods prior to 1 January 2011. Firms must also disclose the periods of non-compliance when presenting non-GIPS-compliant SI-IRR for periods ending prior to 1 January 2006 (I.7.A.20). Similarly to disclosure requirements of the main provisions of the GIPS standards, for gross-of-fees returns firms must disclose if any other fees are deducted in addition to transaction expenses, and for net-of-fees returns they must disclose if any fees other than transaction expenses and investment management fees are deducted (I.7.A.18–19).

Firms must disclose the calculation methodology used for the benchmark. Firms that choose to present a composite's **public market equivalent** (PME) as a benchmark must disclose the index used in calculating it. (I.7.A.16.) In this approach to benchmarking, firms apply the composite's external cash flows to a hypothetical investment that earns the returns of a capital market index. By replicating the timing and amount of composite cash flows in a PME, firms can calculate the internal rate of return of a benchmark to which the composite's SI-IRR is comparable.

Having reviewed the requirements for input data, calculation methodology, composite construction, and disclosure, we are in position to address the GIPS provisions for private equity presentation and reporting.[44] Firms must present, and clearly identify, both the gross-of-fees and the net-of-fees SI-IRR of the composite through the end of each annual period. Firms must initially present at least five years of performance (or, if fewer than five years, performance from the firm's inception or the composite inception date), and each subsequent year they must present an additional year of performance. For periods beginning on or after 1 January 2011, when the initial period is shorter than a full year, firms must present the non-annualized gross-of-fees and net-of-fees SI-IRR through the initial annual period end. For periods ending on or after 1 January 2011, firms must present the gross-of-fees and net-of-fees SI-IRR through the composite's final liquidation date. (I.7.A.21.) Firms must also present the SI-IRR of the benchmark through the end of each annual period; in addition to representing the composite's investment mandate, objective, or strategy, the benchmark must be the same vintage year and presented for the same time period as the composite (I.7.A.24). Firms must not present non-GIPS-compliant SI-IRR for periods ending on or after 1 January 2006 (I.7.A.28).

---

43 The following disclosure provisions do not apply to private equity: I.4.A.5, I.4.A.6.a, I.4.A.6.b, I.4.A.8, I.4.A.15, I.4.A.26, I.4.A.32, I.4.A.33, and I.4.A.34.
44 The following presentation and reporting provisions do not apply to private equity: I.5.A.1.a, I.5.A.1.b, I.5.A.1.c, I.5.A.1.d, I.5.A.1.e, I.5.A.1.i, I.5.A.2, I.5.A.3, I.5.B.2, I.5.B.3, I.5.B.4, and I.5.B.5.

Several requirements apply specifically to private equity fund of fund composites. First, for periods ending on or after 1 January 2011, if a fund of funds composite is defined only by its investment mandate, objective, or strategy,[45] then firms must also present, as of the most recent annual period, the SI-IRR of the underlying investments aggregated by vintage year as well as other measures that are required by provision I.7.A.23 (see below). These measures must be presented gross of the fund of funds investment management fees and must be presented as of the most recent annual period end (I.7.A.22). Second, if fund of funds composite is defined only by its investment mandate, objective, or strategy, and a benchmark is presented for the underlying investments, the benchmark must reflect the same mandate, objective, or strategy and have the same vintage year as the underlying investments (I.7.A.25). Third, for periods ending on or after 1 January 2011, firms must present the percentage, if any, of fund of funds composite assets that is invested in direct investments (rather than fund vehicles) as of each annual period end (I.7.A.26). It is recommended but not required that this percentage be presented for earlier periods (I.7.B.6).

For periods ending on or after 1 January 2011, firms must present the percentage of primary fund vehicle composite assets that is invested in fund investment vehicles (rather than in direct investments) as of the end of each annual period (I.7.A.27). It is recommended but not required that the same percentage be presented for earlier periods (I.7.B.7).

For all private equity composites, firms must present, as of each annual period end, the cumulative committed capital, since-inception paid-in capital, and since-inception distributions. In addition, firms must present the following ratios: total value to since-inception paid-in capital (known as the investment multiple or TVPI); since-inception distributions to since-inception paid-in capital (called the realization multiple or DPI); since-inception paid-in capital to cumulative committed capital (the PIC multiple); and residual value to since-inception paid-in capital (the unrealized multiple or RVPI) (I.7.A.23.). These ratios were mentioned earlier in connection with real estate closed-end fund composites.

Finally, there are some recommendations that we have not previously mentioned. Private equity investments should be valued at least quarterly; for periods ending prior to 1 January 2011, the SI-IRR should be calculated using daily cash flows; and firms should disclose and explain material differences between the valuations used in performance reporting and the valuations used in financial reporting as of each annual period end (I.7.B.1–3).

Just as with real estate investing, the intricacies of performance presentation in compliance with the GIPS provisions for private equity reflect this field's complexity. Of necessity, the introductory treatment given the subject here does not address many nuances or special circumstances that the practitioner may encounter. Further information about these specialized asset classes may be found in the GIPS Guidance Statements on Real Estate and Private Equity, both of which are available on the GIPS website (www.gipsstandards.org).

3.17 Wrap Fee/Separately Managed Account (SMA) Provisions

Wrap fee portfolios, also known as separately managed accounts (SMAs), are typically managed by investment management firms serving as sub-advisors to a sponsor who acts as the client's investment advisor. The sponsor charges the client a single **bundled**

---

45 On the other hand, if the fund of funds composite is defined only by vintage year of the fund of funds, it is recommended but not required that firms present, for periods ending on or after 1 January 2011, the SI-IRR of the underlying investments aggregated by investment mandate, objective, or strategy, along with the other measures listed in provision I.7.A.23. These measures should be gross of the fund of funds investment management fees (I.7.B.5.).

fee which combines fees for various services such as investment management, trading, custody, and administrative functions. Such arrangements create complexities that are specifically addressed by the provisions of the GIPS standards governing the presentation of wrap fee/SMA performance.

The GIPS standards for wrap fee portfolios or separately managed accounts apply to wrap fee/SMA performance presentations to existing and prospective wrap fee/SMA sponsors and prospective wrap fee/SMA clients if they present results for periods beginning on or after 1 January 2006. Furthermore, these provisions apply to portfolios where there are bundled fees and a sponsor serves as an intermediary between an investment firm that claims to comply with the GIPS standards and the end user of the investment services. They do not apply to other types of bundled fee arrangements, nor are they applicable to model or overlay portfolios unless the firm has discretion to manage the actual individual portfolios.

The wrap fee/SMA provisions *supplement* the required and recommended provisions of the GIPS standards, that is to say, they are in addition to the fundamentals of compliance; the provisions for input data, calculation methodology, composite construction, disclosure, and presentation and reporting; and, if applicable, the provisions for real estate and private equity. Of special importance in this context is the requirement to capture and maintain all data and information necessary to support all items included in a compliant presentation (I.1.A.1); recognizing that wrap fee/SMA portfolios are subject to the same level of verification as all other portfolios, firms may have to choose between relying upon the sponsor's performance calculations and engaging in shadow accounting[46] to track the wrap fee/SMA portfolios in their own performance measurement system. Also pertinent is the requirement to calculate returns after the deduction of the actual trading expenses incurred during the measurement period (I.2.A.4). We saw earlier that, if the actual trading expenses cannot be identified and segregated from a bundled fee, returns must be reduced by the entire bundled fee or the portion of the bundled fee that includes the trading expenses (I.2.A.5.a–b). We also made note of disclosure and presentation requirements pertaining to composites that contain portfolios with bundled fees: Firms must disclose the types of fees that are included in the bundled fee (I.4.A.24) and present the percentage of composite assets represented by portfolios with bundled fees as of the end of each annual period (I.5.A.7).

The first provision set forth in the wrap fee/SMA section of the GIPS standards has to do with composite construction. Provision I.8.A.1 requires firms to include the performance record of actual wrap fee/SMA portfolios in appropriate composites in accordance with the firm's established portfolio inclusion policies (discussed in Section 3.9 earlier in this reading). Once established, the portfolios containing wrap fee/SMA portfolios must be used in the firm's compliant presentations to prospective wrap fee/SMA clients.

IMPLEMENTATION (11)

Defining Composites. Firms may have both wrap fee/SMA portfolios and non-wrap fee/SMA portfolios that are managed in accordance with the same investment strategy. In this case, they must decide at the outset whether to include all of them in the same composite for performance presentations to non-wrap fee/SMA prospects or to define a separate composite that only contains the non-wrap fee/SMA portfolios. If they choose to include both types of portfolios in the same composite, their performance presentation will show larger composite assets. However, if they are unable to break out actual trading

---

46 In the present context, a sub-advisory firm that engages in "shadow accounting" independently maintains a parallel set of portfolio accounting records to serve as the basis for calculating and presenting investment performance.

expenses from the sponsor's bundled fee, then they must reduce the wrap fee/SMA port-folio returns by the entire amount of the bundled fee or the portion of the bundled fee that includes trading expenses. This may have a competitively disadvantageous result: A composite that contains both kinds of portfolio is likely to have lower gross-of-fees and net-of-fees returns than the composite would have if it only contained non-wrap fee/SMA portfolios. Firms must consider the trade-off between higher assets and lower returns when defining composites for non-wrap fee/SMA portfolios.

There are several disclosure-related provisions that apply to wrap fee/SMA composite presentations. For all compliant presentations that include periods before an actual wrap fee/SMA portfolio was included in the composite, the firm must disclose for each period that the composite does not contain actual wrap fee/SMA portfolios (I.8.A.2). In addition, for any performance presented for periods prior to 1 January 2006 that does not comply with the GIPS standards, firms must disclose the periods of non-compliance (I.8.A.3). Additional disclosure requirements pertaining to sponsor-specific performance presentations are explained below.

When firms present performance to prospective wrap fee/SMA clients, the composite must include all wrap fee/SMA portfolios, regardless of the sponsor, that are managed according to the composite's investment mandate, objective, or strategy. In other words, firms must present "style-defined" composites to prospective wrap fee/SMA clients (I.8.A.5.). Moreover—and this is a key requirement—when firms present performance to prospective wrap fee/SMA clients, they must present the performance net of the *entire* wrap fee (I.8.A.6). This provision applies regardless of the nature of the services covered by the wrap fee.

The GIPS standards distinguish between style-defined composites that contain wrap fee/SMA portfolios, described in the preceding paragraph, and sponsor-specific wrap fee/SMA composites. Whether to report its investment results or to win additional business, a firm that serves as sub-advisor to a wrap fee/SMA sponsor may wish to prepare a GIPS-compliant performance presentation that includes only the sponsor's wrap fee/SMA portfolios—in other words, a performance presentation of a sponsor-specific composite. When doing so, firms must disclose the name of the sponsor (I.8.A.4.a) and, if the purpose of the presentation is to generate wrap fee/SMA business and does *not* include performance net of the entire wrap fee, the firm must disclose that the sponsor-specific presentation is only for the use of the named sponsor (I.8.A.4.b). The intent of the last-mentioned provision is to discourage sponsors from redistributing purportedly GIPS-compliant performance presentations to prospective wrap fee/SMA clients without reducing returns by the entire wrap fee.

Finally, firms must not link non-GIPS-compliant performance for periods beginning on or after 1 January 2006 to their GIPS-compliant wrap fee/SMA performance (I.8.A.7).

4   GIPS VALUATION PRINCIPLES

The GIPS standards are based on the ethical principles of fair representation and full disclosure. Recalling how rates of return are calculated, it is almost trivially apparent that meaningful performance measurement presupposes the validity of beginning and ending asset values. During the global financial crisis of 2008–2009, however, when market prices were unavailable for many hard-to-value securities, the investment industry and the accounting profession gave renewed attention to the issue of valuation. The International Accounting Standards Board (IASB), the Financial Accounting Standards Board (FASB), and others re-examined the notions of fair value and market value, and studied the problem of valuing assets in inactive markets. The GIPS Valuation Principles were developed in consideration of the work done by these organizations. Effective 1 January 2011, the GIPS standards require firms to apply a fair value methodology following the definition and requirements we are about to summarize.

The GIPS standards define fair value as the amount at which an investment could be exchanged in a current arm's length transaction between willing parties in which the parties each act knowledgeably and prudently. (In this context, the phrase "arm's length" describes a transaction in which the parties are unrelated and acting in their own interests.) The valuation must be determined using the objective, observable, unadjusted quoted market price for an identical investment in an active market on the measurement date if this price is available;[47] otherwise, the valuation must reflect the firm's best estimate of the market value. Fair value must include accrued income. (II.A, Fair Value Definition.)

In delineating the valuation requirements, the GIPS standards restate provisions and, in some cases, clarify the applicability of provisions we have described earlier. For periods beginning on or after 1 January 2011, portfolios must be valued in accordance with the definition of fair value and the GIPS Valuation Principles (I.1.A.2). Firms must comply with all applicable laws and regulations regarding the calculation and presentation of performance (I.0.A.2) and, if a compliant presentation conforms with laws and regulations that conflict with the requirements of the GIPS standards, firms must disclose and describe the conflict (I.4.A.22). Accordingly, firms must comply with applicable laws and regulations relating to valuation, and when there is a conflict they must disclose it (II.B.3-4). Firms must document their policies and procedures and apply them consistently (I.0.A.5); this requirement entails documenting and adhering to their valuation policies, procedures, methodologies, and hierarchy (and any changes to them). Firms must disclose that policies for valuing portfolios, calculating performance, and preparing compliant presentations are available upon request (I.4.A.12). For periods beginning on or after 1 January 2011, firms must disclose the use of subjective, unobservable inputs for valuing portfolio investments if the investments thus valued are material to the composite (I.4.A.27), and they must disclose if a composite's valuation hierarchy materially differs from the recommended hierarchy in the GIPS Valuation Principles (I.4.A.28).

We have referred several times to the GIPS standards' recommended valuation hierarchy, which firms should incorporate into their valuation policies and procedures on a composite-specific basis. Articulated in Section C of the GIPS Valuation Principles, it is a hierarchy in the strong sense that, if the inputs described at one stage are unavailable or inappropriate, then firms should proceed to the next stage. As we have indicated, investments *must* be valued using objective, observable, unadjusted quoted market prices for identical investments in active markets on the measurement date. If such prices are not available, then investments *should* be valued using objective, observable, quoted market prices for similar investments in active markets.

If such prices are unavailable or inappropriate, investments *should* be valued using, in descending order, the bases spelled out in Provision II.C.1:

1   Quoted prices for identical or similar investments in markets that are not active.

2   Market-based inputs other than quoted prices that are observable for the investment.

3   Subjective, unobservable inputs.

---

47 This requirement is reiterated in item II.B.2 in the GIPS Valuation Principles.

The GIPS Valuation Principles clarify that inactive markets include those in which there are few transactions for the investment, the prices are not current, or price quotations vary substantially over time and/or between market makers. Unobservable inputs reflect the firm's assumptions about the assumptions market participants would use in pricing the investment—assumptions about assumptions. They should be developed based on the best information available in the circumstances.

IMPLEMENTATION (12)

Valuation Policies and Procedures. Firms may enter transactions involving a wide range of financial instruments, including derivative securities, in many different markets. It is fitting, therefore, that the GIPS standards not only require firms to document their valuation policies, procedures, methodologies, and hierarchies but also recommend that the valuation hierarchies be composite-specific. Normally, for investment strategies that employ plain-vanilla securities trading in robust markets, quoted prices are readily available. Other composites, however, may represent strategies that materially make use of securities that trade infrequently in relatively illiquid markets where values must be imputed or estimated. Real estate and private equity are obvious examples, but valuing investments in swaps, options, and other derivatives that are tied to underlying securities uniquely issued by specific companies may prove problematic, especially if the firm cannot refer to recent transactions in identical or similar assets. Implementing the GIPS standards offers firms an opportunity to re-examine their valuation policies, procedures, and methodologies and to define valuation hierarchies reflecting the characteristics of the securities held in each composite and the markets in which the composite strategy is executed. For assets that are valued using quantitative models, it is useful to list input factors such as discount rates and risk-adjusted cash flow projections and to review the basis for estimating them. Portfolio managers, security analysts, quantitative analysts, and traders should participate in these discussions. Once established, the valuation policies must be documented, followed consistently, and made available to prospective clients upon request.

The GIPS standards also set forth additional requirements pertaining to real estate valuations. Recalling that real estate investments must have an external valuation (I.6.A.4), the GIPS Valuation Principles further require that the external valuation process adhere to practices of the relevant valuation governing and standard-setting body (II.B.10). The GIPS Valuation Principles also state that the firm *must not* use external valuations where the valuer's or appraiser's fee is contingent upon the appraised value (II.B.11). Clearly, such financial arrangements would incentivize the appraiser to inflate the asset's value. The GIPS Valuation Principles proceed to restate other requirements, chiefly having to do with disclosures, that we mentioned in the section on real estate investing earlier. They also include, however, some additional recommendations. Although appraisal standards may allow for a range of estimated values, the GIPS standards recommend that a single value be obtained from external valuers or appraisers because only one value is used in performance reporting (II.C.6). It is also recommended that the external appraisal firm be rotated every three to five years (II.C.7).

Similarly, the GIPS Valuation Principles restate private equity disclosure requirements that we discussed earlier in this reading and add another requirement: The valuation methodology selected must be the most appropriate for a particular investment based on the nature, facts, and circumstances of the investment (II.B.17). There is also a recommendation having to do with private equity valuations that we have not previously mentioned. The following considerations should be incorporated into the valuation process: (a) the quality and reliability of the data used in each methodology; (b) the comparability of enterprise or transaction data; (c) the stage of development of the enterprise; and (d) any additional considerations unique to the enterprise (II.C.12).

Fair representation means developing and adhering to policies and procedures designed to determine asset values as accurately as possible. Full disclosure means documenting those policies and providing the valuation-related information required by the GIPS standards—and, optimally, the recommended information as well—so that prospective investors can evaluate the reported performance and have a greater degree of confidence in the performance information presented to them.

GIPS ADVERTISING GUIDELINES

5

A firm may wish to claim that it complies with the GIPS standards in advertisements that do not accommodate a compliant performance presentation. For instance, space may be limited, or the creative design and marketing message may not call for communicating investment results in full. To address this need, the GIPS standards include requirements which apply to firms that already satisfy all the requirements of the GIPS standards on a firm-wide basis and claim compliance with the GIPS standards in an advertisement. Firms that choose to claim compliance in an advertisement must either follow the GIPS Advertising Guidelines—for convenience, we will refer to them as "the Guidelines" in this section—or include a compliant presentation in the advertisement.

The Guidelines do not replace the GIPS standards, nor do they in any way exempt firms from providing compliant presentations as the GIPS standards require. Here as elsewhere, in cases where there is a conflict between applicable laws or regulations and the requirements of the GIPS standards, firms must comply with the law or regulation. If an advertisement conforms with legal and/or regulatory requirements that conflict with the GIPS standards and/or the Guidelines, firms must disclose this fact and disclose the manner in which they conflict (III.B.13).

For the purpose of the Guidelines, advertisements include any written or electronic materials addressed to more than one prospective client, whether in newspapers, magazines, firm brochures, letters, media, websites, or any other written or electronic material addressed to more than one prospective client. Under this definition, "one-on-one" presentations and individual client reports are not considered advertisements. This rule applies on a relationship basis. Presentations and reports to a single prospective or existing client are not considered advertisements despite the fact that a number of people may be in attendance, such as a board of trustees or the members of an investment committee. The Guidelines pertain to any written material disseminated more broadly to retain existing clients or solicit new clients.

IMPLEMENTATION (13)

Communicating the GIPS Advertising Guidelines. Applying the Guidelines affects the work of marketing and other departments that may be unfamiliar with the GIPS standards. The firm's performance practitioners might conduct an educational session or workshop to present the Guidelines and discuss implementation with the marketing department, including copywriters and graphic designers, and with other areas of the firm including the firm's legal and compliance experts. Here are some suggestions to facilitate the discussion:

■ Explain that the GIPS standards are ethical standards for fair representation and full disclosure of investment performance.

- Describe in general terms the sections included within the GIPS standards (fundamentals of compliance, input data, calculation methodology, composite construction, disclosures, presentation and reporting, real estate, private equity, and verification, as well as advertising).
- Explain how the firm is defined.
- Distribute the firm's list of composite descriptions.
- Explain how advertisements are defined for the purpose of the Guidelines.
- Explain the relationship between applicable laws and regulations and the GIPS standards, including the Guidelines.
- Present the requirements and recommendations of the Guidelines in detail as they apply to advertisements in which the firm claims compliance with the GIPS standards and (1) does or (2) does not present performance.
- Review the sample advertisements provided in Appendix B of the 2010 edition of the GIPS standards.
- Explain how other information can be used in advertisements.
- Reach agreement on compliance review procedures for new advertising materials. Because information used in advertisements that are subject to the Guidelines must be taken or derived from GIPS-compliant performance presentations, it is advisable for both a legal or compliance professional, and a member of the performance measurement group to approve new advertising materials.

All advertisements that state a claim of compliance must include a definition of the firm and information about how to obtain a compliant presentation and/or a list of the firm's composite descriptions (III.B.1–2). The required wording of the GIPS compliance statement for advertisements is: "[Name of firm] claims compliance with the Global Investment Performance Standards (GIPS®)." (III.B.3).

All advertisements that not only state a claim of compliance, but also present performance, must disclose further information as detailed below, and the relevant information must be taken or derived from a compliant presentation. The required information includes, among other elements, the composite description (III.B.4), an indication whether performance is shown gross of fees, net of fees, or both (III.B.6), and the currency used to express returns (III.B.10). In advertisements presenting performance information for periods prior to 1 January 2000 that does not comply with the GIPS standards, firms must disclose the periods of non-compliance (III.B.12).

Advertisements that state a claim of compliance *and present performance* must also present one of the following sets of total returns:

a   one-, three-, and five-year annualized composite returns through the most recent period;

b   period-to-date composite returns in addition to one-, three-, and five-year annualized composite returns through the same period of time as presented in the corresponding compliant presentation; or

c   period-to-date composite returns in addition to five years of annual composite returns calculated through the same period of time as presented in the corresponding compliant presentation.

If the composite has been in existence for less than five years, firms must also present the corresponding returns since the composite inception date. Under option (a), for instance, if the composite has been in existence for four years, the firm must present the composite's annualized one-year, three-year, and four-year returns. Whichever alternative is chosen, the period-end date must be clearly identified and returns for less than one year must not be annualized. These requirements are set forth in Provision III.B.5.a–c.

Advertisements asserting a claim of compliance with the GIPS standards must also disclose the benchmark description (III.B.8) and present the benchmark total returns for the same periods as those for which composite performance is presented in the advertisement. The benchmark used in the advertisement must be the same benchmark presented in the corresponding compliant presentation. (III.B.7.) If the firm determines no appropriate benchmark for the composite exists, it must disclose why no benchmark is presented (III.B.9).

In advertisements stating compliance with the GIPS standards and presenting performance, firms must also disclose the presence, use, and extent of leverage, derivatives, and short positions, if material, including a description of the frequency of use and the characteristics of the instruments sufficient to identify risks (III.B.11).

Firms may also include other information in advertisements that are subject to the Guidelines, provided it is not given greater prominence than the required information and it does not conflict with the GIPS standards and/or the Guidelines. The Guidelines emphasize that firms must adhere to the principles of fair representation and full disclosure when advertising, and they must not present performance or performance-related information that is false or misleading.

Appendix B in the 2010 edition of the GIPS standards provides sample advertisements which adhere to the requirements of the Guidelines.

VERIFICATION

6

Verification may be informally and unofficially characterized as a process in which an independent expert assesses a firm's policies and procedures for constructing composites and calculating and presenting performance in light of the requirements of the GIPS standards.[48] Verification is intended to provide the firm and the users of its performance presentations greater confidence in its claim of compliance with the GIPS standards. Verification does not ensure the accuracy of any particular composite presentation. However, in addition to making the claim of compliance on a firm-wide basis more credible, the verification process may benefit the firm in other ways: increased knowledge in the performance measurement team, consistently higher quality of performance presentations, improved internal processes and procedures, and potential marketing advantages. Above all, verification supports the guiding principles of fair representation and full disclosure of investment performance.

The GIPS standards strongly encourage firms to undergo **verification**. Chapter IV of the GIPS standards reviews the scope and purpose of verification and sets forth the minimum procedures that verifiers must follow prior to issuing a **verification report** to the firm. The verification procedures attempt to strike a balance between ensuring the quality, accuracy, and relevance of performance presentations and minimizing the cost to firms.

IMPLEMENTATION (14)

Selecting a Verification Firm. Verification is a major undertaking, and it is crucial for the investment management firm to choose an independent verifier whose resources match the firm's needs. At the outset of the selection process, the investment management

---

48 The GIPS Glossary defines verification as "a process by which an independent verifier assesses whether (1) the firm has complied with all the composite construction requirements of the GIPS standards on a firm-wide basis and (2) the firm's policies and procedures are designed to calculate and present performance in compliance with the GIPS standards."

firm approaching verification should consider the scope of its operations and the nature of its products. The requirements of a large investment management organization with a presence in markets around the world will differ from those of a firm operating in only a single country. Similarly, a hedge fund manager, a manager who engages in real estate or private equity investing, a quantitatively oriented manager whose investment strategies rely heavily on the use of derivative securities, or a manager who manages tax-aware portfolios for individuals may have more specialized requirements than a manager who manages funds for tax-exempt institutions such as pension plans and charitable foundations. These factors should be communicated to potential verifiers and reflected in the selection criteria.

Some organizations have standard request-for-proposal templates that can be adapted for specific purposes. The RFP should include a description of the issuing organization and a statement on the scope of the project. Firms investigating verifiers' qualifications might consider conducting an internet search and initially asking RFP respondents for the following information:

■ A description of the verification firm, including its history, ownership, and organizational structure; a description of the performance-related services it offers; and a representative list of verification assignments completed indicating the nature of the investment management firm verified (e.g., "institutional trust division of a regional bank").

■ An explanation of the firm's approach to project management, sampling, and testing.

■ The roles and biographies, including professional designations, of the verifiers who will be assigned to this project.

■ Client references, including contact details, and information about the number of clients added and lost over some period of time (for instance, the last three years).

■ The verification firm's fees.

■ A preliminary project plan setting forth the major tasks and estimated timeframes for completion of the verification.

The reader is also referred to "Suggested Questions to Ask Prospective Verification Firms," a paper published by the former Investment Performance Council (IPC). This resource, which is *not* considered a part of the GIPS standards, is available on the GIPS standards website (www.gipsstandards.org).

Understanding the scope and purpose of verification, as described in Chapter IV.A of the GIPS standards related to verification, is vitally important. Verification, which must be performed by a qualified and independent[49] third party (IV.A.1), assesses whether (a) the firm has complied with all composite construction requirements of the GIPS standards on a firm-wide basis and (b) the firm's policies and procedures are designed to calculate and present performance in compliance with the GIPS standards (IV.A.2). A verification report must opine that the firm meets these two criteria, and a firm must not state that it has been verified unless a verification report has been issued (IV.A.5). A single verification report is issued with respect to the whole firm; verification cannot be carried out on a composite and, accordingly, does not provide assurance about the investment performance of any specific composite. The GIPS standards stress that firms must not state or imply that a particular composite has been "verified." (IV.A.3.) A firm that is verified (as evidenced by a verification report) may additionally choose to have a detailed performance examination conducted on one or more specific composites, and it may state that a composite has been examined *if* a performance examination report has been issued for the specific composite (IV.C).

---

49 The GIPS Guidance Statement on Verifier Independence defines the term *independence* in the context of verification and addresses potential independence issues. It is available on the GIPS standards website.

The minimum initial period for which verification can be performed is one year, or from the firm's inception date through the period-end if that timeframe is less than one year. The GIPS standards recommend that verification cover all periods for which the firm claims compliance (IV.A.4).

We have seen that a firm that does not meet all the requirements of the GIPS standards may not claim compliance; the firm must not represent that it is in compliance with the GIPS standards "except for" certain requirements (I.0.A.6). We have seen, too, that firms must document their policies and procedures for establishing and maintaining compliance with the GIPS standards (I.0.A.5), and they must capture and maintain all data and information necessary to support all items included in a compliant presentation (I.1.A.1). After conducting the required verification procedures summarized below, however, a verifier may conclude that the firm is not in compliance with these or other requirements of the GIPS standards. In such situations, the verifier must provide a statement to the firm explaining why a verification report cannot be issued. The GIPS standards clearly state that a verification report must not be issued when the verifier knows that the firm is not in compliance with the GIPS standards or the records of the firm cannot support a verification (IV.A.8).

In setting forth the scope and purpose of verification, the GIPS standards address the question whether verifiers can rely upon the work of others. As part of the basis for an opinion, a principal verifier may accept the work of another verifier. The principal verifier may also choose to rely on the audit and/or internal control work done by an independent, qualified, reputable third party or by the verification firm itself. However, when deciding whether to rely on the work of another independent third party, the principal verifier must assess the qualifications, competency, objectivity, and reputation of the other party as well as the scope of that party's work, including the time period, and the results of the procedures that were performed. In addition, the principal verifier must document the considerations taken into account in reaching a conclusion about the reliability of the other party's work. The GIPS standards instruct principal verifiers to exercise professional skepticism when making this decision (IV.A.6.)

Because verification is conducted on a firm-wide basis, verifiers must subject the entire firm to testing. (In applying this rule, verifiers may take two factors into account. First, as noted earlier, with due deliberation verifiers may place reliance on work performed by another qualified and reputable independent third party. Second, the GIPS standards allow for verifiers to perform "appropriate alternative control procedures.") However, verifiers may use a sampling methodology to conduct the required firm-wide testing. The minimum factors to be considered when selecting sample portfolios include the number of composites at the firm, the number of portfolios in each composite, and the type of composites. In addition, verifiers must minimally take into account the total assets under management, the internal control structure at the firm, the number of years under examination, the computer applications used to calculate performance and to construct and maintain composites, the method of calculating performance, and whether the firm uses external performance measurement services. The selection of sample accounts for testing is a critical step in the verification process. If the verifier encounters errors or discovers that the firm's record-keeping is deficient, a larger sample or additional verification procedures may be warranted (IV.A.7.)

Chapter IV.A, Scope and Purpose of Verification, has one more requirement: The verification report must state that the verification has been conducted in accordance with the required verification procedures (IV.A.9), to which we now turn. Chapter IV.B, Required Verification Procedures, sets forth the minimum procedures that must be followed.

Under the heading "pre-verification procedures," the GIPS standards describe what is initially required of verifiers. Specifically, verifiers must understand all the requirements and recommendations of the GIPS standards, including any updates, Guidance Statements, interpretations, Questions & Answers (Q&As), and clarifications published by CFA Institute and the GIPS Executive Committee. In addition, verifiers must be knowledgeable about laws and regulations regarding the calculation and presentation of performance, and they must consider any differences between these laws and regulations and the GIPS standards. Equipped with the foregoing expertise, verifiers must learn about the firm, including its corporate structure and how it operates, and they must understand the firm's policies and procedures for complying with all applicable requirements and adopted recommendations of the GIPS standards. It is emphasized that verifiers must not only obtain a copy of the firm's GIPS-related policies and procedures but also ensure that all applicable policies and procedures are properly included and adequately documented. Finally, verifiers must understand the policies, procedures, and methodologies the firm uses to value portfolios and compute investment performance. (IV.B.1.a–e.)

IMPLEMENTATION (15)

Preparing for Verification. The investment management firm undertaking verification should gather the following information. The verifiers may use this information to prepare a fee estimate and a project plan, and they will need it in the course of the review.

- Information about the firm, including its corporate structure and the types of investment product it manages.

- Sample performance presentations and marketing materials.

- *All* of the firm's performance-related policies, such as the firm's definition of discretion, the sources, methods, and review procedures for asset valuations, the time-weighted rate-of-return calculation methodology, the treatment of external cash flows, the computation of composite returns, the correction of errors, etc.

- The complete list of composite descriptions.

- Composite definitions, including benchmarks and the criteria for including portfolios.

- A list of all portfolios under management.

- A list of all the portfolios that have been in each composite during the verification period, the dates they were in the composites, and documentation supporting any changes to the portfolios in the composites.

The verifiers will require the investment management agreements and investment policy statements for selected portfolios and historical portfolio- and composite-level performance data for sampling and testing. The items listed above represent a good start; other information requirements will come to light in the course of the verification.

Having summarized the prerequisites, let us describe some of the verification procedures. Verifiers must perform sufficient procedures to determine that the firm satisfies certain fundamental requirements. They must determine that the firm has been and remains appropriately defined; total firm assets are appropriately calculated and disclosed; the firm's list of composite descriptions is complete; the firm's definition of discretion has been consistently applied over time; and the firm's policies and procedures for ensuring the existence and ownership of client assets are appropriate and have been consistently applied. They must also determine that the firm has defined and maintained composites in compliance with the GIPS standards; the firm's policies and procedures for creating and maintaining composites have been consistently applied; all actual, fee-paying, discretionary portfolios are included in at least one composite; all portfolios are included in their respective composites at all times, and no portfolios that belong in a particular composite have been excluded; and the composite benchmark reflects the investment mandate, objective, or strategy of the composite (IV.B.2.a.i–x.)

Verifiers must review selected portfolios to determine that the treatment of certain input data is consistent with the firm's policies. The GIPS standards specifically identify the classification of portfolio flows (for example, receipts, disbursements, dividends, interest, fees, and taxes) as one such item. Verifiers must perform sufficient procedures to determine that the treatment of the following items is consistent with the firm's policy: income, interest, and dividend accruals and receipts; taxes, tax reclaims, and tax accruals; purchases, sales, and the opening and closing of other positions; and accounting treatment and valuation methodologies for investments, including derivatives (IV.B.2.d.i–v.)

We have already stressed that verification does not provide assurance that specific composite returns are correctly calculated and presented. Nonetheless, testing the firm's performance-related calculations is an important element of the verification process. Verifiers must determine that the firm has calculated and presented performance in accordance with the firm's policies and procedures. In so doing, they must recalculate rates of return for selected portfolios and confirm that a return formula that meets the requirements of the GIPS standards is used. Fees and expenses must be treated in conformity with the GIPS standards and the firm's policies and procedures. Verifiers must also take a sample of composite and benchmark calculations to determine the accuracy of all required numerical data such as risk measures and internal dispersion. In addition, if a custom benchmark or a combination of multiple benchmarks is used, verifiers must take a sample of the firm's benchmark data to determine that the calculation methodology has been correctly applied and the data used are consistent with the benchmark disclosure in the compliant presentation (IV.B.2.e.i–iii.)

In order to validate the discretionary status of portfolios, verifiers must obtain a list of all portfolios, select portfolios for review, and perform sufficient procedures to determine that the selected portfolios are appropriately classified as discretionary or non-discretionary. In making this determination, verifiers will refer to the firm's policies and procedures related to investment discretion and the selected portfolios' investment management agreements and/or investment guidelines (IV.B.2.b.)

Testing the construction and maintenance of composites is central to the verification process. To this end, verifiers must obtain lists of all open portfolios, including both new and existing ones, and of all closed portfolios for all composites for the periods under verification. They must select portfolios from these lists and conduct sufficient procedures to determine that the selected portfolios' investment mandate, objective, or strategy (as appropriately documented, for example, by the investment management agreement, investment guidelines, and/or portfolio summary) is consistent with the composite definition. They must further determine that portfolios are completely and accurately included in composites by tracing selected composites from the investment management agreement and/or investment guidelines to the composites and vice-versa. Verifiers must also determine that portfolios sharing the same investment mandate, objective, or strategy are included in the same composite, and that the timing of portfolios' inclusion in and exclusion from composites is in accordance with the firm's policies and procedures. Finally, verifiers must determine that portfolios' movements from one composite to another are appropriate and consistent with the redefinition of the composite or documented changes to the investment mandate, objective, or strategy (IV.B.2.c.i–vi.) Verifiers must review a sample of composite presentations to ensure that they include all the required information and disclosures. Moreover, the information and disclosures must be consistent with the firm's documented policies and procedures, the firm's records, and the results of the verifier's procedures (IV.B.2.f.)

Finally, under the GIPS standards, verifiers must maintain sufficient information to support all procedures performed in support of the verification report, including all significant judgments made and conclusions reached by the verifier. As part of the supporting documentation, verifiers must obtain a representation letter from the firm confirming that policies and procedures used in establishing and maintaining compliance with the GIPS standards are as described in the firm's documents and have been consistently applied throughout the periods being verified. The representation letter must confirm that the firm complies with the GIPS standards for the periods being verified, and it must also contain any other specific representations made to the verifier during the course of the verification engagement (IV.B.2.g–h.)

We have remarked that verification alone, without a specifically focused performance examination, does not ensure that any particular presentation of composite performance meets the requirements of the GIPS standards or represents investment results fairly, completely, and accurately. However, a verification report issued by a verifier who meets or exceeds the minimum requirements summarized above lends additional credibility to the firm's claim of compliance with the GIPS standards.

7   OTHER ISSUES

We have finished reviewing the 2010 edition of the GIPS standards. In this part of the reading, we will introduce after-tax performance measurement issues and comment on ways to keep informed about future developments affecting the application of the GIPS standards.

7.1 After-Tax Return Calculation Challenges

The GIPS standards do not require compliant firms to present after-tax returns for composites made up of portfolios managed on a tax-aware basis. Many firms engage in investment management on behalf of taxable institutions, individuals, and family offices, however, and they market tax-aware strategies to prospective clients. The interaction of complex regional tax codes with clients' varied circumstances and objectives not only renders tax-aware investing extremely arduous but also complicates performance measurement. In this section, we will discuss major issues surrounding after-tax performance evaluation and present fundamental concepts for after-tax return calculations. Although country-specific tax regulations vary widely, some principles of after-tax performance measurement apply universally.

In writing this section, we consulted the GIPS Guidance Statement for Country-Specific Taxation Issues, among other sources. However, in the interest of fully acknowledging and maintaining a unified, global standard, the GIPS Executive Committee decided to remove this tax-related guidance from the GIPS standards and to transfer responsibility for country-specific provisions and/or guidance to the GIPS country sponsors. Firms that comply with the GIPS standards were encouraged to provide after-tax returns to prospective clients, but effective 1 January 2011, all after-tax performance reporting presented as part of a compliant presentation will be supplemental information and, as such, it will be subject to the requirements and recommendations of the GIPS Guidance Statement on the Use of Supplemental Information.

Let us first consider certain theoretical aspects and practical factors that make valid after-tax performance measurement, analysis, and evaluation problematic.

The timeframe in which estimated tax liabilities are assumed to be realized affects the after-tax rate of return. A pre-liquidation calculation method takes into account only the taxes realized during the measurement period. That is, the before-tax return is reduced by the taxes associated with investment income earned and gains and losses realized during the period. This calculation may understate the tax effect, however, because it does not recognize any tax liability or benefit for unrealized gains and losses embedded in the portfolio's ending value. Although the securities in the portfolio are subject to future price-driven changes in value, and the tax-aware portfolio manager will take advantage of opportunities to offset gains with losses and to defer taxes, the preliquidation method entirely disregards the prospective tax effects that may result from the portfolio's currently unrealized capital gains and losses. In other words, the pre-liquidation method effectively assumes that unrealized capital gains are untaxed.[50]

Another calculation method, the mark-to-liquidation method, assumes that all taxes on unrealized gains are immediately payable as of the end of the measurement period. This method may overstate the tax effect, however, because in addition to disregarding future value changes affecting the actual tax liability, it neglects the time value of money. Portfolios are generally managed on an ongoing basis, and in the normal course of events, taxable gains and losses will be realized as securities are sold, and the proceeds distributed or reinvested, at an indeterminate pace over the planning horizon.

For analytical purposes, we may derive potentially useful information from estimating the timing and amount of future tax assessments over suitably extended periods.[51] Such estimates of the portfolio's "true economic value," however, necessarily rest on debatable assumptions about future returns, among other parameters, and at present no generally accepted guidelines exist for modeling prospective tax outcomes in a manner that ensures the methodological comparability warranted for performance reporting. After-tax returns calculated in accordance with the pre-liquidation and mark-to-liquidation methods are meant to reflect actual before-tax results achieved during the measurement period rather than projected investment experience. Given the known deficiencies of these latter methods, however, the prospective client must interpret after-tax returns with care.

We have seen that the historical cost of securities held in a portfolio is irrelevant to before-tax performance measurement, where assets are valued at fair value and no distinction is made between realized and unrealized gains and losses. The taxable cost basis of portfolio investments is used, however, in determining tax liabilities for the purpose of after-tax return calculations. In addition, different tax regulations and rates may apply depending on the length of the holding period and the types of securities held. Clients' anticipated tax rates—the tax rates that guide the portfolio manager's investment decisions—also vary, contingent on such factors as their level of income and the tax jurisdictions to which they belong. As a practical matter, therefore, substantially more extensive input data must be captured and managed to support reasonable after-tax performance calculations.[52]

Not only is calculating after-tax portfolio returns intricate, selecting or devising appropriate after-tax performance benchmarks is also difficult. Valid before-tax benchmarks have certain properties. Among other attributes, they are unambiguous, investable, measurable, specified or agreed upon in advance, and consistent with the investment strategy or style of the portfolio or composite. After-tax benchmarks should have all the desirable properties of suitable before-tax benchmarks, and one more: They should additionally reflect the client's tax status.

---

50 See Poterba (1999).

51 Stein (1998) proposes a method for estimating a "full cost equivalent" portfolio value. Horan, Lawton, and Johnson (2008) define an after-tax performance measurement methodology that discounts future after-tax cash flows at an appropriate tax-adjusted and risk-adjusted discount rate.

52 From an implementation perspective, the input data requirements and after-tax return calculation methodology have significant implications for the development or selection of portfolio accounting and performance measurement systems. See Rogers and Price (2002) and Simpson (2003).

Financial services firms publish capital market indices representing a wide range of investment strategies and styles. Some providers calculate index returns net of withholding taxes on dividends, but at this writing none have published index returns fully reflecting imputed effects of taxation. Conceptually, given information on the constituent securities or the price and income return components, investment management firms could adjust reported before-tax index results to construct an after-tax benchmark. Adjusting standard before-tax indices is easier said than done, however. The adjustment methodology would have to incorporate the provider's rules for constructing and rebalancing the original index (e.g., whether it is equal weighted, capitalization weighted, or float weighted), the taxable turnover of securities held in the index, and issuers' corporate actions such as stock splits, as well as security-specific dividend and interest payments and price changes. A firm might formulate some simplifying assumptions to lessen the data requirements and reduce the computational intensity introduced by these factors.[53]

Alternatives to modifying standard before-tax indices include using mutual funds or exchange-traded funds as benchmarks, or developing customized shadow portfolios. Mutual funds and exchange-traded funds benchmarked to capital market indices are imperfect benchmarks because they are subject to fees, and their returns may deviate from those of the indices they emulate. The tax liabilities of mutual funds are affected by the portfolio manager's security transactions and by the collective deposit and redemption activities of shareholders. Exchange-traded funds likewise have turnover, but they do not incur taxes as a result of other investors' actions, so they may be better suited as benchmarks for after-tax performance evaluation.

Nonetheless, the investment management firm seeking a valid after-tax benchmark must address the fact that any one particular client's tax experience depends not only on the rates at which the investment income and capital gains are taxed but also the cost of the securities and the sequence of cash flows in the portfolio. The firm that uses custom security-based benchmarks for performance evaluation is well positioned to simulate the tax impact of external cash flows on benchmark results. Firms that use standard indices for before-tax performance evaluation can simulate the effect of client-specific cash flows on estimated after-tax benchmark returns by assuming that the benchmark pays proportionately the same capital gains taxes for withdrawals as the actual portfolio and invests contributions at the cost basis of the index at the time the contribution is made.[54] Alternately, firms can use mutual funds or exchange-traded funds to build shadow portfolios in which simulated purchases and sales are triggered by client-initiated cash flows. These approaches, however, are also data and computation intensive. Moreover, a customized shadow portfolio that works well for a single portfolio is unlikely to be useful for a composite made up of multiple client portfolios. Constructing valid benchmarks remains one of the greatest challenges in after-tax performance evaluation.

We have observed that performance measurement attempts to quantify the value added by a portfolio manager's investment actions. Because managers should not be held accountable for factors beyond their control, the GIPS standards exclude non-discretionary portfolios from composites and prescribe time-weighted returns to eliminate the impact of external cash flows. Portfolio managers may be compelled to liquidate securities to meet client-directed withdrawals, however, and taxes may be realized as a result of the non-discretionary asset sales. Firms may wish to make an adjustment to remove the tax effect of non-discretionary capital gains. In effect, the adjustment adds back the hypothetical realized taxes that were not incurred at

---

53 Stein, Langstraat, and Narasimhan (1999) suggest a method to approximate after-tax benchmark returns.
54 Price (2001) presents three increasingly accurate levels of approximation in constructing after-tax benchmarks from pretax indices and describes the "shadow portfolio" approach to adjusting indices for client-specific cash flows.

the manager's discretion.[55] To avoid creating a perverse incentive for the portfolio manager to maximize the adjustment credit by selecting highly appreciated assets for sale, the adjustment term should reflect the capital gains tax that would be sustained if all the securities in the portfolio were proportionately liquidated.

There is another situation in which client actions affect after-tax returns (in this case, favorably). The client may instruct a portfolio manager to realize tax losses to offset gains realized either within the portfolio or in other assets held outside the portfolio. For the client, such "tax loss harvesting" reduces his tax liability on net capital gains. This practice is entirely consistent with the fundamental wealth management principle that investors should consider all their assets when making investment decisions. For the portfolio manager who has realized gains or who handles only a portion of the client's assets, however, the non-discretionary directive to harvest tax losses improves reported after-tax results. Firms should disclose the percentage benefit of tax-loss harvesting for the composite if realized losses are greater than realized gains during the period. This suggestion implicitly assumes that tax benefits not used within the portfolio in the measurement period can be used outside the portfolio or in the future. The wealth benefit derived from tax-loss harvesting may be computed by applying the appropriate capital gains tax rate to the net losses realized in the period; the percentage benefit may be calculated by dividing the money benefit by the simple average assets in the portfolio.

With this, we conclude the introduction to after-tax return calculations for individual portfolios. It is evident even from this abbreviated, non-mathematical presentation that after-tax performance measurement requires considerable expertise as well as extensive data and powerful technological resources, particularly when advancing from the portfolio to the composite level. After-tax performance measurement and analysis is both a science and an art: "The 'scientific' aspects are manifested in the discrete requirements and details, while the 'artisanal' aspects recognize that cash flows, substantial unrealized capital gains, and composite definitions can have a significant impact on after-tax results." Supplemental information, including tax efficiency measures not presented here, can materially assist prospective clients in evaluating a firm's after-tax performance record.

7.2 Keeping Current with the GIPS Standards

At the beginning of this reading, we surveyed the evolution of performance presentation standards, marking as particularly noteworthy events the publication of Peter Dietz's work in 1966 and the report of the Financial Analysts Federation's Committee for Performance Presentation Standards in 1987. The Global Investment Performance Standards are now fairly comprehensive and well-defined, the integrated product of thoughtful contributions from many academicians and practitioners committed to the ethical ideals of fair representation and full disclosure in reporting investment results. The revised GIPS standards issued in 2010 represent a significant advance in the globalization of performance presentation norms.

Nonetheless, the GIPS standards will continue to evolve over time to address additional aspects of performance presentation. Firms that claim compliance must meet all applicable requirements, including not only the provisions of the GIPS standards but also any updated information, Guidance Statements, interpretations, Questions & Answers (Q&As), and clarifications published by CFA Institute and the GIPS Executive Committee which are available on the GIPS standards website. Practitioners should visit the GIPS standards website frequently in order to stay informed about existing

---

55 Price (1996) presents the logic and implications of this adjustment factor.

and new requirements and recommended best practices. CFA Institute and other organizations also offer publications and conduct conferences and workshops designed to help practitioners implement and maintain compliance with the GIPS standards.

SUMMARY

The Global Investment Performance Standards meet the need for globally accepted standards for investment management firms in calculating and presenting their results to clients and potential clients. This reading has made the following points:

- The GIPS standards are ethical standards that promote fair representation and full disclosure of an investment firm's performance history.

- The GIPS standards were created and funded by CFA Institute (formerly known as the Association for Investment Management and Research, or AIMR) with the participation of many experts and local sponsorship from numerous industry groups. The GIPS Executive Committee is the governance body responsible for developing and interpreting the GIPS standards.

- The GIPS standards include provisions for fundamentals of compliance, input data, calculation methodology, composite construction, disclosure, presentation and reporting, real estate, private equity, and wrap fee/Separately Managed Account (SMA) along with valuation principles, advertising guidelines, and verification requirements.

- Only investment management firms can claim compliance with the GIPS standards. The GIPS standards must be applied on a firm-wide basis, and a firm may claim compliance only when it has satisfied all the requirements of the GIPS standards.

- Accrual accounting must be used for all assets that accrue interest income, and for periods beginning on or after 1 January 2005, trade-date accounting must be used. For periods beginning on or after 1 January 2011, all portfolios must be valued in accordance with the definition of fair value and the GIPS Valuation Principles.

- Firms must calculate total returns that include returns from cash and cash equivalents and are reduced by actual trading expenses. For periods beginning on or after 1 January 2005, if a firm uses approximated rates of return, it must adjust them for daily-weighted external cash flows. For periods beginning on or after 1 January 2010, firms must value portfolios on the date of all large external cash flows.

- Large external cash flows can substantially distort the accuracy of estimated returns when markets are volatile. The GIPS standards require firms to document composite-specific policies for the treatment of external cash flows and to adhere to those policies consistently.

- Composites must be defined according to their investment mandate, objective, or strategy.

- All actual, fee-paying, discretionary portfolios must be included in at least one composite. Portfolios are discretionary if client-imposed restrictions do not prevent the firm from implementing the intended investment strategy.

- Composite returns must be calculated by asset-weighting the individual portfolio returns using beginning-of-period values or a method that reflects both beginning-of-period values and external cash flows.

- Firms must include new portfolios in composites on a timely and consistent basis. Terminated portfolios must be included in the historical performance of the appropriate composite up to the last full measurement period they were under management. A firm cannot switch portfolios from one composite to another unless documented changes to a portfolio's investment mandate, objective, or strategy or the redefinition of a composite makes it appropriate.

- For periods beginning on or after 1 January 2010, the returns of a single asset class (e.g., equities) carved out of a multiple asset class portfolio (e.g., a balanced account invested in equity and fixed-income securities) are not permitted to be included in single asset class composite returns unless the carved-out segment is actually managed separately with its own cash balance.

- The GIPS standards include detailed disclosure requirements related to the firm, performance calculations, benchmarks, fees, composites, composite performance presentations, and other items. Additional disclosures are also recommended.

- The GIPS provisions for presentation and reporting require that at least five years of compliant performance must initially be shown (or from inception if the firm or composite has been existence for a shorter period). The compliant performance record must then be extended each year until at least 10 years of results are presented.

- The GIPS standards specify required items to be contained in composite performance presentations, including composite and benchmark total returns for each annual period presented, the number of portfolios in the composite (if more than five) at annual period end, the amount of assets in the composite at annual period end, either the percentage of the firm's total assets represented by the composite or the amount of total firm assets at the end of each annual period, a measure of dispersion of individual portfolio returns within the composite and, for periods ending on or after 1 January 2011, the three-year annualized ex-post standard deviation of composite and benchmark returns. Other items may be required in certain cases, and additional items are recommended.

- Acceptable measures of internal dispersion include, but are not limited to, high/low, range, and standard deviation.

- Performance of a past firm or affiliation must be linked to or used to represent the historical performance of a new or acquiring firm if all the following conditions are met on a composite specific basis: substantially all the investment decision makers are employed by the new or acquiring firm; the decision-making process remains substantially intact and independent within the new or acquiring firm; and the new or acquiring firm has records that document and support the performance.

- If a firm uses a custom benchmark or a combination of multiple benchmarks, it must disclose the benchmark components, weights, and rebalancing process. The frequency of rebalancing can affect the reported benchmark return.

- For periods beginning on or after 1 January 2008, real estate investments must be valued at least quarterly. For periods beginning on or after 1 January 2011, real estate investments must be valued in accordance with the definition of fair value and the GIPS Valuation Principles. Real estate investments must be valued by an external professionally designated, certified or licensed commercial property valuer or appraiser at least once every 36 months for periods prior to 1 January 2012 and, unless client agreements stipulate otherwise, at least once every 12 months thereafter.

- In addition to total return for real estate, firms must calculate the time-weighted returns of the income and capital return components. For closed-end real estate fund composites, the GIPS standards also require firms to present the net-of-fees since-inception internal rate of return (SI-IRR) of the composite through each annual period-end.

- For periods ending on or after 1 January 2011, private equity investments must be valued in accordance with the definition of fair value and the GIPS Valuation Principles, and the annualized SI-IRR must be calculated using daily cash flows.

- Performance presentations for private equity composites must include the gross-of-fees and net-of-fees SI-IRR of the composite through the end of each annual period. For closed-end real estate and private equity composites, the composite's cumulative committed capital, since-inception paid-in capital, and since-inception distributions must be presented as of each annual period end. In addition, firms must present as of each annual period end the investment multiple (the ratio of total value to since-inception paid-in capital, or TVPI), the realization multiple (the ratio of since-inception distributions to since-inception paid-in capital, or DPI), the PIC multiple (the ratio of since-inception paid-in capital to cumulative committed capital), and the unrealized multiple (the ratio of residual value to since-inception paid-in capital, or RVPI).

- When firms present performance to prospective wrap fee/SMA clients, they must present the performance net of the entire wrap fee.

- Verification is a process by which an independent verifier assesses whether (1) the firm has complied with all the composite construction requirements of the GIPS standards on a firm-wide basis and (2) the firm's policies and procedures are designed to calculate and present performance in compliance with the GIPS standards. A single verification report is issued for the entire firm; verification cannot be carried out for an individual composite. Firms that have been verified may choose to have a further in-depth examination of a specific composite presentation.

- The GIPS Advertising Guidelines allow a firm to claim compliance with the GIPS standards in an advertisement without presenting the compliant presentation. All advertisements stating a claim of compliance following the GIPS Advertising Guidelines must use the prescribed wording for the GIPS compliance statement for advertisements. Advertisements that state this claim of compliance and show performance results must also present in the advertisement additional required information taken or derived from a compliant performance presentation.

- Effective 1 January 2011, after-tax performance reporting, if presented as part of a compliant presentation, will be considered supplemental information and subject to the requirements and recommendations of the GIPS Guidance Statement on the Use of Supplemental Information.

APPENDIX: GIPS GLOSSARY

ACCRUAL ACCOUNTING The recording of financial transactions as they come into existence rather than when they are paid or settled.

ADMINISTRATIVE FEE All fees other than TRADING EXPENSES and the INVESTMENT MANAGEMENT FEE. ADMINISTRATIVE FEES include CUSTODY FEES, accounting fees, auditing fees, consulting fees, legal fees, performance measurement fees, and other related fees. See "BUNDLED FEES."

BENCHMARK DESCRIPTION General information regarding the investments, structure, and/or characteristics of the BENCHMARK. The description MUST include the key features of the BENCHMARK, or the name of the BENCHMARK for a readily recognized index or other point of reference.

BUNDLED FEE A fee that combines multiple fees into one total or "bundled" fee. BUNDLED FEES can include any combination of INVESTMENT MANAGEMENT FEES, TRADING EXPENSES, CUSTODY FEES, and/or ADMINISTRATIVE FEES. Two examples of BUNDLED FEES are WRAP FEES and ALL-IN FEES.

CAPITAL RETURN The change in value of the REAL ESTATE investments and cash and/or cash equivalent assets held throughout the measurement period, adjusted for all capital expenditures (subtracted) and net proceeds from sales (added). The CAPITAL RETURN is computed as a percentage of the CAPITAL EMPLOYED. Also known as "capital appreciation return" or "appreciation return."

CARRIED INTEREST The profits that GENERAL PARTNERS are allocated from the profits on the investments made by the investment vehicle. Also known as "carry" or "promote."

CARVE-OUT A portion of a PORTFOLIO that is by itself representative of a distinct investment strategy. It is used to create a track record for a narrower mandate from a multiple-strategy PORTFOLIO managed to a broader mandate. For periods beginning on or after 1 January 2010, a CARVE-OUT MUST be managed separately with its own cash balance.

CLOSED-END FUNDS A type of investment vehicle where the number of investors, total COMMITTED CAPITAL, and life are fixed and not open for subscriptions and/or redemptions. CLOSED-END FUNDS have a capital call (drawdown) process in place that is controlled by the GENERAL PARTNER.

COMMITTED CAPITAL Pledges of capital to an investment vehicle by investors (LIMITED PARTNERS and the GENERAL PARTNER) or by the FIRM. Committed capital is typically not drawn down at once but drawn down over a period of time. Also known as "commitments."

COMPOSITE An aggregation of one or more PORTFOLIOS managed according to a similar investment mandate, objective, or strategy.

(continued)

COMPOSITE CREATION DATE	The date when the FIRM first groups one or more PORTFOLIOS to create a COMPOSITE. The COMPOSITE CREATION DATE is not necessarily the same as the COMPOSITE INCEPTION DATE.
COMPOSITE DEFINITION	Detailed criteria that determine the assignment of PORTFOLIOS to COMPOSITES. Criteria may include investment mandate, style or strategy, asset class, the use of derivatives, leverage and/or hedging, targeted risk metrics, investment constraints or restrictions, and/or PORTFOLIO type (e.g., segregated or pooled, taxable versus tax exempt).
COMPOSITE DESCRIPTION	General information regarding the investment mandate, objective, or strategy of the COMPOSITE. The COMPOSITE DESCRIPTION may be more abbreviated than the COMPOSITE DEFINITION but MUST include all key features of the COMPOSITE and MUST include enough information to allow a PROSPECTIVE CLIENT to understand the key characteristics of the COMPOSITE's investment mandate, objective, or strategy. (See the Sample List of Composite Descriptions in Appendix C to the Global Investment Performance Standards.)
CUSTODY FEE	The fees payable to the custodian for the safe-keeping of PORTFOLIO assets. CUSTODY FEES are considered to be ADMINISTRATIVE FEES and typically contain an asset-based portion and a transaction-based portion. The CUSTODY FEE may also include charges for additional services, including accounting, securities lending, and/or performance measurement. Custodial fees that are charged per transaction SHOULD be included in the CUSTODY FEE and not included as part of TRADING EXPENSES.
DISTINCT BUSINESS ENTITY	A unit, division, department, or office that is organizationally and functionally segregated from other units, divisions, departments, or offices and that retains discretion over the assets it manages and that should have autonomy over the investment decision-making process. Possible criteria that can be used to determine this include: ■ being a legal entity, ■ having a distinct market or client type (e.g., institutional, retail, private client, etc.), and ■ using a separate and distinct investment process.
DISTRIBUTION	Cash or stock distributed to LIMITED PARTNERS (or investors) from an investment vehicle. DISTRIBUTIONS are typically at the discretion of the GENERAL PARTNER (or the FIRM). DISTRIBUTIONS include both recallable and non-recallable DISTRIBUTIONS.
DPI	SINCE INCEPTION DISTRIBUTIONS divided by SINCE INCEPTION PAID-IN CAPITAL. See "REALIZATION MULTIPLE."
EVERGREEN FUND	An OPEN-END FUND that allows for on-going subscriptions and/or redemptions by investors.
EXTERNAL CASH FLOW	Capital (cash or investments) that enters or exits a PORTFOLIO.

FAIR VALUE	The amount at which an investment could be exchanged in a current arm's length transaction between willing parties in which the parties each act knowledgeably and prudently. The valuation MUST be determined using the objective, observable, unadjusted quoted market price for an identical investment in an active market on the measurement date, if available. In the absence of an objective, observable, unadjusted quoted market price for an identical investment in an active market on the measurement date, the valuation MUST represent the FIRM's best estimate of the MARKET VALUE. FAIR VALUE must include ACCRUED INCOME.
FEE SCHEDULE	The FIRM's current schedule of INVESTMENT MANAGEMENT FEES or BUNDLED FEES relevant to the particular COMPLIANT PRESENTATION.
FINAL LIQUIDATION DATE	The date when the last PORTFOLIO in a COMPOSITE is fully distributed.
FIRM	The entity defined for compliance with the GIPS standards. See "DISTINCT BUSINESS ENTITY."
FUND OF FUNDS	An investment vehicle that invests in underlying investment vehicles. PRIVATE EQUITY FUNDS OF FUNDS predominately invest in CLOSED-END FUNDS and may make opportunistic DIRECT INVESTMENTS.
GENERAL PARTNER	A class of partner in a LIMITED PARTNERSHIP. The GENERAL PARTNER retains liability for the actions of the LIMITED PARTNERSHIP. The GENERAL PARTNER is typically the fund manager, and the LIMITED PARTNERS (LPs) are the other investors in the LIMITED PARTNERSHIP. The GENERAL PARTNER earns an INVESTMENT MANAGEMENT FEE that typically includes a percentage of the LIMITED PARTNERSHIP's profits. See "CARRIED INTEREST."
GROSS-OF-FEES RETURN	The return on investments reduced by any TRADING EXPENSES incurred during the period; in real estate and private equity, the return on investments reduced by any TRANSACTION EXPENSES incurred during the period.
INCOME RETURN	The investment income earned on all investments (including cash and cash equivalents) during the measurement period net of all non-recoverable expenditure, interest expense on debt, and property taxes. The INCOME RETURN is computed as a percentage of the CAPITAL EMPLOYED.
INTERNAL DISPERSION	A measure of the spread of the annual returns of individual PORTFOLIOS within a COMPOSITE. Measures may include, but are not limited to, high/low, range, or STANDARD DEVIATION (asset weighted or equal weighted) of PORTFOLIO returns.
INVESTMENT MANAGEMENT FEE	A fee payable to the FIRM for the management of a PORTFOLIO. INVESTMENT MANAGEMENT FEES are typically asset based (percentage of assets), performance based (see "PERFORMANCE-BASED FEE"), or a combination of the two but may take different forms as well. INVESTMENT MANAGEMENT FEES also include CARRIED INTEREST.

(continued)

INVESTMENT MULTIPLE	TOTAL VALUE divided by SINCE INCEPTION PAID-IN CAPITAL.
LARGE CASH FLOW	The level at which the FIRM determines that an EXTERNAL CASH FLOW may distort performance if the PORTFOLIO is not valued. FIRMS MUST define the amount in terms of the value of cash/asset flow or in terms of a percentage of the PORTFOLIO assets or the COMPOSITE assets.
LIMITED PARTNER	An investor in a LIMITED PARTNERSHIP. The GENERAL PARTNER is liable for the actions of the LIMITED PARTNERSHIP, and the LIMITED PARTNERS are generally protected from legal actions and any losses beyond their COMMITTED CAPITAL.
LIMITED PARTNERSHIP	The legal structure used by most PRIVATE EQUITY and REAL ESTATE CLOSED-END FUNDS. LIMITED PARTNERSHIPS are usually fixed life investment vehicles. The GENERAL PARTNER manages the LIMITED PARTNERSHIP pursuant to the partnership agreement.
LINK	1 Mathematical linking: The method by which sub-period returns are geometrically combined to calculate the period return using the following formula: $$\text{Period return} = [(1 + R_1) \times (1 + R_2) \ldots (1 + R_n)] - 1$$ Where $R_1, R_2 \ldots R_n$ are the sub-period returns sub-period 1 through n, respectively.
	2 Presentational linking: To be visually connected or otherwise associated with a COMPLIANT PRESENTATION (e.g., two pieces of information are LINKED by placing them next to each other.
MARKET VALUE	The price at which investors can buy or sell an investment at a given time multiplied by the quantity held plus any accrued income.
MUST	A provision, task, or action that is mandatory or REQUIRED to be followed or performed. See "REQUIRE/REQUIREMENT."
OPEN-END FUND	A type of investment vehicle where the number of investors and the total COMMITTED CAPITAL is not fixed and is open for subscriptions and/or redemptions. See "EVERGREEN FUND."
PAID-IN CAPITAL	Capital inflows to an investment vehicle. COMMITTED CAPITAL is typically drawn down from LIMITED PARTNERS (or investors) over a period of time through a series of capital calls, which are at the discretion of the GENERAL PARTNER or FIRM. PAID-IN CAPITAL is equal to the amount of COMMITTED CAPITAL that has been drawn down SINCE INCEPTION. PAID-IN CAPITAL includes DISTRIBUTIONS that are subsequently recalled by the GENERAL PARTNER or FIRM and reinvested into the investment vehicle.
PIC MULTIPLE	SINCE INCEPTION PAID-IN CAPITAL divided by cumulative COMMITTED CAPITAL.
PORTFOLIO	An individually managed group of investments. A PORTFOLIO may be an account or pooled investment vehicle.

PRIMARY FUND VEHICLE	An investment vehicle that makes DIRECT INVESTMENTS rather than investing in other investment vehicles.
PRIVATE EQUITY	Investment strategies include, but are not limited to, venture capital, leveraged buyouts, consolidations, mezzanine and distressed debt investments, and a variety of hybrids, such as venture leasing and venture factoring.
PROFESSIONALLY DESIGNATED, CERTIFIED, OR LICENSED COMMERCIAL PROPERTY VALUER/APPRAISER	In Europe, Canada, and parts of Southeast Asia, the predominant professional designation is that of the Royal Institution of Chartered Surveyors (RICS). In the United States, the professional designation is Member [of the] Appraisal Institute (MAI). In addition, each state regulates REAL ESTATE appraisers and registers, licenses, or certifies them based on their experience and test results.
PROSPECTIVE CLIENT	Any person or entity that has expressed interest in one of the FIRM'S COMPOSITE strategies and qualifies to invest in the COMPOSITE. Existing clients may also qualify as PROSPECTIVE CLIENTS for any strategy that is different from their current investment strategy. Investment consultants and other third parties are included as PROSPECTIVE CLIENTS if they represent investors that qualify as PROSPECTIVE CLIENTS.
PUBLIC MARKET EQUIVALENT	The performance of a public market index expressed in terms of an internal rate of return (IRR), using the same cash flows and timing as those of the COMPOSITE over the same time period. A PME can be used as a BENCHMARK by comparing the IRR of a PRIVATE EQUITY COMPOSITE with the PME of a public market index.
REALIZATION MULTIPLE	SINCE INCEPTION DISTRIBUTIONS divided by SINCE INCEPTION PAID-IN CAPITAL.
RECOMMEND/RECOMMENDATION	A suggested provision, task, or action that should be followed or performed. A RECOMMENDATION is considered to be best practice but is not a REQUIREMENT. See "SHOULD."
REQUIRE/REQUIREMENT	A provision, task, or action that must be followed or performed. See "MUST."
RESIDUAL VALUE	The remaining equity that LIMITED PARTNERS (or investors) have in an investment vehicle at the end of the performance reporting period.
RVPI	RESIDUAL VALUE divided by SINCE INCEPTION PAID-IN CAPITAL. See "UNREALIZED MULTIPLE."
SECONDARY FUND VEHICLE	An investment vehicle that buys interests in existing investment vehicles.
SETTLEMENT DATE ACCOUNTING	Recognizing the asset or liability on the date when the exchange of cash and investments is completed.
SHOULD	A provision, task, or action that is RECOMMENDED to be followed or performed and is considered to be best practice, but is not REQUIRED. (See "RECOMMEND/RECOMMENDATION."

(continued)

SINCE INCEPTION INTERNAL RATE OF RETURN (SI-IRR)	The internal rate of return (IRR) is the implied discount rate or effective compounded rate of return that equates the present value of cash outflows with the present value of cash inflows. The SI-IRR is a special case of the IRR that equates the present value of all cash flows (capital calls and DISTRIBUTIONS) with the period end value. The SI-IRR is always annualized except when the reporting period is less than one year, in which case the SI-IRR is not annualized.
SUPPLEMENTAL INFORMATION	Any performance-related information included as part of a COMPLIANT PRESENTATION that supplements or enhances the REQUIRED and/or RECOMMENDED provisions of the GIPS standards.
TEMPORARY NEW ACCOUNT	An account for temporarily holding client-directed EXTERNAL CASH FLOWS until they are invested according to the COMPOSITE strategy or disbursed. FIRMS can use a TEMPORARY NEW ACCOUNT to remove the effect of a SIGNIFICANT CASH FLOW on a PORTFOLIO. When a SIGNIFICANT CASH FLOW occurs in a PORTFOLIO, the FIRM may direct the EXTERNAL CASH FLOW to a TEMPORARY NEW ACCOUNT according to the COMPOSITE'S SIGNIFICANT CASH FLOW policy.
TIME-WEIGHTED RATE OF RETURN	A method of calculating period-by-period returns that negates the effects of EXTERNAL CASH FLOWS.
TOTAL FIRM ASSETS	All discretionary and non-discretionary assets for which a FIRM has investment management responsibility. TOTAL FIRM ASSETS includes assets assigned to a SUB-ADVISOR provided the FIRM has discretion over the selection of the SUB-ADVISOR.
TOTAL VALUE	RESIDUAL VALUE plus DISTRIBUTIONS.
TRADE DATE ACCOUNTING	Recognizing the asset or liability on the date of the purchase or sale and not on the settlement date. Recognizing the asset or liability within three days of the date the transaction is entered into (trade date, T + 1, T + 2, or T + 3) satisfies the TRADE DATE ACCOUNTING REQUIREMENT for purposes of the GIPS standards. See "SETTLEMENT DATE ACCOUNTING."
TRADING EXPENSES	The actual costs of buying or selling investments. These costs typically take the form of brokerage commissions, exchange fees and/or taxes, and/or bid–offer spreads from either internal or external brokers. Custodial fees charged per transaction should be considered CUSTODY FEES and not TRADING EXPENSES.
TRANSACTION EXPENSES	All actual legal, financial, advisory, and investment banking fees related to buying, selling, restructuring, and/or recapitalizing PORTFOLIO investments as well as TRADING EXPENSES, if any.
TVPI	TOTAL VALUE divided by SINCE INCEPTION PAID-IN CAPITAL. See "INVESTMENT MULTIPLE."
UNREALIZED MULTIPLE	RESIDUAL VALUE divided by SINCE INCEPTION PAID-IN CAPITAL.

VERIFICATION	A process by which an independent verifier assesses whether 1) the FIRM has complied with all the COMPOSITE construction REQUIREMENTS of the GIPS standards on a FIRM-wide basis and 2) the FIRM's policies and procedures are designed to calculate and present performance in compliance with the GIPS standards.
VERIFICATION REPORT	A VERIFICATION REPORT is issued after a VERIFICATION has been performed and opines that the FIRM has complied with all the COMPOSITE construction REQUIREMENTS of the GIPS standards on a FIRM-wide basis and that the FIRM's policies and procedures are designed to calculate and present performance in compliance with the GIPS standards.
VINTAGE YEAR	Two methods used to determine VINTAGE YEAR are:

1   The year of the investment vehicle's first drawdown or capital call from its investors; or

2   The year when the first COMMITTED CAPITAL from outside investors is closed and legally binding.

REFERENCES

Committee for Performance Presentation Standards (CPPS). 1987. "A Report on Setting Performance Presentation Standards." *Financial Analysts Journal*, vol. 43, no. 5:8.

Dietz, Peter. 1966. *Pension Funds: Measuring Investment Performance*. New York: The Free Press.

Gaudette, Stephen C., and Philip Lawton. 2007. "Equity Portfolio Characteristics in Performance Analysis." CFA Institute.

Harris, Larry. 2003. *Trading and Exchanges: Market Microstructure for Practitioners*. Oxford University Press.

Horan, Stephen M., Philip Lawton, and Robert R. Johnson. 2008. "After-Tax Performance Measurement." *Journal of Wealth Management*, vol. 11, no. 1:69–83.

Poterba, James. 1999. "Unrealized Capital Gains and the Measurement of After-Tax Portfolio Performance." *Journal of Private Portfolio Management*, vol. 1, no. 4.

Price, Lee. 1996. "Calculation and Reporting of After-Tax Performance." *Journal of Performance Measurement*, vol. 1, no. 2.

Price, Lee. 2001. "Taxable Benchmarks: The Complexity Increases." *AIMR Conference Proceedings: Investment Counseling for Private Clients III*. No. 4.

Rogers, Douglas, and Lee Price. 2002. "Challenges with Developing Portfolio Accounting Software for After-Tax Reporting." *Journal of Performance Measurement*, vol. 6 (Technology Supplement.).

Shilling, James. 2002. *Real Estate*, 13th edition. Mason, OH: South-Western.

Simpson, John. 2003. "Searching for a System to Meet Your After-Tax Performance Reporting Needs." *Journal of Performance Measurement*, vol. 7 (Performance Presentation Standards Supplement).

Stein, David. 1998. "Measuring and Evaluating Portfolio Performance After Taxes." *Journal of Portfolio Management*, vol. 24, no. 2.

Stein, David, Brian Langstraat, and Premkumar Narasimhan. 1999. "Reporting After-Tax Returns: A Pragmatic Approach." *Journal of Private Portfolio Management*. Spring.

PRACTICE PROBLEMS

1   Company C manages money for both retail and institutional clients. There are two autonomous groups within Company C: "Company C Institutional Investment Management," which manages institutional assets, and "Company C Retail Investors," which manages retail assets. How should Company C define itself as a firm to comply with the GIPS standards?

2   Firm A is a multinational investment firm, with offices around the world including Japan, Australia, the United Kingdom, and the United States. Although all of its offices are part of the global parent, each office is registered with the appropriate national regulatory authority and each is held out to clients and potential clients as a distinct business entity. Firm A (US) claims compliance with the GIPS standards. What should the definition of the firm disclosure be?

3   The GIPS standards do **not** require firms to value portfolios in accordance with:

    A   the definition of fair value.

    B   composite-specific valuation policies.

    C   generally accepted principles of financial accounting.

4   For periods beginning on or after 1 January 2011, firms must **not** value portfolios:

    A   when objective, observable market prices are unavailable.

    B   more frequently than required by the composite-specific valuation policy.

    C   as of the last business day of the month unless it is the calendar month-end.

5   Firm A claims compliance with the GIPS standards. It maintains hard copies of the records supporting compliance for three years and discards all records older than three years in an effort to save office space. The performance reported on all its composite presentations shows five years of history. Is the firm in compliance with the GIPS standards?

6   Use the information in the following table to answer this question (amounts in €):

Date	Market Value	External Cash Flow	Market Value Post Cash Flow
31 December 1997	200,000		
31 January 1998	208,000		
16 February 1998	217,000	+40,000	257,000
28 February 1998	263,000		
22 March 1998	270,000	−30,000	240,000
31 March 1998	245,000		

Calculate the rate of return for this portfolio for January, February, March, and the first quarter of 1998 using revaluing for large cash flows methodology (assume "large" is defined as greater than 5%).

7   A European equity composite contains three portfolios. For convenience, the cash flow weighting factors are presented below.

	Cash Flow Weighting Factor	Portfolio (€ millions)		
		A	B	C
Fair value as of 31 July		74.9	127.6	110.4
External cash flows:				
8 August	0.742		−15	
12 August	0.613	7.5		
19 August	0.387		−5	15
Fair value as of 31 August		85.3	109.8	128.4

A Calculate the returns of Portfolio A, Portfolio B, and Portfolio C for the month of August using the Modified Dietz formula.

B Calculate the August composite return by asset-weighting the individual portfolio returns using beginning-of-period values.

C Calculate the August composite return by asset-weighting the individual portfolio returns using a method that reflects both beginning-of-period values and external cash flows.

8 Convenable Capital Management manages an equity portfolio for the Flender Company. Cash held in the portfolio is invested by the Flender's existing custodial bank. Must Convenable include cash and cash equivalents in the portfolio return calculations?

A Yes.

B No; the cash is not invested by Convenable.

C No; Convenable does not have discretion over the selection of the custodian.

9 Under the GIPS standards, the *most* accurate statement is that actual direct trading expenses do **not** include:

A spreads from internal brokers.

B brokerage commissions.

C custody fees charged per transaction.

10 Can a firm include a single portfolio in more than one of the firm's composites?

11 Barry Smith Investment Management (Barry Smith) specializes in balanced account management for midsize pension plans. On 12 March 2006, a contribution of $2,265,000 is made to Dennett Electronics' Pension Plan, which is included in Barry Smith's Balanced Tax-Exempt Composite. This is the only external cash flow for March. Barry Smith invests the contribution on 13 March. The pension plan's portfolio had a fair value of $16,575,000 at the beginning of March. For the purpose of calculating portfolio performance, how should Barry Smith handle the external cash flow? Assume that Barry Smith has adopted a large cash flow policy as of 1 January 2006, all external cash flows are assumed to take place at the end of day, and the 12 March 2006 cash flow meets the definition of "large".

12 In March 2007, Smith & Jones Asset Management, a GIPS-compliant firm, introduced a new technical analysis model that management believed would be a powerful tool in tactical asset allocation. After extensive back-testing, Smith & Jones began to use the model to manage actual "live" portfolios in June 2007, and managers constructed a composite composed of actual, fee-paying, discretionary portfolios managed in accordance with the model. In 2010, after three very successful years of managing client funds in this way, management decided that because the actual performance of live portfolios validated the performance of the model, it should present the simulated performance of the model through the back-testing period to prospective clients. Smith & Jones proceeded to link the back-tested returns to the actual performance of the composite and presents 3-, 5- and 10-year performance as a continuous record to prospects. Does this practice comply with the GIPS standards?

13 A charitable foundation transfers securities in kind to Taurus Asset Management Ltd. to fund a new private equity portfolio. Taurus estimates that, after liquidating the transferred securities, it will take five months to invest the foundation's assets in privately held companies. Which statement *best* describes a requirement of the GIPS standards? Taurus must include the foundation's portfolio in the appropriate private equity composite:

A on a timely and consistent basis.

B when the assets are substantially invested.

C as of the beginning of the next full measurement period.

14 Ord Capital Management, an investment management firm that claims to comply with the GIPS standards, manages a global equity portfolio for a pension plan sponsored by Chimie bio-industrielle. On 15 April, the plan sponsor notifies Ord that the firm will be terminated as of the end of the month and instructs the manager to stop trading immediately. Ord should include the Chimie portfolio in the historical returns of the composite to which it belongs up to:

A 31 March.

B 15 April.

C 30 April.

15 Southwest Capital Advisors LLC manages a fixed-income composite in accordance with an enhanced indexing strategy which makes strategic use of high-yield and emerging market bonds in addition to investment grade bonds issued in developed markets. The Merrimack Company, a family office, has a portfolio that is included in the firm's fixed-income enhanced indexing composite. Merrimack informs Southwest in writing that, due to changes in its investment policy, the portfolio can no longer hold high-yield or emerging market bonds. In accordance with the GIPS standards, Southwest decides to switch the Merrimack portfolio to another composite. The historical performance of the portfolio must be:

A reflected in both composites.

B switched to the new composite.

C retained in the enhanced indexing composite.

The following information relates to Questions 16–18

Belltower Investment Management defines its core-plus fixed-income composite as containing all discretionary portfolios over $10 million that are invested in accordance with a strategy that includes domestic high-yield debt in addition to US government and agency securities and investment-grade bonds issued by US corporations. The composite benchmark is 75% Barclays Capital US Government/Credit Index and 25% Barclays Capital US High Yield Index, rebalanced monthly.

16 The core-plus fixed-income composite includes a portfolio managed on behalf of the Avonfield Academy endowment fund. The trustees of Avonfield inform Belltower in writing that, due to a change in investment policy, the endowment fund is no longer permitted to hold below-investment-grade securities. Belltower determines that henceforth the Avonfield portfolio should be included in the core fixed-income composite, rather than the core-plus fixed-income composite. The historical record of the portfolio must be:

   A included in both composites.

   B kept in the core-plus fixed income composite.

   C excluded from the core-plus fixed income composite.

17 After an extended period of rising interest rates, the market value of Hartford Special Machinery Company's core-plus fixed-income portfolio falls below the composite minimum of $10 million. The Hartford portfolio remains below the composite-specific minimum asset level for nine months until the client makes an additional contribution that brings it back above $10 million in assets. Belltower must:

   A temporarily switch the Hartford portfolio to the firm's miscellaneous composite.

   B include the Hartford portfolio in the core-plus fixed income composite in all measurement periods.

   C exclude the Hartford portfolio from the core-plus fixed income composite for the period it was below the minimum asset level.

18 Kingswood Manufacturing Company, a core-plus fixed-income client, informs Belltower in writing that, in the future, all security transactions must be approved in advance by Kingswood's controller. The *most likely* consequence is that Belltower must prospectively exclude the Kingswood portfolio from:

   A all composites.

   B total firm assets.

   C the core-plus fixed-income composite only.

19 Midwest National Bank manages a domestic equity portfolio for the Springfield Municipal Employees' Retirement Fund (SMERF), a mature defined-benefit pension plan. The SMERF portfolio belongs to Midwest's Institutional Equity composite. The composite description states, "Portfolios included in the Institutional Equity composite are actively managed for long-term capital appreciation." SMERF's investment policy statement includes the following provisions:

   All security transactions must be approved in advance by the SMERF Investment Committee. SMERF anticipates making regular net withdrawals in substantial amounts from the portfolio to meet pension liabilities. SMERF staff will prepare a schedule of withdrawals at the beginning of each fiscal year. The portfolio manager must manage liquidity so as to disburse funds in accordance with the withdrawal schedule.

   In view of these restrictions, discuss whether Midwest National Bank can justify including the SMERF portfolio in the composite.

20 Which statement *most accurately* expresses a requirement of the GIPS standards?

   A Non-fee-paying portfolios must not be included in composites.

B   All actual fee-paying discretionary portfolios must be included in at least one composite.

C   All actual fee-paying discretionary portfolios must be included in one and only one composite.

21 A fixed-income portfolio is *most likely* to be considered non-discretionary if the client's investment policy states that:

A   securities held at a gain must not be sold.

B   the average credit quality must be investment grade.

C   securities held in the portfolio must be issued in developed markets.

22 What is the minimum number of portfolios that a composite must contain to comply with the GIPS standards? Must a firm disclose the number of portfolios in a composite?

23 Firms that claim to comply with the GIPS standards must disclose the use of a sub-advisor and the:

A   identity of the sub-advisors.

B   period the sub-advisors were used.

C   investment strategies employed by the sub-advisors.

24 Gravite Asset Management started managing tax-efficient fixed income portfolios in January 1999. However, because the firm initially did not have a suitable portfolio accounting system, accrued income was not included in market valuations until June 1999. Under the GIPS standards, if Gravite presents the performance of the tax efficient fixed income composite since inception, it must:

A   disclose the period of non-compliance.

B   bring the non-compliant returns into compliance.

C   estimate the return including accrued income in the first half of 1999.

25 The GIPS standards require firms to disclose the presence, use, and extent of leverage, derivatives, and short positions if material, including a description of the:

A   characteristics of the instruments.

B   composite's net exposure to systematic risk.

C   firm's risk management policies and procedures.

26 Bentwood Institutional Asset Management has been managing equity, fixed-income, and balanced accounts since 1986. The firm became GIPS-compliant on 1 January 2001 and prepared composite performance presentations for the 1996-2000 period. Fixed-income performance was poor prior to 2001, when a new team of managers was brought on board. When Christopher Cooper joins Bentwood as marketing director in June 2006, he suggests showing performance starting with calendar 2001, the first year that performance started to improve. He proposes to show composites with returns for the five calendar years 2001 through 2005. Does this course of action comply with the GIPS standards?

27 It is 2011. Bristol Capital Management is the intermediate global fixed-income manager for the Jarvis University endowment fund. Bristol has prepared the performance report shown below. James Chan, consultant to Jarvis University, reviews the report and tells the fund's investment committee that the report does not meet the minimum requirements of the GIPS standards.

Identify *four* omissions that prevent the Bristol Capital Management performance report from being in compliance with GIPS standards. Also identify *four* items included in the Bristol Capital Management performance report (other than omissions) that do not comply with GIPS standards.

Year	Gross-of-Fees Return (%)	Benchmark Return (%)	Number of Portfolios	Composite Dispersion (%)	Composite Assets; End of Period ($ millions)	Percent of Firm Assets	Total Firm Assets ($ millions)
2006	12.7	10.7	8	6.6	512	21	2,438
2007	9.5	7.2	12	4.7	780	23	3,391
2008	2.1	1.5	22	6.5	1,250	27	4,629
2009	14.2	14.1	25	3.0	1,425	32	4,453
2010	4.9	6.1	29	1.9	1,712	32	4,891
1Q 2011	7.1	5.9	34	4.4	1,994	37	5,389

(Returns for 1Q 2011 are annualized.)

Bristol Capital Management has prepared and presented this report in compliance with the Global Investment Performance Standards (GIPS®), except for the use of cash-basis accounting for the recognition of interest income. Allied Verification, Ltd. has verified the Bristol Capital Management Intermediate Global Fixed Income Composite.

Notes:

7   Bristol Capital Management is an independent investment management firm founded in November 1999.

8   Performance results are presented before investment management and custodial fees.

9   Portfolio valuations are computed quarterly and are denominated in US dollars.

10 Bristol Capital Management uses derivative products to enhance portfolio returns.

11 All accounts worth more than $1 million that are invested in the Intermediate Global Fixed Income strategy are included in the composite at the beginning of the first full quarter under management.

12 The Intermediate Global Fixed Income composite includes several non-fee-paying accounts.

The following information relates to Questions 28–30

Tidewater Investment Management's performance presentation for its large cap US value composite is shown below.

Large-Cap US Value Composite
Composite Creation Date: 1 July 2001 ($ in millions)

Period	Composite Return %	Composite Median Return %	Benchmark Return %	Internal Dispersion	Number of Accounts	Total Composite Assets ($)	Total Firm Assets ($)
2005	6.37	6.52	6.14	1.54	15	922.4	9,752.3
2004	12.03	11.97	12.73	2.37	17	985.6	9,889.9
2003	26.52	26.74	26.01	4.05	19	1,028.3	10,779.5
2002	−19.06	−18.11	−21.52	3.97	22	1,354.8	11,845.3
2001	−12.00	−8.51	−12.16	2.13	27	1,227.5	11,253.6

Notes:

■ Tidewater Investment Management has prepared and presented this report in compliance with the Global Investment Performance Standards (GIPS®).

(continued)

- For the purposes of compliance with the GIPS standards, the firm is defined as all institutional accounts managed by Tidewater Investment Management. A complete list and description of all the firm's composites is available upon request.

- The strategy of the US Large Cap Value Composite (formerly the Core Domestic Equity Composite) is to invest in US large cap value equity securities. The composite consists of all fee-paying and non-fee-paying discretionary accounts with a minimum market value of $5 million.

- The benchmark for periods beginning 1 January 2003 is a custom security-based benchmark that is rebalanced to target sector weights monthly. The benchmark for periods prior to 1 January 2003 is the Russell 1000® Value Index.

- Between 25% and 35% of the assets contained in the composite in 2001 and 2002 were carved out of portfolios managed according to the firm's Large Cap Value Balanced style.

- For new clients acquired in periods starting 1 January 2004, Tidewater charges a bundled fee of 1.0% on assets up to $10 million and 0.85% on assets in excess of $10 million. The bundled fee includes investment management and administrative fees.

- Additional information regarding policies for calculating and reporting returns is available upon request.

(There are numerous errors and omissions in Tidewater's performance presentation. The following questions do not address all of them.)

28 Tidewater's performance presentation for the large cap US value composite fails to comply with the GIPS standards because it does **not** present:

A cumulative composite and benchmark returns.

B the percentage of the total firm assets represented by the composite.

C the percentage of composite assets represented by non-fee-paying portfolios.

29 Tidewater's performance presentation *most likely* fails to comply with the GIPS standards because it does **not** disclose the:

A custom benchmark weights and components.

B presence, use, and extent of leverage or derivatives.

C date and reasons for the change in the composite name.

30 In order to comply with the GIPS standards, Tidewater's disclosures related to fees must include the:

A fee schedule for periods prior to 1 January 2004.

B investment management and administrative fees on a segregated basis.

C bundled fee portfolios as a percentage of composite assets for each annual period.

---

31 At Firm T, Manager D is responsible for Firm T's Emerging Market Composite. Although Manager D makes all the investment decisions for the portfolios in the composite, Manager D is supported by Firm T's research department and trading desk. Firm U is seeking to establish an emerging market investment strategy and hires Manager D to join Firm U. Can Firm U link the historical performance of Manager D while at Firm T to the performance of its new strategy and comply with the GIPS standards?

The following information relates to Questions 32–35

Techno Investment Partners serves as general partner in a limited partnership whose strategy is to invest in privately owned software companies with innovative products designed to improve productivity in the service sector of the economy. The investment results of the limited partnership are presented in the firm's GIPS-compliant Service Productivity Enhancement Software (SPES) composite.

Paul Reid, a performance analyst, is updating the SPES composite performance presentation through the end of the third year since inception. The information shown in Exhibit 1 is taken from one of Reid's worksheets.

Exhibit 1	SPES Composite Data as of the End of Year 3 ($ in millions)					
Paid-In Capital	Invested Capital	Cumulative Distributions	Realization Multiple (DPI)	PIC Multiple	Ratio of Residual Value to Paid in Capital (RVPI)
20.0	16.6	2.5	0.13	0.80	0.99

32 The market value of the SPES composite is *closest* to:

   A $16.6 million.

   B $19.8 million.

   C $20.2 million.

33 The SPES composite's investment multiple (TVPI) is *closest* to:

   A 0.13.

   B 0.86.

   C 1.12.

34 What percentage of the limited partners' paid-in capital has been returned to them?

   A 13%

   B 15%

   C 80%

35 The limited partnership's committed capital is *closest* to:

   A $16.6 million.

   B $20.4 million.

   C $25.0 million.

36 Bugle Capital Advisors places an advertisement for its Targeted Maturity Composite in major newspapers on 30 April. The advertisement includes the GIPS Advertising Guidelines compliance statement and presents annualized composite and benchmark returns for the 1-year, 3-year, and 5-year periods ended 31 December. Does the advertisement satisfy the requirements of the GIPS Advertising Guidelines?

   A Yes.

   B No; it omits the period-to-date return.

C No; it omits five years of annual returns.

37 Which of the following is *least likely* to be considered an advertisement for the purposes of the GIPS Advertising Guidelines?

A A letter addressed to prospective clients.

B Written material used in one-on-one presentations.

C A quarterly report e-mailed to multiple existing clients.

38 Greene Springs Asset Management complies with the GIPS standards but has not been verified. The firm wishes to prepare an advertisement that includes a claim of compliance. Which of the following is the correct wording of the GIPS compliance statement for advertisements?

A "Greene Springs Asset Management claims compliance with the Global Investment Performance Standards (GIPS®)."

B "Greene Springs Asset Management claims compliance with the Global Investment Performance Standards (GIPS®). The firm's compliance has not been independently verified."

C "Greene Springs Asset Management claims compliance with the Global Investment Performance Standards (GIPS®). A list of composite descriptions is available upon request."

The following information relates to Questions 39–42

Amelia Gordon, the head of compliance at Herrschaft Asset Management Corporation, is examining an advertisement that promotes the firm's fundamental value strategy. The advertisement is shown in Exhibit 1.

Exhibit 1	"Herrschaft. Master the market."			

		Herrschaft Asset Management **Fundamental Value Composite Performance**		
	3 Months Ended 31 March 2006	**Periods Ended 31 December 2005**		
		1 Year	**3 Years (Annualized**	**5 Years (Annualized)**
Composite	5.51%	14.56%	22.03%	5.17%
Custom Benchmark	5.35%	14.72%	21.47%	4.86%

- Herrschaft Asset Management Corporation meets all applicable requirements of the Global Investment Performance Standards (GIPS®).

- Herrschaft Asset Management Corporation is a registered investment advisory firm offering a full suite of equity and fixed-income products for individuals and institutions.

- The Fundamental Value Composite contains all discretionary portfolios that are invested in accordance with Herrschaft's proprietary fundamental value strategy.

- Portfolios in the Fundamental Value Composite may include futures solely to equitize portfolio cash during inflows and outflows. Futures are not used to add leverage to the portfolio.

Exhibit 1   (Continued)

■ To receive a complete list and description of Herrschaft Asset Management
Corporation's composites, contact Jules Arnauld at (212) 555-0000 or write
Herrschaft Asset Management Corporation, 1250 15th Avenue, New York, NY or
jarnauld@herrschaftam.com

---

39 Which of the following statements is *most* accurate? Herrschaft's advertisement
does **not** meet the requirements of the GIPS Advertising Guidelines because it
fails to disclose:

A a description of the benchmark.

B the benchmark construction rules.

C how often the benchmark is rebalanced.

40 Which of the following statements is *most* accurate? Herrschaft's advertisement
does **not** meet the requirements of the GIPS Advertising Guidelines because it
fails to:

A present five years of annual composite returns.

B present a measure of dispersion of individual portfolio returns.

C disclose whether performance is shown gross or net of investment management fees.

41 Herrschaft's compliance statement does **not** meet the requirements of the GIPS
Advertising Guidelines. The correct statement is:

A Herrschaft Asset Management Corporation claims compliance with the
Global Investment Performance Standards (GIPS®).

B Herrschaft Asset Management Corporation has prepared and presented this
report in compliance with the Global Investment Performance Standards
(GIPS®).

C Herrschaft Asset Management Corporation has prepared and presented this
advertisement in compliance with the Advertising Guidelines of the Global
Investment Performance Standards (GIPS®).

42 Which of the following statements is *most* accurate? Herrschaft's advertisement
does **not** satisfy an applicable requirement of the GIPS Advertising Guidelines
because it fails to include all salient features in its description of the:

A firm.

B composite strategy.

C extent and use of leverage and derivatives.

---

43 It is *most* accurate to say that verification:

A makes the claim of compliance more credible.

B certifies that the firm has adequate internal controls.

C ensures the accuracy of specific composite presentations.

44 Renner, Williams & Woods decides to have its equity and balanced composites
verified. Because the firm has only a handful of fixed-income accounts and does
not present fixed-income management results in marketing materials shown
to prospects, management decides that it would be a waste of time and money

to hire a verification firm to verify such a small composite. Is it possible for Renner, Williams & Woods to obtain a firm-wide verification that covers only the equity and balanced composites?

The following information relates to Questions 45 and 46

Excedent Asset Management hires Maven Performance Consulting, Inc. to verify its claim of compliance with the GIPS standards.

Excedent offers equity and fixed-income portfolio management services to US-based institutional clients. Maven's services include customized training programs, technology and operational consulting, and GIPS verification.

At the outset of the verification process, Maven reviews Excedent's performance-related policies and procedures. The verifier also obtains a list of open and closed accounts for all composites for the years under examination.

While the verification is still in progress, Excedent asks Maven to serve as its technology consultant for the selection and implementation of a new fixed-income performance measurement and attribution system.

45 Which statement *most* accurately describes a requirement of the GIPS standards? Maven must be satisfied that Excedent's composite benchmarks are:

A free from systematic bias.

B consistently applied over time.

C unambiguous, investable, and measurable.

46 Maven asks Excedent to provide the account agreements for certain open and closed accounts. Reviewing the selected account agreements is *least likely* to be useful in determining whether:

A Excedent's treatment of taxes, tax reclaims, and tax accruals are correct.

B Excedent has appropriately classified accounts as discretionary or non-discretionary.

C the accounts' objectives are consistent with the definitions of the composites in which they are included.

SOLUTIONS

1 The GIPS standards encourage firms to adopt the broadest, most meaningful definition of a firm. Company C should consider defining itself to include the assets managed by both the institutional entity and the retail entity for the purposes of claiming compliance with the GIPS standards. However, Company C could define the two autonomous entities as separate firms if each subsidiary is held out to clients and potential clients as a distinct business unit. (See Section 3.1 of the reading.)

2 Sample Disclosure: "Firm A is defined as an independent management firm with offices in Japan, Australia, the United Kingdom, and the United States. Firm A (US) is a subsidiary of Firm A serving US clients. Firm A also has subsidiaries in the United Kingdom, Australia, and Japan." (See Section 3.1 of the reading.)

3 C is correct. Provision 1.1.A.2 states that, for periods beginning on or after 1 January 2011, portfolios must be valued in accordance with the definition of fair value, and Provision 1.1.A.3 states in pertinent part that firms must value portfolios in accordance with the composite-specific valuation policy. The GIPS standards do not require firms to adhere to the principles of financial accounting. (See Section 3.2 of the reading.)

4 B is correct. Provision 1.1.A.3.c states that portfolios must be valued "no more frequently than required by the valuation policy." The definition of fair value includes the statement, "In the absence of an objective, observable, unadjusted quoted market price for an identical investment in an active market on the measurement date, the valuation must represent the firm's best estimate of the market value." Provision 1.1.A.4 states, "For periods beginning on or after 1 January 2010, firms must value portfolios as of the calendar month end or the last business day of the month." (See Section 3.2 of the reading.)

5 No. A firm must maintain data necessary to support a firm's claim of compliance. Because Firm A presents five years of performance history, it must maintain the records to support the firm's five-year history and all other relevant data on the firm's composite presentations. Because the Standards require firms to build a ten-year performance history, the firm must continue to maintain the records to support the firm's eventual ten-year performance history. (See Section 3.2 of the reading.)

6 January:

$$R_{\text{Jan}} = (208{,}000 - 200{,}000)/200{,}000 = \textbf{4.00\%}$$

February:

$$R_{\text{Feb1-15}} = (217{,}000 - 208{,}000)/208{,}000 = 4.33\%$$

$$R_{\text{Feb16-28}} = (263{,}000 - 257{,}000)/257{,}000 = 2.33\%$$

$$R_{\text{Feb1-28}} = [(1 + 0.0433) \times (1 + 0.0233)] - 1 = \textbf{6.76\%}$$

March:

$$R_{\text{Mar1-21}} = (270{,}000 - 263{,}000)/263{,}000 = 2.66\%$$

$$R_{\text{Mar22-31}} = (245{,}000 - 240{,}000)/240{,}000 = 2.08\%$$

$$R_{\text{Mar1-31}} = [(1 + 0.0266) \times (1 + 0.0208)] - 1 = \textbf{4.80\%}$$

Quarter 1:

$$R_{QT1} = [(1 + 0.0400) \times (1 + 0.0676) \times (1 + 0.0480)] - 1 = \mathbf{16.36\%}$$

(See Section 3.3 of the reading.)

7 A Portfolio returns:

$$r_A = \frac{85.3 - 74.9 - 7.5}{74.9 + (7.5 \times 0.613)} = \frac{2.9}{79.5} = 0.0365 = 3.65\%$$

$$r_B = \frac{109.8 - 127.6 - (-15) - (-5)}{127.6 + (-15 \times 0.742) + (-5 \times 0.387)} = \frac{2.2}{114.535} = 0.0192 = 1.92\%$$

$$r_C = \frac{128.4 - 110.4 - 15}{110.4 + (15 \times 0.387)} = \frac{3}{116.205} = 0.0258 = 2.58\%$$

B To calculate the composite return based on beginning assets, first determine the percent of beginning composite assets represented by each portfolio; then determine the weighted-average return for the month:

Beginning composite assets = 74.9 + 127.6 + 110.4 = 312.9

Portfolio A = 74.9/312.9 = 0.239 = 23.9%

Portfolio B = 127.6/312.9 = 0.408 = 40.8%

Portfolio C = 110.4/312.9 = 0.353 = 35.3%

$$r_{Comp} = (0.0365 \times 0.239) + (0.0192 \times 0.408) + (0.0258 \times 0.353)$$
$$= 0.0257 = 2.57\%$$

C To calculate the composite return based on beginning assets plus cash flows, first use the denominator of the Modified Dietz formula to determine the percentage of total beginning assets plus weighted cash flows represented by each portfolio, and then calculate the weighted-average return:

Beginning composite assets + Weighted cash flows = [74.9 + (7.5 × 0.613)] + [127.6 + (−15 × 0.742) + (−5 × 0.387)] + [110.4 + (15 × 0.387)] = 79.5 + 114.535 + 116.205 = 310.24

Portfolio A = 79.5/310.24 = 0.256 = 25.6%

Portfolio B = 114.535/310.24 = 0.369 = 36.9%

Portfolio C = 116.205/310.24 = 0.375 = 37.5%

$$r_{Comp} = (0.0365 \times 0.256) + (0.0192 \times 0.369) + (0.0258 \times 0.375)$$
$$= 0.0261 = 2.61\%$$

A mathematically equivalent method consists simply in summing beginning assets and intra-period external cash flows, treating the entire composite as though it were a single portfolio and then computing the return directly with the Modified Dietz formula.

$$r_{Comp} = \frac{323.5 - 312.9 - (-15 + 7.5 + 10)}{312.9 + [(-15) \times 0.742 + 7.5 \times 0.613 + 10 \times 0.387]}$$
$$= 0.0261 = 2.61\%$$

8 A is correct. Provision 1.2.A.3 states, "Returns from cash and cash equivalents held in portfolios must be included in all return calculations." Lawton writes, "Cash and cash equivalents must be included in the total return calculation even if the cash is not actually invested by the same person or group." Whether the custodian is selected by the client or the manager is pertinent to the calculation of total firm assets but irrelevant to this question. (See Section 3.5 of the reading.)

9 C is correct. The GIPS Glossary defines trading expenses as "the actual costs of buying or selling investments" and states, "These costs typically take the form of brokerage commissions, exchange fees and/ or taxes, and/ or bid-offer spreads from either internal or external brokers. Custodial fees charged per transaction should be considered custody fees and not trading expenses." (See Section 3.5 of the reading.)

10 Yes. The Standards state that firms must include all actual, discretionary, fee-paying portfolios in at least one of the firm's composites. If the portfolio meets the defined criteria for inclusion in more than one composite, the firm must include the portfolio in all the firm's appropriate composites. For example, a firm may have a large-cap composite and a large-cap growth composite. If the firm manages a portfolio that meets the criteria for inclusion in the large-cap composite as well as the large-cap growth composite, the firm must include the portfolio in both composites. (See Section 3.7 of the reading.)

11 Barry Smith must have a documented, composite-specific policy for the treatment of external cash flows and must compute time-weighted total returns that adjust for external cash flows. For periods beginning 1 January 2005, rate-of-return approximation methods must adjust for cash flows on a day-weighted basis (I.2.A.2). Accordingly, Barry Smith must use a return-calculation methodology that adjusts for daily-weighted external cash flows, such as the Modified Dietz method. However, the 12 March 2006 contribution to the Dennett portfolio represents 13.67 percent of the portfolio's value, and it may be classified as a large external cash flow. Barry Smith must establish in advance a policy for the treatment of external cash flows for the Balanced Tax-Exempt composite. "Large" external cash flows may distort approximated returns. (See Sections 3.2, 3.5, and 3.9 of the reading.)

The 2010 version of the Standards includes a recommendation to value portfolios on the date of "all" external cash flows. This recommendation is effective for periods beginning on or after January 1, 2011 (I.1.B.1). As Barry Smith has adopted a large cash flow policy as of 1 January 2006 and assumes all external cash flows take place at the end of the day, given that the 12 March 2006 cash flow meets the definition of "large", the firm must value the portfolio as of the end of the day on 12 March 2006. Barry Smith would then compute sub-period returns for the March partial periods before and after the cash flow and link them to calculate a true time-weighted rate of return for the month of March. Alternately, if Barry Smith had adopted a "significant" cash flow policy for this composite and the 12 March cash flow met this definition, the firm would either determine that this entire portfolio be excluded from the composite for the month of March or treat the cash flow as a temporary new account (I.3.B.2).

12 Smith & Jones may not claim to be in compliance with the GIPS standards if model performance is linked to actual performance. The GIPS standards state that composites must include only actual assets under management within the defined firm, and they expressly prohibit linking the performance of simulated or model portfolios with actual performance (I.3.A.3). (See Section 3.7 of the reading.)

13 A is correct. Provision I.3.A.5 states, "Composites must include new portfolios on a timely and consistent basis after each portfolio comes under management." In this case, it is expected to take an extended period to invest the new client's assets in accordance with the composite strategy. Assuming Taurus complies with the GIPS standards, its documented policy would provide for the inclusion of new private equity portfolios in the composite on a timely basis. For example, Taurus's policy may require new portfolios to be included in the composite as of the first full measurement period that the assets are fully invested. Taurus must apply its policy consistently. (See Section 3.9 of the reading.)

14 A is correct. Provision I.3.A.6 states, "Terminated portfolios must be included in the historical performance of the composite up to the last full measurement period that each portfolio was under management." The last full measurement period that the Chimie bio-industrielle portfolio was under the management of Ord Capital Management was the month of March. (See Section 3.9 of the reading.)

15 C is correct. Provision I.3.A.7 states, "Portfolios must not be switched from one composite to another unless documented changes to a portfolio's investment mandate, objective, or strategy or the redefinition of the composite makes it appropriate. The historical performance of the portfolio must remain with the original composite." (See Section 3.9 of the reading.)

16 B is correct. Provision I.3.A.7 states, "Portfolios must not be switched from one composite to another unless documented changes to a portfolio's investment mandate, objective, or strategy or the redefinition of the composite make it appropriate. *The historical performance of the portfolio must remain with the original composite.*" (Emphasis added.) (See Section 3.9 of the reading.)

17 C is correct. Provision I.3.A.9 states in pertinent part, "If the firm sets a minimum asset level for portfolios to be included in a composite, the firm must not include portfolios below the minimum asset level in that composite." Belltower must remove the Hartford portfolio from the core-plus fixed-income composite when the portfolio's assets fall below the minimum, and return it to the composite when it once again qualifies for inclusion. A is incorrect because composites must be defined according to similar investment objectives and/or strategies; there should be no "miscellaneous" composite. (See Section 3.9 of the reading.)

18 A is correct. The client's prior approval authority for security transactions appears to render the portfolio non-discretionary. Provision I.3.A.1 states, in part, that "non-discretionary portfolios must not be included in a firm's composites." B is incorrect because, in accordance with Provision I.0.A.13, total firm assets must include all discretionary and non-discretionary assets managed by the firm. (See Sections 3.1 and 3.7 of the reading.)

19 The GIPS standards prohibit including non-discretionary portfolios in composites. IPS restrictions do not necessarily render a portfolio non-discretionary. It is up to the investment management firm to define discretion and to determine whether it has the discretion to implement the investment strategy, given the restrictions of the IPS. In this case, however, it appears likely that SMERF's policy requiring transactions to be approved in advance by the Investment Committee and the pension plan's liquidity needs prevent Midwest National Bank from fully implementing the investment objective of achieving long-term capital appreciation through active management. If so, Midwest National Bank should classify the SMERF portfolio as non-discretionary and exclude it from all composites. (See Section 3.7 of the reading.)

20 B is correct. Provision I.3.A.1 states, "All actual, fee-paying, discretionary portfolios must be included in at least one composite. Although non-fee-paying discretionary portfolios may be included in a composite (with appropriate disclosure), non-discretionary portfolios must not be included in a firm's composites." (See Section 3.7 of the reading.)

21 A is correct. Such a restriction would most likely alter portfolio structure and would also be likely client specific. The restrictions in B and C are not necessarily client specific and could already be part of the investment strategy of the manager. (See Section 3.7 of the reading.)

22 Under the Standards, there is no minimum or maximum number of portfolios that a composite may include. The Standards require that firms disclose the number of portfolios in each composite as of the end of each annual period presented, unless there are five or fewer portfolios (I.5.A.1f). (See Section 3.12 of the reading.)

23 B is correct. Provision I.4.A.25 states, "For periods beginning on or after 1 January 2006, firms must disclose the use of a sub-advisor and the periods a sub-advisor was used." (See Section 3.11 of the reading.)

24 A is correct. "For any performance presented for periods prior to 1 January 2000 that does not comply with the GIPS standards, firms must disclose the periods of non-compliance (I.4.A.15)." Provision I.5.B.8 recommends that firms comply with the GIPS Standards for all historical periods. (See Sections 3.11 and 3.13 of the reading.)

25 A is correct. Provision I.4.A.13 states, "Firms must disclose the presence, use, and extent of leverage, derivatives, and short positions, if material, including a description of the frequency of use and characteristics of the instruments sufficient to identify risks." (See Section 3.11 of the reading.)

26 The GIPS standards require that at least five years of GIPS-compliant performance be reported (or for the period since firm's inception or the composite inception date if the firm or the composite has been in existence less than five years). After presenting a minimum of five years of GIPS-compliant performance (or for the period since firm's inception or the composite inception date if the firm or composite has been in existence less than five years), the firm must present an additional year of performance each year, building up to a minimum of 10 years of GIPS-compliant performance (I.5.A.1a). Bentwood Institutional Asset Management could not drop the years prior to 2001 at the time Cooper suggests it do so. In addition to violating a specific requirement, Cooper's suggestion was not in the spirit of fair representation and full disclosure of performance. Technically, the firm will be able drop the early years of its composite presentation once it has established a 10-year GIPS-compliant record, as long as it continues to show at least the most recent 10 years. For instance, it will be able to show just the 10 calendar years 2001-2010 after the composite returns for 2010 become available. However, it is recommended that Bentwood show its entire GIPS-compliant performance record (I.5.B.7). (See Sections 3.12 and 3.13 of the reading.)

27 The report has a large number of omissions and errors.

Omissions that prevent the Bristol Capital Management performance report from being GIPS-compliant includes the following:

- The availability of a list of composite descriptions is not disclosed as is required (I.4.A.11).

- The availability of policies for valuing portfolios, calculating performance, and preparing compliant presentations is not disclosed (I.4.A.12).

- Although Bristol does disclose the use of derivatives, it appears that the firm has not included all the required disclosure in this area. The firm must disclose the presence, use, and extent of leverage, derivatives and short positions, if material, including a description of the frequency of use and characteristics of the instruments sufficient to identify risks (I.4.A.13).

- If the firm has included non-fee-paying portfolios in its composite, the percentage of the composite assets represented by non-fee-paying portfolios must be disclosed as of the end of each annual period (I.5.A.6).

- The composite creation date must be disclosed (I.4.A.10).

- Because the composite represents a global investment strategy, the presentation must include information about the treatment of withholding taxes on dividends, interest income, and capital gains, if material (I.4.A.20).

- Both a composite description and benchmark description must be disclosed (I.4.A.3-4).

- A fee schedule appropriate to the compliant presentation must be disclosed (I.4.A.9).

There are many items included in the Bristol Capital Management performance report that are *not compliant* with GIPS, including the following:

- The GIPS standards state that performance periods of less than one year must not be annualized, as Bristol does for the first quarter of 2011 (I.5.A.4).

- GIPS verification cannot be performed for a single composite as is stated in the presentation. Verification does not provide assurance about the performance of any specific composite. Firms must not state that a particular composite has been "verified" or make any claim to that effect (IV.A.3).

- For periods beginning on or after 1 January 2001, portfolios must be valued at least monthly. For periods beginning on or after 1 January 2010, portfolios must be valued on the date of all large cash flows. Bristol is valuing portfolios quarterly (I.1.A.3).

- A firm must use the appropriate compliance statement as specified in the GIPS standards. There are no allowances for partial compliance. If a firm does not meet all the requirements of the GIPS standards, the firm must not represent or state that it is "in compliance with the Global Investment Performance Standards except for..." or make any other statements that may indicate partial compliance with the GIPS standards. Bristol's use of the "except for" compliance statement violates the Standards (I.0.A.6) and the appropriate compliance statement has not been used (I.4.A.1).

- The firm must disclose which measure of internal dispersion is presented (I.4.A.8).

- The GIPS standards state that accrual accounting must be used for fixed-income securities and all other investments that earn interest income (I.1.A.6). Bristol states that it uses cash-basis accounting for the recognition of interest income.

28 C is correct. The composite description indicates that the composite contains both fee-paying and non-fee-paying portfolios. GIPS Provision I.5.A.6 states, "If a composite includes non-fee-paying portfolios, the firm must present the percentage of composite assets represented by non-fee-paying portfolios as of each annual period end." A is incorrect because the Standards recommend but do not require that firms present cumulative returns for all periods. B is incorrect because the Standards permit firms to present either the percentage of the total firm assets represented by the composite or the amount of total firm assets at the end of each annual period. (See Sections 3.12 and 3.13 of the reading.)

29 A is correct. GIPS Provision I.4.A.31 states, "If a custom benchmark or combination of multiple benchmarks is used, the firm must disclose the benchmark components, weights and re-balancing process." Tidewater discloses the frequency of custom benchmark rebalancing but does not describe the custom benchmark weights and components. B is not the best answer because the

Standards require disclosure of the presence, use, and extent of leverage or derivatives only if the use of leverage or derivatives is material. C is incorrect because the Standards require only that firms disclose any changes to the name of a composite. Firms are not required to disclose the date and reasons for the composite name change. (See Section 3.11 of the reading.)

30 C is correct. GIPS Provision I.5.A.7 states, "If a composite includes portfolios with bundled fees, the firm must present the percentage of composite assets represented by portfolios with bundled fees as of each annual period end." The Standards do not require firms to disclose the fee schedule in effect for prior periods or the segregated components of bundled fees. (See Section 3.12 of the reading.)

31 The firm must determine if the decision-making process remains intact (unchanged) in Firm U. If Firm U continues the original strategy of the composite with all of its continuing factors, appropriate disclosures are made and documentation is in place, the performance must be linked. (See Section 3.12 of the reading.)

32 B is correct. The GIPS Glossary gives this definition of Residual Value (private equity and real estate): "The remaining equity that limited partners (or investors) have in an investment vehicle at the end of the performance reporting period." The GIPS Glossary defines the RVPI (real estate and private equity) as "residual value divided by since inception paid-in capital". Accordingly, the market value of the SPES composite can be estimated by multiplying the paid-in capital by the RVPI measure. The calculation is $20.0 \times 0.99 = $19.8 million. (See Section 3.15 of the reading.)

33 C is correct. The GIPS Glossary defines the TVPI (real estate and private equity) as "total value divided by since inception paid-in capital." The GIPS Glossary defines Total Value (real estate and private equity) as "residual value plus distributions". Using the data given in Exhibit I, the simplest way to find TVPI is to add RVPI and DPI. The calculation is: 0.99 + 0.13 = 1.12. Alternately, one can multiply the monetary amount of paid-in capital by RVPI to determine the residual value, add it to cumulative distributions, and divide the sum by paid-in capital. In this approach, the calculation is [(20 × 0.99) + 2.5]/20 = 1.12. (See Section 3.15 of the reading.)

34 A is correct. The GIPS Glossary defines the Realization Multiple (DPI) (real estate and private equity) as "since inception distributions divided by since inception paid-in capital". The realization multiple (DPI) may be described as a measure of how much of the investors' capital has been returned to them. Exhibit I displays the realization multiple (0.13 or 13%), and it can also be calculated by dividing cumulative distributions by paid-in capital. (See Section 3.15 of the reading.)

35 C is correct. The GIPS Glossary defines the PIC Multiple (real estate and private equity) as "since inception paid-in capital divided by cumulative committed capital". Accordingly, given paid-in capital of $20 million and a PIC multiple of 0.80, committed capital is $20/0.80 = $25.0. (See Section 3.15 of the reading.)

36 B is correct. The GIPS Advertising Guidelines specify that advertisements that include a claim of compliance and that present performance results must include period-to-date composite performance results in addition to either one-, three-, and five-year annualized composite returns or five years of annual composite returns. (See Section 5 of the reading.)

37 B is correct. The following definition of "advertisement" is provided in the GIPS Advertising Guidelines: "For the purposes of these guidelines, an advertisement includes any materials that are distributed to or designed for use in newspapers,

magazines, firm brochures, letters, media, or any other written or electronic material addressed to more than one prospective client. Any written material, other than one-on-one presentations and individual client reporting, distributed to maintain existing clients or solicit new clients for a firm is considered an advertisement." (See Section 5 of the reading.)

38   A is correct. Chapter III.B.3 of the GIPS Advertising Guidelines provides the correct wording of the compliance statement that must be used in advertisements that include a claim of compliance. The advertisements must also state how prospective client can obtain a compliant presentation and/or the firm's list of composite descriptions, but that disclosure is not a part of the GIPS compliance statement for advertisements. (See Section 5 of the reading.)

39   A is correct. GIPS Provision III.B.8 states, "All advertisements that include a claim of compliance with the GIPS standards by following the GIPS Advertising Guidelines must disclose the following: The benchmark description." (See Section 5 of the reading.)

40   C is correct. GIPS Provision III.B.6 states, "All advertisements that include a claim of compliance with the GIPS standards by following the GIPS Advertising Guidelines must disclose the following: Whether returns are presented gross-of-fees and/or net-of-fees". A is incorrect because GIPS-compliant advertisements may show either five years of annual composite returns or period-to-date, one-, three-, and five-year cumulative annualized composite returns. Herrschaft's advertisement shows the latter. B is incorrect because the GIPS Advertising Guidelines do not require firms to present a measure of dispersion. (See Section 5 of the reading.)

41   A is correct. Answer A presents the prescribed wording of the GIPS Advertising Guidelines compliance statement. (See Section 5 of the reading.)

42   B is correct. Herrschaft's description of the composite strategy is uninformative. It would most likely be possible for Herrschaft to provide a more satisfactory description without revealing its trade secrets. A is incorrect because the description of the firm is adequate. C is incorrect because Herrschaft states that derivatives are used solely for the purpose of efficient management of cash flows. GIPS Provision III.B.11 states, "All advertisements that include a claim of compliance with the GIPS standards by following the GIPS Advertising Guidelines must disclose the following: The presence, use, and extent of leverage, derivatives, and short positions, if material, including a description of the frequency of use and characteristics of the instruments sufficient to identify risks". Consequently, a description of the use and extent of leverage or derivatives is not required in this case. (See Sections 3.11 and 5 of the reading.)

43   A is correct. The GIPS standards state that verification "brings additional credibility to the claim of compliance" but that it "does not ensure the accuracy of any specific composite presentation." (IV, Verification.) The Standards do not indicate that verification attests to the adequacy of the firm's internal controls. (See Section 6 of the reading.)

44   Under the GIPS standards, a single verification report is issued with respect to the whole firm. Verification cannot be carried out on a composite, and, accordingly, does not provide assurance about the performance of any specific composite. Firms must not state that a particular composite has been "verified" or make any claim to that effect (See IV.A.3). A qualified verification firm would not accept an assignment from Renner, Williams & Woods to conduct verification only with regard to the firm's equity and balanced account composites while excluding the fixed-income composites from the scope of the verification. (See Section 6 of the reading.)

45 B is correct. GIPS Provision IV.B.2.a.vii states, "Verifiers must perform sufficient procedures to determine that: The composite benchmark reflects the investment mandate, objective, or strategy of the composite." (See Section 6 of the reading.)

46 A is correct. The account agreements are unlikely to shed light on whether the firm's treatment of taxes, tax reclaims, and tax accruals is correct. B is incorrect because GIPS Provision IV.B.2.b states, in part, "Verifiers must obtain a list of all portfolios. Verifiers must select portfolios from this list and perform sufficient procedures to determine that the firm's classification of the portfolios as discretionary or non-discretionary is appropriate by referring to the portfolio's investment management agreement and/or investment guidelines and the firm's policies and procedures for determining investment discretion." C is incorrect because GIPS Provision IV.B.2.c.iii states, in part, "Verifiers must...determine that: The portfolio's investment mandate, objective, or strategy, as indicated by the portfolio's investment management agreement, investment guidelines, portfolio summary, and/or other appropriate documentation, is consistent with the composite definition." (See Section 6 of the reading.)

Glossary

10-year moving average price/earnings A price-to-earnings ratio in which the numerator (in a US context) is defined as the real S&P 500 price index and the denominator as the moving average of the preceding 10 years of real reported earnings on the S&P 500.

AUM fee A fee based on assets under management; an ad valorem fee.

Absolute return benchmark A minimum target return that an investment manager is expected to beat.

Absolute-return vehicles Investments that have no direct benchmark portfolios.

Accounting risk The risk associated with accounting standards that vary from country to country or with any uncertainty about how certain transactions should be recorded.

Accumulated benefit obligation (ABO) The present value of pension benefits, assuming the pension plan terminated immediately such that it had to provide retirement income to all beneficiaries for their years of service up to that date.

Accumulated service Years of service of a pension plan participant as of a specified date.

Active investment strategies An approach to investing in which the portfolio manager seeks to outperform a given benchmark portfolio.

Active management An approach to investing in which the portfolio manager seeks to outperform a given benchmark portfolio.

Active return The portfolio's return in excess of the return on the portfolio's benchmark.

Active risk A synonym for tracking risk.

Active-lives The portion of a pension fund's liabilities associated with active workers.

Active/immunization combination A portfolio with two component portfolios: an immunized portfolio which provides an assured return over the planning horizon and a second portfolio that uses an active high-return/high-risk strategy.

Active/passive combination Allocation of the core component of a portfolio to a passive strategy and the balance to an active component.

Actual extreme events A type of scenario analysis used in stress testing. It involves evaluating how a portfolio would have performed given movements in interest rates, exchange rates, stock prices, or commodity prices at magnitudes such as occurred during past extreme market events (e.g., the stock market crash of October 1987).

Ad valorem fees Fees that are calculated by multiplying a percentage by the value of assets managed; also called assets under management (AUM) fees.

Adaptive markets hypothesis (AMH) A hypothesis that applies principles of evolution—such as competition, adaptation, and natural selection—to financial markets in an attempt to reconcile efficient market theories with behavioral alternatives.

Adverse selection risk The risk associated with information asymmetry; in the context of trading, the risk of trading with a more informed trader.

Algorithmic trading Automated electronic trading subject to quantitative rules and user-specified benchmarks and constraints.

Allocation/selection interaction return A measure of the joint effect of weights assigned to both sectors and individual securities; the difference between the weight of the portfolio in a given sector and the portfolio's benchmark for that sector, times the difference between the portfolio's and the benchmark's returns in that sector, summed across all sectors.

Alpha Excess risk-adjusted return.

Alpha and beta separation An approach to portfolio construction that views investing to earn alpha and investing to establish systematic risk exposures as tasks that can and should be pursued separately.

Alpha research Research related to capturing excess risk-adjusted returns by a particular strategy; a way investment research is organized in some investment management firms.

Alternative investments Groups of investments with risk and return characteristics that differ markedly from those of traditional stock and bond investments.

Anchoring and adjustment An information-processing bias in which the use of a psychological heuristic influences the way people estimate probabilities.

Anchoring and adjustment bias An information-processing bias in which the use of a psychological heuristic influences the way people estimate probabilities.

Anchoring trap The tendency of the mind to give disproportionate weight to the first information it receives on a topic.

Angel investor An accredited individual investing chiefly in seed and early-stage companies.

Anomalies Apparent deviations from market efficiency.

Ask price The price at which a dealer will sell a specified quantity of a security. Also called *ask*, *offer price*, or *offer*.

Ask size The quantity associated with the ask price.

Aspirational risk bucket In goal-based portfolio planning, that part of wealth allocated to investments that have the potential to increase a client's wealth substantially.

Asset allocation reviews A periodic review of the appropriateness of a portfolio's asset allocation.

Asset covariance matrix The covariance matrix for the asset classes or markets under consideration.

Asset location The type of account an asset is held within, e.g., taxable or tax deferred.

Asset-only (AO) approach In the context of determining a strategic asset allocation, an approach that focuses on the characteristics of the assets without explicitly modeling the liabilities.

Asset/liability management The management of financial risks created by the interaction of assets and liabilities.

Asset/liability management (ALM) approach In the context of determining a strategic asset allocation, an asset/liability management approach involves explicitly modeling liabilities and adopting the allocation of assets that is optimal in relationship to funding liabilities.

Assurity of completion   In the context of trading, confidence that trades will settle without problems under all market conditions.

Assurity of the contract   In the context of trading, confidence that the parties to trades will be held to fulfilling their obligations.

Asynchronism   A discrepancy in the dating of observations that occurs because stale (out-of-date) data may be used in the absence of current data.

Automated trading   Any form of trading that is not manual, including trading based on algorithms.

Availability bias   An information-processing bias in which people take a heuristic approach to estimating the probability of an outcome based on how easily the outcome comes to mind.

Average effective spread   A measure of the liquidity of a security's market. The mean effective spread (sometimes dollar weighted) over all transactions in the stock in the period under study.

Back office   Administrative functions at an investment firm such as those pertaining to transaction processing, record keeping, and regulatory compliance.

Backtesting   A method for gaining information about a model using past data. As used in reference to VAR, it is the process of comparing the number of violations of VAR thresholds over a time period with the figure implied by the user-selected probability level.

Backwardation   A condition in the futures markets in which the benefits of holding an asset exceed the costs, leaving the futures price less than the spot price.

Balance of payments   An accounting of all cash flows between residents and nonresidents of a country.

Bancassurance   The sale of insurance by banks.

Barbell portfolio   A portfolio made up of short and long maturities relative to the investment horizon date and interim coupon payments.

Base   With respect to a foreign exchange quotation of the price of one unit of a currency, the currency referred to in "one unit of a currency."

Base-rate neglect   A type of representativeness bias in which the base rate or probability of the categorization is not adequately considered.

Basis   The difference between the cash price and the futures price.

Basis point value (BPV)   The change in the bond price for a 1 basis point change in yield. Also called *present value of a basis point* or *price value of a basis point (PVBP)*.

Basis risk   The risk resulting from using a hedging instrument that is imperfectly matched to the investment being hedged; in general, the risk that the basis will change in an unpredictable way.

Batch auction markets   Auction markets where multilateral trading occurs at a single price at a prespecified point in time.

Bayes' formula   A mathematical rule explaining how existing probability beliefs should be changed given new information; it is essentially an application of conditional probabilities.

Bear spread   An option strategy that involves selling a put with a lower exercise price and buying a put with a higher exercise price. It can also be executed with calls.

Behavioral finance   An approach to finance based on the observation that psychological variables affect and often distort individuals' investment decision making.

Behavioral finance macro   A focus on market level behavior that considers market anomalies that distinguish markets from the efficient markets of traditional finance.

Behavioral finance micro   A focus on individual level behavior that examines the behavioral biases that distinguish individual investors from the rational decision makers of traditional finance.

Benchmark   In an investments context, a standard or point of reference for evaluating the performance of an investment portfolio.

Best efforts order   A type of order that gives the trader's agent discretion to execute the order only when the agent judges market conditions to be favorable.

Beta   A measure of the sensitivity of a given investment or portfolio to movements in the overall market.

Beta research   Research related to systematic (market) risk and return; a way investment research is organized in some investment management firms.

Bid   The price at which a dealer will buy a specified quantity of a security. Also called *bid price*.

Bid price   In a price quotation, the price at which the party making the quotation is willing to buy a specified quantity of an asset or security.

Bid size   The quantity associated with the bid price.

Bid–ask spread   The difference between the current bid price and the current ask price of a security.

Binary credit options   Options that provide payoffs contingent on the occurrence of a specified negative credit event.

Block order   An order to sell or buy in a quantity that is large relative to the liquidity ordinarily available from dealers in the security or in other markets.

Bond-yield-plus-risk-premium method   An approach to estimating the required return on equity which specifies that required return as a bond yield plus a risk premium.

Bottom-up   Focusing on company-specific fundamentals or factors such as revenues, earnings, cash flow, or new product development.

Bounded rationality   The notion that people have informational and cognitive limitations when making decisions and do not necessarily optimize when arriving at their decisions.

Box spread   An option strategy that combines a bull spread and a bear spread having two different exercise prices, which produces a risk-free payoff of the difference in the exercise prices.

Broad market indexes   An index that is intended to measure the performance of an entire asset class. For example, the S&P 500 Index, Wilshire 5000, and Russell 3000 indexes for US common stocks.

Broker   An agent of a trader in executing trades.

Brokered markets   Markets in which transactions are largely effected through a search-brokerage mechanism away from public markets.

Bubbles   Episodes in which asset market prices move to extremely high levels in relation to estimated intrinsic value.

Buffering   With respect to style index construction, rules for maintaining the style assignment of a stock consistent with a previous assignment when the stock has not clearly moved to a new style.

Build-up approach   Synonym for the risk premium approach.

Bull spread   An option strategy that involves buying a call with a lower exercise price and selling a call with a higher exercise price. It can also be executed with puts.

Bullet portfolio A portfolio made up of maturities that are very close to the investment horizon.

Business cycle Fluctuations in GDP in relation to long-term trend growth, usually lasting 9–11 years.

Business risk The equity risk that comes from the nature of the firm's operating activities.

Butterfly spread An option strategy that combines two bull or bear spreads and has three exercise prices.

Buy side Investment management companies and other investors that use the services of brokerages.

Buy-side traders Professional traders that are employed by investment managers and institutional investors.

Calendar rebalancing Rebalancing a portfolio to target weights on a periodic basis; for example, monthly, quarterly, semi-annually, or annually.

Calendar-and-percentage-of-portfolio rebalancing Monitoring a portfolio at regular frequencies, such as quarterly. Rebalancing decisions are then made based upon percentage-of-portfolio principles.

Calmar ratio The compound annualized rate of return over a specified time period divided by the absolute value of maximum drawdown over the same time period.

Cap A combination of interest rate call options designed to hedge a borrower against rate increases on a floating-rate loan.

Cap rate With respect to options, the exercise interest rate for a cap.

Cap weighting See *capitalization weighting*.

Capital adequacy ratio A measure of the adequacy of capital in relation to assets.

Capital allocation line A graph line that describes the combinations of expected return and standard deviation of return available to an investor from combining an optimal portfolio of risky assets with a risk-free asset.

Capital flows forecasting approach An exchange rate forecasting approach that focuses on expected capital flows, particularly long-term flows such as equity investment and foreign direct investment.

Capital market expectations (CME) Expectations concerning the risk and return prospects of asset classes.

Capitalization weighting The most common security weighting scheme in which constituents are held in proportion to their market capitalizations, calculated as price times available shares. Also known as *market value*, *market cap*, or *cap weighting*.

Caplet Each component call option in a cap.

Carried interest A private equity fund manager's incentive fee; the share of the private equity fund's profits that the fund manager is due once the fund has returned the outside investors' capital.

Carry trade A trading strategy of borrowing in low-yield currencies and investing the borrowed amount in high-yield currencies.

Cash balance plan A defined-benefit plan whose benefits are displayed in individual recordkeeping accounts.

Cash flow at risk A variation of VAR that measures the risk to a company's cash flow, instead of its market value; the minimum cash flow loss expected to be exceeded with a given probability over a specified time period.

Cash flow matching An asset/liability management approach that provides the future funding of a liability stream from the coupon and matured principal payments of the portfolio. A type of dedication strategy.

Cell-matching technique (stratified sampling) A portfolio construction technique used in indexing that divides the benchmark index into cells related to the risk factors affecting the index and samples from index securities belonging to those cells.

Certainty equivalent The maximum sum of money a person would pay to participate or the minimum sum of money a person would accept to not participate in an opportunity.

Chain-linking A process for combining periodic returns to produce an overall time-weighted rate of return.

Cheapest-to-deliver A bond in which the amount received for delivering the bond is largest compared with the amount paid in the market for the bond.

Civil law A legal system derived from Roman law, in which judges apply general, abstract rules or concepts to particular cases. In civil systems, law is developed primarily through legislative statutes or executive action.

Claw-back provision With respect to the compensation of private equity fund managers, a provision that specifies that money from the fund manager be returned to investors if, at the end of a fund's life, investors have not received back their capital contributions and contractual share of profits.

Closed-book markets Markets in which a trader does not have real-time access to all quotes in a security.

Closeout netting In a bankruptcy, a process by which multiple obligations between two counterparties are consolidated into a single overall value owed by one of the counterparties to the other.

Cobb-Douglas model A production function (model for economic output) based on factors of labor and capital that exhibits constant returns to scale.

Cobb-Douglas production function A production function (model for economic output) based on factors of labor and capital that exhibits constant returns to scale.

Cognitive dissonance The mental discomfort that occurs when new information conflicts with previously held beliefs or cognitions.

Cognitive errors Behavioral biases resulting from faulty reasoning; cognitive errors stem from basic statistical, information processing, or memory errors.

Collar An option strategy involving the purchase of a put and sale of a call in which the holder of an asset gains protection below a certain level, the exercise price of the put, and pays for it by giving up gains above a certain level, the exercise price of the call. Collars also can be used to provide protection against rising interest rates on a floating-rate loan by giving up gains from lower interest rates.

Collateral return The component of the return on a commodity futures contract that comes from the assumption that the full value of the underlying futures contract is invested to earn the risk-free interest rate. Also called *collateral yield*.

Collateralized debt obligation A securitized pool of fixed-income assets.

Combination matching A cash flow matching technique; a portfolio is duration-matched with a set of liabilities with the added constraint that it also be cash-flow matched in the first few years, usually the first five years. Also called *horizon matching*.

Commingled real estate funds (CREFs) Professionally managed vehicles for substantial commingled (i.e., pooled) investment in real estate properties.

Commitment period The period of time over which committed funds are advanced to a private equity fund.

Commodities   Articles of commerce such as agricultural goods, metals, and petroleum; tangible assets that are typically relatively homogeneous in nature.

Commodity trading advisors   Registered advisors who manage futures funds.

Common law   A legal system which draws abstract rules from specific cases. In common law systems, law is developed primarily through decisions of the courts.

Community property regime   A marital property regime under which each spouse has an indivisible one-half interest in property received during marriage.

Company-specific risk   The non-systematic or idiosyncratic risk specific to a particular company's operations, reputation, and business environment.

Completeness fund   A portfolio that, when added to active managers' positions, establishes an overall portfolio with approximately the same risk exposures as the investor's overall equity benchmark.

Confidence band   With reference to a quality control chart for performance evaluation, a range in which the manager's value-added returns are anticipated to fall a specified percentage of the time.

Confidence interval   An interval that has a given probability of containing the parameter it is intended to estimate.

Confirmation bias   A belief perseverance bias in which people tend to look for and notice what confirms their beliefs, to ignore or undervalue what contradicts their beliefs, and to misinterpret information as support for their beliefs.

Confirming evidence trap   The bias that leads individuals to give greater weight to information that supports an existing or preferred point of view than to evidence that contradicts it.

Conjunction fallacy   An inappropriate combining of probabilities of independent events to support a belief. In fact, the probability of two independent events occurring in conjunction is never greater than the probability of either event occurring alone; the probability of two independent events occurring together is equal to the multiplication of the probabilities of the independent events.

Conservatism bias   A belief perseverance bias in which people maintain their prior views or forecasts by inadequately incorporating new information.

Consistent growth   A growth investment substyle that focuses on companies with consistent growth having a long history of unit-sales growth, superior profitability, and predictable earnings.

Constant returns to scale   A characteristic of a production function such that a given percentage increase in capital stock and labor input results in an equal percentage increase in output.

Contango   A condition in the futures markets in which the costs of holding an asset exceed the benefits, leaving the futures price more than the spot price.

Contingent immunization   A fixed-income strategy in which immunization serves as a fall-back strategy if the actively managed portfolio does not grow at a certain rate.

Continuous auction markets   Auction markets where orders can be executed at any time during the trading day.

Contrarian   A value investment substyle focusing on stocks that have been beset by problems.

Controlled foreign corporation   A company located outside a taxpayer's home country and in which the taxpayer has a controlling interest as defined under the home country law.

Conversion factor   An adjustment used to facilitate delivery on bond futures contracts in which any of a number of bonds with different characteristics are eligible for delivery.

Convexity   A measure of how interest rate sensitivity changes with a change in interest rates.

Convexity adjustment   An estimate of the change in price that is not explained by duration.

Core capital   The amount of capital required to fund spending to maintain a given lifestyle, fund goals, and provide adequate reserves for unexpected commitments.

Core-plus   A fixed-income mandate that permits the portfolio manager to add instruments with relatively high return potential to core holdings of investment-grade debt.

Core-satellite portfolio   A portfolio in which certain investments (often indexed or semiactive) are viewed as the core and the balance are viewed as satellite investments fulfilling specific roles.

Core–satellite   A way of thinking about allocating money that seeks to define each investment's place in the portfolio in relation to specific investment goals or roles.

Corner portfolio   Adjacent corner portfolios define a segment of the minimum-variance frontier within which portfolios hold identical assets and the rate of change of asset weights in moving from one portfolio to another is constant.

Corner portfolio theorem   In a sign-constrained mean–variance optimization, the result that the asset weights of any minimum-variance portfolio are a positive linear combination of the corresponding weights in the two adjacent corner portfolios that bracket it in terms of expected return (or standard deviation of return).

Corporate governance   The system of internal controls and procedures used to define and protect the rights and responsibilities of various stakeholders.

Corporate venturing   Investments by companies in promising young companies in the same or a related industry.

Country beta   A measure of the sensitivity of a specified variable (e.g., yield) to a change in the comparable variable in another country.

Covered call   An option strategy involving the holding of an asset and sale of a call on the asset.

Credit VAR   A variation of VAR related to credit risk; it reflects the minimum loss due to credit exposure with a given probability during a period of time.

Credit default swap   A swap used to transfer credit risk to another party. A protection buyer pays the protection seller in return for the right to receive a payment from the seller in the event of a specified credit event.

Credit derivative   A contract in which one party has the right to claim a payment from another party in the event that a specific credit event occurs over the life of the contract.

Credit event   An event affecting the credit risk of a security or counterparty.

Credit forwards   A type of credit derivative with payoffs based on bond values or credit spreads.

Credit method   When the residence country reduces its taxpayers' domestic tax liability by the amount of taxes paid to a foreign country that exercises source jurisdiction.

Credit protection seller   With respect to a credit derivative, the party that accepts the credit risk of the underlying financial asset.

Credit risk   The risk of loss caused by a counterparty's or debtor's failure to make a timely payment or by the change in value of a financial instrument based on changes in default risk. Also called *default risk*.

Credit spread forward A forward contract used to transfer credit risk to another party; a forward contract on a yield spread.

Credit spread option An option based on the yield spread between two securities that is used to transfer credit risk.

Credit spread risk The risk that the spread between the rate for a risky bond and the rate for a default risk-free bond may vary after the purchase of the risky bond.

Credited rates Rates of interest credited to a policyholder's reserve account.

Cross hedge A hedge involving a hedging instrument that is imperfectly correlated with the asset being hedged; an example is hedging a bond investment with futures on a non-identical bond.

Cross-default provision A provision stipulating that if a borrower defaults on any outstanding credit obligations, the borrower is considered to be in default on all obligations.

Cross-hedge A hedge involving a hedging instrument that is imperfectly correlated with the asset being hedged; an example is hedging a bond investment with futures on a non-identical bond.

Currency overlay programs A currency overlay program is a program to manage a portfolio's currency exposures for the case in which those exposures are managed separately from the management of the portfolio itself.

Currency return The percentage change in the spot exchange rate stated in terms of home currency per unit of foreign currency.

Currency risk The risk associated with the uncertainty about the exchange rate at which proceeds in the foreign currency can be converted into the investor's home currency.

Currency swap A swap in which the parties make payments based on the difference in debt payments in different currencies.

Currency-hedged instruments Investment in nondomestic assets in which currency exposures are neutralized.

Current credit risk The risk of credit-related events happening in the immediate future; it relates to the risk that a payment currently due will not be paid. Also called *jump-to-default risk*.

Cushion spread The difference between the minimum acceptable return and the higher possible immunized rate.

Custom security-based benchmark A custom benchmark created by weighting a manager's research universe using the manager's unique weighting approach.

Custom security-based benchmarks Benchmarks that are custom built to accurately reflect the investment discipline of a particular investment manager. Also called *strategy benchmarks* because they reflect a manager's particular strategy.

Cyclical stocks The shares of companies whose earnings have above-average sensitivity to the business cycle.

Day traders Traders that rapidly buy and sell stocks in the hope that the stocks will continue to rise or fall in value for the seconds or minutes they are prepared to hold a position. Day traders hold a position open somewhat longer than a scalper but closing all positions at the end of the day.

Dealer A business entity that is ready to buy an asset for inventory or sell an asset from inventory to provide the other side of an order. Also called *market maker*.

Decision price The prevailing price when the decision to trade is made. Also called *arrival price* or *strike price*.

Decision risk The risk of changing strategies at the point of maximum loss.

Deduction method When the residence country allows taxpayers to reduce their taxable income by the amount of taxes paid to foreign governments in respect of foreign-source income.

Deemed dispositions Tax treatment that assumes property is sold. It is sometimes seen as an alternative to estate or inheritance tax.

Deemed distribution When shareholders of a controlled foreign corporation are taxed as if the earnings were distributed to shareholders, even though no distribution has been made.

Default risk The risk of loss if an issuer or counterparty does not fulfill its contractual obligations.

Default risk premium Compensation for the possibility that the issue of a debt instrument will fail to make a promised payment at the contracted time and in the contracted amount.

Defaultable debt Debt with some meaningful amount of credit risk.

Defined-benefit plan A pension plan that specifies the plan sponsor's obligations in terms of the benefit to plan participants.

Defined-contribution plan A pension plan that specifies the sponsor's obligations in terms of contributions to the pension fund rather than benefits to plan participants.

Deflation A decrease in the general level of prices; an increase in the purchasing power of a unit of currency.

Delay costs Implicit trading costs that arise from the inability to complete desired trades immediately due to order size or market liquidity. Also called *slippage*.

Delivery option The feature of a futures contract giving the short the right to make decisions about what, when, and where to deliver.

Delta The relationship between the option price and the underlying price, which reflects the sensitivity of the price of the option to changes in the price of the underlying.

Delta hedge An option strategy in which a position in an asset is converted to a risk-free position with a position in a specific number of options. The number of options per unit of the underlying changes through time, and the position must be revised to maintain the hedge.

Delta hedging Hedging that involves matching the price response of the position being hedged over a narrow range of prices.

Delta-normal method A measure of VAR equivalent to the analytical method but that refers to the use of delta to estimate the option's price sensitivity.

Demand deposit A deposit that can be drawn upon without prior notice, such as a checking account.

Demutualizing The process of converting an insurance company from mutual form to stock.

Descriptive statistics Methods for effectively summarizing data to describe important aspects of a dataset.

Differential returns Returns that deviate from a manager's benchmark.

Diffusion index An index that measures how many indicators are pointing up and how many are pointing down.

Direct commodity investment Commodity investment that involves cash market purchase of physical commodities or exposure to changes in spot market values via derivatives, such as futures.

Direct market access Platforms sponsored by brokers that permit buy-side traders to directly access equities, fixed income, futures, and foreign exchange markets, clearing via the broker.

Direct quotation Quotation in terms of domestic currency/ foreign currency.

Discounted cash flow models (DCF models) Valuation models that express the idea that an asset's value is the present value of its (expected) cash flows.

Discretionary trust A trust structure in which the trustee determines whether and how much to distribute in the sole discretion of the trustee.

Disintermediation To withdraw funds from financial intermediaries for placement with other financial intermediaries offering a higher return or yield. Or, to withdraw funds from a financial intermediary for the purposes of direct investment, such as withdrawing from a mutual fund to make direct stock investments.

Disposition effect As a result of loss aversion, an emotional bias whereby investors are reluctant to dispose of losers. This results in an inefficient and gradual adjustment to deterioration in fundamental value.

Distressed debt arbitrage A distressed securities investment discipline that involves purchasing the traded bonds of bankrupt companies and selling the common equity short.

Distressed securities Securities of companies that are in financial distress or near bankruptcy; the name given to various investment disciplines employing securities of companies in distress.

Diversification effect In reference to VAR across several portfolios (for example, across an entire firm), this effect equals the difference between the sum of the individual VARs and total VAR.

Dividend recapitalization A method by which a buyout fund can realize the value of a holding; involves the issuance of debt by the holding to finance a special dividend to owners.

Dollar duration A measure of the change in portfolio value for a 100 bps change in market yields.

Domestic asset An asset that trades in the investor's domestic currency (or home currency).

Domestic currency The currency of the investor, i.e., the currency in which he or she typically makes consumption purchases, e.g., the Swiss franc for an investor domiciled in Switzerland.

Domestic-currency return A rate of return stated in domestic currency terms from the perspective of the investor; reflects both the foreign-currency return on an asset as well as percentage movement in the spot exchange rate between the domestic and foreign currencies.

Donor-advised fund A fund administered by a tax-exempt entity in which the donor advises on where to grant the money that he or she has donated.

Double inflection utility function A utility function that changes based on levels of wealth.

Downgrade risk The risk that one of the major rating agencies will lower its rating for an issuer, based on its specified rating criteria.

Downside deviation A measure of volatility using only rate of return data points below the investor's minimum acceptable return.

Downside risk Risk of loss or negative return.

Due diligence Investigation and analysis in support of an investment action or recommendation, such as the scrutiny of operations and management and the verification of material facts.

Duration A measure of the approximate sensitivity of a security to a change in interest rates (i.e., a measure of interest rate risk).

Dynamic approach With respect to strategic asset allocation, an approach that accounts for links between optimal decisions at different points in time.

Dynamic hedge A hedge requiring adjustment as the price of the hedged asset changes.

ESG risk The risk to a company's market valuation resulting from environmental, social, and governance factors.

Earnings at risk (EAR) A variation of VAR that reflects the risk of a company's earnings instead of its market value.

Earnings momentum A growth investment substyle that focuses on companies with earnings momentum (high quarterly year-over-year earnings growth).

Econometrics The application of quantitative modeling and analysis grounded in economic theory to the analysis of economic data.

Economic exposure The risk associated with changes in the relative attractiveness of products and services offered for sale, arising out of the competitive effects of changes in exchange rates.

Economic indicators Economic statistics provided by government and established private organizations that contain information on an economy's recent past activity or its current or future position in the business cycle.

Economic surplus The market value of assets minus the present value of liabilities.

Effective duration Duration adjusted to account for embedded options.

Effective spread Two times the distance between the actual execution price and the midpoint of the market quote at the time an order is entered; a measure of execution costs that captures the effects of price improvement and market impact.

Efficient frontier The graph of the set of portfolios that maximize expected return for their level of risk (standard deviation of return); the part of the minimum-variance frontier beginning with the global minimum-variance portfolio and continuing above it.

Electronic communications networks (ECNs) Computer-based auctions that operate continuously within the day using a specified set of rules to execute orders.

Emerging market debt The sovereign debt of nondeveloped countries.

Emotional biases Behavioral biases resulting from reasoning influenced by feelings; emotional biases stem from impulse or intuition.

Endogenous variable A variable whose values are determined within the system.

Endowment bias An emotional bias in which people value an asset more when they hold rights to it than when they do not.

Endowments Long-term funds generally owned by operating nonprofit institutions such as universities and colleges, museums, hospitals, and other organizations involved in charitable activities.

Enhanced derivatives products companies A type of subsidiary separate from an entity's other activities and not liable for the parent's debts. They are often used by derivatives dealers to control exposure to ratings downgrades. Also called *special purpose vehicles*.

Enterprise risk management An overall assessment of a company's risk position. A centralized approach to risk management sometimes called firmwide risk management.

Equal probability rebalancing Rebalancing in which the manager specifies a corridor for each asset class as a common multiple of the standard deviation of the asset class's returns. Rebalancing to the target proportions occurs when any asset class weight moves outside its corridor.

Equal weighted In an equal-weighted index, each stock in the index is weighted equally.

Equal weighting Security weighting scheme in which all constituents are held at equal weights at specified rebalancing times.

Equitized Given equity market systematic risk exposure.

Equity forward sale contract A private contract for the forward sale of an equity position.

Equity monetization The realization of cash for an equity position through a manner other than an outright sale.

Equity *q* The ratio of a company's equity market capitalization divided by net worth measured at replacement cost.

Equity risk premium Compensation for the additional risk of equity compared with debt.

Equity-indexed annuity A type of life annuity that provides a guarantee of a minimum fixed payment plus some participation in stock market gains, if any.

Estate All of the property a person owns or controls; may consist of financial assets, tangible personal assets, immovable property, or intellectual property.

Estate planning The process of preparing for the disposition of one's estate (e.g., the transfer of property) upon death and during one's lifetime.

Estate tax freeze A plan usually involving a corporation, partnership, or limited liability company with the goal to transfer *future* appreciation to the next generation at little or no gift or estate tax cost.

Eurozone The region of countries using the euro as a currency.

***Ex post* alpha** (or Jensen's alpha) The average return achieved in a portfolio in excess of what would have been predicted by CAPM given the portfolio's risk level; an after-the-fact measure of excess risk-adjusted return.

Excess capital An investor's capital over and above that which is necessary to fund their lifestyle and reserves.

Excess currency return The expected currency return in excess of the forward premium or discount.

Excess return The difference between the benchmark return and the portfolio return, which may be either positive or negative.

Exchange A regulated venue for the trading of investment instruments.

Exchange fund A fund into which several investors place their different share holdings in exchange for shares in the diversified fund itself.

Execution uncertainty Uncertainty pertaining to the timing of execution, or if execution will even occur at all.

Exemption method When the residence country imposes no tax on foreign-source income by providing taxpayers with an exemption, in effect having only one jurisdiction impose tax.

Exogenous shocks Events from outside the economic system that affect its course. These could be short-lived political events, changes in government policy, or natural disasters, for example.

Exogenous variable A variable whose values are determined outside the system.

Externality Those consequences of a transaction (or process) that do not fall on the parties to the transaction (or process).

Factor covariance matrix The covariance matrix of factors.

Factor push A simple stress test that involves pushing prices and risk factors of an underlying model in the most disadvantageous way to estimate the impact of factor extremes on the portfolio's value.

Factor sensitivities In a multifactor model, the responsiveness of the dependent variable to factor movements. Also called *factor betas* or *factor loadings*.

Factor-model-based benchmark A benchmark that is created by relating one or more systematic sources of returns (factors or exposures) to returns of the benchmark.

Factor-model-based benchmarks Benchmarks constructed by examining a portfolio's sensitivity to a set of factors, such as the return for a broad market index, company earnings growth, industry, or financial leverage.

Fallen angels Debt that has crossed the threshold from investment grade to high yield.

Fed model An equity valuation model that relates the earnings yield on the S&P 500 to the yield to maturity on 10-year US Treasury bonds.

Federal funds rate The interest rate on overnight loans of reserves (deposits) between US Federal Reserve System member banks.

Fee cap A limit on the total fee paid regardless of performance.

Fiduciary A person or entity standing in a special relation of trust and responsibility with respect to other parties.

Financial buyers Buyers who lack a strategic motive.

Financial capital As used in the text, an individual investor's investable wealth; total wealth minus human capital. Consists of assets that can be traded such as cash, stocks, bonds, and real estate.

Financial equilibrium models Models describing relationships between expected return and risk in which supply and demand are in balance.

Financial risk Risks derived from events in the external financial markets, such as changes in equity prices, interest rates, or currency exchange rates.

Fiscal policy Government activity concerning taxation and governmental spending.

Fixed annuity A type of life annuity in which periodic payments are fixed in amount.

Fixed trust A trust structure in which distributions to beneficiaries are prescribed in the trust document to occur at certain times or in certain amounts.

Fixed-rate payer The party to an interest rate swap that is obligated to make periodic payments at a fixed rate.

Flexible-premium variable life A type of life insurance policy that combines the flexibility of universal life with the investment choice flexibility of variable life. Also called *variable universal life*.

Floating supply of shares The number of shares outstanding that are actually available to investors. Also called *free float*.

Floating-rate payer The party to an interest rate swap that is obligated to make periodic payments based on a benchmark floating rate.

Floor A combination of interest rate options designed to provide protection against interest rate decreases.

Floor broker An agent of the broker who, for certain exchanges, physically represents the trade on the exchange floor.

Floorlet Each component put option in a floor.

Forced heirship rules Legal ownership principles whereby children have the right to a fixed share of a parent's estate.

Foreign assets Assets denominated in currencies other than the investor's home currency.

Foreign currency   Currency that is not the currency in which an investor makes consumption purchases, e.g., the US dollar from the perspective of a Swiss investor.

Foreign-currency return   The return of the foreign asset measured in foreign-currency terms.

Formal tools   Established research methods amenable to precise definition and independent replication of results.

Forward conversion with options   The construction of a synthetic short forward position against the asset held long.

Forward discount   The forward rate less the spot rate, divided by the spot rate; called the forward discount if negative, and forward premium if positive. Also called *forward premium*.

Forward hedging   Hedging that involves the use of a forward contract between the foreign asset's currency and the home currency.

Forward rate bias   Persistent violation of uncovered interest rate parity that is exploited by the carry trade.

Foundations   Typically, grant-making institutions funded by gifts and investment assets.

Fourth market   A term occasionally used for direct trading of securities between institutional investors; the fourth market would include trading on electronic crossing networks.

Framing   An information-processing bias in which a person answers a question differently based on the way in which it is asked (framed).

Framing bias   An information-processing bias in which a person answers a question differently based on the way in which it is asked (framed).

Front office   The revenue generating functions at an investment firm such as those pertaining to trading and sales.

Front-run   To trade ahead of the initiator, exploiting privileged information about the initiator's trading intentions.

Full replication   When every issue in an index is represented in the portfolio, and each portfolio position has approximately the same weight in the fund as in the index.

Fully funded plan   A pension plan in which the ratio of the value of plan assets to the present value of plan liabilities is 100 percent or greater.

Functional duration   The key rate duration. Also called *multifunctional duration*.

Fund manager   The professional manager of separate accounts or pooled assets structured in a variety of ways.

Fund of funds   A fund that invests in a number of underlying funds.

Fundamental law of active management   The relation that the information ratio of a portfolio manager is approximately equal to the information coefficient multiplied by the square root of the investment discipline's breadth (the number of independent, active investment decisions made each year).

Fundamental weighting   Patented by Research Affiliates LLC, this scheme uses company characteristics such as sales, cash flow, book value, and dividends to weight securities.

Funded status   The relationship between the value of a plan's assets and the present value of its liabilities.

Funding currencies   The low-yield currencies in which borrowing occurs in a carry trade.

Funding ratio   A measure of the relative size of pension assets compared to the present value of pension liabilities. Calculated by dividing the value of pension assets by the present value of pension liabilities. Also referred to as the *funded ratio* or *funded status*.

Funding risk   The risk that liabilities funding long asset positions cannot be rolled over at reasonable cost.

Futures contract   An enforceable contract between a buyer (seller) and an established exchange or its clearinghouse in which the buyer (seller) agrees to take (make) delivery of something at a specified price at the end of a designated period of time.

Futures price   The price at which the parties to a futures contract agree to exchange the underlying.

Gain-to-loss ratio   The ratio of positive returns to negative returns over a specified period of time.

Gamblers' fallacy   A misunderstanding of probabilities in which people wrongly project reversal to a long-term mean.

Gamma   A numerical measure of the sensitivity of delta to a change in the underlying's value.

Global custodian   An entity that effects trade settlement, safekeeping of assets, and the allocation of trades to individual custody accounts.

Global investable market   A practical proxy for the world market portfolio consisting of traditional and alternative asset classes with sufficient capacity to absorb meaningful investment.

Global minimum-variance (GMV) portfolio   The portfolio on the minimum-variance frontier with smallest variance of return.

Gold standard currency system   A currency regime under which currency could be freely converted into gold at established rates.

Gordon (constant) growth model   A version of the dividend discount model for common share value that assumes a constant growth rate in dividends.

Government structural policies   Government policies that affect the limits of economic growth and incentives within the private sector.

Grinold–Kroner model   An expression for the expected return on a share as the sum of an expected income return, an expected nominal earnings growth return, and an expected repricing return.

Growth in total factor productivity   A component of trend growth in GDP that results from increased efficiency in using capital inputs; also known as technical progress.

Guaranteed investment contract   A debt instrument issued by insurers, usually in large denominations, that pays a guaranteed, generally fixed interest rate for a specified time period.

H-model   A variant of the two-stage dividend discount model in which growth begins at a high rate and declines linearly throughout the supernormal growth period until it reaches a normal growth rate that holds in perpetuity.

Hague Conference on Private International Law   An intergovernmental organization working toward the convergence of private international law. Its 69 members consist of countries and regional economic integration organizations.

Halo effect   An emotional bias that extends a favorable evaluation of some characteristics to other characteristics.

Hedge funds   A historically loosely regulated, pooled investment vehicle that may implement various investment strategies.

Hedge ratio   The relationship of the quantity of an asset being hedged to the quantity of the derivative used for hedging.

Hedged return   The foreign asset return in local currency terms plus the forward discount (premium).

Hedging   A general strategy usually thought of as reducing, if not eliminating, risk.

Herding   When a group of investors trade on the same side of the market in the same securities, or when investors ignore their own private information and act as other investors do.

High yield   A value investment substyle that focuses on stocks offering high dividend yield with prospects of maintaining or increasing the dividend.

High-water mark   A specified net asset value level that a fund must exceed before performance fees are paid to the hedge fund manager.

High-yield investing   A distressed securities investment discipline that involves investment in high-yield bonds perceived to be undervalued.

Hindsight bias   A bias with selective perception and retention aspects in which people may see past events as having been predictable and reasonable to expect.

Historical simulation method   The application of historical price changes to the current portfolio.

Holdings-based style analysis   An approach to style analysis that categorizes individual securities by their characteristics and aggregates results to reach a conclusion about the overall style of the portfolio at a given point in time.

Home bias   An anomaly by which portfolios exhibit a strong bias in favor of domestic securities in the context of global portfolios.

Home currency   See *domestic currency*.

Human capital   An implied asset; the present value of expected future labor income. Also called *net employment capital*.

Hybrid markets   Combinations of market types, which offer elements of batch auction markets and continuous auction markets, as well as quote-driven markets.

Hypothetical events   A type of scenario analysis used in stress testing that involves the evaluation of performance given events that have never happened in the markets or market outcomes to which we attach a small probability.

Illiquidity premium   Compensation for the risk of loss relative to an investment's fair value if an investment needs to be converted to cash quickly.

Illusion of control   A bias in which people tend to believe that they can control or influence outcomes when, in fact, they cannot. Illusion of knowledge and self-attribution biases contribute to the overconfidence bias.

Illusion of control bias   A bias in which people tend to believe that they can control or influence outcomes when, in fact, they cannot. Illusion of knowledge and self-attribution biases contribute to the overconfidence bias.

Immunization   An asset/liability management approach that structures investments in bonds to match (offset) liabilities' weighted-average duration; a type of dedication strategy.

Immunized time horizon   The time horizon over which a portfolio's value is immunized; equal to the portfolio duration.

Implementation shortfall   The difference between the money return on a notional or paper portfolio and the actual portfolio return.

Implementation shortfall strategy   A strategy that attempts to minimize trading costs as measured by the implementation shortfall method. Also called *arrival price strategy*.

Implied yield   A measure of the yield on the underlying bond of a futures contract implied by pricing it as though the underlying will be delivered at the futures expiration.

Incremental VAR   A measure of the incremental effect of an asset on the VAR of a portfolio by measuring the difference between the portfolio's VAR while including a specified asset and the portfolio's VAR with that asset eliminated.

Indexing   A common passive approach to investing that involves holding a portfolio of securities designed to replicate the returns on a specified index of securities.

Indifference curve analysis   A decision-making approach whereby curves of consumption bundles, among which the decision-maker is indifferent, are constructed to identify and choose the curve within budget constraints that generates the highest utility.

Indirect commodity investment   Commodity investment that involves the acquisition of indirect claims on commodities, such as equity in companies specializing in commodity production.

Inferential statistics   Methods for making estimates or forecasts about a larger group from a smaller group actually observed.

Inflation   An increase in the general level of prices; a decrease in the purchasing power of a unit of currency.

Inflation hedge   An asset whose returns are sufficient on average to preserve purchasing power during periods of inflation.

Inflation premium   Compensation for expected inflation.

Information coefficient   The correlation between forecast and actual returns.

Information ratio   The mean excess return of the account over the benchmark (i.e., mean active return) relative to the variability of that excess return (i.e., tracking risk); a measure of risk-adjusted performance.

Information-motivated traders   Traders that seek to trade on information that has limited value if not quickly acted upon.

Infrastructure funds   Funds that make private investment in public infrastructure projects in return for rights to specified revenue streams over a contracted period.

Initial public offering   The initial issuance of common stock registered for public trading by a formerly private corporation.

Input uncertainty   Uncertainty concerning whether the inputs are correct.

Inside ask   The lowest available ask price. Also called *market ask*.

Inside bid   The highest available bid price. Also called *market bid*.

Inside bid–ask spread   Market ask price minus market bid price. Also called *market bid–ask spread, inside spread, or market spread*.

Inside quote   Combination of the highest available bid price with the lowest available ask price. Also called *market quote*.

Inside spread   Market ask price minus market bid price. Also called *market bid–ask spread, inside bid–ask spread, or market spread*.

Institutional investors   Corporations or other legal entities that ultimately serve as financial intermediaries between individuals and investment markets.

Interest rate management effect   With respect to fixed-income attribution analysis, a return component reflecting how well a manager predicts interest rate changes.

Interest rate parity   A formula that expresses the equivalence or parity of spot and forward rates, after adjusting for differences in the interest rates.

Interest rate risk   Risk related to changes in the level of interest rates.

Interest rate swap   A contract between two parties (counterparties) to exchange periodic interest payments based on a specified notional amount of principal.

Interest spread   With respect to banks, the average yield on earning assets minus the average percent cost of interest-bearing liabilities.

Internal rate of return   The growth rate that will link the ending value of the account to its beginning value plus all intermediate cash flows; money-weighted rate of return is a synonym.

Intestate   Having made no valid will; a decedent without a valid will or with a will that does not dispose of their property is considered to have died intestate.

Intrinsic value   The difference between the spot exchange rate and the strike price of a currency option.

Inventory cycle   A cycle measured in terms of fluctuations in inventories, typically lasting 2–4 years.

Inverse floater   A floating-rate note or bond in which the coupon is adjusted to move opposite to a benchmark interest rate.

Investment currencies   The high-yielding currencies in a carry trade.

Investment skill   The ability to outperform an appropriate benchmark consistently over time.

Investment style   A natural grouping of investment disciplines that has some predictive power in explaining the future dispersion of returns across portfolios.

Investment style indexes   Indices that represent specific portions of an asset category. For example, subgroups within the US common stock asset category such as large-capitalization growth stocks.

Investment universe   The set of assets that may be considered for investment.

Investor's benchmark   The benchmark an investor uses to evaluate performance of a given portfolio or asset class.

Irrevocable trust   A trust arrangement wherein the settlor has no ability to revoke the trust relationship.

J factor risk   The risk associated with a judge's track record in adjudicating bankruptcies and restructuring.

Joint ownership with right of survivorship   Jointly owned; assets held in joint ownership with right of survivorship automatically transfer to the surviving joint owner or owners outside the probate process.

Justified P/E   The price-to-earnings ratio that is fair, warranted, or justified on the basis of forecasted fundamentals.

Key rate duration   A method of measuring the interest rate sensitivities of a fixed-income instrument or portfolio to shifts in key points along the yield curve.

Knock-in/knock-out   Features of a vanilla option that is created (or ceases to exist) when the spot exchange rate touches a pre-specified level.

Lagging economic indicators   A set of economic variables whose values correlate with recent past economic activity.

Leading economic indicators   A set of economic variables whose values vary with the business cycle but at a fairly consistent time interval before a turn in the business cycle.

Legal/contract risk   The possibility of loss arising from the legal system's failure to enforce a contract in which an enterprise has a financial stake; for example, if a contract is voided through litigation.

Leverage-adjusted duration gap   A leverage-adjusted measure of the difference between the durations of assets and liabilities which measures a bank's overall interest rate exposure.

Leveraged floating-rate note   (leveraged floater) A floating-rate note or bond in which the coupon is adjusted at a multiple of a benchmark interest rate.

Leveraged recapitalization   A leveraging of a company's balance sheet, usually accomplished by working with a private equity firm.

Liability   As used in the text, a financial obligation.

Liability-based benchmark   A benchmark structured to accurately reflect the return required to meet the future obligations of an investor and to mimic the volatility of the liabilities.

Life annuity   An annuity that guarantees a monthly income to the annuitant for life.

Lifetime gratuitous transfer   A lifetime gift made during the lifetime of the donor; also known as *inter vivos* transfers.

Limit order   An instruction to execute an order when the best price available is at least as good as the limit price specified in the order.

Linear programming   Optimization in which the objective function and constraints are linear.

Liquidity   The ability to trade without delay at relatively low cost and in relatively large quantities.

Liquidity risk   Any risk of economic loss because of the need to sell relatively less liquid assets to meet liquidity requirements; the risk that a financial instrument cannot be purchased or sold without a significant concession in price because of the market's potential inability to efficiently accommodate the desired trading size.

Liquidity-motivated traders   Traders that are motivated to trade based upon reasons other than an information advantage. For example, to release cash proceeds to facilitate the purchase of another security, adjust market exposure, or fund cash needs.

Lock-up period   A minimum initial holding period for investments during which no part of the investment can be withdrawn.

Locked up   Said of investments that cannot be traded at all for some time.

Logical participation strategies   Protocols for breaking up an order for execution over time. Typically used by institutional traders to participate in overall market volumes without being unduly visible.

Longevity risk   The risk of outliving one's financial resources.

Loss-aversion bias   A bias in which people tend to strongly prefer avoiding losses as opposed to achieving gains.

Low P/E   A value investment substyle that focuses on shares selling at low prices relative to current or normal earnings.

M^2   A measure of what a portfolio would have returned if it had taken on the same total risk as the market index.

Macaulay duration   The percentage change in price for a percentage change in yield. The term, named for one of the economists who first derived it, is used to distinguish the calculation from modified duration. (See also *modified duration*).

Macro attribution   Performance attribution analysis conducted on the fund sponsor level.

Macro expectations   Expectations concerning classes of assets.

Managed futures   Pooled investment vehicles, frequently structured as limited partnerships, that invest in futures and options on futures and other instruments.

Managed futures funds   Pools of private capital managed by commodity trading advisors.

Manager continuation policies   Policies adopted to guide the manager evaluations conducted by fund sponsors. The goal of manager continuation policies is to reduce the costs of manager turnover while systematically acting on indications of future poor performance.

Manager monitoring   A formal, documented procedure that assists fund sponsors in consistently collecting information relevant to evaluating the state of their managers' operations; used to identify warning signs of adverse changes in existing managers' organizations.

Manager peer group   See *manager universe*.

Manager review   A detailed examination of a manager that currently exists within a plan sponsor's program. The manager review closely resembles the manager selection process, in both the information considered and the comprehensiveness of the analysis. The staff should review all phases of the manager's operations, just as if the manager were being initially hired.

Manager universe   A broad group of managers with similar investment disciplines. Also called *manager peer group*.

Market ask   The lowest available ask price.

Market bid   The best available bid; highest price any buyer is currently willing to pay.

Market bid–ask spread   Market ask price minus market bid price. Also called *inside bid–ask spread, inside spread,* or *market spread*.

Market cap weighting   See *capitalization weighting*.

Market fragmentation   A condition whereby a market contains no dominant group of sellers (or buyers) that are large enough to unduly influence the market.

Market impact   The effect of the trade on transaction prices. Also called *price impact*.

Market index   Represents the performance of a specified security market, market segment, or asset class.

Market integration   The degree to which there are no impediments or barriers to capital mobility across markets.

Market microstructure   The market structures and processes that affect how the manager's interest in buying or selling an asset is translated into executed trades (represented by trade prices and volumes).

Market model   A regression equation that specifies a linear relationship between the return on a security (or portfolio) and the return on a broad market index.

Market on close order   A market order to be executed at the closing of the market.

Market on open order   A market order to be executed at the opening of the market.

Market order   An instruction to execute an order as soon as possible in the public markets at the best price available.

Market oriented   With reference to equity investing, an intermediate grouping for investment disciplines that cannot be clearly categorized as value or growth.

Market quote   Combination of the highest available bid price with the lowest available ask price. Also called *inside quote*.

Market risk   The risk associated with interest rates, exchange rates, and equity prices.

Market risk bucket   In goal-based portfolio planning, that part of wealth allocated to investments intended to maintain the client's current standard of living.

Market segmentation   The degree to which there are some meaningful impediments to capital movement across markets.

Market spread   Market ask price minus market bid price. Also called *market bid–ask spread, inside spread,* or *inside bid–ask spread*.

Market value weighting   See *capitalization weighting*.

Market-adjusted implementation shortfall   The difference between the money return on a notional or paper portfolio and the actual portfolio return, adjusted using beta to remove the effect of the return on the market.

Market-not-held order   A variation of the market order designed to give the agent greater discretion than a simple market order would allow. "Not held" means that the floor broker is not required to trade at any specific price or in any specific time interval.

Marking to market   A procedure used primarily in futures markets in which the parties to a contract settle the amount owed daily. Also known as the *daily settlement*.

Mass affluent   An industry term for a segment of the private wealth marketplace that is not sufficiently wealthy to command certain individualized services.

Matrix prices   Prices determined by comparisons to other securities of similar credit risk and maturity; the result of matrix pricing.

Matrix pricing   An approach for estimating the prices of thinly traded securities based on the prices of securities with similar attributions, such as similar credit rating, maturity, or economic sector.

Maturity premium   Compensation for the increased sensitivity of the market value of debt to a change in market interest rates as maturity is extended.

Maturity variance   A measure of how much a given immunized portfolio differs from the ideal immunized portfolio consisting of a single pure discount instrument with maturity equal to the time horizon.

Maximum loss optimization   A stress test in which we would try to optimize mathematically the risk variable that would produce the maximum loss.

Mega-cap buy-out funds   A class of buyout funds that take public companies private.

Mental accounting bias   An information-processing bias in which people treat one sum of money differently from another equal-sized sum based on which mental account the money is assigned to.

Micro attribution   Performance attribution analysis carried out on the investment manager level.

Micro expectations   Expectations concerning individual assets.

Middle-market buy-out funds   A class of buyout funds that purchase private companies whose revenues and profits are too small to access capital from the public equity markets.

Midquote   The halfway point between the market bid and ask prices.

Minimum-variance frontier   The graph of the set of portfolios with smallest variances of return for their levels of expected return.

Minimum-variance hedge ratio   A mathematical approach to determining the optimal cross-hedging ratio.

Mismatch in character   The potential tax inefficiency that can result if the instrument being hedged, and the tool that is being used to hedge it, produce income and loss of a different character.

Missed trade opportunity costs   Unrealized profit/loss arising from the failure to execute a trade in a timely manner.

Model risk   The risk that a model is incorrect or misapplied; in investments, it often refers to valuation models.

Model uncertainty   Uncertainty concerning whether a selected model is correct.

Modified duration   An adjustment of the duration for the level of the yield. Contrast with *Macaulay duration*.

Monetary policy   Government activity concerning interest rates and the money supply.

Monetize   To access an item's cash value without transferring ownership of it.

Money markets   Markets for fixed-income securities with maturities of one year or less.

Money-weighted rate of return   Same as the internal rate of return; the growth rate that will link the ending value of the account to its beginning value plus all intermediate cash flows.

Mortality risk   The risk of loss of human capital in the event of premature death.

Multifactor model   A model that explains a variable in terms of the values of a set of factors.

Multifactor model technique   With respect to construction of an indexed portfolio, a technique that attempts to match the primary risk exposures of the indexed portfolio to those of the index.

Multiperiod Sharpe ratio   A Sharpe ratio based on the investment's multiperiod wealth in excess of the wealth generated by the risk-free investment.

Mutuals   With respect to insurance companies, companies that are owned by their policyholders, who share in the company's surplus earnings.

Natural liquidity   An extensive pool of investors who are aware of and have a potential interest in buying and/or selling a security.

Net employment capital   See *human capital*.

Net interest margin   With respect to banks, net interest income (interest income minus interest expense) divided by average earning assets.

Net interest spread   With respect to the operations of insurers, the difference between interest earned and interest credited to policyholders.

Net worth   The difference between the market value of assets and liabilities.

Net worth tax or net wealth tax   A tax based on a person's assets, less liabilities.

Nominal default-free bonds   Conventional bonds that have no (or minimal) default risk.

Nominal gross domestic product   A money measure of the goods and services produced within a country's borders. Also called *nominal GDP*.

Nominal risk-free interest rate   The sum of the real risk-free interest rate and the inflation premium.

Nominal spread   The spread of a bond or portfolio above the yield of a Treasury of equal maturity.

Non-deliverable forwards   Forward contracts that are cash settled (in the non-controlled currency of the currency pair) rather than physically settled (the controlled currency is neither delivered nor received).

Nonfinancial risk   Risks that arise from sources other than the external financial markets, such as changes in accounting rules, legal environment, or tax rates.

Nonparametric   Involving minimal probability-distribution assumptions.

Nonstationarity   A property of a data series that reflects more than one set of underlying statistical properties.

Normal portfolio   A portfolio with exposure to sources of systematic risk that are typical for a manager, using the manager's past portfolios as a guide.

Notional principal amount   The amount specified in a swap that forms the basis for calculating payment streams.

Objective function   A quantitative expression of the objective or goal of a process.

Offer price   The price at which a counterparty is willing to sell one unit of the base currency.

Open market operations   The purchase or sale by a central bank of government securities, which are settled using reserves, to influence interest rates and the supply of credit by banks.

Open outcry auction market   Public auction where representatives of buyers and sellers meet at a specified location and place verbal bids and offers.

Operational risk   The risk of loss from failures in a company's systems and procedures (for example, due to computer failures or human failures) or events completely outside of the control of organizations (which would include "acts of God" and terrorist actions).

Opportunistic participation strategies   Passive trading combined with the opportunistic seizing of liquidity.

Optimization   With respect to portfolio construction, a procedure for determining the best portfolios according to some criterion.

Optimizer   A heuristic, formula, algorithm, or program that uses risk, return, correlation, or other variables to determine the most appropriate asset allocation or asset mix for a portfolio.

Option-adjusted spread (OAS)   The current spread over the benchmark yield minus that component of the spread that is attributable to any embedded optionality in the instrument.

Options on futures   Options on a designated futures contract. Also called *futures options*.

Options on physicals   With respect to options, exchange-traded option contracts that have cash instruments rather than futures contracts on cash instruments as the underlying.

Order-driven markets   Markets in which transaction prices are established by public limit orders to buy or sell a security at specified prices.

Ordinary life insurance   A type of life insurance policy that involves coverage for the whole of the insured's life. Also called *whole life insurance*.

Orphan equities investing   A distressed securities investment discipline that involves investment in orphan equities that are perceived to be undervalued.

Orphan equity   Investment in the newly issued equity of a company emerging from reorganization.

Output gap   The difference between the value of GDP estimated as if the economy were on its trend growth path (potential output) and the actual value of GDP.

Overall trade balance   The sum of the current account (reflecting exports and imports) and the financial account (consisting of portfolio flows).

Overbought   When a market has trended too far in one direction and is vulnerable to a trend reversal, or correction.

Overconfidence bias   A bias in which people demonstrate unwarranted faith in their own intuitive reasoning, judgments, and/or cognitive abilities.

Overconfidence trap   The tendency of individuals to overestimate the accuracy of their forecasts.

Oversold   The opposite of overbought; see *overbought*.

Pairs trade   A basic long–short trade in which an investor is long and short equal currency amounts of two common stocks in a single industry. Also called *pairs arbitrage*.

Panel method   A method of capital market expectations setting that involves using the viewpoints of a panel of experts.

Partial correlation In multivariate problems, the correlation between two variables after controlling for the effects of the other variables in the system.

Partial fill Execution of a purchase or sale for fewer shares than was stipulated in the order.

Participate (do not initiate) order A variant of the market-not-held order. The broker is deliberately low-key and waits for and responds to the initiatives of more active traders.

Passive investment strategies A buy-and-hold strategy to investing in which an investor does not make portfolio changes based upon short-term expectations of changing market or security performance.

Passive management A buy-and-hold approach to investing in which an investor does not make portfolio changes based upon short-term expectations of changing market or security performance.

Passive traders Traders that seek liquidity in their rebalancing transactions, but are much more concerned with the cost of trading.

Payment netting A means of settling payments in which the amount owed by the first party to the second is netted with the amount owed by the second party to the first; only the net difference is paid.

Pension funds Funds consisting of assets set aside to support a promise of retirement income.

Pension surplus Pension assets at market value minus the present value of pension liabilities.

Percentage-of-portfolio rebalancing Rebalancing is triggered based on set thresholds stated as a percentage of the portfolio's value.

Percentage-of-volume strategy A logical participation strategy in which trading takes place in proportion to overall market volume (typically at a rate of 5–20 percent) until the order is completed.

Perfect markets Markets without any frictional costs.

Performance appraisal The evaluation of portfolio performance; a quantitative assessment of a manager's investment skill.

Performance attribution A comparison of an account's performance with that of a designated benchmark and the identification and quantification of sources of differential returns.

Performance evaluation The measurement and assessment of the outcomes of investment management decisions.

Performance measurement A component of performance evaluation; the relatively simple procedure of calculating an asset's or portfolio's rate of return.

Performance netting risk For entities that fund more than one strategy and have asymmetric incentive fee arrangements with the portfolio managers, the potential for loss in cases where the net performance of the group of managers generates insufficient fee revenue to fully cover contractual payout obligations to all portfolio managers with positive performance.

Performance-based fee Fees specified by a combination of a base fee plus an incentive fee for performance in excess of a benchmark's.

Periodic auction markets Auction markets where multilateral trading occurs at a single price at a prespecified point in time.

Permanent income hypothesis The hypothesis that consumers' spending behavior is largely determined by their long-run income expectations.

Personal risk bucket In goal-based portfolio planning, that part of wealth allocated to investments intended to protect the client from a drastic decrease in lifestyle.

Plan sponsor The trustee, company, or employer responsible for a public or private institutional investment plan.

Pledging requirement With respect to banks, a required collateral use of assets.

Point estimate A single-valued estimate of a quantity, as opposed to an estimate in terms of a range of values.

Policy portfolio A synonym of strategic asset allocation; the portfolio resulting from strategic asset allocation considered as a process.

Policyholder reserves With respect to an insurance company, an amount representing the estimated payments to policyholders, as determined by actuaries, based on the types and terms of the various insurance policies issued by the company.

Political risk The risk of war, government collapse, political instability, expropriation, confiscation, or adverse changes in taxation. Also called *geopolitical risk.*

Portable Moveable. With reference to a pension plan, one in which a plan participant can move his or her share of plan assets to a new plan, subject to certain rules, vesting schedules, and possible tax penalties and payments.

Portable alpha A strategy involving the combining of multiple positions (e.g., long and short positions) so as to separate the alpha (unsystematic risk) from beta (systematic risk) in an investment.

Portfolio segmentation The creation of subportfolios according to the product mix for individual segments or lines of business.

Portfolio trade A trade in which a number of securities are traded as a single unit. Also called *program trade* or *basket trade.*

Position a trade To take the other side of a trade, acting as a principal with capital at risk.

Post-trade transparency Degree to which completed trades are quickly and accurately reported to the public.

Potential output The value of GDP if the economy were on its trend growth path.

Preferred return With respect to the compensation of private equity fund managers, a hurdle rate.

Premium Regarding life insurance, the asset paid by the policy holder to an insurer who, in turn, has a contractual obligation to pay death benefit proceeds to the beneficiary named in the policy.

Prepackaged bankruptcy A bankruptcy in which the debtor seeks agreement from creditors on the terms of a reorganization before the reorganization filing.

Prepaid variable forward A collar and loan combined within a single instrument.

Present value distribution of cash flows A list showing what proportion of a portfolio's duration is attributable to each future cash flow.

Present value of a basis point (PVBP) The change in the bond price for a 1 basis point change in yield. Also called *basis point value* (BPV).

Pretrade transparency Ability of individuals to quickly, easily, and inexpensively obtain accurate information about quotes and trades.

Price discovery Adjustment of transaction prices to balance supply and demand.

Price improvement Execution at a price that is better than the price quoted at the time of order placement.

Price risk   The risk of fluctuations in market price.

Price uncertainty   Uncertainty about the price at which an order will execute.

Price value of a basis point   (PVBP) The change in the bond price for a 1 basis point change in yield. Also called *basis point value* (BPV).

Price weighted   With respect to index construction, an index in which each security in the index is weighted according to its absolute share price.

Price weighting   Security weighting scheme in which constituents are weighted in proportion to their prices.

Priced risk   Risk for which investors demand compensation.

Primary capital   Assets held outside a concentrated position that are at least sufficient to provide for the owner's lifetime spending needs.

Primary risk factors   With respect to valuation, the major influences on pricing.

Prime brokerage   A suite of services that is often specified to include support in accounting and reporting, leveraged trade execution, financing, securities lending (related to short-selling activities), and start-up advice (for new entities).

Principal trade   A trade with a broker in which the broker commits capital to facilitate the prompt execution of the trader's order to buy or sell.

Private equity   Ownership interests in non-publicly-traded companies.

Private equity funds   Pooled investment vehicles investing in generally highly illiquid assets; includes venture capital funds and buyout funds.

Private exchange   A method for handling undiversified positions with built-in capital gains in which shares that are a component of an index are exchanged for shares of an index mutual fund in a privately arranged transaction with the fund.

Private placement memorandum   A document used to raise venture capital financing when funds are raised through an agent.

Probate   The legal process to confirm the validity of a will so that executors, heirs, and other interested parties can rely on its authenticity.

Profit-sharing plans   A defined-contribution plan in which contributions are based, at least in part, on the plan sponsor's profits.

Projected benefit obligation (PBO)   A measure of a pension plan's liability that reflects accumulated service in the same manner as the ABO but also projects future variables, such as compensation increases.

Prospect theory   An alternative to expected utility theory, it assigns value to gains and losses (changes in wealth) rather than to final wealth, and probabilities are replaced by decision weights. In prospect theory, the shape of a decision maker's value function is assumed to differ between the domain of gains and the domain of losses.

Protective put   An option strategy in which a long position in an asset is combined with a long position in a put.

Proxy hedging   Hedging that involves the use of a forward contract between the home currency and a currency that is highly correlated with the foreign asset's currency.

Proxy-hedge   See *cross-hedge*.

Prudence trap   The tendency to temper forecasts so that they do not appear extreme; the tendency to be overly cautious in forecasting.

Public good   A good that is not divisible and not excludable (a consumer cannot be denied it).

Purchasing power parity   The theory that movements in an exchange rate should offset any difference in the inflation rates between two countries.

Pure sector allocation return   A component of attribution analysis that relates relative returns to the manager's sector-weighting decisions. Calculated as the difference between the allocation (weight) of the portfolio to a given sector and the portfolio's benchmark weight for that sector, multiplied by the difference between the sector benchmark's return and the overall portfolio's benchmark return, summed across all sectors.

Put spread   A strategy used to reduce the upfront cost of buying a protective put, it involves buying a put option and writing a call option.

Quality control charts   A graphical means of presenting performance appraisal data; charts illustrating the performance of an actively managed account versus a selected benchmark.

Quality option   With respect to Treasury futures, the option of which acceptable Treasury issue to deliver. Also called *swap option*.

Quantitative easing   A policy measure in which a central bank buys financial assets to inject a predetermined quantity of money in the financial system.

Quote-driven markets   Markets that rely on dealers to establish firm prices at which securities can be bought and sold. Also called *dealer markets*.

Quoted depth   The number of shares available for purchase or sale at the quoted bid and ask prices.

Rate duration   A fixed-income instrument's or portfolio's sensitivity to a change in key maturity, holding constant all other points along the yield curve.

Ratio spread   An option strategy in which a long position in a certain number of options is offset by a short position in a certain number of other options on the same underlying, resulting in a risk-free position.

Rational economic man   A self-interested, risk-averse individual who has the ability to make judgments using all available information in order to maximize his/her expected utility.

Re-base   With reference to index construction, to change the time period used as the base of the index.

Real estate   Interests in land or structures attached to land.

Real estate investment trusts (REITs)   Publicly traded equities representing pools of money invested in real estate properties and/or real estate debt.

Real option   An option involving decisions related to tangible assets or processes.

Real risk-free interest rate   The single-period interest rate for a completely risk-free security if no inflation were expected.

Rebalancing ratio   A quantity involved in reestablishing the dollar duration of a portfolio to a desired level, equal to the original dollar duration divided by the new dollar duration.

Recallability trap   The tendency of forecasts to be overly influenced by events that have left a strong impression on a person's memory.

Recession   A broad-based economic downturn, conventionally defined as two successive quarterly declines in GDP.

Reference entity   An entity, such as a bond issuer, specified in a derivatives contract.

Regime   A distinct governing set of relationships.

Regret   The feeling that an opportunity has been missed; typically an expression of *hindsight bias*.

Regret-aversion bias An emotional bias in which people tend to avoid making decisions that will result in action out of fear that the decision will turn out poorly.

Regulatory risk The risk associated with the uncertainty of how a transaction will be regulated or with the potential for regulations to change.

Reinvestment risk The risk of reinvesting coupon income or principal at a rate less than the original coupon or purchase rate.

Relative economic strength forecasting approach An exchange rate forecasting approach that suggests that a strong pace of economic growth in a country creates attractive investment opportunities, increasing the demand for the country's currency and causing it to appreciate.

Relative strength indicators A price momentum indicator that involves comparing a stock's performance during a specific period either to its own past performance or to the performance of some group of stocks.

Remaindermen Beneficiaries of a trust; having a claim on the residue.

Representativeness bias A belief perseverance bias in which people tend to classify new information based on past experiences and classifications.

Repurchase agreement A contract involving the sale of securities such as Treasury instruments coupled with an agreement to repurchase the same securities at a later date.

Repurchase yield The negative of the expected percent change in number of shares outstanding, in the Grinold–Kroner model.

Resampled efficient frontier The set of resampled efficient portfolios.

Resampled efficient portfolio An efficient portfolio based on simulation.

Residence jurisdiction A framework used by a country to determine the basis for taxing income, based on residency.

Residence–residence conflict When two countries claim residence of the same individual, subjecting the individual's income to taxation by both countries.

Residence–source conflict When tax jurisdiction is claimed by an individual's country of residence and the country where some of their assets are sourced; the most common source of double taxation.

Residue With respect to trusts, the funds remaining in a trust when the last income beneficiary dies.

Resistance levels Price points on dealers' order boards where one would expect to see a clustering of offers.

Retired-lives The portion of a pension fund's liabilities associated with retired workers.

Returns-based benchmarks Benchmarks constructed by examining a portfolio's sensitivity to a set of factors, such as the returns for various style indexes (e.g., small-cap value, small-cap growth, large-cap value, and large-cap growth).

Returns-based style analysis An approach to style analysis that focuses on characteristics of the overall portfolio as revealed by a portfolio's realized returns.

Reverse optimization A technique for reverse engineering the expected returns implicit in a diversified market portfolio.

Revocable trust A trust arrangement wherein the settlor (who originally transfers assets to fund the trust) retains the right to rescind the trust relationship and regain title to the trust assets.

Risk budgeting The establishment of objectives for individuals, groups, or divisions of an organization that takes into account the allocation of an acceptable level of risk.

Risk exposure A source of risk. Also, the state of being exposed or vulnerable to a risk.

Risk premium approach An approach to forecasting the return of a risky asset that views its expected return as the sum of the risk-free rate of interest and one or more risk premiums.

Risk profile A detailed tabulation of the index's risk exposures.

Risk reversal With respect to foreign exchange option strategies, one involving a long position in a call option and a short position in a put option.

Risk tolerance The capacity to accept risk; the level of risk an investor (or organization) is willing and able to bear.

Risk tolerance function An assessment of an investor's tolerance to risk over various levels of portfolio outcomes.

Roll return The component of the return on a commodity futures contract that comes from rolling long futures positions forward through time. Also called *roll yield*.

Rolling return The moving average of the holding-period returns for a specified period (e.g., a calendar year) that matches the investor's time horizon.

Sale and leaseback A transaction wherein the owner of a property sells that property and then immediately leases it back from the buyer at a rate and term acceptable to the new owner and on financial terms consistent with the marketplace.

Sample estimator A formula for assigning a unique value (a point estimate) to a population parameter.

Sample-size neglect A type of representativeness bias in which financial market participants incorrectly assume that small sample sizes are representative of populations (or "real" data).

Sandwich spread An option strategy that is equivalent to a short butterfly spread.

Satisfice A combination of "satisfy" and "suffice" describing decisions, actions, and outcomes that may not be optimal, but are adequate.

Savings–investment imbalances forecasting approach An exchange rate forecasting approach that explains currency movements in terms of the effects of domestic savings–investment imbalances on the exchange rate.

Scenario analysis A risk management technique involving the examination of the performance of a portfolio under specified situations. Closely related to *stress testing*.

Seagull spread An extension of the risk reversal foreign exchange option strategy that limits downside risk.

Secondary offering An offering after the initial public offering of securities.

Sector/quality effect In a fixed-income attribution analysis, a measure of a manager's ability to select the "right" issuing sector and quality group.

Security selection effect In a fixed-income attribution analysis, the residual of the security's total return after other effects are accounted for; a measure of the return due to ability in security selection.

Segmentation With respect to the management of insurance company portfolios, the notional subdivision of the overall portfolio into sub-portfolios each of which is associated with a specified group of insurance contracts.

Self-attribution bias A bias in which people take personal credit for successes and attribute failures to external factors outside the individual's control.

Self-control bias A bias in which people fail to act in pursuit of their long-term, overarching goals because of a lack of self-discipline.

Sell side   Broker/dealers that sell securities and make recommendations for various customers, such as investment managers and institutional investors.

Semiactive management   A variant of active management. In a semiactive portfolio, the manager seeks to outperform a given benchmark with tightly controlled risk relative to the benchmark. Also called *enhanced indexing* or *risk-controlled active management*.

Semivariance   A measure of downside risk. The average of squared deviations that fall below the mean.

Separate property regime   A marital property regime under which each spouse is able to own and control property as an individual.

Settlement date   The designated date at which the parties to a trade must transact. Also called *payment date*.

Settlement netting risk   The risk that a liquidator of a counterparty in default could challenge a netting arrangement so that profitable transactions are realized for the benefit of creditors.

Settlement risk   When settling a contract, the risk that one party could be in the process of paying the counterparty while the counterparty is declaring bankruptcy.

Settlor (or grantor)   An entity that transfers assets to a trustee, to be held and managed for the benefit of the trust beneficiaries.

Shari'a   The law of Islam. In addition to the law of the land, some follow guidance provided by Shari'a or Islamic law.

Sharpe ratio   A measure of risk-adjusted performance that compares excess returns to the total risk of the account, where total risk is measured by the account's standard deviation of returns. Also called *reward-to-variability*.

Short sale against the box   Shorting a security that is held long.

Shortfall risk   The risk that portfolio value will fall below some minimum acceptable level during a stated time horizon; the risk of not achieving a specified return target.

Shrinkage estimation   Estimation that involves taking a weighted average of a historical estimate of a parameter and some other parameter estimate, where the weights reflect the analyst's relative belief in the estimates.

Shrinkage estimator   The formula used in shrinkage estimation of a parameter.

Sign-constrained optimization   An optimization that constrains asset class weights to be nonnegative and to sum to 1.

Smart routing   The use of algorithms to intelligently route an order to the most liquid venue.

Smoothing rule   With respect to spending rates, a rule that averages asset values over a period of time in order to dampen the spending rate's response to asset value fluctuation.

Social proof   A bias in which individuals tend to follow the beliefs of a group.

Socially responsible investing   An approach to investing that integrates ethical values and societal concerns with investment decisions. Also called *ethical investing*.

Soft dollars   The use of commissions to buy services other than execution services. Also called *soft dollar arrangements* or *soft commissions*.

Sole ownership   Owned by one person; assets held in sole ownership are typically considered part of a decedent's estate. The transfer of their ownership is dictated by the decedent's will through the probate process.

Solow residual   A measure of the growth in total factor productivity that is based on an economic growth model developed by economist Robert M. Solow.

Sortino ratio   A performance appraisal ratio that replaces standard deviation in the Sharpe ratio with downside deviation.

Source jurisdiction   A framework used by a country to determine the basis for taxing income or transfers. A country that taxes income as a source within its borders imposes source jurisdiction.

Source–source conflict   When two countries claim source jurisdiction of the same asset; both countries may claim that the income is derived from their jurisdiction.

Sovereign risk   A form of credit risk in which the borrower is the government of a sovereign nation.

Spot return   The component of the return on a commodity futures contract that comes from changes in the underlying spot prices via the cost-of-carry model. Also called *price return*.

Spread duration   The sensitivity of a non-Treasury security's price to a widening or narrowing of the spread over Treasuries.

Spread risk   Risk related to changes in the spread between Treasuries and non-Treasuries.

Stale price bias   Bias that arises from using prices that are stale because of infrequent trading.

Static approach   With respect to strategic asset allocation, an approach that does not account for links between optimal decisions in future time periods.

Static hedge   A hedge that is not sensitive to changes in the price of the asset hedged.

Static spread   The constant spread above the Treasury spot curve that equates the calculated price of the security to the market price. Also called *zero-volatility spread*.

Stationary   A series of data for which the parameters that describe a return-generating process are stable.

Status quo bias   An emotional bias in which people do nothing (i.e., maintain the "status quo") instead of making a change.

Status quo trap   The tendency for forecasts to perpetuate recent observations—that is, to predict no change from the recent past.

Sterling ratio   The compound annualized rate of return over a specified time period divided by the average yearly maximum drawdown over the same time period less an arbitrary 10 percent.

Stock companies   With respect to insurance companies, companies that have issued common equity shares.

Stock index futures   Futures contracts on a specified stock index.

Stops   Stop-loss orders involve leaving bids or offers away from the current market price to be filled if the market reaches those levels.

Straddle   An option strategy involving the purchase of a put and a call on the same underlying with the same exercise price and expiration date. If the put and call are held long, it is a long straddle; if they are held short, it is a short straddle.

Straight-through processing   Systems that simplify transaction processing through the minimization of manual and/or duplicative intervention in the process from trade placement to settlement.

Strangle   A variation on a straddle in which the put and call have different exercise prices; if the put and call are held long, it is a long strangle; if they are held short, it is a short strangle.

Strap An option strategy involving the purchase of two calls and one put.

Strategic asset allocation 1) The process of allocating money to IPS-permissible asset classes that integrates the investor's return objectives, risk tolerance, and investment constraints with long-run capital market expectations. 2) The result of the above process, also known as the policy portfolio.

Strategic buyers Buyers who have a strategic motive (e.g., realization of synergies) for seeking to buy a company.

Strategy benchmarks See custom security-based benchmarks.

Stratified sampling A sampling method that guarantees that subpopulations of interest are represented in the sample. Also called *representative sampling*.

Strike spread A spread used to determine the strike price for the payoff of a credit option.

Strip An option strategy involving the purchase of two puts and one call.

Structural level of unemployment The level of unemployment resulting from scarcity of a factor of production.

Structured note A variation of a floating-rate note that has some type of unusual characteristic such as a leverage factor or in which the rate moves opposite to interest rates.

Style drift Inconsistency in style.

Style index A securities index intended to reflect the average returns to a given style.

Stylized scenario A type of analysis often used in stress testing. It involves simulating the movement in at least one interest rate, exchange rate, stock price, or commodity price relevant to the portfolio.

Sunshine trades Public display of a transaction (usually high-volume) in advance of the actual order.

Support levels Price points on dealers' order boards where one would expect to see a clustering of bids.

Surplus The difference between the value of assets and the present value of liabilities. With respect to an insurance company, the net difference between the total assets and total liabilities (equivalent to policyholders' surplus for a mutual insurance company and stockholders' equity for a stock company).

Surplus capital Capital that is in excess of primary capital.

Surplus efficient frontier The graph of the set of portfolios that maximize expected surplus for given levels of standard deviation of surplus.

Survey method A method of capital market expectations setting that involves surveying experts.

Survival probability The probability an individual survives in a given year; used to determine expected cash flow required in retirement.

Survivorship bias Bias that arises in a data series when managers with poor track records exit the business and are dropped from the database whereas managers with good records remain; when a data series as of a given date reflects only entities that have survived to that date.

Swap rate The interest rate applicable to the pay-fixed-rate side of an interest rate swap.

Symmetric cash flow matching A cash flow matching technique that allows cash flows occurring both before and after the liability date to be used to meet a liability; allows for the short-term borrowing of funds to satisfy a liability prior to the liability due date.

Tactical asset allocation Asset allocation that involves making short-term adjustments to asset class weights based on short-term predictions of relative performance among asset classes.

Tactical rebalancing A variation of calendar rebalancing that specifies less frequent rebalancing when markets appear to be trending and more frequent rebalancing when they are characterized by reversals.

Tail value at risk (or conditional tail expectation) The VAR plus the expected loss in excess of VAR, when such excess loss occurs.

Target covariance matrix A component of shrinkage estimation; allows the analyst to model factors that are believed to influence the data over periods longer than observed in the historical sample.

Target semivariance The average squared deviation below a target value.

Target value The value that the portfolio manager seeks to ensure; the value that the life insurance company has guaranteed the policyholder.

Tax avoidance Developing strategies that minimize tax, while conforming to both the spirit and the letter of the tax codes of jurisdictions with taxing authority.

Tax efficiency The proportion of the expected pretax total return that will be retained after taxes.

Tax evasion The practice of circumventing tax obligations by illegal means such as misreporting or not reporting relevant information to tax authorities.

Tax premium Compensation for the effect of taxes on the after-tax return of an asset.

Tax risk The uncertainty associated with tax laws.

Tax-exempt bonds Bonds whose interest payments are in whole or in part exempt from taxation; they are typically issued by governmental or certain government-sponsored entities.

Taylor rule A rule linking a central bank's target short-term interest rate to the rate of growth of the economy and inflation.

Term life insurance A type of life insurance policy that provides coverage for a specified length of time and accumulates little or no cash values.

Territorial tax system A framework used by a country to determine the basis for taxing income or transfers. A country that taxes income as a source within its borders imposes source jurisdiction.

Testamentary gratuitous transfer The bequeathing or transfer of assets upon one's death. From a recipient's perspective, it is called an inheritance.

Testator A person who makes a will.

Theta The change in price of an option associated with a one-day reduction in its time to expiration; the rate at which an option's time value decays.

Tick The smallest possible price movement of a security.

Time deposit A deposit requiring advance notice prior to a withdrawal.

Time to expiration The time remaining in the life of a derivative, typically expressed in years.

Time value The difference between the market price of an option and its intrinsic value, determined by the uncertainty of the underlying over the remaining life of the option.

Time-series estimators Estimators that are based on lagged values of the variable being forecast; often consist of lagged values of other selected variables.

Time-weighted average price (TWAP) strategy   A logical participation strategy that assumes a flat volume profile and trades in proportion to time.

Time-weighted rate of return   The compound rate of growth over a stated evaluation period of one unit of money initially invested in the account.

Timing option   With respect to certain futures contracts, the option that results from the ability of the short position to decide when in the delivery month actual delivery will take place.

Tobin's q   An asset-based valuation measure that is equal to the ratio of the market value of debt and equity to the replacement cost of total assets.

Top-down   Proceeding from the macroeconomy, to the economic sector level, to the industry level, to the firm level.

Total factor productivity (TFP)   A variable which accounts for that part of Y not directly accounted for by the levels of the production factors (K and L).

Total future liability   With respect to defined-benefit pension plans, the present value of accumulated and projected future service benefits, including the effects of projected future compensation increases.

Total rate of return   A measure of the increase in the investor's wealth due to both investment income (for example, dividends and interest) and capital gains (both realized and unrealized).

Total return   The rate of return taking into account capital appreciation/depreciation and income. Often qualified as follows: **Nominal** returns are unadjusted for inflation; **real** returns are adjusted for inflation; **pretax** returns are returns before taxes; **post-tax** returns are returns after taxes are paid on investment income and realized capital gains.

Total return analysis   Analysis of the expected effect of a trade on the portfolio's total return, given an interest rate forecast.

Total return equity swap   A swap contract that involves a series of exchanges of the total return on a specified asset or equity index in return for specified fixed or floating rate payments.

Total return swap   A swap in which one party agrees to pay the total return on a security. Often used as a credit derivative, in which the underlying is a bond.

Tracking risk   The condition in which the performance of a portfolio does not match the performance of an index that serves as the portfolio's benchmark. Also called *tracking error, tracking error volatility*, or *active risk*.

Trade blotter   A device for entering and tracking trade executions and orders to trade.

Trade settlement   Completion of a trade wherein purchased financial instruments are transferred to the buyer and the buyer transfers money to the seller.

Trading activity   In fixed-income attribution analysis, the effect of sales and purchases of bonds over a given period; the total portfolio return minus the other components determining the management effect in an attribution analysis.

Transaction exposure   The risk associated with a foreign exchange rate on a specific business transaction such as a purchase or sale.

Translation exposure   The risk associated with the conversion of foreign financial statements into domestic currency.

Transparency   Availability of timely and accurate market and trade information.

Treasury spot curve   The term structure of Treasury zero coupon bonds.

Twist   With respect to the yield curve, a movement in contrary directions of interest rates at two maturities; a nonparallel movement in the yield curve.

Type I error   With respect to manager selection, keeping (or hiring) managers with zero value-added. (Rejecting the null hypothesis when it is correct).

Type II error   With respect to manager selection, firing (or not hiring) managers with positive value-added. (Not rejecting the null hypothesis when it is incorrect).

Unconstrained optimization   Optimization that places no constraints on asset class weights except that they sum to 1. May produce negative asset weights, which implies borrowing or shorting of assets.

Underfunded plan   A pension plan in which the ratio of the value of plan assets to the present value of plan liabilities is less than 100 percent.

Underlying   An asset that trades in a market in which buyers and sellers meet, decide on a price, and the seller then delivers the asset to the buyer and receives payment. The underlying is the asset or other derivative on which a particular derivative is based. The market for the underlying is also referred to as the spot market.

Underwriting (profitability) cycle   A cycle affecting the profitability of insurance companies' underwriting operations.

Unhedged return   A foreign asset return stated in terms of the investor's home currency.

Unit-linked life insurance   A type of ordinary life insurance in which death benefits and cash values are linked to the investment performance of a policyholder-selected pool of investments held in a so-called separate account. Also called *variable life insurance.*

Universal life insurance   A type of life insurance policy that provides for premium flexibility, an adjustable face amount of death benefits, and current market interest rates on the savings element.

Unrelated business income   With respect to the US tax code, income that is not substantially related to a foundation's charitable purposes.

Unstructured modeling   Modeling without a theory on the underlying structure.

Uptick rules   Trading rules that specify that a short sale must not be on a downtick relative to the last trade at a different price.

Urgency of the trade   The importance of certainty of execution.

Utility   The level of relative satisfaction received from the consumption of goods and services.

Utility theory   Theory whereby people maximize the present value of utility subject to a present value budget constraint.

Valuation reserve   With respect to insurance companies, an allowance, created by a charge against earnings, to provide for losses in the value of the assets.

Value   The amount for which one can sell something, or the amount one must pay to acquire something.

Value at risk (VAR)   A probability-based measure of loss potential for a company, a fund, a portfolio, a transaction, or a strategy over a specified period of time.

Value weighted   With respect to index construction, an index in which each security in the index is weighted according to its market capitalization. Also called *market-capitalization weighted.*

Value-motivated traders   Traders that act on value judgments based on careful, sometimes painstaking research. They trade only when the price moves into their value range.

Variable annuity A life annuity in which the periodic payment varies depending on stock prices.

Variable life insurance A type of ordinary life insurance in which death benefits and cash values are linked to the investment performance of a policyholder-selected pool of investments held in a so-called separate account. Also called *unit-linked life insurance.*

Variable prepaid forward A monetization strategy that involves the combination of a collar with a loan against the value of the underlying shares. When the loan comes due, shares are sold to pay off the loan and part of any appreciation is shared with the lender.

Variable universal life A type of life insurance policy that combines the flexibility of universal life with the investment choice flexibility of variable life. Also called *flexible-premium variable life.*

Vega A measure of the sensitivity of an option's price to changes in the underlying's volatility.

Venture capital The equity financing of new or growing private companies.

Venture capital firms Firms representing dedicated pools of capital for providing equity or equity-linked financing to privately held companies.

Venture capital fund A pooled investment vehicle for venture capital investing.

Venture capital trusts An exchange-traded, closed-end vehicle for venture capital investing.

Venture capitalists Specialists who seek to identify companies that have good business opportunities but need financial, managerial, and strategic support.

Vested With respect to pension benefits or assets, said of an unconditional ownership interest.

Vintage year With reference to a private equity fund, the year it closed.

Vintage year effects The effects on returns shared by private equity funds closed in the same year.

Volatility Represented by the Greek letter sigma (σ), the standard deviation of price outcomes associated with an underlying asset.

Volatility clustering The tendency for large (small) swings in prices to be followed by large (small) swings of random direction.

Volume-weighted average price (VWAP) The average price at which a security is traded during the day, where each trade price is weighted by the fraction of the day's volume associated with the trade.

Volume-weighted average price (VWAP) strategy A logical participation strategy that involves breaking up an order over time according to a prespecified volume profile.

Wealth relative The ending value of one unit of money invested at specified rates of return.

Whole life insurance A type of life insurance policy that involves coverage for the whole of the insured's life. Also called *ordinary life insurance.*

Wild card option A provision allowing a short futures contract holder to delay delivery of the underlying.

Will A document associated with estate planning that outlines the rights others will have over one's property after death. Also called *testament.*

Within-sector selection return In attribution analysis, a measure of the impact of a manager's security selection decisions relative to the holdings of the sector benchmark.

Worst-case scenario analysis A stress test in which we examine the worst case that we actually expect to occur.

Yardeni model An equity valuation model, more complex than the Fed model, that incorporates the expected growth rate in earnings.

Yield beta A measure of the sensitivity of a bond's yield to a general measure of bond yields in the market that is used to refine the hedge ratio.

Yield curve The relationship between yield and time to maturity.

Yield curve risk Risk related to changes in the shape of the yield curve.

Yield to worst The yield on a callable bond that assumes a bond is called at the earliest opportunity.

Zero-cost collar A transaction in which a position in the underlying is protected by buying a put and selling a call with the premium from the sale of the call offsetting the premium from the purchase of the put. It can also be used to protect a floating-rate borrower against interest rate increases with the premium on a long cap offsetting the premium on a short floor.

Zero-premium collar A hedging strategy involving the simultaneous purchase of puts and sale of call options on a stock. The puts are struck below and the calls are struck above the underlying's market price.

Index